# A Private War

The Douglass Series on
Women's Lives and the Meaning of Gender

# A Private War

## LETTERS AND DIARIES OF
## MADGE PRESTON
"1862–1867

## Edited by
## Virginia Walcott Beauchamp

RUTGERS UNIVERSITY PRESS

NEW BRUNSWICK AND LONDON

**Library of Congress Cataloging-in-Publication Data**

Preston, Madge, b. 1815.
  A private war.

  (The Douglass series on women's lives and the meaning of gender)
  Includes index.
  1. Preston, Madge, b. 1815.  2. Abused wives—Maryland—Biography.
3. Maryland—Social life and customs.  I. Beauchamp, Virginia Walcott.  II. Title.
III. Series.
HV6626.P73  1987     306.8'7  [B]     86-15578
ISBN   0-8135-1206-9

British Cataloguing-in-Publication Information Available

IN MEMORY OF MY PARENTS

*Edith Carlson Walcott*
*and*
*Fred G. Walcott*

# Contents

# Acknowledgments

Without the pioneering work of a group of college teachers and scholars whom I do not even know, this book could never have been conceived and written. Members of this group, the Modern Language Association's Commission on the Status of Women in the Profession, originated a project, supported by the Fund for the Improvement of Postsecondary Education (FIPSE), to recover, analyze, and teach the writings of ordinary women. Organized into regional networks, the first participants unearthed incredible stories of women's lives. An account of this project is presented in an MLA volume, edited by Leonore Hoffmann and Deborah Rosenfelt, *Teaching Women's Literature from a Regional Perspective* (1982). Although not a participant, I was sufficiently stimulated by some of the instructional materials this group developed to initiate a course on my own campus which explored and utilized archival and other resources to retrieve the stories of Maryland women.

During the summer of 1979 I was chosen as one of twenty-five college language teachers to participate in the five-week Institute, "Women's Nontraditional Literature, Theory and Practice," which was funded by the National Endowment for the Humanities. Here one of our purposes was to explore further and to try to develop a theory for dealing with the private or out-of-print writings of women. Some of these new ways of thinking about women's culture, women's experience in America, and our own lives as teachers have been recorded in a second MLA volume, edited by Leonore Hoffmann and Margo Culley, *Women's Personal Narratives: Essays in Criticism and Pedagogy* (1985).

A co-editor of both volumes is Leonore Hoffmann. She was a member of the MLA commission which, acting on Cynthia Secor's idea, conceived the original FIPSE project. Hoffmann's enterprise over a three-year period handled the project's administrative details. Later, her proposal won the NEH grant that created the Institute; her skills as a planner and an organizer brought it to fruition. She created the environment of learning which let us look again at what we mean by American history and American literature. Out of our creative rethinking of these disciplines came the impulse that has inspired this book.

Other members of the Institute faculty played indispensable roles as well in the genesis of this book—Ellen DuBois, Florence Howe, Paul Lauter, Elizabeth Meese, and most particularly Margo Culley. Her earlier work with women's diaries offered a model, and her encouragement has provided me with the inspiration to proceed. Her careful critique helped me to polish and improve the book. Without her example of careful, sensitive scholarship with works so closely intertwined with women's lives, the present work would have been inconceivable.

To all of us who participated in the Institute, the experience was transforming. It exposed us to works by women which had rarely been looked at as works of literature. But it also created a network of scholars with similar commitments to the retrieval and study of such works. Short of listing the names of all participants in the Institute, I should like to acknowledge the particular assistance or parallel endeavors of a few whose work has been a continuing reinforcement for my own: Elouise Bell, Alice Gasque, Dure Jo Gillikin, Rose Kamel, Susan Kissel, John Schilb, Judith Stitzel, Carolyn Ruth Swift, Susan Ward, and Susan Waugh.

Outside the Institute group, the support and assistance of Annette Kolodny have been invaluable. Her previous experience with such documents, her articulate defense of their value, and her specific suggestions for shaping this work for publication have been indispensable.

None of us who works with private writings can forget, of course, that in the retrieval of archival resources we are dependent on the many dedicated librarians associated with public and private repositories. When I first decided to teach a course based on such materials, I received the skilled assistance of Mary Boccaccio, then archivist and curator of historical manuscripts at the University of Maryland, College Park. Through her knowledge of the actual contents of the collections—conventionally catalogued under the names of heads-of-households (who are usually male, of course)—she was able to recommend to my students various writings by women, including the diaries of Madge Preston. Boccaccio and her staff, especially Charlotte B. Brown and Jessie Hinkle, provided invaluable support—first to my students and then, as I embarked on the project that culminated in this book, to myself as well. Lauren R. Brown, current curator and archivist, has continued this tradition of gracious and generous assistance.

At the library of the Maryland Historical Society in Baltimore, where about half of the Preston Papers are preserved, I received every kind of assistance to make my research truly a pleasure. I am most particularly indebted to Karen Stuart.

Without the generous permission of these two repositories—the Historical Manuscripts and Archives Department of McKeldin Library, the University of Maryland, for the use of the collection of Preston Family Papers, and the Manuscripts Division of the Maryland Historical Society Library—for use of the Preston Papers (ms. 711), William P. Preston Collection (ms. 978), and Margaret Smith Preston Diaries (ms. 1861)—to publish documents from the respective collections, the task of creating this work could not have been undertaken.

Similarly I am indebted to the Daughters of Charity at St. Joseph's Provincial House, Emmitsburg, Maryland, and most especially to their archivist, Sister Aloysia Dugan, for making available to me information concerning their former student May Preston and the times in which she lived. I am most grateful for their sharing with me their predecessors' eye-witness accounts from the summer of 1863—a unique source that has deepened and enriched my reconstruction of that important time.

Colleagues and friends have also contributed in important ways to this book. Carl Bode, who first tapped the Preston Papers for one chapter of his *Maryland: A Bicentennial History*, has given generous and enthusiastic encouragement. I am particularly grateful to him for reading the Introduction in its original, and much longer, form. Joyce Kornblatt has given similar support. I particularly regret that Shirley Bryant was not able to live to see this book in print, because her contribution was in some ways most valuable of all. She is the only person who read every single page of the original manuscript, both before and after it was typed. Her careful proofreading turned up many errors, but her greatest contribution was to compile an index of proper names that appear in the book. Leo Walder provided psychological references for interpreting Preston's aberrant behavior, and Mary Geiger read the completed manuscript before it went to the publisher.

Clara Schwan, a former student, must be credited with first getting me started with the project on Madge Preston. She brought into class a transcription of the diary passage in which Madge describes being struck to the floor. Clara's transcription of the 1865 diary formed the indispensable nucleus around which the rest of the project has grown. Other students whose work with the Preston Papers has helped to fill out the picture of the remarkable family have been Sally Hudson, Jeannette Subrizi, and Pava Wodiska.

During my work on the Preston Papers, I have had the support of the Department of English of the University of Maryland. A sabbatical semester enabled me to complete the collection and transcription of the documents used in this work. The department has provided me with staff resources to type, photocopy, and collate the manuscript. In particular, I owe a tremendous debt to the two secretaries who typed almost all of the prodigious manuscript from which the present work has been culled—Ann Allen and Julie Bicknell.

My family has been a constant source of encouragement and support throughout the years that I have been absorbed in this project. My son George and my daughter Edith have provided editorial assistance and informed criticism. My son-in-law Seamus Neary helped me with genealogical and other factual research. George E. and Catherine Beauchamp and George E. Beauchamp, Jr., have provided continued encouragement as well. All have read portions of the manuscript.

To move from manuscript to completed book involves manifold skills beyond the author's ability. For that I must express my gratitute to the staff of the Rutgers University Press; to Suzanne Lebsock for her careful reading and helpful suggestions; and most particularly to my editor, Leslie Mitchner, for her encouragement, skilled criticism, and practical advice. I will be ever grateful for her suggestion to shape the immense body of correspondence and diary excerpts of the Preston family around the unifying theme of Madge Preston's contrasting voices. Working with Leslie has been a joy.

# Introduction

## Family History

Madge Preston was born Margaret Smith in 1815, probably on one of the substantial German farms along the Monocacy Creek valley in Frederick County, Maryland. Her birth year is derived from the 1860 census figures that place her age at forty-five—three years her husband's junior. Her tombstone, in Green Mount Cemetery, Baltimore, gives her birth year as 1823; yet this date must be incorrect, since her mother, according to the very precise information given by Madge's sister Louisa Smith, died in 1817. Louisa, answering a request from Madge's daughter for family history, notes that her mother, Anne Wickham Smith, had died between 10 and 11 A.M. on January 24, age 32 years, 2 months, and 10 days—three weeks after the birth of her fifth child. Madge, the next youngest, must have been about two years old. Louisa says little about her father. She does not mention when he died, and no mention of either of her parents appears in Madge's voluminous correspondence or her diary volumes. Descended, according to family legend, from one of four brothers who were early immigrants from Germany, Madge was the daughter of Andrew Smith, one of sixteen children of Christian Smith and Elizabeth Bonar. The 1873 *Atlas of Frederick County, Maryland*, shows many Smith families living on farms within nine to fifteen miles due south of Emmitsburg, where Madge attended school. Following her sojourn there at St. Joseph's Academy, she spent most of 1838 and 1839 with Louisa Smith's family in Gettysburg. Sometime during this period Madge converted to the Catholic faith.

In 1846, in St. John's Catholic Church in Philadelphia, Madge married William P. Preston, a well-established Baltimore lawyer. We do not know where they met—perhaps in Philadelphia, where she had relatives and where he grew up; perhaps near Gettysburg, where both spent some years of their youth. Probably orphaned young, Madge lived for a time, as noted, with her married sister Louisa, whose husband, Joseph Smith, was a country doctor. Some years earlier, Preston had lived north of Gettysburg in Menallen Township. There for a while he was postmaster.

Although Preston is an important name in Baltimore—indeed, it is the name of a well-known street—the William P. Preston whom Madge married was not connected with the distinguished family for whom the street was named. Nor does he seem associated with the prominent Virginia Prestons, whose extensive genealogy appeared in 1842 in Orlando Brown's self-published *Memoranda of the Preston Family.*[1] This family included several lawyers, important clergymen, and not a few distinguished military officers. Although several bore the name of William, if the William of this book was related to them, record of the affiliation has been lost.

According to Preston's obituaries, he was born in Virginia in 1811 and lived in Philadelphia during his youth. He was noted for his fine education; and the *Baltimore Sun* obituary reports that "in the business office of his guardian," Preston "acquired a fine, bold handwriting, for which he was celebrated." From Philadelphia, still in his teens, Preston returned to Virginia, becoming a tutor in the family of President James Monroe.

Following his position with the Monroes, Preston traveled for a while in Europe. In 1828, writing from Alexandria, Virginia, he described in a letter to a friend how he had returned from France, where he had relatives, on the promise of an inheritance. This prospect failed, however, and he was next heard from in Gettysburg. He seems to have embarked for a while on the study of medicine but later turned to the law.

Preston appears to have been a self-made man. His legal career achieved prominence when he served as counsel for creditors of the Bank of Maryland, which failed in 1834. During riots in the following year, Preston published under the name of "Junius" a series of letters that attracted great attention. He was an impassioned and witty orator both in and out of court and was called upon often to address political rallies or to speak at formal ceremonies. Throughout his life he was a Democrat. Although President Andrew Jackson offered him the post of private secretary, Preston chose to follow his law career. Prospering, he accumulated a number of properties, both in the city and within Baltimore County. His principal land holdings in the 1860s were the farm known as Pleasant Plains and the townhouse residence at 65 Fayette Street in the city, where he kept his law office. Here he brought his new bride, and here their daughter, May, was born in 1849. Pleasant Plains, on the Hillen Road, lay two and half miles southeast of the Baltimore County courthouse in Towsontown. Preston traveled often between the two homes.

## MADGE PRESTON AS WRITER

Within the private writings of Madge Preston two voices emerge. One is the voice of her diaries, the other the voice of her letters. The tone of the letters is sociable—a kind of written conversation. She herself called it "a good long talk." If her own words are to be believed, she valued these conversations through letters more than face-to-face interactions with favored friends. Turning down an invitation to visit in the country with former neighbors, Madge shared in her weekly letter to her daughter, May, her "most important" reason for declining: "the losing my Sunday visit to you—nothing that is offered to me can in any wise compensate for that deprivation. I feel the want of it the whole week following. . . ."

Earlier in the same letter Madge had sketched for her schoolgirl daughter an engaging self-portrait—herself in the role she cherished most, letter writer caught in the act of writing. The image, in fact, informs the many pages of the mother's correspondence that have been preserved for all these years. Madge Preston enjoyed writing, and letters were the medium she had practiced and polished and made her own.

> Well my little pet, I suppose you see in your "mind's eye" . . . the vision of an old lady, seated at a convenient and comfortable looking writing desk, with papers and letters and envelopes, books &c &c scattered in an apparent wild confusion over it, and by looking a little closely you are made conscious that old lady is your own dear Mama, and she is engaged in the pleasant task of writing to her darling child. The vision is a reality, my little one, and here I am prepared for a good long talk . . . this stormy sabbath evening. (March 3, 1867)

If the self-portrait displayed in the diary is frequently less serene, it is also unstudied. When Madge writes in this genre, her pen does not pause on the writer viewed from outside herself. It records instead—often movingly, sometimes angrily—her own consciousness as felt from within. It expresses the torment of her private reality.

On the first day of 1867, only two months before the date of the letter, Madge Preston wrote:

> Come here my diary, and thank God with me, that we are once more alone! What a struggle we have had tonight and what a struggle we have had all day to be where the *eyes of intrusion* should not be upon us. Alas! Alas! it is even worse than I feared it would be, when those who have made the house pleasant by their absence, should return. How long, Oh how long is this fearful life to be endured—something must bring about a change or I cannot live!

To whom, we may ask, are the diaries addressed? Who is the intended reader?

That most of the diaries have been saved may imply that Madge imagined a future readership. Perhaps she hoped that someday her daughter, as a comprehending and solicitous adult, would learn of the anguish that the mother had withheld from the growing child. Perhaps Madge wanted her true story eventually to be told. But in one passage the audience she envisions seems more immediate, though probably posthumous. Written at the end of a day full of terror for herself, Madge's final sentence speaks out to possibly official readers—local citizens perhaps, who would need to know what only she had had voice to tell:

> During this afternoon we have all been as unhappy as well could be owing to Mr Preston's humour which unfortunately for me, fulminated this evening and ended by Mr Preston striking [me] to the floor almost senseless. I record this fact, that it may, if necessary, be known to others in the future. (February 24, 1865)

A day earlier Madge had written in her diary: ". . . I have almost made up my mind to report Mr Preston as insane, and a dangerous person to be living with, either that or leave the house!" On the twenty-fifth, she would write again of her terror: "I had some fears for my personal safety last night but notwithstanding, I slept in the bed with Mr Preston."

The truth disclosed in Madge Preston's diaries is her undisguised admission that she was a battered wife. The diaries can thus be read as her strategy for coping with her humiliating secret. Yet, on another level, so also can her letters.

## A Case of Marital Violence: A Possible Cause

We cannot know when Preston's beatings first began. Although we must trust the diary passages that affirm this violence against her, an earlier absence of explicit reports need not imply lack of such occurrences. Denials and suppression take many forms and have many reasons. Nor do exchanges of loving letters between the couple give assurance that all was well in their relationship. Possibly the very separations that engendered the correspondence were a strategy to escape from stress within the family.[2]

If we could be certain that the earliest diary volume that has been preserved—the one for 1860—was the first that Madge began to keep, we might ask why she chose that particular year to begin. Diarists often seek in their self-communing some daily solace when other comfort fails. But if Madge Preston's 1860 diary was the first in a series, the diary does not tell us so—as first diaries often do. If the passage of philosophy with which Madge begins is appropriate to a new endeavor, it would be appropriate also to the first day of a new decade:

> The old year has passed away and this morning ushered upon the world the beginning of another epoch in the Christian era. The past was fraught with

much of pain and of pleasure, but in the labyrinth of the future all will be forgotten except that which smote the heart or thrilled the mind with pleasurable emotions.

In Madge's matched pairs of human experience—"much of pain and of pleasure," "which smote the heart or thrilled the mind"—the darker thought seems to leap to consciousness, the happier to trail along like an afterthought—not so much felt as brought in to complete a rhetorical figure. But nineteenth-century stylists often drew from the dark palette—more a convention, perhaps, than a personal way of seeing.[3]

Clearer evidence that the passage begins a new diary-keeping enterprise comes in the next sentence. Dealing with factual matters, it assumes no knowledge from a previous day's entry. Rather it records what happened on the day before. "May and I returned yesterday, from the city where we had been making a visit to Mrs Hillen & family." Had an entry been written for December 31 in a diary for 1859, Madge would already have recorded their return. Surely the trip's purpose would also have been assumed. Probably the start of a decade—"the beginning of another epoch"—would have felt to Madge like an auspicious moment to take up the task of record keeping—a time sharply marked by the calendar between pains and pleasures of the past, the unknowable mysteries of the future. By her own acts as diarist, events to come could be saved from oblivion. The diary passage, which goes on about cheerful New Year's Day affairs (for the others—she stayed home), ends with a description of the icy weather and the expostulation, "God help the *poor* tonight!" Can one of their party have been "poor Madge"?

Weather is a continuing interest for Madge in the 1860 diary. Most daily entries begin with it—not surprising perhaps in a time when human beings were so vulnerable to its vicissitudes and when the *Farmer's Almanac* was the most well-thumbed book. Despite the philosophical passage with which the book begins, the general tenor of the diary is upbeat—chock-full of accounts of callers received and visits made, of household tasks completed with pleasure, of purchases made and of farm work supervised. Yet in the midst of these annals of a busy life comes a lament of the writer, striking for its sudden dissonance: "I am not very happy tonight. Indeed I am not very often otherwise than unhappy of late!!" The comment, on April 1, returns us to an apparently philosophical passage, which now rings with new overtones. On January 25, when the old, rotting springhouse was pulled down, Madge wrote: "but so it is, the old is constantly giving place to the new, and thus it will be with myself. Some new mistress will take my place and I shall be laid away!" If the 1860 volume was the first in a series of successive diaries, what unhappiness had been growing in Madge Preston's life, prodding her thus to begin to write?

The commencement of the diary is I believe connected with an extraordinary event two months earlier which had prostrated her husband and perhaps left him with permanent injuries. From that moment William P. Preston seems to have undergone a personality change that affected their marriage and required a profound readjustment from his wife. She may have begun the diary to help cope with this change in her life.

Preston, who was an attorney in Baltimore, had run for Congress in 1859. As a member of a reform movement within the Democratic party, he hoped that control of city politics could be regained from nativist Know-Nothing politicians who had held sway through most of the 1850s. In 1854 the Know-Nothing party, organizing through secret societies, had swept the Baltimore city election. In the statewide election of the following year, Know-Nothing candidates won a sufficient number of seats to dominate the Maryland legislature.

Voters in Baltimore (as in other East Coast ports where immigrant populations were concentrated) were attracted to the party because of its anti-Catholic stand, its proposal to limit immigration, and its pro-American rhetoric. By 1850 one-fifth of Baltimore's population had been born outside the United States; by 1860, one-quarter. Thus among blue-collar workers, who felt economically threatened by the influx of foreign-born laborers— primarily Irish and German Catholics, the Know-Nothing platform had strong appeal. At a time too when Southern factionalism threatened to split the country, Know-Nothings sought to uphold the Union.[4]

Although party members who served as elected officials left a record of responsible government, the party's preelection campaigning often took a violent turn. In 1856 four men were killed in the Baltimore city election, and many were wounded. In November of the same year, during the presidential election, ten men died; more than 250 were injured.[5]

In 1859 when Preston accepted the Democratic candidacy for a congressional seat, he could not imagine himself in danger. Yet it is hard to see how he could have expected to win. Although a Democratic president, James Buchanan, was in the White House, his opponent, Millard Fillmore, had carried Maryland; in Baltimore, Know-Nothing politicians dominated every ward but one. Their candidate, the state's current governor, had carried Baltimore by almost 10,000 votes.

Events turned ominous at an October rally shortly before the election. At Baltimore's Battle Monument, a crowd gathered that soon became a chanting, shouting mob—moved by slogans such as "The Awl Is Useful in the Hands of an Artist" and "Come Up and Vote; There Is Room for Awl." In front of the speaker's stand stood a blacksmith at a forge, making awls to hand out among the crowd.[6]

On the evening before the election, Preston retired with an acquaintance to an eating house on Eastern Avenue near Broadway. Seated at a table, he occupied himself in reading a paper. He paid no attention to a party of four who entered the room. Nor did his companion, who had risen beside him and at that moment happened to turn his back. Suddenly, in the words of the other man,

> I heard a crushing noise wheeled around, and saw Mr Preston rising in a staggering way, from the floor—as he staggered passed me I observed one man rushing out of the door another with an uplifted chair which he hurled toward the part of the room where I was standing. I rushed to the relief of Mr Preston and found him almost senseless and bleeding profusely. His face was dreadfully crushed and his clothing covered with blood. The blow was the work of an instant, there was no noise or commotion at the time—not a word was spoken—so quick was the act that I did not see the blow struck.

These words, inscribed carefully in Madge's handwriting, come from a notarized statement made by Preston's companion, a man named Royster Betts.[7] It in part denies, and in part supports, the description in a *Baltimore Sun* article on November 3 reporting the incident. This article, which places the assault outside a polling place on the morning of the election, November 2, describes "a severe blow on the back of the head with a slung shot" and "a blow across the nose with brass knuckles, breaking the bridge of the nose. . . . The wound . . . in the back of the head is very severe, and the injury is serious. —Last night he was somewhat easier, but his condition is considered dangerous by his friends."

Betts's version of the affair concludes with a specific denial, evidently addressing an interpretation that must have been circulating as gossip: "It is not true that Mr Preston was in company with 'ruffians' he was not conversing with anyone at the time of the occurrence. . . . It is not true that the occurrance took place on the 'Causeway.'" The implications of the notarized statement are clear: the assault was premeditated. Perhaps it was carried out by hired thugs.

The only concrete record of the victim's physical condition following the attack appears in Preston's personal diary of 1860. "I feel constantly troubled in the back part of my head," he wrote on February 13. "I cannot doubt that this suffering arises from the injury I sustained in November last." On March 23, following a morning of planting seeds in the new greenhouse, he wrote again: "Feel very sensibly the effects of the injury I received in my head in November last, physical or mental efforts affect me. —The exertions of today chiefly physical cause me by evening to feel greatly fatigued and depressed."

Depression dogged him thereafter for many years. Moreover, evidence— besides Madge's frightened comments in the 1865 diary—suggests that

Preston received some mental impairment as well. In a biographical piece in the *Baltimore Daily News* (October 23, 1880) at the time of his death, the assault is remembered—although attributed to 1856, the wrong year. Then this judgment is added: "It is doubtful whether he ever fully recovered from its effects."

Madge would have taken personally any changes in Preston's behavior toward herself and within the family. His sudden, unexplained rages, known to us first in a discreet reference in Madge's 1860 diary three days after a "blow up," appeared as early as February—three months after the election trauma. By September quarrels between the couple were so frequent—but perhaps confined to the times when a drive on country roads provided privacy—that Madge was beginning to think of avoiding such rides again. By the summer of 1864, Preston's actions had become truly bizarre.[8]

Despite whatever stresses were created for Preston by headaches and physical debilitation, he was engaged in those early months after the election in what was clearly also a stressful effort to reverse its results. As part of a group of leading Baltimore citizens, he helped to organize a lobbying effort with the legislature to protest the election.

In fact, the political climate within Maryland was changing. No longer were immigrants seen as the major worry for those who had traditionally enjoyed political and economic control. The new threat was the large numbers of free blacks now residing in Maryland—greater than in any other state in the Union. (The 1860 census lists 83,942 free blacks, as compared with 87,189 slaves.)[9] Not only did the free blacks create a large population into which escaping slaves could disappear, but they formed a pool of cheap labor which seemed to threaten the economic stability of lower-class whites. Added to these concerns were the political implications within abolitionist rhetoric, which endorsed the equality of blacks and whites. All these anxieties were of course exacerbated in October 1859, shortly before the election, when John Brown carried out his raid on Harpers Ferry.

Thus by the end of the year, many of Maryland's traditional Democrats were returning to the fold. To them the growth of the Republican party seemed a greater threat than economic pressure from the immigrants. In line with these changes, at the end of the state legislative session in 1860, the Maryland House of Delegates, on the grounds of a fraudulent election, annulled the right of the nine Know-Nothing members from Baltimore to continue to hold their seats.[10]

But Preston's appeal to the U.S. House of Representatives met a different fate. On November 30, 1859, Preston wrote an official letter of complaint to his opponent, describing in explicit detail both fraud and violence during the election. On December 28 Harris formally denied the complaint.[11] Preston then appealed to the House Committee of Elections. Nine months later—on February 27, 1861—this committee reported in favor of their colleague.[12]

Preston, in his own words, expected no other result. On January 12, 1860, two weeks after Harris's denial of Preston's complaint, Preston had recorded in his diary a day spent in Baltimore

> in company with several politicians, discussing the propriety of the contesting the seat of J. Morrison Harris in the Congress of the U.S. My own judgment is that it is utterly futile to do so—the political partisanship of the dominant party in the House of Rep. will make members deaf to justice principle however demand contest.

He seemed to see his own colleagues in a similarly dismal light. On the next day he wrote: "I am still among the politicians and a heartless set they are—every expression and look betrays a selfishness beyond the power of language to express—the miserable juggle sickens me—would that I were out of the reach of everything akin to political influence." Yet against his personal perception of political reality, he apparently acceded to whatever pressures —selfish or principled—his party members exerted.

On January 16, Preston put into motion a chain of events that would engage him in difficult hours of data gathering, legal consultation, and lengthy interviews. His logs of some of his days of travel and business equal those of a modern businessman—entailing, for example, all-day trips to Washington, often beginning with an early rising at 4 A.M. and lasting until an exhausted return to the farm north of Baltimore at 9 P.M. On one such trip he traveled by carriage and train and held interviews with President Buchanan, the postmaster general, and his victorious—and no doubt smug and hostile—opponent. During other long days he worked on the legal papers, preparing subpoenas for witnesses, consulting with influential friends, mailing off petitions. On February 17 he spent a second long grueling day in the nation's capital, going and coming on the same day. It is understandable, no doubt, that his accumulated frustration and fatigue spilled over on to the family on the twenty-first—the day of the "blow up."

While Preston awaited a response from the House committee, he underwent further anxiety as an aftermath of the assault. On April 4 he appeared in criminal court as a witness against his assailant. "The trial was commenced at the regular time," his diary records, "and finished at 2.30 P.M. when the jury retired. —Some of the Defendants witnesses swore to infamous falsehoods —will the jury be believe them? We shall see. . . ." Apparently they did not, for the assailant was sentenced to the state penitentiary.[13] Full, daily accounts in Preston's diary end with the entry of April 4. He does not describe the day in Washington on May 11 when he testified before the House committee. And although Madge's diary records her husband's fatigue (he went straight to bed upon returning that night to Pleasant Plains), her letters and diaries make no mention either of his political ambitions or of the injustices that he must have felt so keenly.

Very little evidence remains concerning Preston's convalescence. Aside from his November 30 letter to Harris and the notarized statement, only three documents seem to have survived between the date of the election and the first day of 1860, when Madge's and his own diaries begin.[14] The only reference to the assault occurs in a business letter on a legal matter, dated November 28 and referring to one received from Preston, "of the 25th inst." Thus, only three weeks after the attack, Preston had turned again to his law business.

In his law office on December 8, Preston received a note from Madge. They were out of flour at Pleasant Plains, and Madge had delegated Mr. Canoles at the end of the day to bring some back. "I hope you will be at the office when he reaches there, and able to attend at once to him, as it is now late when he leaves. . . ." She does not appear to feel this unexpected task will tax her husband's health unduly. In case he could not return home that evening, she sent fresh clothing for his use.

Mr. Canoles must have brought back, with the flour, the following letter, also dated December 8:

> Dear Madge,
> I spent yesterday in Washington—a miserable rainy day—but necessary I should be there. I did not go on with Mr. Lindsley—went on very suddenly to see the Prest. of U.S. about a pressing affair— . . . in compliance with your request shall detain Mr. Canoles as short a time as possible—will endeavor to send by him the things mentioned in your note. I shall not be out tonight—probably shall be tomorrow. If I come out I will come by the evening omnibus—and then I will *walk over* unless it be *raining* or *snowing* —in which *event send* for me. If the weather be dry I prefer to walk from Towsontown home. If I do not reach you tomorrow night, come in for me or send for me on Saturday. I shall be able on Saturday to leave for home at one or 2 P.M. —
> God bless you.                                        W. P. Preston

The letter is almost an illegible scrawl—not like Preston's usual, large, legible script. Was it only the hurry of the moment that produced that effect? Perhaps we are observing some damage, not yet healed, to Preston's motor control. His 1860 diary has the same crowded, hurried scrawl.[15]

## MADGE'S LIFE AT PLEASANT PLAINS

If Madge's 1860 diary makes no note of the stressful business affairs that absorbed her husband, what then were her concerns? In contrast to later volumes of her diary, at first reading this one seems fairly unrevealing. Yet themes build and recur. Some aspects of daily life stand out more boldly than others. For example, as I have mentioned, the weather; and gardening, the building and planting of a greenhouse, which Madge primarily supervised and accomplished. Also traveling. When I first read her diary, I was struck by the details about comings and goings at Pleasant Plains: Madge catalogued every wagon or carriage trip to the nearby village, for whatever purpose, and all of Preston's journeys to Baltimore or farther afield.[16]

All his peregrinations are logged in the diary of 1860. If Preston stays home, the event is recorded. If he travels abroad, we know that too. During the first three months of the year, for instance, he traveled into Baltimore thirty-eight times, spending twenty-three nights away from Pleasant Plains. That he returned home so often on the same day is perhaps the wonder, for the trip one-way by horse and carriage usually took two hours. Occasionally Madge shows her disapproval of all this traveling. When Preston left unusually early on a January day to be in the city before courthouse hours and returned that afternoon "in the midst of a drenching rain," Madge was not surprised that he felt "quite poorly—his head being much affected. I feel certain," she wrote, "*that* is from riding so much, but Mr Preston won't hear to such a thing."

Another theme in the diary is Madge's recurring, prostrating headaches and sickness among members of the family and servants, whom Madge attends with care and concern—Clara's toothache, the birth of Aunt Nancy's new baby, May's influenza. Special events, in which white and black house servants alike sometimes participate—the trip to Baltimore for the first arrival in the United States of ambassadors from Japan, for example, or another trip to the harbor to see the astounding steamship, *The Great Eastern*—also receive detailed attention. On a July day Madge and May went to the city to hear the piano pyrotechnics of "little Negro Tom." Truly "the wonder of the world," Madge wrote.

Much of the traveling was made possible by the Prestons' decision to operate from their own back yard the York Line omnibus between Baltimore and Towsontown. In April Preston, who all his life showed interest in and invested in road improvements, street railways, telegraph lines, and railroads, rebuilt the barn basement, turning it into a stable for the omnibus horses. A young slave, Jim, became the driver. And with so convenient a mode of transportation available, all members of the household—Madge included—could readily go to the city for a day's shopping or to call on friends; and May and the neighbors' children could catch free rides near the journey's end. But on August 31 the Prestons' management of the omnibus, which had not been the moneymaker they had hoped for, ceased.

Three women at Pleasant Plains appear repeatedly in the pages of the diary. One, Miss Fanny Healy, remains a shadowy figure, hired in March as a governess for young May but let go with relief in early July. It is strange, perhaps, that so little is said of Miss Fanny, when Clara, the housekeeper, looms so large. Madge's eye seems to be sharply on household management, not the events of the schoolroom. Yet perhaps other anxieties kept Madge's attention on Clara, as chapter 3 suggests.

In the 1860 diary we first meet Lizzie, an important member of the Preston household until she disappears in the summer of 1863. According to the 1860 census, Elizabeth Johnson, described as a mulatto, was thirty—just Clara's age. She was also a free woman. But she was married to Jim, the driver, whose name is omitted from the census because he was a slave. In the same way, Uncle Isaac Woodlands, the senior black on the place, was a free man, married to a slave, Aunt Nancy. The other black member of the household was the child Kitty, the personal slave of the Prestons' daughter, May—her Christmas gift from a family friend, when May was six.[17] In microcosm, the blacks at Pleasant Plains represent roughly the proportions of slaves to free blacks present in the larger black community of Maryland.

By inference they must also have represented the changing consciousness of their race. As the possibilities for freedom in the 1860s seemed to approach, they were no longer the docile, good-humored servants that the Prestons had depended on. Jim followed with avidity the arguments of the most passionate orators among the abolitionists; and soon the behavior of both Jim and Lizzie began to change.

Madge, their troubled mistress, records a series of incidents involving the black servants which she interprets as a breakdown of discipline, if not outright crime. Since none of the Preston blacks could read or write, their views of their own situation can only be read between the lines. But as Southern slaveowners well knew: ". . . let any number of [slaves] be indulged with the hope of freedom, one must have but little knowledge of their nature, who is to be informed that they reject restraint and become almost wholly unmanageable."[18]

The first of such instances with Jim and Lizzie occurred during the summer of 1860, when Preston departed for a lengthy vacation at Cape May. During his absence things blew up at the farm. On July 23 Madge's diary records the first of four miserable days revolving around Lizzie: "I have had great trouble with Lizzie this evening and intend sending for the Constable in the morning and shall have her sent to Jail. I am sorry for it, but I would not have her another day on any account."

What unnamed crime on Lizzie's part could have caused such an apparently extreme response? If she had taken to the bottle, as on earlier occasions (which Madge labeled "frolics"), or stolen change from Madge's purse, of which Lizzie was probably guilty three years later, Madge would surely have said as much. Perhaps Lizzie spoke the unspeakable, expressed a truth Madge was still unready to hear. Clearly the other black woman, Aunt Nancy, disapproved of Madge's action. She must have seen in it something in excess of the deed that set it off.

Yet Madge persisted in her intention to send Lizzie away to jail. She justified the action because "the experience of last night taught me a lesson not soon to be forgotten." Yet, she wrote, it almost broke her heart. Lizzie came home, however, before Preston's return.

Of the servants who surface from time to time in the pages of the Preston diaries and letters in 1860, only Lizzie, Jim, and Kitty remained in 1862. Sometime during 1861—a year for which Madge's diary is missing—the Woodlands couple left the Prestons' employ, taking up residence on Maryland's Eastern Shore. Clara, a native of Italy, also left. In her place old Mrs. Pent (or Pentz) assumed the duties of housekeeper, and a succession of other servants and hired hands required Madge's anxious supervision. Some now came from the mixed population of immigrants which was crowding into Baltimore. Others were free—or after the Emancipation Proclamation, newly freed—blacks.

While European immigrants were settling into eastern coastal cities and freed blacks were moving northward into the more hospitable environment of Maryland, young people from the disadvantaged rural regions also flocked to the city in search of opportunity. Both Madge's nephews, Hamilton and Crick Smith, came down at different times from their homes in Pennsylvania, hoping for advancement through contacts made at the law office of their uncle. (Hamilton was the son of Madge's brother, Crick of her sister, whose husband's name was also Smith.) After May's departure for school at St. Joseph's Academy, Crick's sisters, Rose and Theodosia, became for a time the Prestons' live-in household help. Such a role was often played in the nineteenth century by unmarried women in the houses of more affluent relatives. Apparently in their teens, the two girls were probably May's senior by two or three years. At times they offered pleasant companionship for Madge; at other times they caused her excruciating pain.

In Baltimore, at the house in town where Preston kept his law office, an immigrant German woman, Mrs. Beer, functioned as housekeeper. A long-time employee, she seems to have shared with Madge certain suspicions concerning William. She is, I believe, the unnamed woman of a mysterious passage near the end of Madge's 1860 diary. On November 14 Madge recorded a hurried trip to the city, made "by arrangement" with "Mrs ——," who "communicated to me strange things. I am not surprised at them neither am I at all annoyed." But the next sentence contradicts this protestation. "I wish however the gentleman would not conduct himself in such a suspicious manner, as I feel perfectly convinced the conduct is innocent though it lays him liable to illnatured remarks." In the light of developments in later years—those spread before us in the documents that make up this volume—we can guess at the other characters in this strange scene. Madge's proprietary interest in the man in question suggests her unnamed husband. And although a Baltimore woman of Madge's own class and upbringing would have hesitated to distress Madge with matters so seemingly sensitive, Mrs. Beer appears to have busied herself with other folks' affairs. Her role in the marital relations between the Prestons will speak for itself in later chapters of this book.

Clara's story, the episode with Lizzie, the cryptic message from Baltimore —all three events remain mysteries never fully explained in Madge's guarded, oblique accounts. But they seem intimations of what in later years becomes more certain—Preston's philandering. His embarrassing attentions to Madge's two nieces are dominant themes in later chapters of this book, and the angry tallies in Madge's diaries of his nights spent away confirm her usually never-quite-named suspicions.

## THE TROUBLED AND TROUBLING SPOUSE

Although we know much, through the diaries, of what Madge was feeling, the internal landscape of the other central figure in this nineteenth-century household is only occasionally revealed in documents he left himself. William Preston's own efforts at the diary form always dwindled off after a month or two. Nevertheless, his inner emotions absorbed him at certain periods almost to paralysis. Thus his serial letter to his daughter, started in December of 1863 and posted at last on her fifteenth birthday in May, describes a deep depression over the first four and a half months of 1864. And in the birthday letter a year later, he begins in the same lugubrious vein, claiming sympathy for a chronic pain in the side from which he suffers: "People see me in court, listen attentively to my arguments or laugh at my smart sayings—alas how little do they dream of the pain which at the same time is gnawing at my vitals." The pity he solicits, through a sentimental quatrain he quotes on "ev'ry man's *internal* care," is grudgingly shared with his wife—"like myself—but poorly." Yet her pains are more evident and intrusive. Although Preston suppresses the truth, they were caused by himself.

Why does a man beat his wife? The brutal events on that election eve may have haunted Preston for years; yet I do not suggest that that trauma alone made him a wife beater; but rather that wife beating, as for many men, was how he reacted when under stress.[19] In a perhaps similar case from today's popular press, the victim of serious injuries from an almost fatal auto accident describes the rage he felt afterwards: "I was trying to learn to walk by holding on to the walls, and was giving my wife headaches. I hate to use the word, but I was a bastard. I was furious at life."[20] Although this modern man did not describe how he mistreated his wife, his behavior was serious enough that she divorced him—an option that Madge ruled out for herself, though she considered it.

For a man to be furious at life, and to displace that fury on his most intimate companion—the theme persists within the annals of Western culture. Throughout European and American history, wife beating has at times been not only condoned but advocated. In America a bill legitimating wife beating was passed by the state legislature of Mississippi as recently as 1824; it was not repealed for seventy years.[21] In Alabama and Massachusetts wife beating was at last made illegal in 1871.[22] In Maryland a bill passed in 1882 punished wife beaters "by flogging at the whipping post."[23] By this time Preston had been dead two years.

As such legal changes illustrate, interpretations of marital relationships and responsibilities were undergoing readjustment during the nineteenth century. In matters of law, most states liberalized their divorce codes, including as acceptable grounds for divorce physical and mental cruelty. Divorce proceedings were also moved out of the realm of state legislatures and into the jurisdiction of the courts. When Madge's friend, Mrs. Stout, sought to divorce her alcoholic husband in Delaware, she had to secure a legislative act to support her petition; but in Maryland Madge could have gone to court.[24]

Preston, as he emerges in Madge's sketchy, often oblique records, seems to have shown regret for his behavior. On occasion he tried to apologize and was rebuffed. "I so detest a Judas kiss," Madge wrote, "that I could not receive it." Once he even played the household servant, preparing breakfast for his disbelieving wife. Yet his birthday letter to May in 1865, attributing Madge's indisposition to catching cold at Mass, seems a denial of stunning proportions.

At the same time, Preston adhered philosophically to a paternalistic system. In 1856, when Madge was visiting friends in Philadelphia, she seems in some way to have blundered—revealing too much about a business negotiation. After learning about the matter, Preston wrote her an abusive letter. Later, contrite, he followed with a letter of apology in which he asked her to forgive and forget—never to refer again to his earlier letter. Although their full exchange was doubtless destroyed, a surviving answer to her reply makes clear that she nevertheless expressed her unhappiness over the accusatory letter. His response, written in the heat of his continuing anger, articulates the cultural assumptions upon which their relationship—in his mind, at least—rested:

> I make a request—you violate it. . . . I simply ask ought I or not to curse my unlucky stars. The old lady who upon her death bed had said "Always let your husband have his own way" uttered a philosophic truth—a truth however which you have not the capacity to comprehend—which from lack of capacity you will neglect or despised [sic] until you sink into your grave.[25]

From the beginning to the middle of the nineteenth century, a clear shift occurs in the theory of child rearing. Early advice literature emphasized strong discipline for the child, with the father as chief authority within the family.[36] But by mid-century the emphasis had changed. "The great agent in executing family law," wrote the Reverend T. J. Moore, "is love. This should manifest itself in words, looks, and tones, to be properly effective."[37] The mother was counseled to study her infant, to learn the meaning of its every cry. She was expected to be "as indulgent as possible; not to be irritated by children's faults, but to pity their weaknesses."[38] At the same time the mother should screen from her children any trace of her own discomfort or distress. Serenity and cheerfulness were to characterize her own demeanor. Mothers were enjoined to reflect a world of Christian benevolence and "gentle kindliness."[39]

If mothers were to be their children's teachers, it followed that the education of future mothers assumed new importance: "educate a man and you have educated one person,—educate a mother and you have educated a family."[40] In the first two decades of the century, girls of the middle and upper classes received educations designed to be useless—smatterings of foreign languages, music, embroidery;[41] but as the new philosophy took hold, more serious instruction was offered—in spelling, reading, writing, English grammar, and arithmetic. The best schools also offered literature, languages, mathematics, science, and history.

Female academies and seminaries, some founded by religious orders, were the most common type of institution for young women. Quakers and other nonconformist groups especially emphasized careful academic training and moral instruction. Other seminaries were private schools, catering to local needs. These might be set up in farmhouses and last only a year or two. Others were long-standing, drawing on a student body from throughout the nation. One of the more distinguished schools of this type was St. Joseph's Academy, founded by Mother Elizabeth Seton (later canonized as America's first saint) at Emmitsburg, Maryland. May Preston's account of her training there in the letters she wrote home to her mother, reveals the values, practices, and personnel of this school as it operated during the 1860s.[42]

## CATHOLICISM IN MARYLAND

That Mother Seton chose Maryland as the site for her school was not an accident. Historically, since the founding of the colony by the Catholic Lord Baltimore, Maryland had been a haven for those of his faith. And when the widow Elizabeth Seton, as a Catholic convert, sought a hospitable environment in which to practice her religion, she came to the state where socially prominent families such as the Calverts and Carrolls had given Catholicism a respectability of a kind denied in sections of the United States which had been founded by Protestants.

By the mid-nineteenth century, membership in the Catholic church had expanded as a result of increasing numbers of impoverished immigrants. Many of the novices with the Sisters of Charity, the order founded by Mother Seton, were drawn from this class. But the administrators of St. Joseph's and the other institutions operated by the order were often drawn from a middle- or upper-class population of Catholic Louisiana.

Although a Catholic, Madge Preston belonged to none of these groups. Her immigrant German forebears, some three generations earlier, were Protestants. Madge, who had been influenced by the example of her own teachers at St. Joseph's, was a convert to the faith. Preston seems to have tolerated his wife's strong commitment to her religion. Although apparently not a practicing member of any established church, he appears to have supported his wife and their daughter in their personal devotions. When the notorious anti-Catholic legal suit, the Mount Hope case of 1866, was brought against the Sisters of Charity, Preston offered his services as defense counsel. The grateful Madge regarded his action as a sign of support for the gentle workers of her faith. But his motivation probably had more to do with his desire to check the political ambitions of figures who had previously flourished in Baltimore as powers in the Know-Nothing movement. Surely he had a score to settle. (The story of his involvement in this legal case is told in chapter 13.)

Madge's committed Catholicism probably caused her to rule out divorce as a way of escaping from domestic tyranny. But the cultural constraints of her time seem even stronger. What appears to have moved her was the quiet principle of feminine self-sacrifice and endurance. On the topic of divorce she never refers to church law.

## The Civil War

Underlying the Prestons' story is the immense cataclysm of the American Civil War. As a border state Maryland in some ways played out in miniature the conflict of values between the slave-holding South and the urban, industrial North. The Prestons, who were landed gentry dependent on a host of servants and hired hands, sympathized with the Confederate cause. Yet they were sourrounded in both city and country by associates who were fiercely partisan Union supporters. Major and minor battles of the war were fought on Maryland soil, and minor eruptions of hostility parted neighbors as well. But of more consequence was Maryland's location as staging ground for the movements of armies on either side, with the Shenandoah Valley providing access

From Madge's diary of a decade later, it is clear that Preston's physical assaults upon his wife were triggered on some occasions when she disputed his right to do as he pleased. But she learned to avoid provoking such occasions. Submitting instead to the prevailing domestic ideology, she adopted the traditional nineteenth-century mother's responsibility of transmitting that ideology to her daughter.

Perhaps she was shaping her letter to May rather more for the others at St. Joseph's who would also read it, but the message epitomizes this philosophy: "My visit with Papa to the mill yesterday was really one of great self-denial but you know it is *part of my religion* to gratify Papa in all his little whims and wishes." Possibly Madge realized that this verbal portrait of Preston cast him as immature. Or perhaps she recognized that to the Sisters of Charity, whose lives had been dedicated to God, her own deference to Preston's wishes for a Sunday picnic in place of her going to Catholic Mass appeared to place the couple's religious values in an unfavorable light. The next sentence seems an effort to correct both undesirable interpretations:

> . . . very likely if I had told Papa my *reason* for not going to the mill, he would at once have yielded his wish to have me with him but then you know it would have been a great disappointment to him and the disappointment had better fall on me than on Papa. (April 28, 1867)

Madge's real message is hidden: disappointment was easier to bear than blows.

## SEPARATE SPHERES

Through most of the nineteenth century, the world of men was changing rapidly. This evolution is documented in the records of technological developments, an expanding frontier, upward and downward mobility, populist political movements, and various movements of social reform. It is documented also in the anxiety latent in the large numbers of self-help books and advice manuals for young men turned out by physicians and teachers in the period after 1830.[26] The nineteenth-century world view for men, reflected in these books, pictured them engaged in a raging competitive battle in a psychic wilderness, alone and surrounded by savages.[27] The imagery is similar in a letter from one of Preston's correspondents: "It seems to me that mankind is but one menagerie of wild beasts, preying on each other."[28]

Probably because of the unrelenting pressures felt by men whose educational advantages and entrepreneurial incentives made them upwardly mobile, the cultural distinctions between male and female, as well as between the races after Emancipation, became markedly pronounced. If life were an unforgiving competition, men could take some comfort in having eliminated from that economic warfare more than half the human race.[29] This may have been the real, though generally unacknowledged, reason for the ideology of separate spheres for men and women.[30]

The economic changes of the nineteenth century transformed an agrarian culture into an industrial giant, pushed the frontier from the Appalachians to the Pacific coast, assimilated immense populations of immigrants, and encompassed several episodes of war. This is the content of formal history— primarily, of course, the story of men. Because women remained for the most part in what was assumed to be a center of stability, the home, historians have also assumed that they escaped the stresses of a world rapidly modernizing.

But historians of women, looking at family life and the separate world of women in nineteenth-century America, have recognized the effect of these changes on women as well. The same economic uncertainty that affected men also affected women. Today one might have servants and supervisory responsibilities; yet tomorrow one might have to do the work oneself. In many households the mother and children were the continuing group. The deserting, absent, or ineffectual husband is, in fact, a common nineteenth-century motif, especially in private writings.[31] Adding to the stresses of the period, women were often pulled out of their networks of extended family by husbands pursuing economic opportunity in the West or in the city.

Middle-class women could often, of course, find a certain power in their acknowledged sphere. There they controlled the moral side of life. "Womanhood and virtue became almost synonymous," Barbara Welter notes.[32] Clearly Madge Preston, saying her daily prayers before the home altar and making her almost twice-daily visits to her church, internalized this view. In the values of the home could be created a world set apart from the competition of business and corrupting influences of the ways of men—a place dedicated to renewal of the spirit. Since a woman's function was to be found primarily in serving others—fulfilling their needs, not her own—submission became the ultimate feminine virtue and training for obedience a daughter's primary education.

Mothers had the major responsibility for educating their daughters. In the nineteenth century, for the first time, childhood seems to have been clearly set off as a special stage of life—not, as in earlier eras, a kind of miniature adulthood.[33] A major industry developed in theories of child raising and in the production of child-guidance manuals and a special literature for children.[34] This celebration of childhood, in the middle and upper classes, was probably causally related to industrialization.[35] Since in urban centers children had no economic role, their leisure, which set them apart from men, forced them to be perceived in a new way; mothers, who were also increasingly separated from productive roles in the economy, assumed responsibility for directing their children's time.

to both North and South. The Prestons felt the economic pinch of wartime inflation and the scarcity of goods. They followed with concern, and sometimes enthusiasm, the shifting territorial boundaries. In their own travels— taking May to school or in visiting back and forth in Pennsylvania with Madge's sister Louisa—they were involved in episodes concerning the movements of troops. Both Preston and Madge, separately, visited Gettysburg after the battle. But in matters of life and death within their own family, the war seems not to have touched them deeply. They had no sons, and Preston himself was too old to fight.

## THE VALUES OF PRIVATE WRITINGS

When the three of Madge's diaries in the collection of the Maryland Historical Society were acquired, they were characterized in the inventory as dealing with trivial events. Similarly Jessie Bernard deplores "the trivia and banalities of daily life" that constituted the major content of letters she exchanged with her son.[43] Yet in rereading their communications Bernard discovered that the letters gave "a perspective to the times in which they were written." She notes how "war and fear of war did, in fact, run like a red thread through the letters. I was surprised to find how much they intruded in our lives."[44]

Both judgments are founded on an unexpressed assumption in the word *trivial* about what we mean by history. Somehow it encompasses great events —disruptions of large populations, conflicts between and within governments, structures of power. But when we read the personal papers of those who lived in such times, we discover that we stand history on its head. As Robert Fothergill, from his reading of diaries of the past, so well appreciates:

> They were so concretely *there*, so firmly embedded in the centre of their own existence, each consciousness composing all the elements of its experience into a unique and incommunicable set of relations, with itself as the focal point of history. One's sense of the substance of history is turned inside out. Where one habitually thought of "ordinary lives" forming a vast background to historical "events," now one's vision is of the great events dimly passing behind the immediate realities that comprise an individual's experience.[45]

The urge is in fact compelling to know that single life. Joanna Field describes once observing a woman from a train window: "I was seized with an impulse to know more about her. . . . I wanted to know that woman as a person, a unique individual, not a specimen. . . . [I]t seemed to be just the unique qualities of particular experience that I wanted."[46] And another psy-

chologist, Gordon Allport, reinforces Field's view: "A person is a self-regard-
ing focus of value. What we *want* to know is what life does look like from this
focus of value . . . and a document produced precisely from this point of view
is exactly what we desire."[47]

The reality of American experience has only occasionally encompassed
war. Throughout most of the centuries of the building of this nation, people
have gone about their daily lives in wholly personal ways. But what were those
ways? And how did those people regard their lives? As the scholarly field of
women's history opens up, our desire to know seems insatiable.

Out of this desire came my impulse to browse through the files of letters,
handwritten in faded ink, that fill out the two collections of Preston family papers from which this book is drawn, and to open Madge's diaries, with their
crumbling leather covers. Out of these pages come tumbling forth all the
"multitude of details about daily thoughts, emotions, and actions" which
make our lives as we live them[48]—inconsistent, rapidly fading, obsessive, or
circling back. Reading nineteenth-century women's diaries and letters highlights how separate were the men's and women's cultures of that time and
how sharply both men and women of our own century have been cut off from
those earlier women's lives.[49] Conventional history speaks of the world of our
male forebears—and then most usually of the elite group that wielded power.
But for all people outside such groups, to discover their own history is to em-
power themselves. Through women's history, all of us can learn to respect the
women who went before us—drawing strength from their examples of endurance and from the structures and models of relatedness in the female culture
that supported them.

But the reading of diaries takes a special kind of detective work. One cannot
peruse them as one reads a novel where the writer has arranged details and
imagery in consciously patterned ways. In diaries some of the mysteries they
contain—workings of the unconscious mind—are unfathomed as well by the
writer. Other mysteries, of names unidentified, of references assumed, come
about because the writer—who is also often the intended reader—knows
them all too well. Hindsight helps to break the code of the mysteries of the
psyche. Knowing what happened in later years to Madge Preston, I could look
back on the diary of 1860 with new insights.

To unravel some of the latter mysteries, I began to read Madge Preston's
letters—and found a treasure-trove. The vast correspondence exchanged between Madge and her young daughter during the five years that May was away
at school evokes a whole way of life. Before these years were over, May had
developed into a letter writer almost as skillful as her mother. To illuminate
the bonding between the two which the letters set forth was this book's original purpose.

But sometimes projects assume their own direction, defying outside control. This began to happen with Madge Preston's story. As I consulted the diaries to flesh out and provide connections between the letters, the real story became Madge Preston's hidden life, the suppressed story of her battering. Diaries and letters, read side by side, illuminated each other. Not only did such juxtaposition more fully illuminate the facts and the content of her life, but the two literary genres in which these facts found expression also achieved definition. What did the two different acts of writing mean to Madge as she tried to cope with her problem?

Wife beating was not an uncommon event in nineteenth-century America, any more than it is today. Some women's private writings refer to it—always with disapproval. But in the instances of which I am aware, this abuse has happened to someone besides the writer. Civil War diarist Mary Chesnut speaks of a banker's wife "whose husband beats her."[50] In the 1850s Susan B. Anthony and Elizabeth Cady Stanton, becoming interested in the desperate situations of women with drunken husbands, sought for the right of divorce for wives who had been abused.[51] Elizabeth Hampsten quotes the private journal of a male physician concerning a patient who had been beaten: "The husband a devil. Will not allow her to do any fancy work or anything that would be a pleasure to her."[52] But as far as I know, Madge Preston's letters and diaries provide the only extended account of what it was like to be a battered wife.

And yet the record is imperfect. For the five-year period from 1862 to 1867, when May's absence from home generated the wide-ranging correspondence between mother and daughter which forms the boundaries of this book, one of Madge Preston's diaries—the volume for 1866—is missing. Since the absent diary immediately precedes the New Year's Day cry of rage—"Come here my diary"—quoted earlier, a crucial piece of the total picture appears lost. But Madge Preston's story is not fiction. Like any historical piece, it can be drawn only from what remains of the real record. If that record is partial, so be it. In any case, the cumulative documents prior to 1867 make the hidden meaning of Madge's language of disguise sufficiently clear to prevent us from taking at face value the cheerful optimism with which her letters could otherwise be (and must have been at the time) received.

The popularity of diary keeping as a literary activity exploded during the nineteenth century. In part this new literature reflected a new kind of consciousness "shaped by print culture," as Walter Ong has observed.[53] Diary keeping reflected also a new concern with individualism which was finding expression in democratic modes of government, in the Romantic movement in literature, and in laissez-faire capitalism. The diary also reflected a new, and modern, conceptualization of time.[54] Yet for nineteenth-century women—cut off from the means men drew on in the larger world of commerce, government, and the arts to develop their individual potential—the diary was the quintessentially female form: no document could be more private and therefore modest. Yet in the very tangibleness of its form, it could preserve for an unknown posterity the record of a life lived, of thoughts registered on a living mind. It could outlast the oblivion of death.[55]

The daily moments of personal record keeping must have reinforced for Madge that sense of apartness that Margo Culley has described as the basis of all diary keeping.[56] To the extent that Madge internalized the idealized nineteenth-century cultural role of wife and mother, manager of the female sphere, she must have felt a failure. The home, as it appeared in contemporary women's fiction and in instructional works such as Catharine Beecher's *Treatise on Domestic Economy*, was described as a retreat rich in culture, in sensitive understanding, in loving companionship.[57] But as Jessie Bernard has pointed out, since the woman's "sphere did not define abuse as part of the female role, the solution to abuse . . . was secrecy"; its victims could only feel "unique, alone."[58]

Culley has commented on "the smaller 'deaths' or dislocations" that have encouraged the keeping of diaries: "marriage, travel, leaving behind loved ones not to be seen again in this life, widowhood." Moments that produce "a sense of discrete self" particularly shaped nineteenth-century women's lives.[59] As I have pointed out, the stresses of rapid change were felt by women as well as men, and the stresses of separation from family and friends were for women even greater. For one unhappy patient made "hysterical" perhaps by such an experience of loss and stress, a nineteenth-century female physician prescribed: "Abandon all medicine; *commence a diary*, go back into the chambers of the past."[60]

Modern psychologist Joanna Field confirms the insight. Using the diary as a form of self-analysis, a way of discovering those things in her life that made her happy, she has recorded: "I found the act of writing curiously calming, so that I gradually came to use it whenever I was over-burdened with worry.[61] In periods of dissatisfaction with her life she would write down what she describes as brief, explosive notes "in response to some blind impulse. . . . I can now remember," Field says, "the feeling of being cut off from other people, separate, shut away from whatever might be real in living."[62]

Another nineteenth-century diarist put into words what Madge Preston must often have felt: "I cannot tell anyone how I feel. . . . I feel the want of sympathy very much."[63] Putting her feelings into words—naming her terror, expressing her anger—in this act Madge must have found what a modern diarist calls "some illusion of control."[64]

The word is compelling. In Susan Schechter's research on male violence, she took this quotation from a female interviewee on the way violence relates to insecurity: "When we become overwhelmed, we have a reason to act controlling where we can. When you feel powerless, you resort to what makes you feel powerful. Violence is controlling; control makes you feel better and it pays."[65] In language reminiscent of this passage, Elizabeth Hampsten reflects about diary keeping: "There may be . . . some comfort in writing it down; forming the event into sentences both in diaries and in letters is a way of gaining control when events themselves have proved so unruly."[66]

Preston's violence, Madge's diary. Were they two sides of the same discomfort in a changing world? Perhaps in the nineteenth century these were the male and the female paradigms.[67]

## MADGE'S LETTERS

Had Madge been less careful in meeting the responsibility of motherhood, this book could not exist. From the first moment of the mother's return to Pleasant Plains after leaving the thirteen-year-old in the care of Sister Raphael, Madge intervened in the only way she could to stay the pangs of homesickness she was sure would come. Communications that today would vanish into the thin air of the long-distance telephone are set down in her correspondence in the most comprehensive detail—all the worries about proper sizes, colors, and fit; whether the trunks and parcels have arrived safely; special food treats. The logging of the letters themselves is also recorded—when sent, how mailed, when received; and how the reader felt about what was communicated and with whom it was shared within the neighborhood or among the circle of friends.

All these letters (except for a rare inserted private note on secret business, like gifts for Papa) were written for an audience of more than one. And each of May's letters from school was written first in draft form, read by the Sister who instructed in writing, corrected, and then carefully copied. What these letters only rarely show is a private, truly intimate relationship between this pair.

Not only were Madge's letters written to be read by a larger circle of friends, but literary pretensions of some sort are apparent. Whether Madge supposed her letters would some day be published we cannot know. But they were important to her: she saved them with care, and she cautioned May to tuck away her own share of the exchange in the bottom of her school trunk. Preston once likened his wife as letter writer to Lady Mary Wortley Montagu. Such a reference to one celebrated through her posthumously published letters would have been the most delicious flattery if Madge held secret ambitions toward literary fame.[68] But of course she could never express those openly. She would have had to protest, as did Sophia Peabody (later Nathaniel Hawthorne's wife), when she wrote to her family in the journal posted regularly from her sojourn in Cuba: "I do not like at all that my journal should be made such public property of . . . just as if it were a published book."[69]

Keeping up the ties of family and friendships through the medium of letters was seen as a woman's task. As it tightened the connections within the extended family and the larger social circle, it was also a woman's comfort. One feels strongly the tug of affiliation and support in the many exchanges among nineteenth-century women which have been preserved. The phenomenon is so universal and conspicuous that it forms the centerpiece of Carroll Smith-Rosenberg's now classic article on American women's social relationships.[70]

Madge Preston—isolated not by space and the great distances of overland travel that generated so many of these exchanges of letters, but by the psychological distancing of the abuse that set her apart—reached out to that network of kindly women and schoolgirls in the sisterhood at St. Joseph's. Though she was silent about the afflictions that she endured from day to day, still the knowledge that these women shared her values, that they approved of her playing out the role that her culture had defined for her, must have kept her going.[71]

Madge's relationships changed with all the Sisters of Charity following her husband's spectacular role in their legal defense in the infamous Mount Hope case. The five years of the correspondence take Madge through her period of lowest ebb, following her post-Christmas visit to St. Joseph's in 1862, when she smarted under Sister Raphael's mild rebuke, to her highest point, when she and Kate Parr led the procession of schoolgirls to May's pregraduation rehearsal. After the Prestons' move from their country home to an abode in the city, Madge's ever-greater absorption with the practices of her Catholic religion becomes a dominant theme of the letters to May and of Madge's diary. With her marriage clearly deteriorating, Madge seems to have found her greatest solace in the hours she spent in quiet worship at her church.

Nevertheless, a striking feature of the collection of letters is a kind of counterpoint in development which they highlight between May and Madge. As May grows to greater maturity, she takes on increasingly her mother's mode as correspondent. The last letters before her graduation respond carefully, point by point, to each subject introduced in the letter that May is answering; and she reflects strongly also her mother's piety. In May's June 5 letter for Madge's birthday in 1867, May echoes her mother's theme that this written conversation weighs more with her than a party with the girls: "I am much happier writing to you than doing anything else."

Madge, by degrees, seems to grow immature, identifying strongly with activities of the St. Joseph's girls. She throws herself into all the excitement of the graduation conspiracies; she keeps up correspondence with May's former schoolmates; she embraces a greater intimacy with the Sisters on her visits at St. Joseph's which allow her to resume again something of her early schoolgirl role; and she relives her own youthful conversion to Catholicism in her support of the young Kate Parr.

Madge also seems to adopt a juvenile stance of tractability with her husband. She does not cross him when he seeks her company in excursions that conflict with her own desires. She also often drops the conventional address of her early letters—"Dear Mr Preston"—in favor of "Dear Papa," as though Madge were her daughter's sister.

## The Two Worlds of Madge Preston

This is a book about one woman's silences. There were the desperate messages of her diaries—trapped within leather covers, read by no one. The other silence—those in her coded letters—went out to the public, but could not be read. In the letters we move primarily through the ordered world of solicitous mother, devoted wife, and kindly mistress of a varied household. By means of her diary, we enter a different reality. The diary is the only witness to how her life departed in fact from the idealization of the female role by which women of her time sought to shape their lives. In re-creating the historical woman behind these documents, we find her record of pain as important as the details of daily life and concern for others which are reflected in her letters. The letters tied her to a female network of shared values and sustaining love; the diary named for herself alone the monstrous circumstance with which she lived. Without both, our sense of her life would be incomplete.

# Editorial Policies

In order to distinguish between the writings of Madge Preston which were intended for an audience, and those kept in secret, I have distinguished them typographically. Thus all diary passages are set in italics. I have modernized both spellings and punctuation, although Madge's -*our* endings (as in *neighbours*) remain. Words such as *to day* and *any thing*, which she regularly wrote as two words, I have closed up. One eccentric spelling, her invariable rendering of the verb *seemes*, I have corrected. In general Madge Preston—in accord with nineteenth-century practice—capitalized many nouns, such as *City* and *Depot*. These I have lower cased. Where it is impossible to tell whether the initial letter in her handwriting is intended as capital or lower case, I have followed modern practice. I have also added apostrophes to show possession or contraction. Generally I have quietly corrected inadvertent misspellings, except in those cases where they may be read as Freudian slips or indications of the writer's emotional state. Madge almost never used a period after abbreviated titles such as Mr or Mrs, an idiosyncrasy I have preserved.

May's early schoolgirl letters appear as written, with misspellings and other errors intact, to establish a scale against which her later competence as a writer can be measured. In general, her later punctuation and capitalization were quite similar to ours, and I have made very few alterations, except to correct inadvertent miswritings.

Preston tended to rely solely on long dashes as punctuation. He rarely used commas either after complimentary openings of letters, for interrupting elements within sentences, or to separate units in a series. To try to preserve his hurried style—so markedly different from the styles of Madge and May—I have introduced additional punctuation only where necessary for grammatical clarity. Preston enjoyed reproducing the dialects of black or immigrant speakers, whom he frequently quotes. Such passages I have preserved in their original spellings and punctuation.

Preston and May kept diaries only sporadically. The rare excerpts from their personal journals which I have included are, like those from Madge's diaries, set in italics.

The letters and diaries of all three of the Prestons were usually written as continuous texts, without paragraphing. To break up such long passages, I have inserted paragraph indentations where changes in topic seemed to make them appropriate.

Both Madge and William Preston were inconsistent in their spelling of names of persons. *Mollie* is sometimes *Molly*, for example; and Madge fairly regularly refers to May's friend Anna as *Anne*. To avoid confusion, I have chosen to render the names consistently. The one exception is the name of Mary Elizabeth Stansbury, who at the beginning of the book, while still a child, is called by her nickname *Mamie*. When she reaches her teens, she seems to have adopted *Mary Lizzie*.

Because the volume of the correspondence is too extensive to render completely in a book of publishable size, I have been forced to make many deletions. In general I have eliminated passages introducing characters whose connection with the main story is peripheral. I have also cut most of the long complimentary closes on both May's and Madge's letters, with their extended lists of persons to receive greetings from the writer—unless it seemed important to establish which particular persons were on the writer's mind. I have also eliminated most postscripts, which are usually extraneous to the letter's major themes. In letters of others—Preston, May, Sister Raphael—I have preserved only those passages that bear directly on what was on Madge's mind.

One type of elision, however, somewhat distorts the overall effect of Madge's letters. These are the rather dull and dreary passages that she wrote when she seemed to feel acutely depressed. Many of her letters for 1866 contain such segments. Since this is also the year of the missing diary, where interspersed diary passages might have offered some contrast in tone to the monotony of the letters, it seemed wise for the sake of the reader's interest to cut drastically some of the duller passages. Many have to do with reflections on her religious practices. I also cut some extended renderings of sermons she had heard or detailed descriptions of fairs and similar events which tell little about her inner life.

Very few diary pages are rendered in full—sometimes because they repeat events more interestingly described in her letters, sometimes because the routine events of a day's work seem tedious. I have almost always eliminated accounts concerning the day's weather.

Insertions to replace accidentally omitted words or explanatory material are set in brackets. Three ellipses indicate elisions within a sentence. A fourth ellipsis indicates the period at the end of a sentence or an elision of more than one sentence.

# A Private War

# 1

# A Daughter Leaves Home

"WE THINK THE BLESSING of Heaven is certainly upon this event, as today is St. Bernard's day, and he is May's patron saint." This is how Madge Preston's diary reveals her feelings on the change soon to come into her own life and that of her young daughter. For in accord with the decision made that day—August 20, 1862—young May Preston would soon leave home to attend St. Joseph's Academy in the northern Maryland town of Emmitsburg. Madge had barely time to get the child's things together. She was to leave on September 1.

May was then just thirteen years old, an only child. And until this moment, like most young girls of her social class, she had never left her mother's side. Madge had been her sole teacher, except for three months two years earlier when the Prestons had employed a governess. It may have seemed time for May to receive the more formal training and kind discipline for which the Sisters of Charity, who ran the school, were so justly famous.

The idea had been broached four days earlier by the young sons of Baltimore publisher A. S. Abell, founder of the *Baltimore Sun*. Charley and Walter had come out to spend the day at Pleasant Plains, the Prestons' comfortable farmhouse near Towsontown. They were to leave soon for Mount St. Mary's, the Emmitsburg school for boys not far from St. Joseph's. Mollie and Jeannette Sanders, May's Baltimore friends, would be enrolling at St. Joseph's, the boys reported. But how would William Preston regard the departure of his only child? And would he be willing to meet the considerable costs of such an education? The two female members of the family could only wait until he made his decision.

Clearly the *we* of the diary passage could refer only to Madge and May. Preston was not a Catholic, though he seems to have supported his wife's and daughter's commitment to their faith. That the decision was made on St.

Bernard's day would have seemed to the two women a happy answer to their prayers. But Preston would have had other motives for agreeing to his daughter's departure—the social influence of those prominent Baltimore friends, for example.

Yet why did Madge have so strong a commitment to supporting her child's leaving? Perhaps the invocation of the saint's name was a hedge against unforeseen consequences of this decision. May's departure would at the least wrench from the mother's side her cherished child. Though the nation was at war, military actions seemed still remote from the Prestons' quiet homeland north of Baltimore. Thoughts of the war do not seem to have been a part of the decision-making process for either Madge or Preston.

Perhaps Madge's share in the child's excitement at the prospect of a new turn in her life came from the mother's strong sense of nostalgia. She too had been a student at St. Joseph's, in long ago and happier days. Orphaned early in life, Madge must have found there a warm haven. Certainly she found the religion that would sustain her through the rest of a troubled life. At some time before or shortly after Madge's departure from the school, under the guidance of Father Elder, who had been the school's chaplain, she converted to Catholicism. Father Elder later presided at May's christening. He would remain for many years a strong influence in both women's lives. Perhaps Madge wanted for her daughter a happy period of intense childhood friendships similar to what she must have experienced at St. Joseph's. And perhaps even more she hoped for May the quiet, careful instruction in her religion that the good Sisters could so well supply.

But Madge may have been most strongly motivated by the desire to send May away from the troubled home. It must have become increasingly difficult to protect the child from scenes of quarreling. Preston's rages were flaring up with increasing violence. Even more urgent for Madge was the need to protect this innocent daughter from knowledge of certain scandalous episodes involving her father. Since that November night in 1859 when Preston had been brought back to the Fayette Street townhouse, bleeding from wounds to his face and the back of his head, Madge's life had shifted into a darker phase. The kind husband of the early years of their marriage occasionally reappeared, but an unfortunate word or a minor frustration could set off a violent torrent of abusive language. Madge seemed to be both the focus of these rages and the unwilling audience for whom his gallantries to other women were played out. It would be a relief to have May protected from the troubling events within her family.

St. Joseph's was the headquarters for the Sisters of Charity, the first native order of female religious, which had been founded by the sainted Mother Seton. Emmitsburg was almost at the Pennsylvania border, just south from Gettysburg. There the Sisters maintained a seminary for novitiates, a school for destitute orphans, and the academy for prosperous young girls like May Preston. Catholic daughters from most parts of the United States came there to school—from as far away as New Orleans and St. Louis. But non-Catholic girls from nearby Maryland, Pennsylvania, and Virginia farms and villages were also attracted to this well-run school. Here from September till June they received the best in contemporary education then available for girls.

When the Prestons learned that Mollie and Jeannette Sanders, who were to be May's school companions at St. Joseph's, were putting off their departure for a week, May's parting time was postponed also. During this interim Madge was occupied in readying May's clothing. Madge made over her own "flowered ducal frock" for her daughter; and Mrs. Schaeffer, a local seamstress, helped make three aprons. May's father contributed by bringing home May's "card a visite," a very handsome portfolio and a silver cup.

September 7 would be the last Sunday that May would spend at home for a long time. "God grant," her mother wrote, "she may be restored safely to me again at the end of the time for which she leaves us."

Yet the Prestons' plan to depart the next day was disrupted after all—by the very war that they seemed so thoughtlessly to have ignored. Something was delaying "the cars"—the Western Maryland Railway that the small party would take for a portion of their journey. The line had recently been completed beyond Westminster, to a spot called Union Bridge. From this point the group of Abells, Hillens, Sanderses, and Prestons planned to proceed by stagecoach to Emmitsburg. Yet no trains left Baltimore on the seventh, because a train sent out the previous day had disappeared. Union sympathizers at Westminster flagged down the succeeding train and hopped aboard, directing it back to Baltimore. Later Baltimoreans learned that the missing train had been cut off when Confederates—members of a contingent of the First Virginia Cavalry—had partially destroyed a bridge. What was not known until much later was that 70,000 of McClellan's troops and 40,000 of Lee's men had missed each other by only a day in the city of Frederick.

Preston may have been wary about sending his womenfolk through a countryside so rampant with militia. Yet if so, he does not seem to have imparted his worries to Madge. On the other hand, she grew greatly frustrated, as the departure was repeatedly postponed. She found it disagreeable to make the long trip back to Pleasant Plains after all the goodbyes had been said. But she was also uncomfortable intruding on city acquaintances such as the Sanders, as the group waited for things to change. Madge's diary, with its stop-and-start form, makes palpable these ongoing disappointments and frustrations. Five days after the first trip to the depot, Madge could still write:

> We were engaged the greater part of the day in preparing and packing up the
> "last things" for May to take away with her and as usual Mr Preston was so

dilatory that we were not able to leave home for the city till quite late; consequently it was sometime after dark when we reached Aunty's. Mr Preston
stopped at the depot to ascertain if the cars were running and finding they
were *not*, we cannot go up tomorrow.

The Hillens, father and son, had departed earlier—before the bridge near
Westminster was destroyed. Returning to Baltimore, Hillen treated the others
to what he described in a diary entry for the fourteenth as "a most glowing account" of their trip northwestward "& of their going to Frederick and seeing
the Grand Confederate Army." Like most residents of southern Maryland, the
Prestons and their friends sympathized with the South.

At last, after a full week of hesitations and thwarted desires, Preston accompanied his wife and daughter as far as Union Bridge. From there, on September 15, Madge and Ned Abell took the children on the final lap of the
journey. Though Abell returned at once, Madge spent the next day at St. Joseph's, a visit she described "as one of the bright spots for memory to rest
upon." At the end of that day, a carriage arrived to transport her to an Emmitsburg inn where, early the next morning, she was to take the stage coach
back to Union Bridge. Her September 16 diary entry records that moment:

> I bade farewell to the Sisters, the girls and my own dear little child, who be-
> haved like a little heroine; she trembled slightly and her eyes filled on bid-
> ding me 'goodbye' and I jumped in the carriage and drove back to town
> *alone*. God knows if I shall ever see her again!

———————————

Pleasant Plains
September 20th 1862

My dear child,

I have risen early, to write you a few lines, to allay any anxiety you may
have felt as to my safety in reaching the city. After I left you on Wednesday, I
drove to Emmitsburg feeling sad and lonely from parting with my good little
girl, yet perfectly content and satisfied to leave her in that beautiful retreat of
piety and learning and surrounded by the influence and protection of those
holy Sisters. I found Mr Dielman awaiting me there, and quite pleased to
hear "all the children," boys and girls, were safely moored in their happy
havens. . . .

After Mr Dielman left me the tea bell rang, and on taking my seat at the
table, I found there was only an old gentleman and myself for supper. Strange
to say—in the course of conversation, I discovered this old gentleman was
from Philadelphia originally and contemporary and quite intimately acquainted with many of my former friends. . . . It was so pleasant to talk over

old times and old friends, some of them long since gone to their graves, that I sat till nine o'clock, and almost forgetting that the barbarous stage driver had told me I must be ready for traveling by four o'clock the next morning. I tried to excite the sympathies of the old gentleman in my annoyance of getting up so early, but I found he was, like your father, an advocate for early rising and only laughed at my apparent distress. Of course I slept very little the first night away from my dear little daughter and was not sorry to hear the rough voice of the driver, at three o'clock in the morning, at my door telling me to "get up." We left Emmitsburg, before four o'clock—too early for me to hear once more the sound of the old convent bell and to know that you also were listening to the same sweet tones.

There were no passengers in the stage but myself, and the consequence was, that the great lumbering clumsy old stage (which by the way, was sufficiently old to have satisfied even a greater lover of antiquity than yourself) went jumping from side to side and pitching forward and backwards, heaving up and down for want of ballast, like a huge vessel in a storm at sea, or some mighty animal in convulsions. I tried to stay myself by seizing hold of the sides of the coach, and again by gathering together the soft cushions on the seats and lying down, but all to no purpose. The old stage in its eagerness to get to its journey's end went tumbling about worse than ever, until I was forced to give in, and let the hysterical creature bounce me down at Union Bridge, only too thankful that none of my bones were broken and that I still retained sufficient of my senses to ask the good, kind old lady with the lump on her neck, for the breakfast, of which I stood so much in need; for be it remembered, that this long journey of sixteen miles, over these terrible rough roads were taken on an empty stomach and part of the time so dark I could scarcely see houses, trees or even the fine barns so much admired by little Walter. The old lady gave me a good breakfast and in the kindness of her heart filled the empty spaces of my basket with fine *rambo* apples.

I left her neat, tidy house about eight o'clock, and took my seat in the car, which I did not leave again till I reached the Baltimore Depot, where I was agreeably surprised to find the first person to greet me was dear, kind, good Ned Abell who . . . had come to the depot to escort me to Mr Sanders'. . . . Immediately I was surrounded by the whole family, all eager to hear the last accounts from the "dear children"; even Mary lingered at the door to hear and to laugh at my recital of all. Their kind *Ma and Aunt Lizzie* wept for joy and thankfulness to learn they were happy and content in their new home. Every little incident that occurred during my stay with them was listened to with the greatest eagerness and they laughed heartily at my imitation of their stately step, with their long trains minus their hoops. . . .

Papa came in for me during the afternoon, and we started for Pleasant Plains about half past six in the evening, but not before I went down to see

Aunty & Miss Malone to give them also an account of my journey. I really believe Aunty was disappointed that I had not brought you "home again"; she seemed to think it almost impossible that I could leave you behind and looked at me with astonishment that I was not overwhelmed with grief at our separation and I fear she scarcely believed me, when I told her I was only too happy at being able to give you to the Sisters!

It was sometime after eight o'clock when we drove up to the house. You may be sure all the family were on hand, to make eager inquiries about Miss May—poor little Kitty could scarcely utter the words, "How did you leave Miss May, Mistress?" for the big tears which filled her eyes, and Mrs Schaeffer's kind & affectionate questions after "that child" told plainly of the strong hold you have on her maternal heart. Papa also listened with beaming eyes at all I had to tell as did Lizzie, Jim and dear old Mrs Pent. Kitty bids me say Juliet's little puppies are well and very beautiful; one is marked like Romeo. . . .

I found on opening my valise, a pair of drawers and body of yours, which I have sent up to you, and Papa also sends by mail your communion veil, two night caps and a guard chain for your keys. . . .

Give my affectionate regards to dear Sister Raphael and Sister Genevieve, and say to them the day spent at St Joseph's shall be marked as one of the bright spots for memory to rest upon, and kiss Mollie & Jeannette and Josephine for me. May our Blessed Mother & all good angels have you now and ever in their holy keeping.

Mama

---

At home Madge had other preoccupations, some very disturbing. These she withheld from her letters but began more and more to confide in her diary.

### Monday, September 22, 1862

*. . . Jim went in for Mrs Beer; during the day we had a very unpleasant scene and Mr Preston as usual behaved very foolishly. The men are to boil the butter all night and Mr Preston will attend to it. Mrs Schaeffer, Mrs Beer & myself are going to bed.*

### Tuesday, September 23, 1862

*I found on getting up this morning that Mr Preston had gone off without saying anything to anybody only leaving me a note telling me I could employ the men as I pleased. I put them to boiling another kettle of apple butter and in the meanwhile we made in the house some pear & apple marmalade which is very fine. We finished the apple butter about nine o'clock. Mr Preston has not come home tonight.*

---

Although he returned in a day or two, he went away again later that week. On Friday, Madge confided to her diary: "I can't account for Mr P. remaining so much in the city lately." But whatever distress she may have felt, Madge wrote a cheerful letter to May that same day. The counterpoint struck here—negative passages in her diary on her marital situation; positive, cheerful letters to May—continues as the year progresses.

Pleasant Plains
Sept 26th 1862

My darling little "Incumbrance,"

I have been greatly disappointed at not hearing from you during the past week. I hope however there is a letter for me now at the post office, which your Papa will bring out to me tomorrow—he and Mrs Schaeffer, together with Mrs Beer, having gone in to town this afternoon to remain all night. You will perceive from this I am altogether alone tonight. After the carriage drove off, I concluded to go over to Eudowood and make a visit which I have been contemplating ever since my return from St Joseph's. I found the ladies, with the exception of Mrs Carman, all home and delighted to see me, and to hear all the particulars of "little May's" going to school &c &c. They spoke of you with the greatest affection. . . .

Johnny also sent his regards and said, "If May was only home now, I would share with her the birds I expect to shoot tomorrow." I laughingly told him I would accept them for you!—The poor little innocent birds, sleeping so quietly in their leafy nests tonight little think of the "Sharpshooter" and his butcherous intentions towards them; if they did they would follow the prudent example of our would-be-valorous soldiers and "Skeddadle" before he got a chance at them. . . .

We have wished for you very often this week, knowing you would have been interested in the domestic duties going on. Last Monday and Tuesday the men, with Jim, as he says, "acting Boss over them," made cider and boiled two large kettles of apple butter; one night they were up all night, having a goodly number of them. Jim acted the McClellan policy over them, allowing some to retire for a while and then calling for reinforcements—in other words, part of them slept, while others worked, and vice versa; I also have been engaged superintending the preserving of sundry kinds of fruit. I have put up some very nice pear and apple marmalade, which I design you shall enjoy, by testing its good qualities on some of St Joseph's good bread at lunch time. . . .

By the way, when I sent your little packet up the other day, I quite forgot the English jacket belonging to your green dress. I will try and send it to you next week; in the meanwhile if you wear the dress, you can wear your red flannel jozey.[1]

While on the subject of dress, let me impress upon you the necessity of being comfortably clad when the weather changes, be sure your clothing is in accordance with the change, and do not run out of doors without throwing something over your shoulders. . . . I regret I did not pack in your trunk the shawl I wished you to take—if you think it would be desirable to have it or any other one, let me know. . . . I have been thinking now that you sleep alone, perhaps it would be as well if you did not take off your drawers body at night; unbutton your drawers, but keep the body on. I have also thought I had better send you some woolen undershirts for the winter. If you find the weather colder, or the house not so well heated as you have been accustomed to, let me know if the articles I have mentioned would be desirable.

My dear child, if you find any difficulty in reading my letters, ask one of the Sisters to be kind enough to read it for you. Each and every member of the family desires to be affectionately remembered to you. Good night. God bless you my dear child.

Mama

### Saturday, September 27, 1862

. . . Mr Preston came home about dark, but did not bring Mrs Morrison as I had hoped. Consequently we are alone for the first night for many years. I did not receive a letter from May as I expected and am very much disappointed.

St. Joseph's Sept 30th /62

My dear Mama,

I received your two letters the last one yesterday evening; and this morning Sister Raphael very kindly told me I could write to you to-day. I would have written to you before, but we are only allowed to write once every two weeks. That being the case, I can write my dear Mama but a very short letter; on next Friday you may expect to receive a very long one from me, it is already commenced. I am as happy as I can be and always have been. I am not in the least "homesick". My good kind Mama, your ansiaty about my not being warm enough may be put rest. I will be sure to take care of number 1. The other night I felt rather cold but forgot to say any thing about it till the next evening and when I did speak of it the Sister of the dormitory was horrified to think I was in the least uncomfortable and immediately brought me a blanket. You may see by this whether I am cold or not. I had a good laugh with one of the Sisters about the "*Wollen Shirts*" there is not the least necessity for them. Sister Teresa of the clothes room is so kind and lets us wear any thing we want and is always anxious to know whether we are warm enough or not. I have just been "*combed*" that is what we call having our hair combed here. Tuesdays and Fridays are combing days. Dear Mother, good bye the bell has rung for plain sewing and I must go. Give my love to Papa and every body home. From your little daughter

May

St. Joseph. Oct 3d 1862

My dear Mama,

I am not homesick yet, I know this will please Papa, for he has always admired fortitude and I am sure he could not have helped being pleased at the way in which I parted from you and acted afterwards, When I left you I did as you told me and ran up to the house, as I neared it I saw Mollie and Mary Ward looking out of one of the windows I laughed and called up to them "see! I have braved it out, I have braved it out." That night when I went to bed I thought I must feel very strange but I experienced no such feeling not a tear escaped me. Next morning I was asked by every one if I was "home sick yet" and I could always answer truly "non." Dear Mother I received your lovely letter of 14 pages. Sister Raphael sent for me one night and when I went to her she asked me if I would like "to have a letter" of course I said "yes Sister" and then Sister handed your dear letter Mama. By the time I was able to read it bed time had arrived so I had to be satisfied with the little I had read till the next evening. Every one was asking me if I had *really* got a letter 14 pages long, it was quite an *occurence*. Dear Mama please write to me as often as you can and make your letters as long as possible, please get every body I know to write to me it is such a comfort, tell them too, not to stand on ceremony. The day after I came here (which was Thursday) the boys from the mountain[2] paid a visit to their Sisters. We were all in the study room and Sister brought in a large basket of apples and at the same time told us the boys were in the parlor. In the commotion caused by so many girls we made quite a laughable mistake, and thought Sister said "here are some apples from the mountain, the girls who have brothers come first" Mollie and Jeannette were to go and see Tour but hearing this Jeannette held back (for she had no brother to make room for *those* that had. Sister had to tell it over two or three times. I wanted to go but Sister Raphal said as I had seen him so recently she could not let me see him then, but perhaps she would let me next time.

Dear Mama I began this letter Sunday and now it is Friday. I suppose you will get the two letters I have written since; before you get this one. Jeannette was in the infirmary for a day or so but is out now, please do not say any thing about it to Mrs Sanders as she will think Jeannette is very ill which is *far* from being the case.

When you see Mamie and Alice ask them to write to me, give my love to them and say I often think of them and wish we could be to gether. Please tell Kitty we have a gay time, but that I would often give it all up for one day with her. Yet still I am not "home sick."

I knew there was some thing I wanted to tell you but could not think what it was. I remember now that it was our takeing supper down at the creek. We had a delightful time. In the morning at breakfast Sister Raphal said we would "take supper at the creek" accordingly about 1 oclock in the afternoon we began to move. Georgie Davis and Pepa Miles were the only ones that stayed home Georgie because she had the neuralgia and Pepa becaused she got poisoned every time she went there, many of the Sisters went too. Father Gairdolpha rowed us in the little boat called the "Mary May" that was after supper. Lulie Jenkins and Tillie Harris came during the after-noon, to stay, they, had been here before. Mrs Jenkins was very much affected at leaving Lulie, Tillie had been here before and her Mother did not mind it so much. . . .

How I wish I could have taken a peep at Jim and the men making apple butter. Tell my Lizzie if I could only have a good long talk with her I should be so happy. . . .

. . . Dear Mama, write soon, and give all the love you can to my Papa and tell him if he sends up the linen I will make him a shirt. Sister Johana [allows] me to do so she says I can sew well enough to make one. Please do not send the bosom already made as I want to make it myself. Sister Mary Elizabeth returned from a Mission a few days ago she gave me a lesson day before yesterday. Sister Mary Edwards (my own music teacher) was sick, she had been delicate for a long time and a few days ago heard of the death of her brother since then she has been very poorly. I love her dearly. Please send my mass veil when you send my English jacket we are obliged to have a fine one for communion thicker one for mass everyday. Will you please get me a looking glass (just a small one) and send me a tooth-brush for my comb. Yesterday we took a long walk up the road and passed the bridge we stoped at a house belonging to the Sisters, we had not been home very long before the boys from the Colledge came over, Tommy and Willie Jenkins had gotten permission tickets to see us but used them to go nut hunting with, so we did not see them. Mr Deilman came over in the course of the afternoon, I forgot to tell you he [came] to see us the day we were down at the creek but did not see us.

Dear Mama I must now stop I think you must almost be tired. I will try to be a good little girl. Tell Papa to write to me soon.

From your affectionate little girl,

May

Pleasant Plains
Oct 5th 1862

My darling child,

Your letter will be a day later this week, owing to Papa not going to the city yesterday; I am sorry for it, as I would not willingly give you even a momentary disappointment, much less a whole day—but this time it is unavoidable—therefore kiss and forgive Mama!

Your two letters reached me on Friday evening; Papa having remained in the city Thursday night consequently he brought them out together. I can't tell you my sweet child, how earnestly I had yearned to hear from you. I did not know, or rather I had forgotten, you were restricted in your time for writing. I thought you could, if you so desired, write at all times during recreation hours, provided you were supplied with the necessary articles, and in no wise interfered with the school supplies and its hours. I even hope it is so yet, at all events, I would like (always with the "Sisters" permission be it distinctly understood) that you could *keep a letter on hand* and write a little in it, whenever you feel so disposed, so that when "letter writing day" comes you would have a good long one, well filled with all your little doings—your thoughts and emotions—your feelings and wishes, jotted down just as they come into that teeming little brain of yours, to send to me. Such a letter would make me feel as though we were not so widely separated. . . .

Your letters were a great comfort and pleasure to us all. I never doubted your being "happy" at St Joseph's, but it was a great satisfaction to have the assurance from yourself. And you escaped the *almost* universal contagion of boarding school children, "Homesickness"? Well! to what shall I attribute your exemption?—Surely not to indifference to your home, to Papa, Mama, "old Kitt"—and "darling Lizzie"?—perhaps the strong philosophic strain running through your character has sustained you in these days. Ah! I have hit upon the real and true cause. Your going to St Joseph's has been but a transfer from *one* home to *another*—the dear Sisters have supplied the place of parents—the children around you, of old friends at home, and the green fields—the grand old woods, the murmuring stream, the song of birds and hum of busy insects are but another phase of your own country home, and thus my "little incumbrance" has been spared that most painful of all diseases, a longing for home and its dear inmates!

I am inclined to think, when the "north wind blow, and falls the hail and snow," you and "Sister" won't laugh, or be inclined to reject the "woollen shirts" now offered to you. It is true, just now, with the pleasant summer sunshine and balmy breezes, a superabundance of clothing is not desirable. . . .

I am very grateful to the kind Sister for supplying you with an extra blanket the night you were cold. As soon after you receive this letter, as you can conveniently—go to the Sister and give her a sweet kiss and tell her I sent it for taking such good care of my little daughter, and tell her I said would she please tuck you up occasionally during the coming cold winter nights.

You say the "bell has rung for plain sewing"—"goodbye &c"—I judge from that, you attend the class—please tell me darling, what kind of sewing you are engaged at? Are you working those sleeves & band you took away with you? When you finish them or even before, I should like you to work me, for Miss Mary Grady, a pair of sleeves and band. . . . Miss Mary is so very fond of you, I am sure she would be gratified by your showing that little attention to her. . . .[3]

You will be surprised to learn I have not been to the city, since I came home from St Joseph's. I have been busy at home, but on Friday evening when your Papa came home, he brought me the sad intelligence, that little Nannie was very ill of typhoid fever, and not expected to recover. I hope however their fears have exaggerated the child's danger. . . . She is a bright talented child and I would be sorry her mother should lose her.

Mrs Schaeffer received a letter from Major Schaeffer a day or two since; he was well and was in Richmond on the 29th of September the date of the letter, and was not as she feared he might be, in any of the battles in Maryland. . . .

Give my warmest love to [Mollie and Jeannette] and tell them I wish I had one of those carpets so famous in the Arabian Nights; I would wrap you all in it, and by one sweep of my wand, transfer it to Pleasant Plains, roll you out, and keep you with me tonight, and have you back again to your comfortable dormitory before the bell rouses you in the morning. . . .

Mary Lizzie and Alice come up very often to see me. . . . They send much love and wish you would write to them. . . . Papa and I, together with Lizzie and Kitty, made a frolic of gathering those fine apples in front of the house. . . . I am sure I have not laughed so much for a very long time as I did in the gathering of them. Papa was on the cherry ladder reaching them down to us, or throwing them in our aprons; occasionally they would glance off from the right direction and come bump upon our heads, or hit us on the shoulder; indeed several came in too close contact with our noses, cheeks and eyes, and when you consider the size of them and the height from which they came, you will know it was no trifling thing to be struck by one. Buck & the colts are well and receive very complacently the caresses I give them for you. Juliet and her little puppies are beautiful and Jewell is looking magnificently. Kitty and Lizzie send a great deal of love and Papa and Mama pray God to bless their little girl.

Pleasant Plains
October 10th 1862

I have been greatly disappointed this week, my dear child. I had fully calculated on sending you a box of "sundries" by the wagon which I am told goes to

Emmitsburg today (Friday), but owing to your Papa being engaged in an important trial in the city for several days, I have not been able to accomplish it; however if nothing occurs to prevent, you may look for it some day in the coming week. Your dear friends, Mamie and Alice, have contributed a nice jelly cake made by themselves; if it should be a little stale when you receive it, recollect it is no fault of theirs, but has become so in consequence of the delay in sending it to you. . . .

I am actually inclined to think that dear Aunty Stansbury, *in her heart*, if she don't really say so, is fully impressed with the idea that we parents who have parted with our children are quite deficient in maternal affection, and you children, who have left us, are wanting in that love which all mothers are so desirous of possessing. As yet they have made no arrangement with regard to a teacher. . . .

Alice spent the day & night with me last Wednesday. The rest of the family had gone to Mr Brady's to spend the day, but Alice, true to the eccentricity of her character, preferred coming up to Aunty Preston's and staying. While here, she wrote you a letter. . . .

While on the subject of letters, let me express to you my very great satisfaction and gratification from all your letters—really my little darling, *I did not expect such clever ones* from a child so unaccustomed to writing as yourself; Papa also was very much pleased and expressed himself so repeatedly while I was reading your letters aloud to him. When you write again, address your letter to him and I am sure you will receive an answer, very soon. . . .

After you left, and while I was still absent, Lizzie took the curtain, laces &c &c off your altar, and washed and ironed them beautifully. I then arranged them on the altar, together with the books and images, and a glass of flowers, and each night, in spirit, I am with you in my prayers. . . .

As soon as I possibly could, after receiving your letter, I went to the city, to see Sister Raphael. I had but a moment to speak to her. . . . She . . . took time to say—you were well, *and doing well.* If she has returned, give my kindest love to her and say I almost regret I did not *capture* her and carry her out to Pleasant Plains by main force. President Lincoln would certainly have held me guiltless, as he so fully believes in such doings himself. . . .

Papa sends much love as does also Lizzie & Kitty. Jim says, "He misses Miss May so much." God bless you my dear child and believe me your devoted Mama. . . .

## Monday, October 13, 1862

*. . . Mr Preston drove to the city this morning, and said he would not be home this evening but contrary to our expectations he returned just at tea time, and brought with him a nice tin box to send up to May with sundry little things. He also brought the papers, containing an account of Stuart's raid into Pa.[4]*

## Tuesday, October 14, 1862

. . . I cut out, this afternoon for May, the set of chemises the first she has ever had.

## Thursday, October 16, 1862

. . . We were quite surprised by a visit from Mrs Hay—in company with a Federal officer, Major Beverage. She . . . was very agreeable. The gentleman was quiet & dignified. . . .

## Tuesday, October 21, 1862

. . . this evening I have been sewing very hard to make up for lost time, and finished May's little chemises, having made the four in less than five days. I hope they will fit her & please her. I am about changing my lodgings tonight, coming down to Mr Preston's room and leaving my own!

## Wednesday, October 22, 1862

I slept excellently in my new quarters, and on awaking this morning found the wind was blowing a perfect gale. We all rose early, to enable the men to get in the corn they had husked, and I, thinking the wind had brought down some chestnuts, started out directly after breakfast and remained out till dinner and gathered 5½ quarts. This afternoon I cut out four pairs of drawers for May. Mr Preston remained home today.

## Saturday, October 25, 1862

We rose early this morning and were glad to find we were likely to have a pleasant day, as we were going to the city. John Kaniff went as far as Towsontown with us, and there gave himself to the sheriff and went to jail, to avoid being given up to the military in consequences of the draft. . . .

## Wednesday, October 29, 1862

. . . this morning I walked over to Eudowood, but seeing the carriage harnessed to take the ladies to the city I did not go in. . . . Shortly after my return to the house, Mr Preston came, he having been absent since Monday morning; something evidently has gone wrong, as he is wretchedly nervous tonight.

**Thursday, October 30, 1862**

*I rose very early to accompany Mr Preston to the city and return again with Jim. On reaching town we drove about apparently to consume time, as I could see no other reason. I went to Akers and purchased myself a fine black merino. . . . While in the city I was the more convinced my conjectures were right about Mr Preston, as he was impatient to have me off and watched me in my intercourse with the inmates of the house. We reached home about one o'clock, and I have had a bad headache ever since.*

Pleasant Plains<br>Oct 30th 1862

My darling child,

I have been anxiously looking for a letter from you for the last week, but thus far I have been doomed to disappointment—why is this? Surely you are not becoming indifferent to your home and parents! or what would be equally as strange—you certainly are not prohibited writing to your Mother and Father at least *once a week*, or even oftener, if you desired. In future, I desire you to write either to Papa or myself *weekly*, and to enable you to do so, and not to infringe upon school hours or duties, let part of Thursday, (your holy day) be devoted to writing to us. As I do not wish to abridge your pleasures and recreations, I shall be satisfied with as *short a letter* as you choose to write. . . . On receiving this letter, make my wishes known to the Sister who controls this department. . . .

Your Papa has been engaged all the week in the city on important business connected with his profession; consequently I have been alone, occasionally however cheered and enlivened by visits from our kind neighbours—Miss Rachael and Johnny (the latter supplying me at times with a little bird, making a savoury morsel for either breakfast or tea). . . .

We have had very exciting times in the county during the last two weeks. The "drafting" so long talked of, took place, and I am happy to be able to inform you that none of our immediate *young* friends, were so unfortunate as to be drawn. Mr Owens, however, was not so lucky; he, as was to be supposed, has provided himself with a substitute, who being accepted, places our good friend "at home" again. Poor Kaniff was also drafted, but as he was already under bond to the court, he could not be taken. One of Mrs Sheeley's boys was drawn, as was also Longneckers' son, which . . . has given great satisfaction to those persons in the neighbourhood to whom they have made themselves obnoxious by their upholding the tyranny of the present government. You have doubtless heard through the "girls" of Hillen's *raid* into Baltimore; I call it "raid," for like Stuart in Pennsylvania he took the people literally by storm.[5]

On Saturday . . . I purchased for you a blue merino dress, of that new and exquisite shade called Humbolt, and also solforino[6] flannel to make you a "Garibaldi"[7] to wear with the striped grey skirt I gave you—these, with the winter dress you already have and which I am now "fixing up" and those you have with you, you must try and make answer for this winter. . . .

Lizzie amuses herself very much, wondering how you will look with your new drawers and chemise on.

With your change of attire, you will be fulfilling the Scriptures and literally "putting away childish things." I wish you also to measure exactly the length of the dress that pleases you best, measure the back width and enclose it in your next letter; a piece of spool cotton will do and will not increase the weight of your letter. I have nothing as a guide. Have you grown any, or will the pattern of your body that I had cut, do for you now?

Pleasant Plains
Novr 6th 1862

Dear child,

As Papa goes to the city in the morning, you will receive your letter a day earlier . . . than usual. I wonder if you know my child that it is almost three weeks since we have heard from you! Both your father and myself have been rendered very anxious in consequence of your long silence—to ascertain if possible the cause of it I went to the city yesterday and called on Mrs Sanders —from her, I heard that Miss Jenkins had come down from St Joseph's to attend a wedding in the city and of course had brought news of yourself and the girls. It satisfied me at all events that you were well when she left the Vale, and I trust you have so continued, but you must in future my little pet, write to us *weekly*; tell Sister it is your Father's request as well as my own. It matters not *how brief* the communication—if you simply say—"I am well," or "I am sick"—as the case may be—at all events, if you find your school duties too much, or if you feel it too great a tax on your time and inclination, let not more than a *fortnight* at furthest ever pass without our hearing from you, and when you do write, always acknowledge having received my letters, so that I may know they do not miscarry or are [not] detained at the post office. Mrs Sweet . . . says all her letters from Baltimore are opened. Consequently I feel some anxiety to know if mine to you are received regularly. The detectives would find little in my letters to pay for their trouble in opening them, but that would hardly deter them in their great anxiety to discover treason lurking somewhere.

Last night the fashionable world of Baltimore was all alive with excitement arising from a grand wedding to come off—Mr Kremlinbury and Miss Jenkins. The bride was to be resplendent in white silk and lace—and one hundred and fifty dear friends were to congratulate her after the ceremony was performed, altogether such a wedding has not been given for a long time and tonight, the happy couple receive *five hundred* more dear friends at their own house.

I forgot to tell you that I also called on Father Elder, thinking he would soon be going to St Joseph's and I could send a message or two to you by him: but judge of my surprise when he told me [he] had already been up there, that he saw you &c &c. I was . . . more pleased than I can tell you to hear good accounts of you. I do so hope my little one that you will in every respect improve the opportunities so graciously given you. I place at the head of everything—your religious duties. . . .

Are you able to get up without any trouble to yourself and to others, and do you dress in the usual time allotted—and do you ever wish Mama was along side of you, to comb those unruly locks of yours? What a comfort to you combing day must be. I suspect you would like it to be every day. Above all my child have you had any of your "sick spells" yet?[8] Do let me know, and let me know also, if you have been sick, how you got along without Mama? . . .

The family are all well and desire much love to you. Papa has been quite well of late, and everything is going on better than for a long time. *Indeed I am very happy just now!*

Lizzie & Kitty talk constantly of you, and whenever anything unusual occurs that would be pleasing to you, they always wish Miss May was here. . . .

God bless you my child.
Your devoted
Mama

St. Joseph's Nov. 5th 1862

My dear Mrs Preston

I am sorry that May's silence should have given you so much anxiety, the ordinary term for letter-writing has been interrupted, but in future you will hear from her more frequently. I am very much pleased with your little darling's exertions & deportment. I find her naturally bright, & with a mind stored with general information for one so young. Now she is learning more methodically & systematically, and I may add more thoroughly. Grammar she has *commenced* & will I trust prove a good grammarian, so essential for conversation & writing. She is very docile respectful & polite to teachers & companions with whom she is a favorite. I suppose she has given you an account of her *personification* or rather representation of the Archangel &c— She acted her part very well.

I trust she will realize her fond parents' expectations. The report in January will show the result of the examinations of next month. Present my kind regards to Mr Preston.

Yours sincerely<br>
S M Raphael

St. Joseph's Nov. 7th / 62

My dear dear Mama,

I take this favorable opportunity of writing to you, for as it is All-Saints-day we have holiday and tomorrow being letter day we can write now. . . .

But if I had all today and all tomorrow it would not [be] sufficient time for me to write all I wish. Since you last heard from me I have been promoted, not in the way that such things generally are . . . done (by degrees) but I was suddenly transported from a mortal to an angel and that too the angel Raphael. As Saint Raphael's day approched the Sisters began to think of some way to celebrate it, of course without Sister Raphael's knowledge, and this you may know was very hard to do, particularly as Sister had strictly forbidden any thing to be done on her day. But Saint Raphael put into the minds of the Sisters, and this was the plan they adopted. One morning as I was finishing my bed making Sister Cephas who has charge of our dormitory called me to her and said "as soon as you have finished your bed go up to Sister Caroline in the middle dormitory" I immediately expected a scolding (that is what we call a piece of advice) for something I had unconsciously done wrong. When I went up Sister Caroline took me through her classroom and into ours. I knew of course something grand was going to happen. When Sister had seated herself I ventured to ask if I had gotten into trouble, and Sister asked me in return if I had any thing on my conscience. After a pause I said "no Sister" she aske me severl times but I still gave the same answer Sister then asked if I could keep a secret and I said yes indeed Sister. It seemed to me then that I was not going to get a scolding and in this I was quite right. Sister then told me that as Sister Raphael had forbidden them to do any thing on her day they had gotten St. Raphael to come down and pay Sister [a] visit, and had determined upon me to personate him. Sister Caroline said she was going to dress me as an angel, and Mary Jane Byrne one of the sweetest little girls in the house and about eleven years old was to take the part of a mortal and ask me why I had come from heaven, and I was to reply. . . . At first I did not think I would be able to cary out my part with becoming dignity. It was on Tuesday and we were to know our piece by Thursday the 24th therefore we immediately began to learn it. Friday was Sister Raphael's day, but the eve of the day is generaly celabrated not the day itself. But on Thursday Sister again said nothing was to be done on Thursday not so with Friday, every thing was gotten ready. As we take dinner at half past eleven, Sister Caroline began to dress me about a quarter before eleven. . . . The girls had already suspected something, for Mary Jane and I had to be absent so often. I am sure you would have laughed if you could have seen us, the minuet any of the girls asked us any thing we make some excuse and go off. After Sister had dressed me she took me dwon in the Clothes-room where Mother and severl of the Sisters had come to see the "angel" The "mortal" was not present being at dinner prayrs. We stood in the passage near the door of the study room so as to be ready as soon as prayrs were over to make our grand entrance. Sister Caroline and the singing class were to sing a hymn to Saint Raphael, so the instant prayers were over Sister Gabrielle who was inside the room beconed for us to come in, and then they commenced the hymn and sang it while St Raphael walked up to Sister Raphael and was joined by the little mortal. Indeed Mother you may imagin how I felt when every where I would look some one was ready to laught at me and I felt like returning it when I thought of my short worked skirt over skirt of half a dozen veils, and white kid slippers an inch and a half too long for me, and sandles of striped purple ribbon bound around and across my stockings.

Mary Jane said her piece very loud and well neither of us broke down. As soon as I could I got my clothes off and went into dinner. But this was not all in the evening we had to go over to the community and speak for Mother and the Sisters. Mother gave me a large apple and both of us some candies. Dear Mother please forgive me for writing this long description, but I was so anxious to tell you all I could not help it. . . .

Dear Mother write soon. Good bye. From your devoted child

May

### Sunday, November 9, 1862

. . . *Mrs Beer, Mr Preston & myself took a short walk to the barn & the cottage, but it was too cold to remain out long. This afternoon Mr Preston went to the city to remain all night leaving Mrs Beer out till Tuesday. We were not much surprised at his doing so, as he generally continues to be in the city one night while she is out here.*

### Monday, November 10, 1862

. . . *Mr Preston returned home this evening, evidently nervous and abashed! We feel assured there was company in his office last night! . . .*

Pleasant Plains
Novr 13th 1862

If I had only been made aware, my precious little "Immortal" that you were about donning the embroidered tunics, the misty veils, the flowing locks and sandaled slippers of the Angelical host, I might have been spared a vast amount of sewing—some considerable expense—and no little anxiety about the fit of sundry "Garibaldies"—"Balmorals"[9] "Secession Hoods" &c &c, I have been manufacturing for the wear and comfort of the above little immortal when I foolishly considered her "of the Earth, Earthy"—but the things are now done, and unless St Raphael's "Substitute" should descend from the high pedestal upon which the fancy of her kind friends have placed her, I can think of no alternative but the transferring of these substantials to the "little mortal, one of the sweetest children in the school."

Your letter my darling child amused and interested us greatly. Papa brought it home the other night, and of course I opened it immediately and began reading it aloud. Mrs Beer was with us, and Kitty as usual standing by my chair—when I came to the description of the dress and the "white kid slippers an inch and a half longer than the feet"—Kitty could contain herself no long[er], but yielded to the most hearty fit of laughter I have heard since you left us—of course it was contagious, and—Papa—Mrs Beer, myself and Lizzie (who was peeping in) joined in concert.—It must have been quite an interesting incident, [compared] to the monotony of school life and one in which I am pleased to know you acted so fair a part. Dear Sister Raphael—how astonished she must have been. . . .

I would like to know what you do with my letters—surely by this time your portfolio must be full to overflowing. If such is the case, and you wish to keep them, you had better put them at the bottom of your trunk where they will be out of your way and give room for those to be written in the future.

Darling, send in your next letter a copy of St Raphael's speech, which you must have forgotten to enclose in your last. I have heard of pulpit oratory and should like to have a specimen of celestial eloquence.

Mama. . . .


## Sunday, November 16, 1862

. . . Mrs Beer & Louis spent the morning under the persimmon tree and Mr Preston as usual pottering about and making excuses for going to the city this afternoon. Of course I knew he would go, but my countenance must have expressed my suspicions, as he took Mrs Beer as well as Louis with him to the city this afternoon leaving here, a little after four o'clock. I have not been at all well today and shall retire early tonight.

## Monday, November 17, 1862

. . . *I went out this morning to overlook the men at their work and found them scattered round in various ways quite different from the arrangement Mr Preston made. I soon put them in order and they have kept pretty well to their work. Mr Preston has not come home tonight.* . . .

Pleasant Plains
Novr 17th 1862

My darling child,

I have just finished a long letter to your God Mother, and as it is somewhat earlier than I wish to retire, I will talk to you a little before bed-time. Mrs Beer and Louis came out with Papa and I, on Saturday evening, and owing to a new tenant going into the offices this morning, they were all obliged to be there so early they determined to drive in last night; consequently I was alone last evening and am so again tonight, the rain having kept Papa in the city. I hope you received, and have read tonight, my long last letter to you. . . . There is reading enough in that one to occupy all your spare time for half the week. I think I see you pouring over its pages, trying to *make out* Mama's scratchings. . . . I do my darling endeavour to write distinctly, but just as I get a little in the way of it, the pen starts off in a gallop to keep pace with my thoughts, and then alas for the writing—one of your favourite spiders, scampering away from a bottle of ink into which he had suddenly fallen would not make more wonderful hieroglyphics than the steel instrument with which I try to communicate my thoughts and wishes to you. . . .

I was only in the city a few hours, having gone in to purchase you a blanket shawl, but instead of which I got you a new article, a kind of talmer[10] made of woven worsted yarn. . . . I have also purchased you a net, which of course is too pretty to be worn in common—you must wear it on highdays and holy days, and take good care of it. I send you a Balmoral, which to my taste is also beautiful. All the ladies who have seen it say you must wear it with the Garibaldi I have made for you, hence I have put brass buttons on the belt to enable you to do so. . . .

Tuesday

I have had quite a pleasant day, my darling child, down at Mrs Stansbury's. I felt anxious about the fit of your dress &c, and concluded to send them down for Alice to try on. I packed them in the tin box, and Kitty and I wended our way to Union Hall. As usual they were delighted to see me, and quite amused at my errand. In a short time we had our little May with us, and when she was entirely herself, Garibaldi, talman, hood &c &c, we called Uncle Willie and the rest of the family to see her. Alice assumed the ways and attitudes of May to perfection, *even her affection for me.* The dear child had been amusing herself making a little present for you, which you will find on the top of your box. She sends her love and hopes the article she has made will be useful to you. I have some fears myself of the propriety of sending it in juxta-position with your nuts & candies; indeed you may consider yourself fortunate if your clothing is not nibbled by its little teeth. She also sends one of the same kind, which she desires you to ask Sister Raphael to accept and use as a pen wiper. . . .

Papa ordered the box today and William has had great pleasure in making it. Lizzie, Kitty, Jim and dear old Mrs Pent assisted in packing it. The chest-nuts were partly gathered at P. Plains and Retirement.[11]. . .The corn is a specimen of Johnny's crop and sent by himself, the cakes Lizzie made and most unaccountably forgot to put the sugar in them, but we thought we would send them up as they were, better than nothing. . . .

Good night my darling child
Mama

### Tuesday, November 18, 1862

. . . *Mr Preston returned this evening and says he has been quite sick ever since he has been away.*

Just a word my dr Mrs Preston to say that I received your letter. May & I have made a compact, that is when she feels inconvenienced by one of these migraines as the French term them, she is to inform me without delay, & she will remain in the Infirmary that night so as to have a rest in the morning, whenever she suffers from them.

She is a bright little creature, & I guess if she had made you acquainted with a schoolgirls' trick the other night, you would not be uneasy about her being melancholy. She continues to do well in her studies.

Yours sincerely
S. M. Raphael

Nov. 20th 1862

### Sunday, November 23, 1862

. . . *Mr. Preston as usual has gone to the city to remain tonight, this is the third Sunday in succession. Alas! alas! will he never be reclaimed!* . . .

Baltimore
Novr 29th 1862

My darling little pet,

In my last letter written since I came to the city, I promised to write to you the next day, but the next was Thanksgiving and we had constant visiting. . . .

Aunty[12] and I have missed you so much during my visit. You must remember this is the first time since you were born, that I have come to the city to remain over night without having you with me. . . .

You will be pleased to learn and to communicate to the girls . . . the gratifying information that our respected but unfortunate "fellow citizens" who have so unjustly been incarcerated in the walls of those gloomy forts in the North have been *unconditionally* released, their release dating from Thanksgiving day. Marshall Kane and Mayor Brown are expected home this evening; the other gentlemen returned last night.[13] There was no public demonstration of course, but they were received with quiet joy and satisfaction by all their friends. . . .

Your devoted
Mama

Pleasant Plains
Decr 3d 1862

My precious child,

Owing to a spell of headache with which I have been troubled for the last few days, I have not written to you since I returned to P. Plains after my agreeable visit to the city. I am quite well again and to beguile an hour or two this evening, I have seated myself to have a talk with my little daughter. Tomorrow will be two weeks since your box left us, and yet my darling you have not written us one line to say you have rec'd it. This is altogether wrong, and I am sorry to say, it very much displeases your Papa. . . . If you have not yet rec'd the box, and we knew the fact, we could institute some inquiry as to where it might be retained, and not let it be altogether lost or mislaid. I have another dress to make you for Christmas, but I fear you will not get it, as I cannot have it cut till I know something about the fit of those I have already sent you. I design coming up myself about that time, and wish you to write to me at once, and tell me at what time you would prefer my coming. Shall I come before Christmas and New Year? Your father has thought of driving up in our own carriage, and I rather inclined to that way myself at first, but now I think if the roads should be bad, and in the winter time we cannot look for anything else, we should find it so very unpleasant, that I disposed to discourage that mode and adopt the old beaten track of railroads and stage coaches. . . .

I suppose you will like to know what wonderful amount of shopping I did while in Baltimore and what kind of winter fixings I got for myself. . . . I have a little brown felt bonnet, the attraction to me being that its shape is modest and I think becoming, and not like those now in vogue among the fashionable damsels, an inverted coal scuttle with a cavity large enough to hold a dozen good sized peonies, dahlias or cabbage roses. . . . The trimmings on the little bonnet, being one long white and brown feather—a brown or rather, black worsted dress with brown flowers on it, and a long loose sack of very dark brown cloth, you will perceive I am like little "Jenny wren" of childish memory, "but I will wear my brown gown and never dress too fine." All this nonsense about dress to a young lady deep in the mysteries of Mathematics, Algebra, Grammar &c &c, must appear very puerile, but as Mama's appearance has always been a matter of considerable importance to you, I thought you would be gratified to be able to picture, in your mind's eye, her looks this winter.

I had a pleasant visit from Johnny this afternoon. The boy has taken a fancy to attempt the grafting of fruit trees. So he came over to get some grafts from our fine apple & cherry trees. I walked out with him to cut the grafts and select from such trees as I thought most desirable. . . .

The girls have as yet no governess and one would think from Mamie's great turn out in the dressing line this winter that she had altogether put aside all thoughts of school life and duties. I am very sorry to see it, but I suppose they know their own business best. . . . Lizzie and Kitty talk constantly of you and often wish you were home. . . .

God bless you darling
Mama

St. Joseph's Nov [n.d.] 1862

My dear Mama

I have received your last three letters the one you wrote before I got my box and two since. . . . I never can thank you enough for my box every thing was just as nice and pretty as it could be. I have nearly demolished the good things. The Garibaldi is lovely, and the ballmoral too. I have not flourished in my new underclothes yet but expect to do so tomorrow. . . .

You have asked several times "What my studies are" of course you know I do not learn anything but english, music, and plain sewing. All I can tell you is the way I have my time distributed. We get up a quarter after 5, leave a half an hour to dress, go down to prayers after which we study that is if it is not time to go to Mass. Then we hear Mass almost every day except Sunday then come home and go to breakfast, then up stairs and make our beds then 20 minutes recreation before studies of which we have one hour then go to class (I do not know [how] long and then the next half hour I go to music, afterwards to class, one quarter, for reading on geography and the other quater for catechism, then prayrs and dinner at half past eleven, then I have recreation until half past one, go to plain sewing for an hour, writing class half an hour, arithmetic one hour, between studies half an hour, music half an hour, and general studies one hour, supper and recreation until eight oclock, prayers, and then we go to bed. So you can now tell what I do all day. . . .[14]

Good bye my darling Mama Please write to me soon. From your loveling little daughter May. . . .

## Tuesday, December 9, 1862

*It was not so cold today, & the snow is disappearing, the ice however is forming very nicely on the pond, and if it continues as good till Mr Preston comes home, I will get him to take it in at once. I finished today the 1st of May's nightgowns, and now I have nothing else to make for her this winter. I would make her a black silk apron, if I had the material and send it up with her blue merino dress; if I can get to the city in time to buy the silk and make one, I will do so. Lizzie & I have been looking over trunks, boxes &c &c and we took out the carpet belonging to my room, to mend and fix it up. Jim & William tacked it down this evening. . . .*

Pleasant Plains
Decr 9th 1862

My dear baby,

I write tonight, from the mere pleasure of writing, as I have not the slightest idea, *when* I can have my letter taken to the post office. Papa is again away to Ellicott's Mills, *trying*, to try, the case of Haman and Kaniff, which was set for yesterday week; but owing to the absence of some important witnesses, it was put off from day to day, until the present time; poor dear papa has been worried more than enough with it, having to go so far from home; it is necessary he should remain in town at nights, which you know is at times very unpleasant to him, consequently I have been much alone for the last week. . . .

You would have been amused and indignant also (as I was) at an incident that occurred on the farm last Friday during the fiercest of the snowstorm. Kitty came running into the sitting room, greatly excited crying out, "O Mistress, there is a whole squad of Union Soldiers on horseback riding round the house, what can they want?" Of course I became excited also, and stepped to the conservatory porch to see what it all meant, and sure enough, there were some six or eight men on horseback dressed in cavalry uniforms, looking very consequential and talking in a pompous manner to the workmen who had gathered around them. Without waiting for bonnet or wrapping up and regardless of the snow, which was falling fast, I started down to meet them and ascertain their business. On approaching them, an officer rode forward, whom I accosted thus—"Have you any business here, Sir?" "Yes Madam! but step under this shed, and protect yourself from the storm." I did so, and then said, "Now Sir, tell me your business, that it may be settled as soon as possible." The tone of my voice, and my determined manner, had the most amusing effect upon the man; he blushed up to the roots of his hair, stuttered and stammered and at length faltered out, "We want Mr Kaniff." I looked him full in the face and replied, "You will find him down at Howard Court House." I then began to have a glimmering of who these people were. They came from Camp Bradford and were in search of the poor drafted creatures who had not reported themselves at Headquarters. It gave me infinite satisfaction to tell them where Kaniff was, as I knew he was beyond their reach. He then asked for Chenowith, who has been cutting wood on the farm for the past month. On being told that the men had not been at work during the day, they consulted together, and two of them started off to scour the woods in search of the poor fellow, while the rest remained riding round the house, evidently thinking the man was concealed somewhere about. Finding they were likely to remain sometime, I turned to him who was standing by me and said, "When these men leave the premises, see that the gates are well fastened after them!!" and entered the house. In the meanwhile the two who had gone in pursuit of the man found him at his own house, where he had hoped to conceal himself, and they and their comrades rode off, taking the poor man with them. I understand they have been doing this same thing all through the county. Is it not shameful that the quiet of one's home should be thus disturbed, and men in the peaceful pursuit of their daily avocations ruthlessly carried off to fight the battles of a cause in which they have no sympathy and indeed are altogether opposed to? . . .

You have not answered Alice's letter yet; will you be so kind as to tell me *why* you have not done so? The poor child asks me every time she sees me, if you have not sent her any message in any of my letters, and as I can not tell an untruth, I am obliged to say no!

Poor little Kitty is just recovering from one of her bad spells of cold, sore throat, ear ache, and head ache, indeed for two or three days she was sick, but Lizzie and I nursed her, and she is now nearly well. The family all send their loves to you. . . .
God bless you!

Mama

## Wednesday, December 10, 1862

*Treanor brought me a piece of ice this morning, which looked very fine, and as all hands seemed desirous of cutting, I put them at it. They took in six loads in the four horse wagon. . . .*

## Thursday, December 11, 1862

*The ice hardened considerably on the pond during the night and this morning the men were at work at an early hour; during the day the weather became quite warm, and the snow disappeared quite rapidly. The men took in today eight loads of ice and tomorrow by noon they expect to finish. I walked over to Aunty Stansbury's this morning & they insisted on my remaining to dinner; soon after dinner Kitty came over for me. On reaching home, the old lady told me she was going to town in the morning and I could go with her. I have arranged to do so. As Mr Preston is not yet home.*

## Monday, December 15, 1862

*. . . Mr Preston & I rose early this morning as he wished to get to the city early to fill an engagement. Mr Preston left here about eight o'clock and as usual when he has not remained in the city on Sunday night, he generally does on Monday so he has remained tonight, though I expected him home to take me to the city tomorrow to attend a lecture at the Maryland Institute.[15] Aunty Stansbury spent the afternoon with me.*

## Friday, December 19, 1862

*It was bright & clear, and though not quite so cold as yesterday, it nevertheless has not snowed any. Mr Preston remained home all day, till after four o'clock, at which time he drove to the city evidently to remain all night, very nervous and feeling badly and looking still more so. Mr Preston superintended the killing of the hogs today five in number; they looked tolerably well. . . .*

Pleasant Plains
Decr 19th 1862

My darling child,

 I wrote you so hastily and imperfectly yesterday, that I avail myself of Papa going to the city today, to write again. . . . The "Christmas box" has been a pleasant contemplation to all of us for some time past, and now that it has really gone and the excitement attendant on it has passed away—I feel as if I could exclaim with Othello my "occupation's gone."[16] Papa took the box to the bookstore of Kelly Hedian & Pet, yesterday at noon, when much to my disappointment, he was told that the college wagon . . . owing to the holiday times, would not make its usual trip on Thursday, but would leave the city on next Wednesday the 24th, as you know *just one* day before Christmas. Now if the wagoner will leave your box at St Joseph's as he passes, all will be right, and you will receive your things to flourish on Christmas. . . . I am anxious . . . as I wish you to wear *new clothing* in honor of the birth of our Blessed Saviour. You know that has always been one of my fancies—to have you freshly attired on these religious festivals!

Perhaps little darling this may be the last letter I shall write till I see you, which I hope will be on Friday, the day after Christmas. . . .

# 2

# Getting an Education

THE PRESTONS' PERSONAL PAPERS take no note of a momentous event in the history of this nation—the bloody battle of Antietam. The engagement, one of the costliest in human life ever recorded, occurred only one day after Madge's return from the trip to Emmitsburg and in a part of Maryland not unknown to her. Although the Union army under General George McClellan failed to pursue the retreating Southern forces across the Potomac, they nevertheless had blocked the Confederate advance into the North. In Washington the outcome was seen as sufficiently decisive that on January 1, 1863, Lincoln put into effect his previously proclaimed intention to emancipate all slaves in the rebelling states. Although this action did not apply to states such as Maryland which had remained loyal to the Union, the implications of the president's plan were already being felt by both slaves and slaveholders in the Preston household.

Preston seemed more aware of these implications than did his wife. Yet the burden of coping with changing relationships with the servants fell most heavily upon her in the family's day-to-day affairs. While Madge was writing excitedly about her difficulties in getting a Christmas box shipped to her daughter ("I have been like a teetotim—half the time on my head and more than half the time on my heels"), Preston wrote May a long, solemn letter informing her that he would be unable to accompany Madge on the holiday trip to Emmitsburg.[1] In a long passage Preston described his low spirits, "caused by the miserable condition of our distressed and distructed country. . . . I have out-lived," he wrote, "the liberty of my country—I have lived to see good men like T. Parkin Scott and others at the dead hour of the night torn from their homes and the bosoms of their families and unjustly and cruelly consigned to the deprivations and horrors of distant and unwholesome dungeons." The irony that his own household included the slaves Jim and Kitty, whose sole freedoms depended on the favor of a relatively benign master and mistress, escaped Preston altogether. Yet he was not unaware of some of the ideas then percolating in Jim's mind. These he alluded to in a charming word picture for May of the personalities, both human and animal, that were still at home.

---

Pleasant Plains
22nd December 1862

My dear daughter,

. . . The routine of our occupation is but little changed since you were here. Aunt Lizzie bustles about as usual. Kit makes as many mistakes as ever, but looks forward I am certain with pleasure and anxiety to the day when she will again be able to join you in the sacred songs of Dixie. Old Mrs. Pent grows fatter every day and looks as rosy as a Dutch cabbage, the shape of which she somewhat resembles. William is about as usual—active, ingenious and scrupulously faithful to the chickens. Jim has been behaving very well and I think will one day turn out to be a very respectable "man of color." The only objection to Jim is he worships Wendell Phillips and like Bishop Whittingham offers up a special prayer for Abraham Lincoln. Old Christie is still the Andy Handy of the Establishment, annoys your mother as much as ever by his awful fits of forgetfulness. Treanor is still Treanor—and is at this time busily employed on a *new* shanty constructed of *old* materials. The horses are generally in good health and Buck is as fat as a rabbit—Jewell jumps and runs as he used to and howls a plaintive "God be praised" whenever Mrs. Pent rings her bell. The cows are as sober as ever, the sheep are cheerful and frisky and the cats as I had occasion to observe this morning are able to climb the trees with surprising agility. In a word the whole of our surroundings animate and inanimate manifest in various degrees God's goodness and providence. . . . May God protect and bless you is the prayer of your affectionate father.

P. S. I would like you to write to our dear good old friend Aunty Carlon.

---

The fiery abolitionist Wendell Phillips, whose influence had reached out to the Prestons' coachman, had been a frequent speaker at antislavery rallies; and the Rev. William Rollin Whittingham, the Episcopal bishop of Maryland, had outraged Southern sympathizers with a prayer of thanksgiving for Union victories, which he had composed and directed should be used at all churches within his jurisdiction.[2] Apparently Jim was already speaking out about the end of slavery. Soon he and Lizzie would be acting out as well.

But in the meantime Madge's concerns with Jim were on matters more mundane.

## Wednesday, December 24, 1862

*The weather still continues mild though the clouded condition of the atmosphere strongly indicates rain. Mr Preston remained home today, and superintended the killing of a cow. Jim took the skin to the city this afternoon and got $4.20 for it; he brought home with him my new dress & cloak, both of which I think are beautiful.*

*This is Christmas Eve and the first one for more than 13 years that I have not had the dear face of my little child near me and her soft arms round my neck, but I am satisfied, well knowing she is happier than I could make her where she is. God bless her tonight and ever.*

## Thursday, December 25, 1862

*A bright and clear day but not very cold, lovely for Christmas. Mr Preston & I went by invitation to Mr Wm Stansbury this morning took a glass of apple toddy & a piece of cake & returned home. After dinner we drove to the city reaching there before dark. I stopped to see Aunty & to bid her goodbye and tomorrow I go to Emmitsburg to visit dear little May. . . .*

## Friday, December 26, 1862

*Rose early to be ready for my journey. Mr Preston came up to Sanders & took breakfast, we went to the cars at 8 o'clock, and I bade them goodbye and went on my way rejoicing.*

*I arrived at St Joseph's about five o'clock, met my dear child, and took her with me to Emmitsburg to remain all night. May looks very well and is apparently very happy at having me with her tonight, as I am also.*

## Saturday, December 27, 1862

*This morning May & myself . . . went out to St Joseph's for the girls, we then went to the Mountain and had a pleasant visit of a couple hours. . . . The girls and May are enjoying themselves to the utmost. . . .*

## Monday, December 29, 1862

*. . . Mr Turner & I asked to see the Southern girls, and Sister granted them permission to come to us. They appeared pleased & gratified at our expressions of sympathy for them. . . .*

Baltimore 30th Decr. 1862

Dear Madge,

I have just recd your letters of the 27th & 28th, the latter post marked at Emmitsburg *this* day—I reached town about an hour ago. Judge Stump went out with me yesterday and came in with me this morning. It is now 2 P.M. I scarcely know how to communicate to you an event which will fill your heart with grief—an event which has moved me more than any event which has occurred within the circle of my movements for many years past. Our beloved Aunty Carlon is no more—she departed this life at 11 o'clock last night. Shortly after my arrival in town I met a gentleman in the street who told me the old lady was very ill. Without going to my office I parted with Judge Stump in the street determining to at once pay the old lady a visit. You may judge of my consternation and grief when as I grew near her abode I saw the crape streaming from the bell pull. It was the dark inanimate messenger that first announced her death to me. On entering the house the poor faithful Anne met me in speechless agony—and within the room the boy Frank overpowered with grief. From the expression on the poor old lady's dead face, she must have died without much pain. She looked as natural as life—except that the roseate hue was wanting. She will be buried tomorrow afternoon. Of the sad event it is not likely you will receive any intimation until she has been folded within the embrace of our common mother—everything in relation to her funeral &c &c devolves upon me as I am her executor. I shall lay her by the side of her beloved "John" and shall endeavor to discharge the melancholy duty as my dear friend the Judge[3] would have done had he been living. I know how deep will be your grief—but sacred as that grief may be, you must not allow its manifestation to turn aside your current duties to yourself—to your child, to those around you and to the occasion which carried you from home. God only knows which of us may next pay the debt of nature.

Affectionately yours—
W. P. Preston

---

The unexpected, sad news of the death of her best and dearest friend suddenly erased the joyfulness of Madge's reunion with May. The older woman could not forgive herself that she had been frolicking in the north at the very moment that the words of Aunty Carlon's funeral service were being read. One last look at the kind old face—a chance to say farewell—would have meant much to Madge. With Aunty Carlon's death, Madge lost the one refuge and support that had sustained her when events in her life seemed overwhelming.

On the return train Madge brooded over conditions at St. Joseph's which her daughter's schoolgirl chatter had revealed or which she had seen herself.

Once at home, she seemed obsessed by these concerns. Probably such brooding distracted her from nearer miseries—the erratic comportment of her husband, the changed behavior of Lizzie and Jim, and consuming grief over the death of her friend. Depression seemed to settle around Madge's shoulders as winter closed in at Pleasant Plains.

Pleasant Plains<br>Jany 9th 1863

My very dear child,

You must not be surprised at my first letter to you after my return home being short. I am desirous to make it as *emphatic* as I can and simple and easily to be understood as I wish all I say to be acted upon. Of course on my reaching home your father was anxious to hear all about his little daughter. With some things I told him he was exceedingly well pleased, but there were others that pained and annoyed him, as well as they had done myself, though when you laughingly told me of them at Emmitsburg, I said very little on the subject and nothing objectionable, as I wished to consult with your father before so doing. I *have* consulted with him and under his suggestion I now give you . . . his decision in the matter. He said, I have always considered physical comfort the chief foundation and stimulus of mental excellence and improvement. I would therefore consider myself remiss in my duty, and it would make me positively unhappy to feel that an attempt was made to improve the condition of my daughter's mind at the expense of hazard to her bodily health. I not only want her piously educated, but she must be *comfortably* educated—if this cannot be done at a public institution—it must be done at home. However unbounded may be my confidence in the piety and wisdom of the ladies of St Joseph's, I shall have to tax their kind consideration in several particulars. I will send May a rug which must be placed at the side of her bed, that she may stand on it when she gets out of bed, instead of having the heat extracted from her limbs by the cold floor. My daughter is more or less subject to hereditary nervous headache—even if her usual place be at the cold water table, she must be furnished with a cup of tea or coffee whenever in her judgment her condition of health or appetite requires it.

These requisites are reasonable and in my judgment necessary—if unfortunately, the gratification of my wishes conflicts with the regulations of St Joseph's Academy, I regret it. If my wishes as I have stated cannot be *strictly* complied with—much as I may deplore it, I am not willing that May shall commence another session! Her health and comfort are dear to me and as I have already said essential . . . to her mental improvement.

My dear child, I have thus given you verbatim your father's views. I do not wish you to be made in the least unhappy or dejected by what is here written. As soon as you read this letter, take it at once to your head angel and ask her to be kind enough to hand it to the Mother—her determination I desire to have without delay. I hope you may be able cheerfully to commence the coming session—but this depends upon the Mother's decision on our views.

Devotedly Your Mama. . . .

**Tuesday, January 13, 1863**

*Another pleasant day. Mr Preston came in this evening with Wm and Jim also brought a load of wood for the house [in Baltimore]. Mr Preston was very nervous & unpleasant when he came in. He brought them, for the purpose of having some boxes made to put Judge LeGrand's pictures in, but he did not have it done. Mr Preston remained in town and sent me home with Wm this afternoon. I found Lizzie drinking again, and she had been doing so since Friday. . . .*

St. Joseph's Jany 13th 1863

My dear Mama,

I received your letter last night and Sister Raphael gave me permission to answer it today. I am very sorry that you and Papa have worried yourselves so much on my account, for although I have many boarding school discomfotures still they are not suffcent to make me unhappy. When you were here I spoke of my wish to take milk but Sister Raphael says they have not got it to give and I think it would make me sick to drink tea or coffee. Sister says that if the rug is sent it can be placed at the foot of my bed, but that we are not allowed to put our shoes on off the bed. Sister Raphael says also perhaps Papa does not know that we have not any fire in the dormitory and she thinks he should. Now dear Mama if you have no objections I should prefer begining the next session for when I told you about our school trials and troubles I did not mean you to be unhappy about me. Please do not think that I have written this because I was told to do so, or that what I have said was dictated to me for I done all at my own free will. I am glad to be able to say, for I know you will be pleased to hear it, I am even *happier* and more contented now than in the earlier part of the year. I will write again on friday my letter is already composed. Good bye. Love to all

Your little daughter
May.

**Wednesday, January 14, 1863**

*. . . William went to the city this morning, and came home again tonight. Mr Preston remained in town, but sent me a letter saying he was not very well —Of course not. . . .*

Pleasant Plains
Jany 14th 1863

My darling child,

I hope you have not been fretted by Mama's not writing to you as frequently as formerly. Many little things have occurred to prevent, almost too trifling to relate yet of sufficient importance to keep me from doing what is really now you are away from me, my chief pleasure, that is, writing to . . . you. Since the New Year, your father's professional duties have kept him almost constantly in the city. Last Saturday, I drove to the city to bring your father home, but just as I reached the house, it began to rain and continued so violent that I was obliged to remain in, all night; I did not reach home again till last evening.

On Monday I spent the day at "Uncle Beverley's."[4] Tell Mollie, the family were all well, as was also her "dear Uncle Wilson," to whom I had the pleasure of an introduction, and with whom I was perfectly charmed! The old gentleman . . . has been in the city for several days. . . . From him I learned a great many interesting things about the Rebels . . . it may please you and the "girls" to hear. On the return of Stuart after his raid into Penna he and his brave little army passed over the Potomac just three miles above Uncle Wilson's farm, and he told me, he supplied food to *fifteen hundred soldiers* on that day. Think of that, what a pleasure it would have been to you girls to have assisted in the waiting on those wearied and toil-worn men! Many other things he told me . . . but as they might possibly be construed into treason, for the good & perhaps safety of all parties I had better not relate them, here at least. . . .

Let me express to you my great pleasure and satisfaction at the reception & contents of you[r] Christmas and New Year's letters. You will make me very happy and gratify your father very much by carrying out the good resolves mentioned in your last. If you should remain at St Joseph's the whole year, and at the end of that time, you were not a recipient of an "honor," I really think your father would be greatly mortified, and he would also think you had not done yourself justice, as he believes it is no very difficult matter to be . . . amiable, obedient and attentive to your duties. . . . While I was with you, from your own account I feared you were a little wild and perhaps reckless, but I was pleased to learn not only from the Sisters but your young companions, that you were a tolerably good little child. . . .

My dear child, thus far I have forborne mentioning anything about our dear Aunty Carlon for the reason the subject is so painful to me, and I do not wish to sadden you with a long recital of a painful subject—suffice it, the dear old lady was only sick three days, and during that time she had the kindest and most devoted attention from her numerous friends; she retained her faculties to the last, and received all the last Sacraments, and thus passed away, one of the best and kindest friends I have ever known. . . .

Good night my darling.

Your affectionate Mother. . . .

## Friday, January 16, 1863

*. . . At four Mr Preston drove into Baltimore where he is staying all night. This agrees with Mrs Beer's story about Friday's doings!*

Baltimore Jany 19th 1863

My darling child,

On going to the p. office with your father this morning, I was gratified with the reception of your two letters. . . . I am most gratified with the contents of the one in reply to mine respecting my "objections." Your father is also pleased to know our wishes can be satisfied, with regard to the "rug"—one of which, we send by tomorrow's "Express" together with undershirts, and a "Confederate uniform"[5] which you are to put on to sleep in. I have made it long that you may wrap your feet in it and make yourself comfortable. The undershirts are not to be taken off at night—indeed sleeping in a cold room as you do, I think you had better . . . keep your muslin chemise on also. I send a few cakes, some candies, which I hope you will find beneficial to your cough —if however your cough is very troublesome, take three or four pills of Nux Vomico twice a day, dry on your tongue—if you have fever with your cough, take three drops of tincture of Aconite in a cup half full of cold water and take a teaspoonful every time you cough. . . . The little bottle of glycerine keep on your washstand and use it on your hands. It will preserve them from chapping, and put the rug by the side of your bed or in the alcove, wherever it is you dress, so that you do not stand on the floor during that operation. . . .

Papa sends his love to you and says you are quite welcome to begin the coming session—don't forget the singing lessons. . . .

Yours devotedly
Mama

## Wednesday, January 21, 1863

*. . . I have engaged all day in the sad occupation of looking over letters and papers, putting some away and burning others. I am so nervous and wretched tonight. I can scarcely contain myself. I wrote a long letter to _____ this morning and sent over to Eudowood to have it put in the post office.*

**Thursday, January 22, 1863**

*. . . Another sad lonely day. Mr Preston has remained again in town.*

---

Madge, of course, could not share with May the depression she felt over Preston's unexplained absences. But as her mood darkened, she seems to have sublimated that more engrossing despair by writing at length—and critically—on a subject less covert.

> Pleasant Plains
> Jany 23d 1863

My darling child,

 . . . I wrote you a very hasty letter in reply to yours of the 14th inst. I will now write more at length. In my letter, I agreed to your wish to commence the coming session—simply because it *was your wish*; but not that it gives me the same satisfaction it did formerly to have you at St Joseph's. I cannot tell *why* it is, but from the most ardent desire to have you placed at that Institution, I now feel an equal repugnance to your being there. I have however made up my mind, and given my consent to your remaining and despite my emotions, I shall, as far as it lays in my power, do everything to promote your happiness, comfort and improvement. I pray you, therefore, let nothing I have written influence you in one iota—*act* and *feel*, for the future, as if I had not expressed myself as above: unless I write and utter my true sentiments, I cannot write and speak at all.

In justice to the institution and the ladies who preside over it, I will say to you, I have not the least objections to the rules, regulations or government of that establishment *collectively*—only *individually* do I presume to question the wisdom of their method!

To *me*, it is absurd to believe that the one mode of instruction is equally good for fifty or a hundred children. That the child with a dull, stultified intellect, that frowns over her studies for hours and then scarcely comprehends the first elements of her lessons, should be put upon the same platform with one whom God in his beneficent kindness and for his *own wise purpose*, has endowed with a mind to understand and a capacity to grasp at conclusions without the lengthened struggle it has taken her fellow student. If such be the case, does it not follow as a matter of course, that the mind of the bright child is brought down to a level with the stupid one, and that its intellectual wings, being clipped or burthened by its surroundings, should in time lose the power to rise above a common height, when its Maker had destined it with *proper culture* to soar beyond the mass and be a shining light to its companions?

Now I do not mean you to infer from this, that I think any of your young friends peculiarly stupid, or that I wish to flatter you with the idea that there may be some among you particularly brilliant. I only mèan that I am the more confirmed in my opinion . . . that no two minds can be instructed or cultivated by the one method—injustice must be done to one or the other —perhaps to both. I am not however foolish enough to think the condition of affairs that has existed for so many years at St Joseph's will be changed to suit any expressed wish of mine, or that I shall ever find an institution for the education of the young formed on a model to please my own exclusive views, unless I become the foundress of one myself! One thing I must be permitted to say, and I wish you to make note of it, as I have sufficient confidence in your own judgment to be guided by what you may think or say in the premises. Are you satisfied that the present mode by which you are instructed is the one best calculated to develop such intellect or capacity as you may possess? and do you not feel that if the opportunities were given you, or if you had a *sufficient incentive,* you could with a reasonable effort on your part, give satisfaction to your teachers in much higher or rather more lengthy studies than those in which you are now engaged? You need not reply to these queries in your letters, only let them be subjects for reflection now, and discussion when we meet. I was looking over, the other day, some of your writing books, and I do assure you my dear child, those written as far back as Jany 1860 are much better written than your letters of the present time, and those written just before you went to St Joseph's are really beautiful in comparison. Now my darling, what does that mean? Surely you are not retrograding!

When you first went to St Joseph's I was anxious you should attach yourself to all the societies or confraternities of a religious character which were instituted there, but . . . I am now perfectly satisfied to have you remain outside of their influence. I saw and heard enough during my visit to convince me they were fruitful sources of bickerings and disquietudes, and perhaps the Protestants who could have nothing to do with them were in the main the happier. . . . Let your devotion to our Blessed Mother be in the heart, then it will not fail to show itself in all your outward doings. —There is error into which we Catholics can readily fall, therefore it behooves us at all times to be watchful; it is this—that in our zeal and attachment to the *forms* and *ceremonies* of our religion, we do not become forgetful or lukewarm in the *spirit* of our beautiful faith. . . .

I believe I have forgotten to tell you in my former letters . . . that you have an increase in your flock of sheep of six little lambs. There are *two* pairs of twins, and the mother of one of the pairs, was so cruel as to refuse to acknowledge one of the little lambs; consequently we were obliged to bring it to the house and raise it by hand. Lizzie is its nurse, and you never saw anything so devoted as the lamb is to Lizzie. We call one pair Willie & May—the other pair are Mollie and Jeannette—and one is Nettie and the other is not yet named. . . .

your devoted Mother. . . .[6]

---

Diary passages for Monday, January 26, provide a rare view into the interactions between the Prestons. His diary keeping was so irregular that almost no entries exist for the period during which May was away at school. But on this day his depression—or perhaps a sense of contrition—seems to have prompted him to record his own emotional world. How that emotion spilled over on to Madge is preserved in her matching record of the same day.

*Monday, Jan. 26th—Pleasant Plains. Heavy fog. Arose with sad depression of mind & pain of body. I feel that I am wearing fast. Perhaps it is better thus. I have outlived the freedom, happiness and prosperity of my country. What is there left for me to live for. —*

*Rambled about the farm with Mr. Bartlett until 11 A.M. Then drove into Balto. Jim came in with a load of wood which I gave to a poor old woman. Dined with Bartlett and had an interview with Shanabrook & Gittings and Mathers. Jim left the wagon to be repaired. Retired at 8 P.M.*

## Monday, January 26, 1863

*. . . We have spent a delightful day, but it would not do for Mr Preston to retire with pleasant feelings or let me do so, consequently we had a "scene" tonight, but I hope Mr Bartlett did not know of it.*

Pleasant Plains<br>Jany 27th 1863

My little pet,

I just remember that you asked me in your last letter to send you some flannel like your Garibaldi to make Mollie's doll a frock. On looking over "Akers" I happened to see the enclosed, partly made baby frock and thought it might answer your purpose better than the article for which you wrote. . . .

I also send a torn one dollar note, which I rec'd in your part of the country as change for half a dollar, but which I am unable to pass down here—you can try it at the stores in town—perhaps you can buy some candy or nuts with it. They seemed to be passing readily as change, among the stage drivers, and at the hotels—but if it is worthless let me know and I will send you something better. . . .

I have been reading over your last letter, and as it expresses so much satisfaction and pleasure at remaining at St Joseph's I begin to feel more reconciled, indeed I believe there is nothing to which I could *not become reconciled*, if I felt sure it contributed in any way to your happiness and pleasure. . . .

Love from all the family—
Mama

### Wednesday, January 28, 1863

*. . . Mr Preston drove home this morning, remained to dinner and returned to the city in all the storm. I cannot see why he should have come home, he never even went out of the house.*

### Friday, January 30, 1863

*. . . I put William to making some little coops in the chicken house today and he had made them [in] his own fashion, instead of mine and the consequence is I am terribly annoyed, and I fear Mr Preston will be also. It is strange that people cannot do as you ask them to do. . . .*

Pleasant Plains
Jany 30th 1863

My dear child,

I have before me the "Report" of your doings at St Joseph's during the past session. Do you know I am greatly surprised at that part which tells of imperfect lessons!—When I recollect what excellent lessons you generally brought me, when I was your teacher, I scarcely know how to account for the discrepancy. In Geography particularly, your recitations were usually almost faultless. I have known you to repeat your Geography lesson, almost verbatim. I hope my darling as you have now had some experience in school life, I shall begin to see some improvement in you. It was not reasonable to suppose the first sessions would show any great change but unless . . . you are retrograding, I shall expect a decided improvement . . . at the close of the session upon which you are now entering. With regard to your deportment, both in class, and out of it—I find you "fail in school rules" and "sometimes fail in silence and attention." All that must rest entirely with yourself; for my own part, I find the rules so excessively stringent that I can make great allowances for you, if you do occasionally "fail" in their observance. There is one thing I must insist upon for *my sake*, and that is, you receive in a docile and gentle manner the reproof it may be found necessary to give you for dereliction of duties and for faulty lessons. . . .

I do not recollect to have mentioned in any of my letters to you that I made inquiry . . . about . . . Dr Berry the dentist. I learned . . . that Dr Berry is a "first class" dentist, every way fully competent to operate on the most delicate teeth. I regretted so much I had not known it . . . that I might have had your tooth refilled while I was with you. . . . Speak to Sister Raphael . . . and ask her to please have the Dr . . . operate on your tooth at once. When you see the Dr, tell him that your Mama would like the cavity of your tooth filled without enlarging it any. If he is as skillful as they tell me he is, he will not do anything to the tooth but merely fill it. . . . Do not let him on any account touch any of your other teeth or *file* any of them; all that can be attended to when you return home. Ask Sister Raphael to speak to Dr Berry for you—if you have not courage to do so yourself.

I am glad Pauline wrote to you, and hope you will answer her letter; while on the subject of letters, let me give you a little instruction on that subject— Be sure always to *date* your letters distinctly—and *do not* begin them *so far down the page* as you do, a letter so commenced has an exceedingly awkward appearance—if you write on ruled paper, it is usually ruled so as to show you where to begin—let me see my child that you remember in future what I have suggested—your Papa says the first letters you wrote to us from St Joseph's are better written and better expressed than the later ones. I believe Papa thinks he has made a mistake in changing your teacher, that while you were under *my* instruction, he constantly saw an improvement, now *it is not so visible*! . . .

Each and all of the family send love to you. Papa says "give my love to May." . . .

Mama

### Monday, February 2, 1863

. . . *Mr Preston has remained all night in town. This evening I took Lizzie and Kitty and went down to spend the evening at Mrs Stansbury's; on arriving home the [Stansbury] girls came up with me & are staying all night. I have just rec'd by Mr Treanor a letter from Mr Preston enclosing one from May and a note from Sr Raphael, which does not please me very much.*

Baltimore 5 P.M.
2nd Feby 1863

Dear Madge

On calling at the post office I found a letter from May & postscript thereto, from Sr. Raphael. I read both—Having done so I concluded not to send your letter to May until I could have an interview with you. What is the meaning of Sr. Raphael's intimation to "withdraw" May? I suppose they do not find her sufficiently profitable as a pupil. I will endeavor to get out tomorrow: and we will talk of the matter—in the meantime say nothing to our neighbours. . . . My head aches dreadfully—

Yours affectionately<br>
W. P. P.

St Joseph's January 30th 1863

Dear Mama,

I received, yesterday, your letter in which you expressed some disatisfaction to my remaining longer at St. Joseph's, but said that you left it entirely to myself whether I did so or not; for my part I am perfectly happy and contented, and should like to continue at school but if you feel as if you would be happier if I were at home I could not think of staying any longer. I have to some extent put my good resolutions in practice for I have not missed any of my lessons since school commenced except those that were missed by the whole class. I am sure you will be pleased to hear this. Please do not judge my writing by my letter and I will try in future to do better. I am in the third class writing and Sister Cephas says that my book looks quite nicely. I am going to write next Friday and give you full account of the celabration of Father Burlando's day, but will tell you this much now. I danced so much that this morning when we got up which was at the usual time I was so sleepy and tired that I could scarcely dress myself. Sister Raphael is so kind as to write you a few lines. Therefore I must say Good bye to my dear Mama.

With love to Papa and all home I remain your loving little daughter

May.

My dear Mrs Preston,

The tone of your letters to May since your recent visit have expressed such decided dissatisfaction with the system of boarding-school education and our domestic arrangements for the comfort of our pupils, that I feel urged to advise you to withdraw May, and pursue the course to which you give the preference. Home education has certainly its advantages, and where parents suffer from extreme solicitude for their children, their anxiety is greatly relieved. We could not change our method, & if May is to continue with us, it is a pity that she or her companions should be prejudiced against it. As the Session has just commenced, it would be a favorable moment to remove her if you determine to do so—

Respectfully<br>
Sister Mary Raphael<br>
Directress[7]

Madge could not bring herself to answer directly Sister Raphael's letter. Like a chastened child, she put on a guise of gaiety to hide her discomfiture. In the next day's letter Madge turned again to the playful style of the first she had written to May at St. Joseph's. Sister Raphael had remarked on the critical tone of the recent letters. Looking back to her happy reunion with May in Emmitsburg, perhaps Madge understood how these last letters could have seemed to the kind Sister like expressions of ingratitude; indirectly Madge tried to apologize.

Madge kept her letter, however, at Pleasant Plains, unsent. And after a second night's sleep she knew she had to confront explicitly the proposal in Sister Raphael's note. Embarrassed, Madge chose to distort the time of arrival of the letter from St. Joseph's. Better to let yesterday's letter stand as an independent expression of cheerful contentment with the school than to suggest that its altered tone was a form of response—as of course it was—to the crisp letter from Sister Raphael.

Pleasant Plains
Feby 3d 1863

Do you know my darling child, I am almost ashamed to send another letter so soon after the two long ones despatched to you on Monday—I think I hear Sr Raphael exclaim "The cry is still, they come"!—Excuse me, all of you —and lay my overwhelming you with letters to my great solicitude about the reception of your box or rather the contents of it. I am beginning to fear it is lost, and I . . . *feel* that you must need the underclothing I sent you: and I do not know how to supply the loss, unless, after you receive this letter, you take it to one of the Sisters . . . and ask her—if—after your boots are purchased, she would be kind enough to purchase you either two little undershirts or materials to make some bodies for you, or such articles as the Sister's own judgment should think proper—but remember, this is only to be done in case the box does not make its appearance. The shocking roads the recent rains & snows have made might well be a good reason for the delay of the wagon. . . .

Do you recollect my asking you, before you went to St Joseph's, to choose for your patron St. whilst there St Aloysius—the patron saint of young students? Have you done so? and if you have not, do you think it too late to do so now? Ask Sister Raphael to let you have the life of that young saint to read; I think you will be greatly pleased with it. I do not know whether it is permissible, but if it were, I could occasionally send you such books for perusal during recreation hours as would not only amuse, but instruct and edify you; but I forgot—you have a fine library at St Joseph's. . . . Do not fail to avail yourself of it, as there is much to be learned, beside the knowledge contained in your school books.

Feby 4th 1863

My dear child,

    I open my letter to say, yours of the 30th ult—has been rec'd—I have not time to answer it at length—suffice it at present to say—I had not the slightest idea of bringing you home this winter, if you yourself desired to remain. You are the one to best judge of what is likely to be of advantage to you, and as you are, and express yourself in warm terms, happy and satisfied at St Joseph's —stay there in welcome, and try by your improvement to reflect credit, not only on your teachers, *but let Mama share a little of it,* for having laid the foundation of the education upon which the Sisters are raising their super-structure. . . .

Yours in great haste
but most affectionately
Mama

## Monday, February 9, 1863

*. . . I reached the office [after a day in the city] about ½ past 3 o'clock . . . it was after 5 when we left and after 7 when we reached home. Lizzie was in a terrible condition and everything topsy turvy.*

## Tuesday, February 10, 1863

*. . . I have passed a most unpleasant & annoying day. Lizzie has been in a ter-rible frolic, and Jim has been so excessively impertinent that I really felt like sending a constable after him.*

Baltimore Feby 9th 1863

My sweet child,

    I have this instant rec'd and read your charming little letter dated 6th Feby, in which you give me so clever an account of the celebration of Father Bur-lando's Feast day—I should not wonder if you would all be willing to give your dear Father the entire catalogue of Saints, provided each of his Patrons were honored with so joyous a day as that. . . .

    We also have had party doings at our house *in town.* Last week—all the la-dies, together with Johnny, from Eudowood, came to the city on Wednesday

& remained till Saturday afternoon, for the purpose of attending two grand parties given respectively by Mr Courtland & Mr George Bartlett. The ladies remained at our house and went from here. I did not come in, but I had a full description of their dresses &c &c. Miss Rachael, who is always *the flower of the flock*, wore to Mrs Courtland's party a violet color silk dress, with Mechlin lace trimmings and jewels; her hair was arranged by a head dresser who by the way dressed all of the ladies' heads. . . . Mrs Carman wore a black watered moire dress, certainly the most beautiful black dress I ever saw—*low in the neck—short sleeves* and illusion cape[8] &c &c, with splendid head dress. . . . At Mrs Bartlett's party, Miss Rachael wore a garnet velvet dress, with flowing sleeves of the same materials lined with white satin, and pearl ornaments. Mrs Carman having presented her for the occasion a beautiful set of pearl together with the most exquisite comb I ever beheld, she must have looked from all accounts magnificently. The ladies tell me the table at Courtland's was gorgeous in the extreme. Cut glass, silver and flowers in such profusion as to seem almost like fairy land. Laura Courtland looked innocence personified in a simple white french muslin dress, full and flowing, with twisted strings of pearl round her neck & arms. The great feature of Mrs Bartlett's ball was the presence of several French naval officers, resplendent in military ornaments and French gallantry.[9] It seems they were the envy of our American gentlemen by the peculiar grace and elegance with which they threw the ladies' long gossamer skirts over their arms, while waltzing and dancing and thus preventing the destruction of those frail articles, an event you know that is constantly occurring in our ballrooms. . . .

Yours devotedly Mama

Pleasant Plains<br>Feby 13th 1863

My darling child,

I scribbled you a hasty reply last Monday to your pleasant little letter of the 6th inst[ance]. I wrote with bonnet and cloak on, ready equipped for a visiting and shopping expedition—therefore very imperfectly & I suppose unsatisfactorily also. . . .

Poor Kitty has just left me after expressing her regrets that Miss May cannot receive any valentines tomorrow, I believe it was her wish to have purchased one and sent it to you, but she is impressed with the idea that it would be placed in your trunk for safe keeping and you would know nothing about it, till, unpacking your trunk next summer, the loving missive should present itself; under these impressions she thinks it best to save her money and send her love and respects in "Missis letter," as she feels sure you will receive that.

Kitty is very unhappy tonight—and she seeks comfort & consolation in talking about you. Owing to sundry misdemeanors of which she has been guilty of late I found it necessary today to deprive her for a month of her baby house—consequently the little wooden edifice you had William make for her was put away, parlour, kitchen and chamber furniture packed up, the dolls, from Anne down to the india rubber monster, laid carefully in boxes, together with their heterogeneous wardrobe, and Kitty sobbing and sighing, watched Lizzie locking them up with as much childish grief as if the dearest object to her in life had actually been buried. I am inclined to think this punishment will have a better effect than greater severity—at all events, she seems *now* very penitent.

I believe I told you in one of my letters, we had a little pet lamb—we call it Mollie, and its twin sister Jeannette. The little thing—strange to say, has attached itself in a most wonderful manner to the dog Jewell—she makes a bed of him . . . and follows him all over the place—if he gets out of her sight, which you may be sure often happens, she cries and bleats about till she sees him and then she starts off and runs and when she reaches him, she rubs her sweet white face against his big black one with the utmost joy and satisfaction at having found him again; sometimes, as I saw myself this afternoon, the dog hears her calling him Ma-a Ma-a, and he walks up quietly and deliberately and places himself by her side, with an inquiring look on his good and honest face as if to say—"What is your pleasure little pet?" . . . I certainly think this is unmistakable evidence of his goodness. . . .

I don't recollect if I mentioned in my last letter . . . my great satisfaction at your evident effort to please me in your hand writing and the beginning of your letter. Papa also noticed it and made satisfactory comments upon both. So you see my child nothing is lost upon us, and when you do not come up to our reasonable expectations, the pain is in proportion to the pleasure your efforts to improve give us. We are particularly anxious about your writing, as we class that among the higher accomplishments; your letters also are often read by our neighbours, and I do not like them to see evidence of carelessness, though I must give you the satisfaction of knowing that your letters are read with great pleasure and receive warm commendations from all quarters. . . .

You ask for some plain sewing. I have a wish to send you the material for a shirt for Papa—but I am afraid my little darling you will find it a tedious piece of work—half an hour of sewing a day. . . .

I understand you have all been vaccinated at St Joseph's. I am very glad if there is any danger of that terrible scourge smallpox, that Mother has taken the precaution to have you all vaccinated. It can do no harm and may prevent the breaking out among you that shocking disease. . . . Good night

Mama

**Tuesday, February 17, 1863**

*. . . This is the night Mr Preston's favour lecture was to come off at the Mary-land Institute. I fear the bad weather will diminish the number of his audience; be there many or few, I hope he will acquit himself creditably.*[10] *I have re-sumed my practicing on the piano about three weeks ago; since that time I have practised an hour or two daily and I really feel I have done very well in that time.*

Pleasant Plains
Feby 19th 1863

My dear child,

I think I have told you that the "19th of Feby" was *to me*, one of those bright spots upon which memory loves to look back and rest with pleasure?—Long years ago, when I was but little older than you are now, I had a dear friend, who was to me almost as a sister, and I am sure I held in her heart the same warm place she has in mine. A pleasant little circumstance occurred to both of us, on the 19th of February. In our girlish enthusiasm we promised each other, always on the anniversary of *that day*, if we could not be together, to write to each other on the evening of the 19th and communicate all that had taken place during the day. For many years we kept our promise faith-fully—till at last time and distance, those great dissolvents of human affec-tions and interests, crept between us. . . .

Now, mingled with those memories, comes one of sadness; the early and loved friend "sleeps the sleep that knows no awakening" and her ear is deaf to the voice of affection and heart has long since ceased to throb in unison with that of friendship. . . .

Have you ever known such weather? It is universally admitted by all the oldest inhabitants in this part of the world that such continued bad weather, and per consequence, such shocking bad roads, have never been known be-fore. We are literally blockaded on our farms—the roads around are really dangerous, nothing has so effectually reconciled me to your being away from us this winter as the very unfavourable weather we have had. . . . Yesterday in a fit of desperation, Mr Stansbury and little Willie drove up in a sleigh, to take me down to spend the day with Aunt Eliza, who has been out a week and I did not know it; while I was hesitating about going—the weather decided for me; it began to rain so hard that my kind gallants were obliged to jump in their sleigh and hasten home, fearing the snow would disappear before they got there. If I had gone, I should have been there yet, as it has never ceased to rain sufficiently long to have enabled me to get home through the drops.

Your father left home Monday morning intending to return on Wednesday morning, but he has not been able to do so. Only think of Lizzie and I wading through the mud to the chicken house to look after some dear little chickens we have and which we are afraid to trust to the tender mercies of William as we have long since learned by experience that he is much more attentive to chickens on the table than chickens in the coop, and when he is not luxuriating over a stew, he is very apt to put me in a "stew" by his negligence in respect to my pretty little pets. — Speaking of pets reminds me of dear little Mollie, the lamb; she is the cutest little thing you ever saw. She domiciles in the "tub room," Lizzie having partitioned off a few feet for her especial comfort and benefit. In the morning nothing can induce her to come out of her house, as Kitty calls it, till she has had her breakfast, and as she is all unmindful of the present season of Lent, her breakfast consists of a good large basin of warm milk. Soon as she drinks it up, she looks pleasantly at Lizzie, evidently acknowledging her obligations to her, steps out and off she goes in search of Jewell; if she does not see him as soon as she wishes, she cries till his huge form looms up, and then with a bound she is by his side frisking & playing as only lambs can frisk & play. In the evening, she lingers round Lizzie, following her to the dairy, to the ice house &c &c, and by her pantomimic gestures asks as plainly as one of the Ravels,[11] to be put to bed, which as soon as Lizzie does, she quietly lies down and that is the last of her till the next morning. Kitty thinks "Miss May, would love the little lamb more than any pet she ever had." By the way, before Kitty went to bed, she tapped at my door, and on permission given to "Come in," she put her bright face in the room, saying "please Misses give my love to Miss May, Miss Mollie and Miss Jeannette"—I promised to do so, so you must tell the girls, and give my love also.

February 22d

I am gratified that you are in possession of your box &c &c. Hope you find comfort in the folds of the "Confederate uniform" and renewed patriotism under the confederate flag, which I herewith enclose and which dear little Alice made, sitting with me some days ago and which she desired me to send you. Now my darling child, be cautious in the use you make of it, and do not let it be the cause of unpleasantness between you and any of your young companions, or of disobedience and punishment between you and your teachers. Now that you have entered on your second session and may fairly be supposed to know *some little* of your own grammar—if you would like to do so, you can take French lessons. Ask Sister Raphael, if she can give you the loan of a French dictionary & grammar, till I can send one of each which I have at home. . . .

We are in the midst of a terrible snowstorm, just such an one, as you may remember, we had years ago on this very day (Washington's birthday)—when "German Mary" was tumbled off the sled with her bucket full of milk and you as a little child stood on the porch, clapping your hands in childish glee at what you thought "great fun," but to poor Mary it was no fun to be tumbled in a snow bank. . . .

God bless you darling—
Your affectionate Mother.

Pleasant Plains
March 10th 1863

My darling child,

Your Papa has just decided to drive to the city this afternoon. I therefore avail myself of the opportunity to write. I fear however my letter must be brief, as there is no detaining Papa, when Mars and Black Hawk are prancing before the door. . . .

I am invited over to Eudowood this afternoon to meet the Stansbury family, together with the Taylors, and a Miss Gatch from Norfolk, who somewhat fantastically calls herself the "Southern Exile." I think however I shall scarcely venture to cross the muddy fields on foot, and the short distance hardly justifies going in a carriage, so the "Exile" and "Mrs Preston" are not likely to exchange compliments for the present at least, unless the said "Exile" waives ceremony and comes to Pleasant Plains. . . .

Yours devotedly—love from papa & Mama
Lizzie and Kitty send love to Miss May.

### Tuesday, March 10, 1863

*On awaking this morning I was sorry to find the sky overcast and with strong evidences of snow before night. I gave orders immediately after breakfast to Jim to begin to plough for early potatoes, and in the meanwhile all hands including Lizzie & Kitty went to burning brush in front of the house. Just as we finished the last pile, it began to snow but fortunately Jim finished ploughing and harrowing by the time the afternoon proved too bad for planting; consequently I set the men grinding corn. A large flock of wild geese flew northward this morning. Mr Preston has remained in town tonight.*

### Wednesday, March 11, 1863

*. . . read some in Madam Campan's life of Marie Antoinette of France. . . .*

### Sunday, March 15, 1863

*. . . We heard very singular sounds for several hours this afternoon. Mr Preston thought they were heavy cannonading at a distance.*

Pleasant Plains
March 13th 1863

My dear little daughter,

Your very pretty and interesting letter of the 6th of this month, I only last night had the satisfaction of reading. . . . I am not only delighted, but *quite astonished* at the improved appearance of your letters, the contents also are most satisfactory—you have an agreeable faculty of catching at those little incidents in a somewhat monotonous life that are pleasant and interesting to know, and a sprightly way of expressing yourself, which is well calculated by practice to make you, what is so desirable all should be, an easy and graceful letter writer. Your orthography has also greatly improved. —It gives me great pleasure . . . to be able thus to express my satisfaction with your efforts. I am sure you will be delighted to know that Papa joins in my declarations to that effect. . . .

. . . You remember the dear old gentleman that gave you Nannie[12]—or rather can you ever forget him?—Well last Saturday he sent out to the farm a beautiful cream coloured mare with black mane & tail, between three and four years old, as a *present to you* for a riding horse. . . . As the animal has Arabian blood in it, I have named her Peri, which in Oriental language means, a spirit of the air. She is gentle as a lamb, having been petted and fondled by the children of that gentleman since it was a colt, and raised expressly for you. . . .

Clouds as well as sunshine follow us in this world; you have had the bright view, now you must be reconciled to the loss of dear little Mollie the lamb. . . . Lizzie found her dead last Monday morning; instead of the frisky little pet that was wont to greet her as she approached with her pail of warm milk, she almost stepped on the lifeless body of the lamb—poor Lizzie was quite affected by it; she said in the most pitiful manner, "I am so sorry Mollie is dead, I thought Miss May would be so pleased with her when she came home." I consoled her by telling her you would have Peri to pet. . . .

Please give my kind regards to Sister Teresa, and say to her, let your stockings be darned as long as they can be made to look well. Dry goods of every description are so exorbitantly high that it has become quite necessary to make clothing of every description last as long as possible. . . .

Love from Papa and
Mama.

# 3

# A Long Winter Ends

ST. PATRICK'S DAY, 1863, marks an anguished passage in Madge's diary. The date stirred painful recollections of events in the preceding spring. Perhaps Preston was doing his best to drown his own memories at "some St. Patrick celebration," where Madge presumed he could be found. "Alas!" she wrote, "what memories must sweep over his soul, if he permits himself to remember that this is the anniversary of that poor unfortunate woman's death. God forgive me but I cannot bring myself to say—'God have mercy on her Soul!'"

On March 17, 1862, Clara Stephans, the former housekeeper for the Prestons, had died after the birth of an apparently illegitimate child. Madge's 1862 diary contains cryptic passages about the event and its aftermath. These suggest her husband's involvement. "Mr Preston planted a grape vine in front of the springhouse this morning," Madge had written on March 17, "(to commemorate the birthday of C——'s baby I suppose)." But wherever in Madge's diary the name of the man in the case should have been inserted, Madge drew a suggestive blank line.

On the week after Clara's death, Preston ordered his city housekeeper, Mrs. Beer, to spend a night and a day at Pleasant Plains—an act prompting Madge to imagine "some diablerie!" Her suspicions were confirmed the next day, on a perhaps not so innocent shopping trip to the city with May. There, Madge wrote, they saw "a furniture car, in front of the office, and the driver taking in furniture . . . , consisting of bedstead &c &c. I understood at once, *why* Mr Preston wanted Mrs Beer away from the house today." At day's end Madge recorded, "Mr Preston seems nervous and irritable." Then she added; "I don't wonder!"

Many references to quarrels between the couple followed thereafter, and before long the decision was made for May to go to St. Joseph's. Perhaps both parents wanted her away from what inadvertently might be revealed. On May's last birthday as a girl at home—May 19, 1862—Madge wrote: "God bless the child, and keep her as free from evil in future as she has been preserved from harm during the past." The Prestons were living in an island of calm surrounded by civil war. Yet war seems not the "harm" Madge had in mind.

In the spring of 1863, however, consciousness of the impact of the war intruded more and more frequently into the family's correspondence and into Madge's diary. Although the long, severe winter lingered well past the normal planting and blossoming season, eventually it ended. As fields and roads began to dry out, Madge's life took on more variety. Turning down an opportunity to accompany her friend Mrs. Hillen on a visit to Emmitsburg, Madge chose instead to make a visit to Philadelphia and then to the Batemans in Brooklyn, New York. This theatrical family included among its members the internationally famous young actress, Kate. While Madge was there, an old schoolmate of her childhood turned up—back with exciting talk of the wealth to be realized in the gold fields of California. With these stimulating changes Madge's brooding on Clara's story seemed to fade away.

---

### Wednesday, March 18, 1863

*Cloudy and dull again today, with a slight sprinkle of rain during the day. This morning a German came and bought old Bob the horse, giving me ten dollars for him. I walked down to Mrs Stansbury's this morning to borrow a card of hooks & eyes, and I remained an hour or two with her. On my return, I had a most unpleasant scene with Jim. I am really afraid I shall be obliged to tell Mr Preston he must send Jim away. He makes Lizzie impertinent also. I am fixing another of my dresses up. Money is so scarce and dry goods so very dear, it makes it necessary for everyone to observe as much economy as possible. I must get clothing for May, and will have to do without myself. Mr Preston is still in the city.*

Pleasant Plains March 18th 1863

My darling child,

On last Monday, I folded up (after cutting & fixing it as nicely as I could) the linen for the shirt you were so desirous of making for Papa, together with some French books, which . . . Papa was to have put in a box, after purchasing stockings for you, and then to send them off. . . . Professional duties and *St Patrick's day* have detained Papa in town, consequently I am uninformed with regard to the fate of your package. I can only think, trusting to Papa's usual attention to our little commissions, that all is right. . . .

Your last letter mentioned a retreat which was to commence on Saturday, and I suppose to end on the 25 the "Annunciation." This will be altogether a new thing for you, but judging from your meditative disposition, I trust you will derive much spiritual benefit from your temporary retirement from the cares and anxieties of everyday life. These are great privileges my child that you are permitted to enjoy, and while in possession of them, forget not to pray for those who are deprived of them, but who thirst after the "living waters," with an ardour more acceptable to our Lord than the lukewarmness of those, who while partaking of the life-giving draught are unmindful of its precious blessings. I am quite desirous of giving little Kitty an opportunity of instruction and confession—for that purpose, I contemplate making a visit to the city of several days; . . . while there, I will take Kitty to Rev Mr Foley, and ask him to initiate her into the mysteries of Confession. I would take her to Father Elder . . . but she would not be able to go to him by herself if it were necessary. . . . She herself is most anxious, and is "trying" *to be good*, before she goes. Lately she has talked constantly of you; I suppose as the time approaches for your return, she becomes more anxious to see you. She, together with Lizzie, when they found I was writing to you this evening asked me to please give their loves to Miss May. . . .

I must not forget to tell you of an unexpected visitor we had last Sunday. I had just returned from my usual Sunday walk with Papa when the peculiar barking of dogs announced the approach of strangers. In a short time, a carriage drew up to the door and Adolphus and his mother alighted. If you recollect, last Sunday was a very cold day, but plenty of furs and a fine robe had protected them from the cold and they told me they had a pleasant drive all the way from the city. Mrs S—— was apparently so well pleased with Papa & myself, that a cordial invitation extended to them to remain to dinner was at once accepted, and I really do not know when I have spent so pleasant a day. . . .

### Monday, March 23, 1863

. . . *Lizzie & Kitty planted me a bed of strawberries in the greenhouse, and I have nearly made a frock for Kitty out of May's old red plaid dress.*

### Tuesday, March 24, 1863

. . . *I finished Kitty's frock and remodeled her Shaker[i] for her, all which pleased her greatly. . . .*

### Wednesday, March 25, 1863

. . . *I have been greatly shocked by intelligence brought me from town today by Louis. It seems my poor nephew Hamilton was killed yesterday on the railroad.*

*His body was to have been brought to the city today. I shall go to the city tomorrow, when I hope to learn the particulars.*

### Thursday, March 26, 1863

*Made an early start for the city this morning, driving in the market wagon & two horses on account of the bad roads; the weather was excessively unpleasant, spitting snow & rain, and was cold raw & disagreeable. As soon as I reached the city, I went up to see Mrs Hammond and in the afternoon Tommy & I went down to see the body of poor Ham, which had come on in the night accompanied by Tommy. Tommy is terribly distressed. As the funeral will not take place till tomorrow I am obliged to remain in town all night and have sent Jim home to let Mr Preston know. Tommy is sleeping with me tonight and she & Mr Bartlett go to Washington in the 4 o'clock train tomorrow morning. Hamilton's remains look as natural as life. It seems the car crushed the back part of his head and his right arm. One would not take him to have been more than 22 years of age though he was almost 30.*

### Friday, March 27, 1863

*Tommy & Mr Bartlett got off early this morning, and returned by one o'clock. Mr Preston came in from the country, and the arrangements being completed, we met at Mr Weaver's to take the body to its final resting place. It was deposited in the Gist family vault in Green Mount Cemetery, and it was really gratifying to his relatives to see so many of his friends in attendance. . . .*

### Thursday, April 2, 1863

*. . . I had quite an agreeable surprise this afternoon. An old friend Isaac Hartman came out to see me. As I had not seen him since long before we were both married, we had much to say to each other and passed an agreeable hour. He lives in California, his wife & two children are dead and he is alone in the world. He tells me he is likely to be a wealthy man soon. I am glad to hear it. . . .*

### Saturday, April 4, 1863

*. . . Mr Hartman came out to spend the day with me. I have enjoyed talking over olden times, and hearing Mr Hartman tell of the wonders of that great Eldorado, California, where he resides. He has given me a strong inclination to go there, but I doubt if Mr Preston would ever be willing to go far from this part of the world. . . .*

**Sunday, April 12, 1863**

*A warm delightful day with several slight April showers. Rose tolerably early this morning to pack and arrange for my journey [to Philadelphia]. About ten o'clock I walked down to Mrs Stansbury, sat with her an hour and returned, packed my trunk, walked round with Lizzie telling her what I wished her particularly to attend to during my absence. . . at five o'clock we left home, reaching the city at seven all safe and comfortable. Mrs Beer & Mrs Stuntz have spent the evening with me, while Mr Preston went out to hear the news; he has just come in and says, it is thought the Rebels have whipped the Federals terribly at Charleston.*[2]

Philadelphia<br>April 13th 1863

My darling child,

You will hardly be surprised at the postmark of this letter, as Mrs Hillen must have informed you of my intention to visit our friends both in this city and also in New York. . . . I came in company with Mr Price and his daughter; the latter is a pupil at Madam Chagerey's, and had been home spending the Easter holidays. What would you think of a boarding school where young ladies went to the opera and theatre, rec'd visitors and visited from school, and read novels in the[ir] own rooms? I congratulated myself most sincerely that the Fates had not dotted you down in such a school. I found our friend Mrs Simmons and her most interesting little boys anxiously awaiting my coming. . . . You will be pleased to learn that dear, little, bright Charley had the great happiness, young as he is (just eleven years old) to make his first communion during the holy time of Lent. The little fellow . . . seemed fully impressed with the importance of the occasion, and since then at times his conduct has been quit[e] edifying. . . . I was thinking constantly of you and regretted not being there to enjoy seeing your happiness. . . .

Your<br>Mama

---

While Madge was in Philadelphia, Preston sent on to her a scrawled note from May. May's letter, misdated, differs from all her earlier correspondence, which had been composed under the watchful eye of the writing teacher and copied in May's most careful script. The new letter was crossed out, smudged, and carefree.

Emmittsburg Mar [April] 13th 1863

My dear Mama,

I have for once an opportunity to write to you without anyone but yourself seeing it and I avail myself of it with the *greatest pleasure*. I have staid out with Mrs. Hillen (Mollie and Jeannette of course being along) for two nights. . . . I suppose you would like to hear all our adventures since Mrs Hillen's arrivle infact before. As I did not know that Mrs Hillen was coming up on Saturday I had nothing to look forward to, and went up to sewing class and was stitching away on Papa's shirt when Jeannette came in and asked for Mollie. I thought Mrs Harris only had come so I did not expect to be called out but Jeannette looked up and saw me for the first time and she immediately beckoned to me to come also as I thought she was in fun and was on the point of giving her a black look for teasing me. But when she asked Sister Johanna for me and she told me to go I began to think I had made a mistake, folded up my work and followed them out of the room. Tillie was all ready waiting for us and it was not long before we too were decked out in hoops. Miss Addie Shorb and her brother Bartie . . . had come over from Clairvoix . . . and took us over. Neither Mr Hillen nor Mrs Hillen had arrived but we enjoyed ourselves very much until the stage. . . . Your little

May

We are as happy as Queens

## Wednesday, April 22, 1863

*. . . we arranged this morning to go to Central Park. . . . I am free to pronounce that place when completed the most beautiful spot of the kind on earth. . . .*

## Thursday, April 23, 1863

*This morning Mr H—— [Hartman] came early for us, and Mrs B—— [Bateman] Mr H— and myself went over to N. York where we spent the day till five o'clock looking at pictures. We went to Fredericks and Mrs B and myself had our pictures taken, we then went to the Academy of Designs and from thence to Church's picture of Cotopaxi.[3] I merely record these things for reference not to criticize. I will simply say, I have never looked on such a picture; it is glorious! Mr H left us at the Brooklyn ferry, and Mrs B went home and I went to Mrs Sweet's, where I spent a delightful evening, reaching home about half past ten o'clock, and rec'd a letter from Mr Preston, said letter being 16 pages long and filled with censure against me for receiving and introducing Mr H into Mrs B——'s family &c &c[4] I did not answer it tonight because I must reflect upon it.*

**Friday, April 24, 1863**

*On arising this morning I found I was to have one of my bad headaches today,
brought on in a great measure by the excitement produced by Mr Preston's letter. I have been obliged to keep my bed all day. . . .*

———————————

While Madge was still indisposed, a second letter, milder in tone, came
from her husband. But a news clipping folded within its pages disturbed her
greatly.

Baltimore 22 April 1863

I have just received your letter of the 21st. It gives me pleasure to know that
you are enjoying yourself—Still it would be well not to tax your powers too
far. Crossing ferries at 1 o'clock A.M. is very questionable so far as health is
concerned, particularly to a woman of your quiet country habits. This is the
third day I have been away from Pleasant Plains—consequently am not able
to say anything about movements there. . . .

I inclose to you a slip which I have cut from one of our daily papers announcing the death of our old and esteemed friend Judge Stump—his departure very naturally filled me with painful emotions. I felt however consoled in
the knowledge that the old gentleman had died in the bosom of his brother's
family and not in some cold-hearted miserable hotel. His death created a
painful sensation throughout the community—and a number of his friends
on the evening of the announcement were seated in Barnums Hotel sadly discussing his merits, when to the utter astonishment of the party, in walked the
old judge—never were men more amazed—one old gentleman actually
fainted. I have not seen the Judge . . . but I have no doubt he is alive and well.
Mention me kindly to our friends and let them understand that you have my
approbation as to the time you may determine to stay with them.

Yours truly
W P Preston

Brooklyn April 25th /63

Dear Mr Preston,
    We spent the greater part of Thursday looking at pictures in N. York. On
reaching Brooklyn about five o'clock P.M. Mrs Bateman went home and drove
round to Mrs Sweet's to spend the evening with the family and some friends,
who had been invited to meet me. The evening passed off pleasantly, but
on leaving, we found there had been a heavy shower of rain . . . and . . . my
feet were soaking by the time I reached Mr Bateman's. Your letter or . . .

"bundle," as dear little Chip called it . . . was handed to me. In the joy of the moment at having rec'd such a lengthy evidence of kindly feeling, as I foolishly imagined, towards your absent wife—I opened the document and read it to the end.—The revulsion of feeling occasioned by its painful and undeserved remarks, together with the length of time I had sat with my cold and wet feet, threw me into such a state of nervous excitement that I went to bed with a severe chill upon me. A restless and unhappy night was followed by a day of terrible nervous headache, which confined me the whole day to my bed. This morning I am somewhat relieved in my head but I feel shattered and depressed to a great degree—perhaps I have "overtaxed" myself and to a "woman of my quiet country habits" the unusual physical exertion and exposure "crossing ferries at one o'clock at night," and undeserved censure in letters, when I had expected pleasant domestic communications and satisfaction on the part of others that the "quiet country woman" was enjoying herself, has been too much for me, and I am now paying the penalty of my imprudence. . . . I am not well enough today to do anything but finish this letter, write another one to Mrs Simmons . . . and loaf about the house and be petted by Mrs Bateman and the children, who are the kindest and most sympathizing creatures in the world to those who need their kindness and sympathy. . . . I shall go to Phila on Tuesday—and remain till Saturday. . . . Now my dear Mr Preston, I think you might so arrange it, as to meet me in Phila if only for one night. Come on Friday, attend to your business with Mrs Simmons, and see Kate play Leah for the last time before she leaves for Europe, from which place she may perhaps never return. . . . Now do . . . gratify me in this particular.

Yours of the 23d postmark was brought to me while in bed yesterday. The tears rushed to my eyes on reading the slip announcing the death of the dear old Judge, and then I felt as if I could give you a good pounding for your own feeling remarks on the subject when the saving clause in your letter revealed the inaccuracy of the publication. . . .

Love to Mrs Beer and the family.
Truly yours
Madge

### Sunday, May 3, 1863

*. . . Mrs Simmons and I went to St John's Church—Oh what emotions crowded on my heart, when I look at the altar, where 17 years ago Mr Preston & I were made man & wife. Good God what terrible events have happened since that time. . . .*

## Wednesday, May 6, 1863

*We had a terrific storm of wind and rain during the night, it was quite alarming, so much so as to prevent my sleeping; all day the storm has still been raging, and tonight there is no abatement of it. The consequence is I have been obliged to remain still at Mr Hood's. I do not regret it, as it is more agreeable to be with Mrs Hood and her family than the little woman [Mrs Simmons], though she is amiable and cheerful and tries to be agreeable. We have news of a terrible battle having been fought on the Rappahannock, occupying several days. From the reports, the Confederates have completely routed the Union Army.[5] I am quite astonished at the strong Southern sentiment in this city.*

## Thursday, May 7, 1863

*It stormed all night, and it has been cloudy with occasional sprinkles of rain, but notwithstanding I left Hoods and went up to Simmons, as I designed to leave for Balt in the half past eleven o'clock train. Mrs Simmons seemed very much annoyed at my staying away so long, and I became rather indignant at some of her remarks. I left at eleven o'clock, reached the train in good time . . . and in a few hours found myself at the Balt depot; not meeting Mr Preston I got in a carriage and drove to the house. In a short time Mr P. came and seemed glad to see me. I walked up to see Mrs Hillen and she gave me glowing accounts of May &c &c. We shall stay in tonight.*

Pleasant Plains
May 10th 1863

My dear child,

I had fully intended to devote a large part of today to you; but unfortunately visitors came in and they did not leave us till nearly dark. . . . You know I have been absent one month today, a very long time for me to be away from home. Wonderful changes had taken place during that time—the trees which I had left with bare branches, I found clothed with young and tender leaves, and covered with their beautiful white or pink blossoms, the fields are green with grass, and your favourite flowers, the modest violet and delicate little forget-me-not, are smiling through woods and meadows. . . .

Mrs Beer has been staying out on the farm during my absence and she, together with Lizzie, Kitty and Mrs Pentz were greatly delighted to see me, and I assure you my darling child, I was just as glad to be here again. It is all very well to travel about occasionally. It enlarges one's mind—it makes them acquainted with new and improved modes of doing things and prevents them

from becoming narrow-minded and contracted in their views—but notwithstanding all its advantages, we return with a feeling of satisfaction and firm
conviction in our own hearts that there is, in the truthful and beautiful language of the poet—"no place like home." Everything seems to have gone on
very well. . . . Papa has enjoyed good health as well as the rest of the family.
Lambs have grown—chickens have increased wonderfully, and turkeys and
ducks are trying to do likewise—altogether I am quite satisfied with the condition of affairs during my absence. . . .

I suppose you have heard of the last great battle fought near Fredericksburg
—and of the really disgraceful defeat of Hooker's army—the more contempt-
ible as Hooker had boasted that the Southern army would be annihilated, as
soon as he (Hooker) should meet them in battle. You will regret to learn that
the good and brave General Stonewall Jackson was severely wounded in his
arm, and he has been obliged to have it amputated. Pray that he may soon be
restored to health and usefulness again. . . . Papa sends love to you as to all
the rest of the family. Good night your loving

Mother

### Wednesday, May 13, 1863

. . . *Mrs Stansbury's grand entertainment came off tonight and truly a great
affair it proved. The company were assembling from seven to ten. It being an
exceedingly dark & rainy night those who came from the city found it very unpleasant, yet notwithstanding, they numbered . . . two hundred & fifty. It
was a beautiful sight. The large room finely lighted and so many young and
beautiful women gaily dressed, the music and dancing lending a peculiar grace
to the scene. The party did not begin to disperse till daylight, it being thought
almost dangerous to start during the darkness of the night. I remained, together with Mrs Beer & some other friends till after breakfast this morning.
About nine o'clock all had gone but myself. And now begins a laughable, but
at the same time, a most distressing part of the affair. Among the many good
things provided for refreshments were lobster salad—and deviled crabs. These
articles, from some unknown cause, began to show themselves obnoxious to the
stomachs of those who had partaken of them. Christie was the first taken, and
while . . . attending to her, George—then Ike—after him Mr Potee, and
lastly Dan. The entire day Mrs Stansbury, Miss Julia Battie & myself were attending the sick. The doctor was sent for and when he came in the afternoon he
said he had been very sick & only was able to keep about by taking large quantities of whiskey. We heard that nearly every person at the party . . . had
suffered in like manner. I never in my life witnessed such suffering. I can't help
thinking the food was impure and slightly poisoned those who ate it. I remained all night again . . . and came home this morning. Mr Preston has com-*

*plained a good deal today of sickness at the stomach, but tonight he feels a little better. Mrs Beer escaped altogether, but Jim and Lizzie have been very sick. . . .*

### Saturday, May 16, 1863

*. . . Mr Preston & Mrs Beer went to the city this morning, the latter having been out here more than a month. I am glad to be alone again, tho' I was satisfied to make a convenience of her while I went to New York. . . .*

### Tuesday, May 19, 1863

*. . . This afternoon Mr Preston came home; he brought with him a packet brought by Adam Express from Phila containing a beautiful writing desk sent by Mrs Hood to May for a birthday gift. May will be delighted. . . .*

### Friday, May 22, 1863

*. . . I have finished reading Aurora Floyd,[6] a book Mrs Bateman gave, which I think beautifully written and very interesting. I am alone tonight!*

### Monday, May 25, 1863

*Mr Preston came up early this morning to tell me of heavy cannonading he had been hearing the greater part of the night, and still heard it after day-break. I am inclined to think it was heaven's artillery and was only a thunder storm. . . .*

### Tuesday, May 26, 1863

*. . . I forgot to mention yesterday that Mr Preston permitted Lizzie & Jim to take his carriage & horse and drive to the city and spend the day, it being Whitmonday. They came home "all right" but unfortunately broke the carriage.*

> Pleasant Plains
> May 26th 1863

My darling child,

Your welcome favor of the 22d came safely to hand late last evening and notwithstanding Papa leaves this morning, I shall endeavour to send by him a letter. . . . I want you as soon as you receive this, to go at once to her Majesty the fair Queen of the South—or more affectionately speaking, to my dear

Mollie and tell her though I did not write to her on her birthday, I nevertheless had she and my equally dear Jeannette in my mind and heart and *in my prayers* on that day. I really wanted to write to both of them, but since my return from the North I have had so much to look after—seed planting—little chickens—house cleaning—and spring sewing, together with a number of letters to answer . . . that I have scarcely been able to write to you. . . . Kiss them both and give them as much love as they desire and tell them Aunty Preston sent it; tell them also, while we are looking forward with so much pleasure to your return, we are not unmindful that they are to come also. It is quite amusing to notice how completely they are associated with you in all our arrangements and fixings; whatever Papa plans for you has the "girls" attached to it, and so it is with our neighbours; "They are to do so and so, when May and the 'girls' come home"—"May and the girls" are always blended— the one, *not* talked or thought of without the other. I am pleased to know you are so lovingly united at St Joseph's. These early and youthful friendships are the most pleasant and lasting of any you will ever make. In future years when the cares and trials insuperable to mature life surround you, it will be one of your great pleasures to look back upon your school days and those young and gay companions with whom you are now so happily associated—and fortunate may you all consider yourselves, if your paths through life sometimes mingle together and that you do not find yourselves late in life and at its close among comparative strangers and those who have not known you in childhood and girlish days. . . .

You say your examinations have commenced; believe me my pet, I sympathize with you every hour in the day and sincerely hope and trust you have been sufficiently attentive to your lessons . . . to pass through this trying ordeal with credit to yourself and satisfaction to your kind instructresses. What do you mean by a private Distribution? Does it mean that honors and premiums (if any are to be awarded) will be given without the presence of parents and friends? If so, I am very sorry for it, as I had intended bringing up with me several ladies who have long wanted to see St Joseph's. . . . I wish you to give my love to Sister Raphael and ask her to please tell you if you will require any other dressing than that you now have and what kind is desirable. . . . Another thing—ask the clothes Sister, if it will be necessary for me to bring up another trunk to put your clothing in, or will she be able to pack some of them in the boxes in which they have been sent. . . . When you are packing up for home—please *do not* forget the carte de visites that I have sent you at different times, and be sure you bring with you all the letters you may have received during your stay at St Joseph's. . . .

God bless you all—

Yours
Mama & Aunty.

Pleasant Plains
May 31st 1863

My darling child,

Papa, *Kitty* and myself have been wandering about this glorious night till it is almost ten o'clock and even now we come in reluctantly. The country, with its fresh spring growth, looks beautifully under this bright moonlight, indeed I think I have never seen Pleasant Plains so beautiful as it is *just now*. The yellow roses . . . are in their first full flush of bloom, some of our finest pink roses are also very abundant and they, together with the fragrant and graceful locust flowers . . . present a varied and gay scene, lovely as the eye would care to look upon. Papa and I gathered a few very fine strawberries on some vines we have in the greenhouse today—the first . . . we have had, and . . . we wished you were here to enjoy them with us. My garden is beginning to look promising—we only want rain, to start the plants and seed to growing. . . .

Papa sends love to you, as also poor little Kitty, who is not very well tonight. Kiss all the young ladies that I know at St Joseph's, and give my love particularly to Mollie and Jeannette. . . . Good night—God bless you—

Mama

2 o'clock in the morning
Aigburth Vale
June 6th 1863

My dear child,

The place from whence my letter is dated and the unusual hour . . . will suggest to you some strange and unusual event. . . . I am sitting up in company with Delia, in attendance on the lifeless body of our dear old friend Mrs Owens, who died quite suddenly yesterday morning. The circumstances surrounding were melancholy in the extreme. Mr and Mrs John E. Owens had just returned the day before, from an absence of several months' duration, and found their mother in her usual health and cheerful spirits, —of course there was much to tell and much to hear from both sides. Yesterday morning while engaged in pleasant conversation, the old lady suddenly complained of pain and oppression at the heart and breast; . . . she gave a slight cough and on her son raising her head to enable her to cough more freely, she looked lovingly in his face and from the son, to the dear old husband by her side, then raised her eyes to Heaven and was gone. We pray to be delivered from a sudden death; but when such a death comes to one who has passed a long, peaceful, good and pure life, we cannot help feeling thankful that our friend is spared the pang of sufferings and trials to which perhaps poor human nature might not be equal without showing a degree of fretfulness and impatience, unbecoming a Christian. I was with the family all day and am here tonight and shall not leave till after the funeral. The old lady looks beautifully. Delia and I have just come in from the garden where we have been gathering, by moonlight, quantities of lovely roses and other flowers and have strewn the body with them. . . .

I went to the city today and received your letter dated May 30th. Owing to Papa having been engaged in a trial all this week at Towsontown . . . it has lain all this time in the . . . post office. In reply to your wish for the blue lawn, you shall surely have it if you desire one, but I think the pretty blue dress you already have, which I made for you last summer just before you left home, is prettier than any lawn I could buy. It has short sleeves and low neck, which I know are objectionable, but I will make a white body with high neck and long sleeves, if you think you would like it, and they are very much worn by young girls this season. I will come up for you the day before Distribution and bring it with me in a trunk, and then Sister can pack your extra clothes in it. . . .

Good night

affectionately your Mama

## Wednesday, June 17, 1863

. . . I finished May's little frock I designed her to wear at the Distribution but in a letter I rec'd from her this evening, she tells me she cannot wear a thin body; this being thin, I know not what the poor child will do, I shall send it up, as it is too late for me to get her another one.

## Thursday, June 18, 1863

. . . Lizzie has been in one her "spells" all this week and tomorrow being churning day, I fear the butter will be spoiled.

## Friday, June 19, 1863

. . . Mr Preston & I went to the city this morning intending to send May's clothing up for Distribution, but when I got to the p. office a letter from May informed me that the Distribution was over and the girls wanted to come down with the Sisters on Monday. . . . I wrote at once and sent her money to come down. . . .

# 4

## The Gettysburg Summer

UNKNOWN TO THE PRESTONS AND their neighbors, and to others in the city, thousands of troops were beginning to move through Maryland in the last week of June. Probably Sister Raphael caught wind of something afoot. Many of the Sisters of Charity had for some time been working among the troops, wherever the wounded lay in need of care, so possibly rumors floated back to the central headquarters in Emmitsburg. In any case, Sister Raphael seems to have acted quickly to finish the term and to get the girls back home. Since the Distribution ceremony at year's end, when the girls received their special commendations, was normally an occasion of great pomp—an opportunity to show the school at best advantage to the parents—the good Sister must have had special reasons to carry it out so abruptly. But whatever they were, she did not share them with the girls. No somber note colors the entries in Madge's diary as she awaited the reunion with May. All members of the household, including May's doll, Nannie, were decked out to receive the newcomer; and the place had an air of festive gaiety.

---

**Tuesday, June 23, 1863**

*Rose in good time this morning, and as it was a pleasant clear windy day Lizzie, Kitty & myself set to work cleaning and fixing up the house; thinking there was a slight propect of May coming home this evening, we took the stove from the parlour, and hung the pictures up in the library, and cleaned the parlour thoroughly; it looks beautifully. We put all May's presents on the table ready for her, we also fixed up her bedroom and arranged her altar, & put fresh flowers on it. Nannie was dressed, Kitty & Lizzie, and sure enough when Mr Preston came home he brought May with him. It seems she and the girls, to-*

*gether with the Baltimore girls, came down yesterday with the Sisters. May re-*
*mained at Sanders' and came out tonight. Christie, Johnny, Jo Grindel &*
*Mamie & Alice, all came up to see her. May does not look so well as she did in*
*the winter; she tells me she has suffered greatly with headaches lately. We are to*
*sleep in Mr Preston's room tonight.*

### Wednesday, June 24, 1863

*Another pleasant day, and May & I have enjoyed being together once more; we*
*have wandered about and I have shown her all round the place; she is delighted*
*at being home again. . . .*

### Saturday, June 27, 1863

*This has been a delightful day, and May and I have enjoyed it greatly. Mr*
*Preston harnessed up Buck in the little carriage today and it proved quite a suc-*
*cess. Buck seems as gentle as one could desire him to be and he and the carriage*
*look very well together. Mrs Stansbury brought May's trunk up this afternoon,*
*and this evening we opened it, and I was gratified by seeing May's cards of*
*merit. She rec'd twelve premiums, nine the first in her class, and three the sec-*
*ond. . . .*

---

While May was renewing her acquaintance with animals and people at
Pleasant Plains during this serene late June day, thousands of men of both armies were traveling along the very roads that May and her school friends had
traversed so recently. Almost 6,000 men—three brigades of General J. E. B.
Stuart's Confederate cavalry—crossed the Potomac on June 27, passing
through Rockville and then north toward the rail hub at Westminster. There
on the twenty-ninth a large unit of Stuart's men had an encounter with a
small Union force, the First Delaware Volunteer Cavalry. Most of the Union
men were captured, but a small contingent, including their commander, got
away. They fled toward safety in Baltimore, pursued almost to Reisterstown
by Stuart's men, within hearing distance of Pleasant Plains.[1]

Lee's plan was to carry the war into Pennsylvania, where he hoped to pick
up much needed supplies. Stuart had been permitted to swing east and to the
rear of the enemy's troops, where he unfortunately lost contact with the rest of
the Southern forces. In the meantime, large contingents of Union troops under General Hooker were crossing the Potomac along the river's northern
reaches, near Williamsport, or further south, near Point of Rocks. As they
moved through the countryside, they converged on the city of Frederick and
then funneled north between the mountains toward Emmitsburg. Northern
forces received a warm welcome, gratifying in this part of the state.[2]

Madge and May were unaware at first of what was happening. Madge was busy with work about the farm. She had enlisted Lizzie's assistance, in fact, with one major, unpleasant task. But the Sisters at St. Joseph's were in the thick of things. On the night of June 27, they became aware of the arrival of men and horses at the very campus of the school. A Union general commandeered the cupola atop the school building as a look-out post, and a Northern cavalry unit was bedding down in a fine field of clover on the farm belonging to the institution. The next morning, when the Sisters looked out, they saw their field, as one of them described it, "barren and bare as a board."

Through all of the next few days the Sisters were wholly absorbed in trying to cope with the complex emergency that had been thrust upon them. All day they worked ceaselessly, offering coffee and bread to the hungry troops, as the men seemed to come in a never-ending line. All night Father Burlando and two of the Sisters stood guard inside the main hall in the dark, alert to possible threats to their colleagues or to the half-dozen schoolgirls from the Southern states who had had to remain at the school because it was impossible to send them home. The young convent novices, excited by the presence of hundreds of men, also had to be closely supervised. At one point, fearing that a battle could break out in the school premises, the Mother Superior planned to send these young women back to their families. But in the early morning hours of July 1, between two and three o'clock, the soldiers pulled out to a man; for a short few hours, the Sisters were able to breathe normally again.[3]

Slowly, over a matter of days, some of this news began to filter down to Pleasant Plains.

### Monday, June 29, 1863

*It rained during the night and rained the greater part of the day, and we had in the midst of it the misfortune to have our chickenhouse burn & cow stable burn to the ground. It happened in this wise. I took Lizzie and went to the chickenhouse about ten o'clock to fumigate the nests and it is supposed, the first must have fallen behind the plaster and we did not see it; a few minutes after we left it blazed up, and in less than two hours the whole range of buildings were burned to the ground. The neighbours came far & near, but could afford no assistance. Mr Preston & our people are worn down with fatigue tonight. . . .*

---

It is possible that the burning of the chickenhouse was no accident. Students of black history of this period describe frequent cases of arson carried out by slaves against the property of the slaveholders. Lizzie was certainly affected by the conversations of her husband, Jim, who was still a slave. Evidently he felt secure enough to speak in Preston's presence about his admiration for the abolitionist Wendell Phillips. Lizzie, ordered by Mrs. Preston to help fumigate the chicken house, would have had ample opportunity to drop a spark in a hidden place.[4]

---

### Tuesday, June 30, 1863

*It rained quite heavily nearly all this morning, which put out very effectively all the fire of yesterday. Several of our friends have been here today, to condole with us in our misfortune. . . . There seems to be very exciting news from the city. The Confederates are invading Pennsylvania and are determined to make the North feel some of the horrors of what the [people of the] South have suffered for two years past. This is a glorious night. May & I think we hear the tramping of cavalry tonight in the distance.*

---

Scarcely had the Union troops moved north from Emmitsburg than Confederate forces came in to take their place. The transfer of men occurred so quickly, and under the cover of darkness, that Father Gandolfo, walking over to St. Joseph's before dawn to conduct early mass, assumed that the pickets who stopped him belonged to General Meade, who had been occupying a house on the premises. Now, for a short time, a few Confederate officers took lodging in the orphanage building on St. Joseph's campus. Then these forces also moved on in the direction of Gettysburg, the Pennsylvania town about ten miles to the north. The encounter between the two armies, which took place by chance at Gettysburg, could well have occurred near the site where May Preston went to school.

From their headquarters at St. Joseph's, the Sisters of Charity and the two chaplains were appalled as the terrible booming of cannons commenced. This happened around noon on the first day of July. For three more days the sound did not cease. Soon the sky darkened as though a storm were brewing; but the clouds, created of black smoke, had been made by the engines of men.

"Whilst the booming of the cannon announced that God was punishing the iniquities of men," wrote Sister Camilla in later years, "our Sisters were in the church praying, and imploring mercy for all mankind."[5]

At Pleasant Plains, too far to see the smoke, but near enough to hear the distant boom, the impact was different. Curiously, Madge seemed oblivious to concerns for the safety of her many Pennsylvania relatives and friends. She could not imagine, of course, that the most significant battle of the Civil War was taking place at a town where she had spent so much time in her youth and to which she had returned often on holiday visits in the years since her marriage.

To Madge, domestic affairs were more all-consuming. Since Lincoln's Emancipation Proclamation, which took effect on January 1, 1863, Lizzie and Jim had become increasingly unruly. The Proclamation applied only to slaves held in rebelling states—not to states such as Maryland, which had remained in the Union. Yet the large numbers of freed slaves who had headed north and were now mingling with the rest of the black population in Maryland made it easy for those who were technically still slaves to disappear. Slaveowners in Maryland found it was hard to control their slaves. Military authorities were forbidden to interfere with the fleeing blacks, and no one dared reclaim fugitives before a civil magistrate. For both slaves and masters, the moral contradictions built into the Proclamation were also difficult to resolve. How could blacks from the rebel states become free men and women, while those in the North were still property?

Although Lizzie and Jim remained at Pleasant Plains, they too heard the cannonading and understood the change in their status its sound implied was forthcoming.[6]

### Thursday, July 2, 1863

. . . *We have been greatly excited this afternoon & evening by the most continued cannonading in the direction of Gettysburg. The battle wherever it is must be a fearful one.* . . .

### Friday, July 3, 1863

. . . *We heard various reports of the battle at Gettysburg. The prevailing opinion is that the Confederates have been rather successful.* . . .

### Saturday, July 4, 1863

*I have had a most unhappy day. Lizzie has been in a terrible frolic for sometime past and culminated today. Everything seems to have gone wrong—dairy duties have been neglected, no ironing done, and everything wrong.*

---

At St. Joseph's more compelling problems came into focus. Aghast as news of the carnage, carried by Confederate stragglers, drifted south from Gettysburg, Father Burlando and eight of the Sisters set out in a carriage and the school's omnibus on Sunday, July 5. They were carrying medicine and supplies for the wounded. Within the next few days, every Sister who could be spared was sent to Gettysburg. There they set up headquarters in McLellan's Hotel and, dispersed among several makeshift hospitals, worked as nurses. Throughout the summer they endured conditions of the most extreme discomfort in their care of the wounded.

Other battlefield visitors, however, arrived in Gettysburg with intentions less serious.

### Monday, July 6, 1863

*. . . Mr Preston told me that he & Mr Hillen had determined to take a trip to Gettysburg to view the battlefields whereon has been fought the greatest battle of modern times. They will start sometime tomorrow. I made a nice jar of raspberry jam today.*

---

It would come out later that among those Preston met was Sister Genevieve of St. Joseph's. Relieved of her duties in the school's Infirmary by the summer vacation, she brought her medical knowledge to those whose need was greater. She was the first of the Sisters Preston knew, and he came to respect her greatly.

### Sunday, July 12, 1863

*. . . It was very interesting to hear Mr Preston's account of the battlefield, and meeting with Louisa and her family. I have never had so correct an idea of a battlefield, as since hearing Mr Preston's account of it. . . .*

---

Some time later Preston must have sought Madge's aid in preparing a written version of his experience. Among his papers is a folded sheaf of several pages inscribed on the outside "A Letter from Battle field of Gettysburg. July 7, 1863." The first five paragraphs of this document have been written out in Madge's neat script. Across this copy, occasional changes in wording are marked in Preston's larger, conspicuous hand; then the rest of the account continues in his handwriting, ending abruptly and inconclusively. Neither addressee nor signature appears on the manuscript. It is dated July 9, with the heading "Gettysburg."

Among the paragraphs inscribed by Madge is a passage in which Preston struck a note of contrasting moods—a before-and-after sequence—that perhaps characterized the national response at the two ends of the summer of 1863:

The Carlisle turnpike leads through a beautiful valley, at this time rich in all the blessings of a fruitful harvest. As we journeyed along last evening . . .

engaged in social chat or quietly contemplating the waving fields of ripened wheat lit with radiance from a long line of mountains fringed with the glory of the setting sun, how little did I conceive of the awful contrast between the quiet lovely scene and the frightful ruin and carnage we have seen today! We reached the village of Oxford ten miles from Gettysburg about six o'clock. At this point the turnpikes cross and we soon found the road leading from Gettysburg to York crowded with all sorts of vehicles—men on horseback and pedestrians; some were going, others returning. I have often seen large crowds, religious assemblages, political meetings, fetes, funerals &c &c. On every occasion I have been able to detect in the faces of the crowd something expressive of the governing emotion—the ruling passion. On this occasion the gestures and features of all who were on their way to the scene of conflict betrayed an active and eager curiousity. Those who were returning wore a very different aspect. Never have I seen such an unmistakable manifestation of wrath and horror—every man's features were painfully rigid and many looked as if all their preconceived opinions of humanity had been suddenly unsettled.

---

More was unsettled than the faces of the curious. The pleasant mood of summer's early days within the Preston household changed as well.

### Wednesday, August 5, 1863

*This has been one of the most unhappy days I have ever spent. Lizzie seems to have determined to trouble us as much as she can with her drinking, and not satisfied with that, she was so dreadfully impertinent that I felt the absolute necessity of leaving the house as I knew Mr Preston would give me no remedy.(?) [sic] I went to Eudowood & spent the day; about 6 o'clock Mr Preston sent for me as he wished to see me before going to the city and May also wrote to me to return as she thought it best I should do so. I came home & found Mr Preston so violent to me that I regretted having come home. . . .*

### Thursday, August 6, 1863

*. . . I have felt greatly annoyed with Mr Preston today as I was fully under the impression that he was going to the city, in relation to Lizzie, but I fear I am doomed to keeping her, to more troubles. . . . Mr Preston has remained home all day and thank Heaven Lizzie has been all right today. I have been fixing her up some clothing today as everything she has seems to have got out of order. . . .*

### Friday, August 14, 1863

*. . . Old Mrs Newberger has been washing for me today. She is a good industrious woman. Lizzie I fear has been drinking again.*

### Monday, August 17, 1863

*. . . I made a very unpleasant discovery today. I find someone has taken several notes from my purse altogether amounting to 2$ and twenty cents.*

### Tuesday, August 18, 1863

*. . . Much to my annoyance and chagrin I have discovered another note taken this morning from my purse making in all 3$ and twenty cts. From all the surroundings I am convinced that Lizzie is the delinquent party. . . .*

---

On August 22 May went into Baltimore for an extended visit with the Sanders family and her school friends Mollie and Jeannette. The next afternoon, Sunday, during a quiet time Madge found solace from other difficulties, as she had in the past, by writing a cheerful letter to her daughter. But the day's diary entry tells clearly how much was wrong at home.

Pleasant Plains
August 23d /63

My dear child,

As papa goes to the city this evening, it gives me an opportunity of writing a few lines to you. . . . After you left me yesterday I was so much occupied . . . with sundry duties pertaining to household affairs, that I had no chance to feel lonely—fearing such a spell might overtake me, I betook myself to that never failing comfort "balmy sleep" "tired nature's sweet restorer"—and snoozed it off most luxuriously till nearly five o'clock, at which time I arose much refreshed, and taking a spring water bath, and "putting on by way of variety" an old flounced dress, . . . smoothing my disheveled locks, and *brushing my teeth*—I soon found "Richard was himself again," and quite equal to combat with the spirit of ennui, let it come in what form it might. I had scarcely reached the cool and darkened sitting room and thrown the door and windows open, when the well known sound of carriage wheels announced the coming of the lord of the mansion. As he drove up, I discovered Frank was in the carriage. I was glad to see the young gentleman and so gave him a cordial welcome. . . .

I have missed you all greatly today—my mind is constantly turning back to last Sunday—the picnic in the woods, and the plentiful supply of peaches provided by your generous beaux and then I contrast the cheerful faces and ringing voices of my merry young friends and my own little daughter and the dear boy Charley, with the sombre and grave looks of Frank, and the antiquated phiz of papa and the lugubrious aspect of poor Kitty, who saunters about, looking as if "Othello's occupation was surely yours"—in other words as the opportunity does not offer, she cannot get into mischief. I console myself with the hope that you are enjoying yourself with our kind friends, to whom please give love and kisses. . . .

Mama

### Sunday, August 23, 1863

*. . . We have spent an exciting day, Mr Preston & I, with the servants Jim & Lizzie. Mr P—— told them this morning, if the stolen money was not forthcoming or a confession made about it, he would certainly put them both in the penitentiary. Neither Mr Preston nor myself have the slightest idea that they are not guilty. Mr Preston says he is determined to prosecute this business to the end. Mr Preston & William drove to the city this evening after 6 o'clock. Mr P—— remained in town but William returned. After Frank went to bed, and about ½ past 9 o'clock, Jim & Lizzie stole out of the house, leaving the door ajar; they have been gone till now 11 o'clock, and have not yet returned. I am sitting here alone waiting for them. A pleasant position truly!*

### Monday, August 24, 1863

*Still very warm. My conjectures were correct. I thought Jim & Lizzie had skeddadled last night, and this morning finding they did not come home I knew that to be the case. I wrote a note to Mr P—— at Towsontown, telling him of the circumstance; after dark Mr P—— came home, apparently like myself greatly relieved from their absence. . . .*

### Tuesday, August 25, 1863

*I feel very much relieved at not having that poor drunken woman about the kitchen. . . .*

### Friday, August 28, 1863

*Thus far we have heard nothing of Jim & Lizzie and I care not if we never see them again. Their ingratitude is so shameful. I have secured the services of a*

*very nice looking girl and one who bears a good character; she is to come to me*
*on Monday next. . . .*

---

*Ingratitude.* When Madge spoke that word, she repeated a term now reverberating among slaveholders throughout the South. As long-time, faithful servants began to drift away, former owners felt betrayed. They had expected loyalty—especially from house slaves and drivers whom they liked to think of as members of the family. Madge would have been remembering their many kindnesses to Lizzie and Jim—the generous permission to use the family wagon on a recent holiday, the dresses Madge had fixed for Lizzie, the times she had nursed her, sick or drunk. And the training they had given to Jim, the trust they had placed in him, when they put him in charge of the omnibus run.

He was a fiery young man, quoting the words of wild abolitionists to his rather indulgent master. Preston could not plead, as did other slaveowners, that he was unaware of Jim's thoughts. And on some level both Preston and Madge must have recognized the covert message in Lizzie's drinking and intractability. If Madge looked on Lizzie's pilfering as a criminal act punishable by time in the penitentiary, Lizzie doubtless regarded her own labor as uncompensated. Her signals seemed conspicuous. And in any case, she had not forgotten how it felt to be locked away in the penitentiary. Had Madge forgotten that? Signals of discomfort were clear enough on both sides with this relationship.

But that word *ingratitude* must have hung in the air during the days after Lizzie's and Jim's departure. Kitty, who never seemed to overcome the insecurity of being set down alone in this household at the age of three, who always felt threatened when newcomers joined the family, quite clearly heard Madge's message. She would act out her own reply on a future shopping trip. Madge recorded the occasion, but she missed Kitty's message: one in the household, at least, could not be accused of ingratitude.

### Monday, August 31, 1863

*. . . I have had a great disappointment today; the girl that I expected to come this morning did not make her appearance but during the afternoon Mrs Kaniff came over and told me she heard that Eliza, the woman that I expected, had got a situation on Charles St Avenue. I can't blame the girl if she gets higher wages than I offered her, but I think she ought to have informed me of her intention not to come. . . .*

**Tuesday, September 1, 1863**

*. . . Mr Preston drove to the city this morning, taking Kitty with him. While in the city, Kitty made several purchases that were very funny—buying me a paper of pins, and May a cornelian ring. . . .*

---

At St. Joseph's, Sister Raphael had struggled throughout the summer to keep the Southern girls reasonably restrained and quiet. But the stimulations had been enormous. When the Northern troops encamped around them in the days before Gettysburg, Sister Raphael urged the girls to "something like civility." But when small detachments of Confederates followed, also heading north, Sister Raphael could not suppress the girls' demonstrations of delight. When a few cavalrymen approached one evening, girlish voices called out from the avenue: "Give me a button. I'm from South Carolina!" "I'm from Louisiana!" another said.

Now, with the summer winding down, Sister Raphael's administrative load could have only increased. Plans were underway for a new term; yet the unruly Southern girls were an unrelenting responsibility, as a letter to May from one of them, sarcastically dated from "Paradise," clearly revealed: "May you will be very much supprised when I tell you you are in the second class that is if you come back, I hope you will, I am still in third. I am all in tremble afraid I will be caught. Last night we had a good *Lecture* about singing *political* songs we are forbidden to do it any longer we got the very *mischiev* for it every day we get a scholding."[7]

A year earlier Madge had been preoccupied with arrangements for sending May to school. This August other matters absorbed the older woman.

**Monday, September 7, 1863**

*. . . Before I left the city a nice old colored woman came to hire with me; as her looks pleased me I at once employed her; she is to come out tomorrow with Mr Preston. . . .*

**Thursday, September 10, 1863**

*. . . Mr Preston reached home just at dark bringing with him the old woman Lucy, who is to live with us. I like her looks and if she only proves as good a worker I shall be much gratified.*

### Friday, September 11, 1863

*I rose as usual to [illegible] the dairy this morning, John assisting me. I took the old woman with us, but found to my great annoyance that the poor old creature really understands nothing about butter making or attending to a dairy. She seems disposed to learn but it is a great trouble to be teaching all the time. . . .*

---

Madge was running last-minute errands past the middle of September as she and May prepared to leave for St. Joseph's. This time the journey by train would take them directly to Gettysburg. Madge planned to spend time there, as Preston had done earlier, touring the battlefield site.

### Friday, September 18, 1863

*. . . Mr Preston reached town in good time to take us to the depot and we started in a heavy shower of rain, which continued to increase in violence till we had one of the most fearful storms of rain that I ever witnessed, fortunately just as we reached Gettysburg the rain ceased. . . .*

### Saturday, September 19, 1863

*. . . I called on George McLellan this morning and asked him to send May's trunk by the stage to St Joseph's today and tomorrow I shall take her over if possible. . . .*[8]

### Sunday, September 20, 1863

*After a good night's sleep we rose and prepared ourselves for church, after which George hired a comfortable hack to take us over to St Joseph's. Before going however we drove to the hospital, where I saw much that pained me, and much that gratified me also. I paid a visit to Major Goldsborough's tents, was introduced to Dr Mirror, Capt Livingston & several others and saw one poor man who had just died prepared for the grave. After leaving the hospital we drove over to Emmitsburg, and directly out to the Mountain, saw Crick, Mr Dielman and all the boys I knew. We left there and drove to . . . St Joseph's. The Sisters & girls seemed greatly delighted at seeing May again, and Sister Raphael gratified me very much by telling me she had promoted May to the 2d class. We bid the girls goodbye and drove home. . . . I have a violent headache to night.*

## Tuesday, September 22, 1863

. . . *Directly after breakfast George Codori brought the buggy to the door and he and I started for an inspection of the battlefield; we began on the Confederate side, and after witnessing all that was interesting there, we drove to the granite spur of Round Top where the desperate artillery duel between the Federals and Rebels took place. . . .*[9] *After gathering relics of a warlike character & also flowers &c we came home. . . . It is one of the most interesting days I ever spent in all my life. . . .*

## Thursday, September 24, 1863

. . . *Louisa, Josephine & George drove out to the camp and after remaining a few hours came in and insisted on my going out. I did so, and was perfectly disgusted at some of the exhibitions going up to amuse the poor sick soldiers with. I had however the satisfaction of visiting the Confederate wounded soldiers and remaining in the tents with them till near dark, at which time Louisa & I drove to town and then out to a house which was said to be the one in which Gen Lee made his headquarters during the battle of G——g; we found however it was not, but were told which was the one and we will visit it another time. . . .*

While Madge was in the north, she received a letter from her husband.

Pleasant Plains
25 Sep. 1863

Dear Madge

. . . I now write to notice more at length your letters. . . . You are quite right in supposing that I well remember the rain of the day on which you started. It gave me great uneasiness, as I was apprehensive that you would be caught in the midst of it at Hanover Junction. It is a vile outrage that rail road cos. have not at all their junctions & stations some cover and protection for passengers against sun or storm. In many places there is not even a shed and these companies without remorse leave the passengers by whom they so largely profit to buffet as they can the inclemency of every kind of weather. . . . I shall make it my duty to thank the conductor who was so civil to you and May in the cars—I am gratified to know that you met several of your old friends at Gettysburg. . . .

You may observe that my hand writing is heavy and occasionally abrupt. I am writing with considerable pain—both of my hands are crippled with rheumatism. I think it was brought about by my riding in an open buggy a considerable distance with Mr Abell, without gloves. . . .

Poor Louis Beer is still in Fort McHenry—the war Christians whose trump of salvation is blown in the battlefield, who preach the peaceful doctrines of Jesus Christ while breathing fire and sword—and who write their daily Christian progress in the bloody characters of violence and desolation, have passed an order precluding his mother from seeing the boy. Yesterday while I was in town, Georgia, who had washed the boy's clothes, gave them to a lady who also has a son there and who promised to take them to the Fort. The lady took them, but was refused admittance for herself and the clothes, [and] therefore had to bring them back—the high-minded men in power I suppose think that keeping a poor boy, sixteen years of age in a filthy condition tormented by bugs, fleas, or lice will restore the Union.—I find my hand so painful that I must close with this page. Mrs Beer, Mrs Pent, old Lucy and Kit send their love. . . . Remain as long as you feel comfortable. . . . When you come bring with you whomsoever you please. Your choice shall have my welcome. Give me a day or two's notice of your coming. My affectionate regards to all. Good night. W. P. Preston

### Monday, October 5, 1863

*We rose early to be ready to start in good time for Gettysburg, which Louisa & I did about ½ past 10, reaching Gettysburg at ½ past 1. After staying with Josephine a while, we went visiting. The first place to see my old friend Jane Welsby. . . . Her house was one of the most terribly riddled with balls of any in town. They were obliged to live in their cellar for several days. They gave me bullets which had passed through one of their windows. . . .*

### Tuesday, October 6, 1863

*. . . Josephine & I drove out to camp this afternoon. We called on Major Goldsborough, Norton & others. Goldsborough told me it was Gen. Edward Johnson who gave the order to charge that hill and Gen John E. Stuart of Baltimore led the charge himself. Mr Jackson took my address to visit us in Baltimore when he should come with the army. . . .*

### Wednesday, October 7, 1863

*It was cold and unpleasant this morning, with every indication of rain, but notwithstanding Simon & I drove over to St Joseph's. I provided myself with crackers, cakes and candy. On our arrival at St Joseph's, we found May ready for us and at once took her with us to the Mountain to see Crick and the boys,*

*but they were all in retreat. . . . We returned to St Joseph's and remained with
May and the girls till after three, at which time we bade them goodbye till next
summer. . . .*

Pleasant Plains
Oct 11th 1863

My dear child,

Notwithstanding the day after I left you was so very stormy, I still cheerfully
encountered it and turned my face homeward. . . . Papa and little Kitty had
been in town during the day, but left before I reached them, thinking the
storm would prevent my coming. I remained at our house all night. . . . The
next day (Friday) Papa came to town and I went out to Pleasant Plains with
him. Mrs Beer, Kitty & Aunt Lucy vied with each other in giving me a warm
welcome so that I soon began to feel the charm of being "home again." . . .

A great change has taken place during my absence. The trees have put on
their autumn robes, and they shine now in gorgeous purple, scarlet, yellow
and the more sombre brown, presenting a charming sight to one who loves
this varied hue as much [as] I do. Our fruit unfortunately has nearly all disappeared. I have scarcely apples enough left to make jelly, and apply jelly you
know with us, is the . . . preserve of all others I would least desire to do without. Peaches of course I have none, but quinces sufficient for my purposes. As
you are now interested in the "kitchen department," I write these things to
give you some views on that subject. I shall expect to find you so finished a
housewife when you leave school, that I shall be relieved altogether of looking
after the cooking, the only part of housekeeping about which I can never feel
very deeply interested—not that I don't love the good things of this world
quite as well as most people, but my *taste* does not turn that way.

I went to the city with Papa on Saturday as I had some shopping to do for
the girls,[10] who will be down I hope the last of this week. I am having dresses
made for them, which I should like to have finished and ready for them as
soon as they come that they may have the full benefit of them during their
stay. . . . Mrs Stansbury intends giving an "entertainment" this fall, but will
not send her invitations out till the "girls" are with me. Papa, Mrs Beer, Kitty,
Mrs Pentz & Aunt Lucy join me in much love to you. . . . Hoping you are
well and happy, and studying nicely, I am as ever your devoted

Mama.

# 5

# New Arrivals at Pleasant Plains

ONLY ONE LETTER SURVIVES of the correspondence between St. Joseph's and Pleasant Plains during the second autumn May spent apart from her parents. Madge was busy introducing her two nieces into the social networks of the neighborhood. Rose and Theodosia Smith, who were finding stimulation and opportunity within this affluent household, also contributed to its smooth functioning. They were delighted to leave the confinement of their isolated home in the Pennsylvania hills.

Daily life at Pleasant Plains was initially further brightened by the arrival of the Greppo couple from Brooklyn. They were friends with whom Madge had visited at Easter time. Ellen Greppo, daughter of the Batemans, had been a famous child actor. A surviving photograph shows her, bearded, dressed for the role of Richard III.[1] During the three weeks the Greppos spent in Maryland, the whole neighborhood gathered from time to time for singing and parlor games.

May, though absent, was of course, not forgotten. At the end of their visit, the Greppos bought a set of silver articles, engraved with her name, to be sent to her at St. Joseph's and used as her table service at the school. Madge added a goblet "of the finest cut glass" and also a veil for May to wear at religious services.

Madge seems to have cherished this happy time. She was genuinely saddened to see her guests depart. Probably she had kept hidden from them the more somber news from her Delaware friend, Mrs. Stout. In the world of Madge's secret thoughts, depression was just below the surface. This fact seems revealed in a curiously garbled diary entry of November 3, where Madge's report of a letter from May describing "an extreme depression of spirits" blurs in mid-sentence into Madge's own disabling spiritless mood. The passage seems to confirm the subconscious bonding Madge had with May.

Perhaps she was similarly paralleling her own domestic circumstances with those of Mrs. Stout.

_____

### Friday, October 30, 1863

*. . . Mr Preston rec'd a letter from Mrs Stout telling him there was a petition before the legislature for divorce between herself & husband. I regret it should be so, as I think it better to submit to almost any hardship rather than be a divorced woman.*

### Saturday, October 31, 1863

*I rose early this morning & before breakfast, I answered Mrs Stout's letter, expressing our regret for her situation and telling her we would do anything to assist her &c &c. . . . . . . . Mrs Hillen made us a visit, and this evening Aunt Christie came over & remained all night and all hands have had, what Rose calls a "high old time," boiling taffy, drinking toddy, and playing masquerades!*

### Tuesday, November 3, 1863

*. . . I rec'd a letter from May this evening, the contents of which have made me quite sad, as the child evidently writes under an extreme depression of spirits produced by constant headaches so much so as to be obliged to go to bed where I remained till after tea, and after Mr Lyman had come I then rose and dressed, and by the time I went to the sitting room Mrs Eudocia Stansbury had come in, and Christie was already here. Father Lyman was in excellent spirits and sang and played most exquisitely. Ellen [Greppo] also sang several songs in her best style. Altogether we spent a most charming evening. Mr Greppo & Mr Bartlett walked over with the ladies, who could not be prevailed upon to remain with us all night.*

### Monday, November 9, 1863

*. . . our friends left us this morning for Brooklyn. Mr Preston drove them to the city. . . . When the time came for parting we found we felt it very keenly— three weeks of pleasant intercourse cannot be changed without causing some emotion. . . .*

### Wednesday, November 11, 1863

*. . . This afternoon I was greatly astonished by the sudden entrance of our old friend Mrs Stout. It seems she came from Dover today and not finding Mr*

*Preston in the city, rode out in the cars & walked over from Towsontown. She is here to have a conversation with Mr Preston on the subject of a separation from her husband.*

### Thursday, November 12, 1863

*. . . Mrs Stout has been giving me a terrible account of the doings of her husband & of her unhappiness in consequence. . . .*

### Thursday, November 19, 1863

*. . . This is an important day in Gettysburg. It is the day the consecration of the national cemetery takes place. Lincoln (and many of the grandees of the Federal party) is expected to be there. I wonder if everything will pass off without a disturbance. . . .*

### Friday, November 20, 1863

*. . . Directly after [Mr. Preston and Mr. Bartlett] left, we all started to work, took up the sitting room carpet, as it has become so ragged it was quite dangerous to walk over. William shook the carpet and hung it up to air and tomorrow we will patch & darn it and tack it down. . . .*

### Saturday, November 21, 1863

*We have . . . had a regular day of fixing and patching, cutting & sewing but our labours have been rewarded by the nice appearance of our carpet, which looks very well indeed, and the whole room has a clean & sweet air about it. Now my house is in good order and I am satisfied once more.*

---

Keeping house was infinitely more difficult than it had been when one knew and could count on one's kitchen staff. Ever since Lizzie's erratic behavior had begun, Madge had done more of the work herself. And although the two Smith girls were now helping out, Madge needed more staff to help with the worst of the drudgery. During this time Madge's diary entries are preoccupied with accounts of the search for, the hiring of, and the departure of household employees. Many changes within the staff occurred over the course of the winter.

Preston seems a less conspicuous figure during this period. We know from a letter that he began writing and finally posted to his daughter on her birthday in May, that through most of this winter he was suffering from a debilitating depression. His dark mood must have been palpable. Ever since his visit to the Gettysburg battlefield, he seems to have sunk within himself. Any optimism concerning the chances for Confederate victory had been wiped out wholly by the carnage there. But sometime during the fall, according to Madge's diary entry of November 30, Preston roused himself to write a long poem commemorating the consecration of the cemetery for those who had fallen in that desperate battle.

### Tuesday, December 8, 1863

*It was still intensely cold this morning and as old Lucy left yesterday Kitty and I got breakfast. About nine o'clock old Aunt Harriet made her appearance, and in a short time she was in full discharge of her kitchen duties. I think I shall like the old woman, she appears humble and kind and disposed to do as desired. . . .*

### Saturday, December 12, 1863

*Cloudy again this morning and at ten o'clock it began to rain and continued till nearly 2 o'clock, consequently I could not go out in the car [from Baltimore to Towsontown] as previously arranged by Mr Preston, but fortunately Mr Stansbury came to the office and gave me a seat in his wagon. . . . On reaching home I was not only pained but greatly mortified by a most unkind reception from Mr P——. The reason given for his anger was that I had disappointed him in not being at Towsontown at the time appointed. He has retired evidently much annoyed by his own conduct.*

### Sunday, December 13, 1863

*Mr Preston by his extreme kindness this morning tried to do away with the ugly impression of last night. . . .*

### Thursday, December 31, 1863

*. . . This is the last day of the year and a sad and wretched one it has been— perhaps all time has never known one more productive of misery. Tonight brings a memory of dear old Aunty Carlon to my mind—in losing her I lost one of my best friends. May she rest in peace! Amidst all the troubles of the past year I hope I am not unmindful of the blessings I have enjoyed. The greatest of which is my darling child with whose dear name let me close this record.*

The following day Madge opened a new diary volume with an inventory of persons and animals at Pleasant Plains and its subsidiary properties.

*The household at Pleasant Plains consists this day, January 1st 1864 of six persons. Namely—*

*Mr Preston*
*Mrs Preston*
*Theodosia W. Smith* ⎱
*Rose E. G. Smith* ⎰ *nieces of M. W. Preston*
*Aunt Harriet a colored woman*
*Kitty Mason a little colored girl*
*As adjuncts to the family and living in the Cottage are Mrs Pent, an old German woman, William Pent, son of the above person, and employed as a Jack of all trades at P. P.*
*On "Indian Hill," resides also a man employed as a farm hand at P. P. named John Enge*
*Martha Enge his wife and one little child a boy about 18 months old.*
*At "Glen May" we have an interesting Swiss family living there, consisting of 3 persons*
*Mrs Julia Roder*
*Adolph Roder and*
*Frederick Roder, sons of that lady. Consequently we number, all told, on the farm—fourteen persons!*
*The stock consists of 7 horses, Mars, Black Hawk, Peri, Jack, the Mare, Barney and little Buck.*
*2 cows and 2 calves*
*26 sheep and one lamb*
*2 dogs. Jewell and Romeo.*
*7 ducks and*
*57 chickens and*
*2 cats, Tom and Phil*

### Friday, January 1, 1864

*. . . The stormy day of yesterday seemed to me a fitting close for the past most wild reckless and disturbed year. Let us hope as the storm of yesterday passed away and this morning we have a bright sunshine and cloudless sky so may it be in the moral and political world and the brutal inhuman and unkind feelings so widely disseminated over a once prosperous and happy land may pass away and the "Peace that passeth all understanding" once more resume*

*her empire. I have begun today a kind of journal or daily letter for May, which
I will send as opportunity offers; thus the child will be kept informed of the
principal events of our home life, at least such as are pleasant—the unhappy
ones I will retain for myself alone. . . .*

Pleasant Plains
January 1st 1864

My darling child—

To open the New Year by wishing you a happy one, I was going to write
and *many returns* of this season, but I check myself in that wish, as I think it
rather questionable happiness to live too long in this wearisome world. I
therefore cheerfully leave you in the hands of Providence feeling that "He
who doeth all things well" will call you at His own proper time! . . .

You will perceive I have begun the year by writing to you. I design to keep a
letter constantly on hand, so that when I, or any of the family think of something we would like to mention to you, we can at once open the sheet and dot
down the said something. . . .

Kitty has just come up with a handful of beautiful feathers plucked from
our New Year's turkey. She says "Please Missus put two of them in your letter
one for Miss May and one for Miss Bruce, and please Missus give my *respects*
to the young ladies!" Rose, who was sitting by me at the time laughed and said
I think dear little May would rather have a *piece* of the turkey than all of its
feathers—She also says, You ought to tell May of our delicious fritters for
dinner today, but then I think that would be too tantalizing—I thought myself it would be placing you in the condition of our poor little goats, who have
been fastened in one corner of the greenhouse, in full view of several piles of
beautiful green cabbage and turnips without the power of getting near them,
and with the sight and fragrance forever before them.

Mentioning the goats, reminds me to tell you, you have had an addition of
six full-grown sheep to your flock lately, making in all twenty-six. So you may
calculate on a goodly quantity of wool, this coming summer. You also have
one little wee lamb—about a week old.

Do you recollect how pleasantly we all spent last New Year's day at Mr
Dielman's? How much I should liked to have passed this one in the same
way. Yours lovingly Mama.

Papa, Rose, Theodosia, Kitty, Aunty and Mrs Pent wish you a Happy New
Year, and send much love. . . .

3d A glorious winter's day! And we have really enjoyed it greatly. The intense cold of the last few days froze the pond over, and it now presents one
unbroken smooth sheet of ice, more beautiful than I have ever seen it. Cold
as it was, we could not resist the temptation of a frolic—so donning our most

picturesque costume, we wended our way to the pond, where Mr Preston, having provided us all the concomitants for a sledding party consisting of the goats' carriage put on runners, your little sled, rocking chairs and the dog Jewell. It was really beautiful to witness; while there, we were joined by the Eudowood party, together with some from Union Hall, making altogether some sixteen or eighteen persons. Papa drew me in the goat carriage all over the pond for half an hour or more, and the rest of the party alternated with each other in sledding with the other conveyances. My old cane-bottom rocking chair made the most pleasant and agreeable of sleds; by placing yourself firmly in the chair and putting your feet on the runners, a strong person could send it flying half over the pond. You will imagine we wished for you and the girls. I doubt however if all the St Joseph's girls could have made a gayer or noisier party than we did. Majestic old Jewell was harnessed to my sled and he actually drew me the length of the pond, and when the harness was taken off him, he frisked and jumped about as if to be admired for his great prowess. We did not leave till near dark. . . .

Yours lovingly
Mama

### Tuesday, January 5, 1864

*. . . We have had a most extraordinary performance here today. Rose has been suffering for several days with an aggravated toothache, and this morning in a fit of hysterics, she insisted on Theodosia taking it out, which strange to say she did in the most skillful manner, much to our surprise and Rose's satisfaction. It was a large back tooth with three prongs, and must have been very painful. I don't know whom most to admire, Rose's courage or Theodosia's skill.*

### Wednesday, January 6, 1864

*. . . Theodosia has taken Rose's place in suffering today, she having had a violent toothache and pain generally in her face, we made a bed for her on the sofa, where she has remained all day. . . .*

### Thursday, January 7, 1864

*. . . We have been greatly annoyed today, at discovering that poor Kitty cannot resist the temptation of the cream crocks. I am unhappy on that poor child's account, for if she does not mend her ways, she must come to evil. . . . I have been neglecting my darling child for several days past not feeling the least inclination to write to anyone.*

Pleasant Plains
January 8th 1864

My darling child,

This is the first moment for days I have had the hope of being able to send to the city with a letter. . . . We received a few days since the "report" on your doings during the past session. I need not say my darling child, that both Papa and I were very much pleased with it. Indeed my little pet it is far beyond my expectations; knowing how much you have had to do in the lesson line, I scarcely thought you would accomplish as much as your report admits you have. . . . Rose & Theodosia are greatly delighted with the St Joseph's account of you—and say We think dear Little May must be a "clever child." We all send quantities of love to you—

Goodbye
Mama

### Saturday, January 9, 1864

. . . *Mr Preston brought me a long letter from May and a long letter from Aunt Louisa. . . . May's letter is quite a little gem; she describes most graphically their doings during Christmas holidays and judging from the cheerful tenor of the letter, she and her young companions must be enjoying themselves. Thank God for the blessing of having so good a child.*

### Sunday, January 10, 1864

. . . *After dinner Mr Preston and Rose drove dear old Aunt Harriet home, as the old thing has become so "painy" she thinks she cannot remain at service any longer. The old woman has been so faithful and kind and attentive to her duties during her stay with us that we have become very much attached to her. . . .*

Pleasant Plains
January 10th 1864

My very dear child,

Your delightfully written and good long letter, dated 2d Jan . . . was rec'd last evening. Papa having gone to the city the day before and remained all night, and on his return last evening, the little moonbeam in the form of your cheerful letter shed its pleasant light over our happy group. *As usual* I had begun to imagine all sorts of things as having happened to prevent your writing. The cough of which you wrote in a former letter being the principal cause of your silence. It was a great joy to me to know . . . it was only an excess of pleasure that had prevented your writing before. While on the subject of letter writing, let me tell you that we are all much pleased with the very evident improvement in your style of writing. Your sentiments are good and well expressed, indeed at times, they become "quite eloquent" "for a little girl"—as Mr Stewart said the other day. I tell you this my pet, not for the purpose of exciting vanity in your breast or a feeling akin to so worldly an emotion, but simply that you may know we are pleased with you, and that our affection for you makes us keenly alive to all your *perfections*!

Jany 11th Johnny was here this afternoon, looking as happy and pleased as—to use an old simile (the fitness of which I have never been able to perceive) "a basket of chips." On bouncing into the room, he exclaimed, "Mrs Preston I have just got a letter from May do you want to read it"—Of course I said, "Yes indeed Johnny," and on opening it, I read it aloud for the benefit of all present. Rose, in her satisfaction, said—"Why Johnny, I really think your letter is the most interesting that May has written yet." The dear boy blushed up and replied, "I feel very much obliged to May for answering my letter, knowing how little time she can have for letter writing—and another thing I was afraid the "Sisters" might not consent to her doing so. It was very kind in them to let her write to me, don't you think so Mrs Preston?" I told Johnny I thought it was, but added: The Sisters had *my* permission to allow May to receive and reply to any and all the letters which should be sent to her, as I well knew May had no correspondents of whom I did not approve. I learned from others that poor Johnny had been watching the post office daily since his letter might have reached you, hoping, I fear, "against hope," for the looked for answer. I hope my child by this time you have written to Mamie—if you have not, and have not the time, I would prefer your devoting your regular letter-writing day to that purpose. You know her family are somewhat narrow-minded and I sometimes think they are foolish enough to believe that you do not receive the letters they send you. Indeed they have even hinted, nay almost said as much.[2] As I wish no misrepresentation on their part and no chance of their doing so—please gratify me by writing a good long letter, and fill it with your pleasant doings.

January 14th. The account you gave of your tableaux was very interesting. It was rather strange you should have taken the character of a Magdalene for this reason. I have always looked upon with loathing and disgust the many representations I have seen of that character. Many of them exquisite works of art, but the *half nude* condition of the figure seemed so unlike what the reality of a poor heart-broken penitent would be that my feelings revolted even at the painting or engravings as they might be. I am pleased to know that I was correct in my dissatisfaction, as the judgment and good taste of those who dressed you for the tableau can be fully relied upon. Your simple white dress and flowing hair—seems to me a proper garb for the wretched and unhappy, but

sorrow-stricken woman. Jeannette, as Faith—must have been perfection!—
Papa says, she must have made an admirable personification of that glorious
virtue; poor little Fanny Abell being "squeezed up" made us laugh heartily. I
am curious to know how you manage these things. I suppose however the Sisters must assist you, by giving you suggestions &c and also in enabling you to
put up frames, curtains and the etcetera pertaining to a successful getting up
of your pictures. It is a beautiful way to spend your holiday times, and gratifying to me to know that you are thus engaged—infinitely more so than it
would be to see you as poor Mamie & Alice have been for the last three
weeks, dressing in the extreme of the fashions and going nightly to entertain-
ments. . . . How will it be possible for either of those girls to fall into their
quiet mode of life and to their studies, after a month of city dissipations? . . . I
would not say so to Mrs Stansbury—but I can't help thinking she is sending
her young girls into society much too early for their interest or benefit—
however each to their own liking—perhaps, she, good kind woman as she
is, thinks that I err in keeping you too much excluded from the world—be
that as it may—you are satisfied and I too, by having you at "dear old St
Joseph's!" . . .

Kitty has been wishing for you all day. The servants are engaged cutting up
some of the nicest young pork I ever saw, and as "spare ribs" and "sausage" are
just now the order of the day, she wishes you were here to enjoy them. Another thing—we are having this winter the greatest quantity of milk. Consequently cream and good butter flourish at Pleasant Plains. Your cousins are
constantly saying—If May only had some of this or that—or the other (dainties made of these articles) how pleased she would be &c &c.

Love from Papa—the girls—Mrs Stansbury—Christie & Johnny. Yours
lovingly

Mama—

## Monday, January 11, 1864

*. . . We have gotten along pretty well today notwithstanding we were without
any servant but Kitty.*

---

On the following Saturday, opening her diary to write the day's entry,
Madge turned back to the inside cover, where she had written her year's opening inventory of living creatures at Pleasant Plains. Dipping her pen in the
inkwell, she wrote:

*January 16th. John Mathews came to live with us. Said John is a nice little
[boy] about eleven years old, an orphan; indeed the boy is so completely iso-*

*lated as to have no one on whom he has the least claim. I like him the better for*
*being so alone.*

### Saturday, January 16, 1864

*The day has been very delightful as regards weather, but it has also been a very*
*busy one. I sent for Mrs Newberger to assist in cleaning and fixing up the*
*kitchen, which has been very untidy since Aunty left us. I also churned six*
*pounds of butter, which is certainly delicious; indeed it is as good butter as I*
*ever ate. The little boy came up from Mr Whiteford's this morning to remain*
*with us. I am greatly impressed with the little fellow's good countenance and*
*pleasant gentle manners. Unless I am much deceived he is the making of a*
*good boy. It seems he is to be brought up a Catholic and to that end has al-*
*ready been to see Father Lyman. I shall do all in my power to enable him to*
*make his first communion with the other children under preparation. . . .*

### Sunday, January 17, 1864

*. . . This afternoon Mr and Mrs Owens drove over to see us, and we persuaded*
*them to remain and take tea with us, which they did and left us after ten*
*o'clock. I have my doubts about the propriety of their going home so late; in*
*future I will insist on their remaining all night. . . .*

### Friday, January 22, 1864

*. . . .While in the city yesterday Mr Preston purchased a stereoscope together*
*with some very pretty pictures. Ellen [Greppo] sent us several representing her*
*house & her mother's—interior & exterior.*

Pleasant Plains
January 24 1864

My dear child
   As your cousin Rose sent you a letter this week, I felt less scrupulous about
my own silence, which has really been unavoidable. For instance poor Kitty
has had her usual winter cold, sore throat and cough—poor child has been
confined to her bed nearly all the week; she is now going about the house, yet
she had by no means entirely recovered—thus you see my child the spare
moments otherwise devoted to you were obliged to be given to Kitty. Another
thing, I believe I told you dear old Aunt Harriet got so "painy" that she
thought she had better go home for awhile and remain with her "daters," she
did not like to be a trouble to "Missus," but when she got well she would come

back again. You can readily imagine without old Aunty and Kitty being sick, I have had quite as much as I could accomplish lately. Rose told you of a newcomer [whom] we have about the establishment, or rather of *two*—George, the German man, we used to have and whom you may recollect as a very excellent hand on the farm is back again, and as he says—"Mr Preston I will never leave you again." . . .

But to return to the newcomer—he is a little boy about ten or eleven years of age, and the nicest little fellow you ever saw. The poor child is a little waif in this wearisome and sad world without a human being on whom he feels he has the slightest claim. Papa came across him at Whitefords the miller, who recommended your Papa to take him. Of course his being an orphan was claim sufficient on my sympathies and I at once gave my consent, and then the boy came—I "took to him" at first sight & I think the feeling was mutual, for the child seems to live almost in my shadow, and to be as happy as he can be when he is by my side. — You will be pleased to know he is a penitent of Father Lyman, and has gone down to church this morning and is to remain this afternoon and attend catechism and instruction for those who are preparing for their first communion. I really think he is one of the finest disposed children I have ever known—good principled—warm hearted, truthful . . . affectionate . . . and intelligent to a degree beyond his years. As soon as I can make suitable arrangements, I intend to give him lessons in reading, writing, spelling and arithmetic, *perhaps a little grammar* if I find I can accomplish so much, or else I shall leave *that* for you. . . .

### Wednesday, January 27, 1864

*Rose at our usual hour and started at once into work. . . . We commenced churning before breakfast and finished in a short [while]. Johnny came to give me the pleasant information the "butter had come." I also made mince pies and cheese cake, the latter a new article which when done proved very good. Thomas Taylor brought up three tons of hay at 30 dollars pr ton. John & William have been engaged this afternoon loading up a small load of wood to take to the city in the morning. . . .*

### Monday, February 1, 1864

*. . . I rec'd a letter from my niece Anne Smith this evening in relation to some vaccine matter I sent to her for; she was not able to send us any, but it does not matter as I shall go to a homeopathic doctor when I go to the city and have myself vaccinated with "cow pox" matter. . . .*

Pleasant Plains
Feby 4th 1864

My dear child—

The family have retired early . . . I, not feeling inclined to retire without a little chat with you . . . have taken my writing implements and will give you an account of our doings. Yesterday was the day set apart for the visit to Mrs Owens, but owing to the stormy condition of the weather we were obliged to postpone our going. . . . On awaking this morning and finding the weather suited, we rose early and made arrangements for an early start as we had promised Mrs Owens to be at Aigburth Vale by ten o'clock. Papa . . . could not accompany us there but it was agreed that he would meet us at the Vale by dinner time. . . .

We found the roads in a shocking condition and the weather much colder than we had anticipated, but as we were bent on enjoying ourselves, we wrapped ourselves the closer in our furs and defied the frost. Mrs Owens, Delia and Laura were at the window awaiting our arrival, which was hailed with apparent great joy and a hearty welcome awarded us. . . .

Do you recollect a medal Delia gave you last summer, which had belonged to a Confederate soldier? . . . Well the poor man died some few months ago of wounds rec'd in the Battle of Gettysburg. He was a married man with several children—a good Catholic and a brave soldier—as you are in the possession of the medal he wore on the battlefield I think you should really feel it almost a duty to say a few prayers for him. I must not forget to mention that Kitty accompanied us to Aigburth by *special invitation*.

How does it happen, my dear child, that we have not heard from you lately? . . . You cannot imagine the anxiety we all feel if your letters do not come on their regular days. You know I begged you to send me *just one line*, if you were not able to write—do so in future my pet.

Love from all Good night
Mama

---

May had spent the weekend of January 30 and 31 in Gettysburg at the Fairmount boarding house. Mollie and Jeannette Sander's elder married sister, Nettie Stuart, who had gone to Emmitsburg to visit the girls, received permission to withdraw them for a brief respite from the school environment. May's letter from that place is scribbled, crowded, sometimes crossed out— wholly unlike the neat, carefully copied versions she had been sending from school. A schoolgirl letter to Madge from Mollie Sanders, which has also survived, illustrates the common practice of nineteenth-century girls of adopting a friend's mother as a substitute parent.[3] Mollie's babyish tone contrasts sharply with May's more dignified letters. Mollie's letter must have amused the Prestons greatly, for "the pudding was grand" became a family catch-phrase.

Fairmont
Jan 30th 1864

My precious Momma
    No doubt you will be very much surprised to recieve a letter or rather a note from your <u>itty baby</u> but as <u>Sissie</u> May is writing I could not let such a good opportunity pass without writing you a few lines hoping they will meet with a welcome reception from my dear Momma
    We are all together once more having a <u>gay old time</u> as May would say. How is Papa give my <u>very very</u> "<u>bestest</u>" love to him. I forgot to tell you that the pudding was <u>luscious.</u> Give my love to the girls and also to Cousin Thomas, & Caleb when you see them. Jeannette & Tom are well and send much love they have retired and left May & Mollie writing, the latter is as great a writer as ever. I am almost crazy with the headache so you must excuse all imperfections. Give my love to Johnny. Oh! the pudding was grand.
Goodbye
Mollie

*"Bed bed bed thou heaven on earth to the wearied head"*
Oh! Momma I am so sleepy and May will keep me up until she finishes that grand letter to you. Please tell her to go to bed call loud enough for her to hear you.
    Remember me kindly to dear Cousin Rose and Theodocia. Oh! the pudding was splended Please make May come to bed I am so sleepy. Get Mrs Pent to ring the bell and then maybe she will come.
Your loving *itty* baby
Mollie

"Bed, bed, bed, thou heaven on *earth to the wearied head.*"
Original
Oh! dear what can the matter be May & Mollie tied to an apple tree
"May are you coming to bed"
*"May has come at last"*

Fairmount
Jan. 30th 1863 [misdated for 1864]

Darling Mama,
    No doubt you will be surprised to received a letter from me headed from any place but Saint Joseph's but your astonishment will be answered when

you know that Mollie Jeannette and myself are out at St. Francis (as you used to call it) with Nettie and Mr. Stuart. They came up on Friday and took M. & J. out with them as they were in a great hurry to let the man who drove them return to Gettysburg and as I was in the library and no one knew it, they were obliged to leave without seeing me, but came over this Saturday morning and Sister Raphael thinking you would have no objections let me accompany them to the "Hill-house." . . . This is why my letter is commenced "Fairmount" for by this name the present proprietors call the place. Dear Mama I declare I hardly know what to say first I think I had better begin by begging you to excuse all mistakes indeed to *shut* your *eyes* to *them, if that is possible.* I am writing by lamp light and obliged to sit in such away that unless I hold my pen 2 or 3 *yards* from the point my hand shades every word I write and besides dearest Mother I feel so easy in writing to you here that I have not troubled myself much about the *othography.* The other day Sister Mary Eliza in the close-room told me I would have to write home for some undershirts. She wanted me to write for thick ones but I must say I do not see the good of them for I wore these net shirts all last winter and found them plenty warm enough and now that the winter is nearly over and the house is fully warmed this year I think it would be useless to send me thicker ones now besides I do not think I would feel as comfortable in any others as I do in these Three will be quite enough If you have a chance to send them to me please send me a little bronze needle-book well filled and some pretty things if they will be any trouble to you or Papa. The needles-book I want for my *favourite Sister* don't be amazed at hearing that word from *me* That illustrious May who last year defied all attempts at touching her heart in that point at least before her companions for . . . I never made the least fuss over *Sister Cephas.* This Sisters name is Sr. Leopoldine and she is as kind to me as you could wish her to be and that is saying a great deal For instance when we have permission to go out in the yard if I do not feel like going (you know I never had any partiality for going out in winter) she goes out just to get me to do so. Now that is what I call real kindness. Dear Momma you must be *jealous* but remember *your dear Sister Josephine* and you will understand all Ah! Mama I never knew how to apprechate you feelings on *that point* until *this year* Now I know why since before I can remember you used to talk to me of that dear Sister and taught my baby lips to lisp her name. . . . If you can send me about a quater of a yard of broad white ribbon and several skeins of Solfareria sewing silk to make Agnes Deis with.[4] Now about every thing in the whole world don't say any thing about the important part of this letter (Alias Sister part) for that is a delicate point with us school girls. Please be careful about this when you write. All the love in my heart to dear Papa Cousins and all home not forgetting your precious self which I believe becomes more so every day *Sister Leopoldine* looks so much *like you.* Thank Rose Johnny & the girls for writing to me.

I will answer when I can. Don't say any thing about it but *I am* praised very much for my letters. It has done me so much good to tell you about S. M. L. Mollie is yelling like for of us as we so at last good bye Your—well I don't know how to express myself

May.

Mollie says she would not like to see me paint a piece for I would never finish *touching it up.*

Baltimore Feby 11th /64

My dear child,

I sent off by the wagon yesterday a *tiny* box, containing two undershirts, some pictures—a paper of tooth powder, ¼ yd of white ribband and three skeins of embroidering silk. . . . I would have sent you something in the "confectionary line," but as we are just entering upon the holy season of Lent, I knew you would feel no inclination to indulge in such luxuries. . . .

I am delighted to think and know you have found a friend who so nearly supplies my place to you—do not fear that I shall feel the least "jealous." I should not deserve to have so good a little daughter, as I believe I have, if I supposed for one moment she did not give me all the affection the most loving child could give a mother. Give my love to dear Sister Leopoldine and tell her I say as a "child of St Joseph's" I feel privileged to send her an abundance of it.

I have been quite busy during the few days I have been in the city. Yesterday (Ash Wednesday) I went to church at the cathedral and by the sprinkling of the ashes on my forehead by *your dear* Father Foley, was reminded of the *dust* from when[ce] I came and to which this poor frail body must again return. In the course of the morning I made a visit to *my* Father Elder, made an appointment to see him again this afternoon, which appointment I most *faithfully* kept. I then went up to Mrs Pinkney's, where I had a pleasant interview with all the ladies of the family including Mrs Owens, who is spending a few days with them. . . .

. . . Good night God bless you my child. Love to Mollie Jeannette & Bruce.

Mama

## Sunday, February 21, 1864

*. . . One of our old servants came over to see me today and desired to come and live with us—Emily Sheridan. I have employed her and she is to be here on Wednesday provided the weather is fine.*[5]

**Monday, February 29, 1864**

*. . . Emily is doing her first washing today and a terribly large one it is, she has no less than thirteen sheets in the wash—and other articles in proportion.*

Pleasant Plains 1864 (n. d.)

My dear child

I fear the hasty letters I have been obliged to write you lately have given you very little satisfaction. . . .

I believe I told you sometime ago that we had lost good old Aunt Harriet. . . . About a week ago a woman who formerly lived with us—Emily—the wife of that dandy servant man we used to have and whom you may remember by his wearing scarlet bows of ribbons fastened over his clothes—Sam Sheridan. Well this woman came to see if I would employ her. Knowing she was a good faithful servant when with me before, I very cheerfully did so. She could not come however without bringing with her one of her children—to that I also consented—for you know I love a child about the house even if it is a black one. Well the little thing came—and she is the nicest, prettiest, best little child I think I ever saw of *that color.* She is not yet four years old and we are really astonished at her intelligence—the little thing comprehends everything that is said to her—is perfectly obedient—and never cries unless something occurs more than her little baby philosophy or forbearance is equal to. One of her most excellent traits is going to bed and getting up without annoying anyone. She comes to me a little after sun down to bid me good night and to "say her prayers." "Goodnight Master Willie and good night Missus"— then she kneels down and I assist her in making the sign of the cross &c &c. She is put to bed and her mother or Kitty at once leave the room and that is the last of her till the next morning when we are at breakfast—during which time we generally hear a little birdlike sound—calling out *Mamaaae Mamaaa*—and then Emily goes up to the child and there she is, bright & cheerful and "ready for her breakfast." The little thing has wound herself so round us that we do not like to be long without her in the room with us. Even Papa asks constantly for her when she is not near him, and strange to say Kitty too, "Takes to her" kindly. Johnny is still the good little boy I wrote you of— and Kitty is only so-so.

I do not recollect if I mentioned to you a wonderful feat performed by your cat Phil—about a month ago—she came to the front of the house, and scratched about till Theodosia, who was in the sitting room, noticed her, and then she had a strange looking animal in her mouth; not seeing me there, Phil walked round to the back part of the house and came into the area where I was standing and laid down at my feet *two* rats—both of which she had in her mouth at once—Now we all think *that* places Phil at the top round of celebrity in the cat line of mouse catching!

Enclosed you will find a handkerchief which it has given me great pleasure to chain stitch in *your* color for you and also to embroider your cipher in the corner, which cipher by the way Papa made and we all think beautiful. I shall adopt it in future in marking your clothing, but on a small scale for underclothing. I am somewhat out of practice in embroidery but a few letters will soon bring me back to my former skill. . . .

You will perceive several days have elapsed since I began this letter. Goodbye Yours affectionately

Mama

## Sunday, March 6, 1864

*. . . Rose has been confined to the bed in our room the greater part of the day with toothache and owing to her having it yet she and Theodosia will sleep in our room tonight. . . .*

## Wednesday, March, 9, 1864

*. . . I was greatly annoyed today by a troop of colored soldiers coming to the house to get recruits on the place, but not finding any here, they went to our neighbours. What they accomplished there I do not know. . . .*

## Monday, March 14, 1864

*. . . Emily & I cleaned out our dairy and also the storeroom, but unfortunately Emily could not resist the temptation of the liquor and the consequence is that this evening she has been perfectly overcome by drinking. Thede was obliged to assist Kitty in putting her to bed tonight.*

## Tuesday, March 15, 1864

*. . . John started to town with the raspberry plants, 18 bundles of them. As I design to give May the benefit of the profits I hope they will turn out well. . . . Another squabble with Mr P—— this evening. Emily has also given me trouble again today.*

## Wednesday, March 16, 1864

*. . . I have been overlooking the cleaning of Emily's & Kitty's room; the back bedroom and the spare room; they* look *and* feel *very much better than they*

*have done for a long time past. Emily is decidedly better today, for which I am extremely glad. . . . During the day I have managed to sew sufficiently to finish the yoke on which I have been engaged for several days. I have therefore only been ten days embroidering the sleeves & yoke, which considering the many interruptions I have, is doing pretty well.*

### Thursday, March 17, 1864

*I was pleased this morning on awaking to find we were likely to have a pleasant day for our trip to the city. . . . At the hour appointed we went to the theatre and had the pleasure of seeing Mrs Powers play Leah,[6] and truly a splendid piece of acting it was. I was constantly reminded of Kate Bateman and I cannot help thinking she herself had seen Kate in that character. . . .*

### Saturday, March 19, 1864

*. . . Mr Preston has been singularly nervous all day, in consequence of the expected visit of Mr Hartman. Thank Heaven he did not come tonight and I hope he may not come tomorrow, indeed he never will come again with my consent.[7]*

### Monday, March 21, 1864

*. . . This morning we were much surprised at William coming to the door and telling Mr Preston that George had left the place during the night and took his trunk with him. As he left without any apparent cause, Mr Preston was resolved to have him back again or else prevent any other person from employing him. Consequently I went to the city and . . . had a notice put in the German paper and also served a notice on Mr Goldenhouse, the man whom we think enticed George away from us. . . .*

### Wednesday, March 23, 1864

*. . . Mr Preston has been remodelling the work of the men. Johnny has had given him the care of the cattle, sheep, chickens and Buck together with making the slop, and little chores about the house. This I think will keep him pretty well employed and be all the better for him. I commenced making a new dress for May. It is very pretty indeed. The ground in the new leather color with a crimson strip. I shall embroider it with black, which I think will make it look very pretty. . . .*

### [Easter] Sunday, March 27, 1864

*The day never opened to a more glorious spring morning after the storm of yesterday and last night. I hoped to have passed a peaceful and quiet day, but an unfortunate expression of mine at the breakfast table kindled the embers of a latent fire in the breast of a certain individual, and the feelings displayed were terrible to behold. The consequence has been an unhappy day for me and him also. The girls have endeavoured to be agreeable, and partly succeeded, but the gentleman has been ill at ease—and greatly disconcerted. Johnny went to church this morning riding Jack down; no one has been here and the day has passed alone. I wrote a long and confidential letter to Louisa today.*

Pleasant Plains
March 28th 1864

My darling child,

I have rec'd your letter of the 21st and as you do not mention the reception of the last "tiny box" I dispatched some days ago, I fear you have not rec'd it. . . . I am pleased my dear child, to know you do not allow yourself to be made unhappy or annoyed by my long silence at any time. It is really as you suppose—a want of an opportunity to send our letters to the city. . . .

. . . I suppose you have heard of the death of Mr Scott, and also of his having become a Catholic on his death bed. Is it not strange that so intelligent a man as he truly was—with, as he avowed, a thorough conviction of the truth of the Catholic religion *for a long* time, should have put off, till Death actually stood before him, the acknowledging of his convictions and receiving the consolations and happiness imparted to those who are faithful members of the church?—It is one of my great pleasures to feel, that when these conversions take place during the seasons that the church has particularly set apart for spiritual devotions, that our Lord has heard the prayers of his children and has answered them. When you write again do not forget to enclose me a piece of blest palm, I will do as you request with regard to it and I am sure Papa will wear it for "your sake." How much I wish, my darling child, that your dear cousins and the rest of our family could enjoy some of the privileges of which you have so many. Your retreat and the happy termination of it to so many dear young children must have been a beautiful sight. . . .

You will know of course that I could not go to church on Easter Sunday—but of that, we will say nothing. I sent Johnny, who came home, happy and gratified. The boy still continues good & obedient and is greatly delighted when I read that part of your letter in which you mention him, as is Kitty also, and our dear little black baby (Ruthy). When Emily first came and the child with her, I believe Papa thought she would be quite a trouble, but *now*, I think he would not like to be without the child. It is his great pleasure to have her brought in the room, before she goes to bed, and to see her kneel down by me and say her prayers. Under *no circumstances* will he have it neglected. The other evening I had not yet returned from the city when it was time for her to be put to bed. Kitty was made to bring the child to Papa and she knelt before him, and he took her little hand and formed the sign of the cross with it on her breast & taught her to say—"In the name &c &c." Was not that very pretty in Papa, and do you not argue good from it? I regret so much that I am not in the city now. I really believe, if Rose & Theodosia had the opportunity, they would become Catholics while with me. . . . You have no idea what excellent good girls they are, and so intelligent. I feel sometimes as if I must take them to Father Foley and leave them in his hands. . . . They send much love, as does every member of the family

Good night God bless you<br>
Mama

### Tuesday, March 29, 1864

*. . . I have been engaged in a new occupation today, cutting and fixing a pair of pantaloons for Johnny. I made them out of an old cloth cloak very much moth eaten and as I thought, good for nothing. . . .*

### Friday, April 1, 1864

*Another cloudy morning but it has not prevented our doing what we have been so desirous to accomplish for a long time. . . . Mr Preston going to the city yesterday . . . we rose early, and all hands at once set to work to clean our bedroom out. We took up the carpet and made a thorough renovation of all things in the room and really by its looks I feel we are amply rewarded for our trouble. . . .*

### Sunday, April 3, 1864

*. . . Mr Preston has scolded considerably about the room being cleaned, but as I expected that, I was fully prepared. . . .*

### Friday, April 8, 1864

*The weather was beautiful this morning for which I was very glad as Mr Preston wished me to drive to the city for him. . . before leaving the house we discovered much to our great annoyance that Emily had been drinking and was very much intoxicated. . . . We started for home reaching here about dark, and found Emily wretchedly drunk and behaving very badly—put Kitty in a bed by herself tonight.*

Pleasant Plains
April 10th 1864

My darling child,

After a night of wind and rain such as we all think has never visited this part of the country in our time, we rose to the pleasant consciousness that we were having the second edition of Noah's flood, and that too, on no very limited scale—and unfortunately without Mount Arrarat near us, on which we might hope to find a resting place for the soles of our feet! On stepping into the library this morning to ascertain the full extent of the damage done during the night—I found a stream of water meandering slowly over the heavy Brussels carpet and here and there breaking into ponds and lakes, and dallying as it were with the said carpet, which in the darkness of the night it had evidently mistook for green mossy banks and flowery meadows—the chairs looked as if they had been dancing a fandango and had found some difficulty in avoiding too close embrace with the huge piano, which was only kept from taking a voyage of discovery round the room by the tightness of its *chords* and the extent of its *bass*! Having no canoe in which to stem the waves I was fain to plunge not headlong, but feet foremost into the element which had so unceremoniously intruded itself in our quarters. With the united efforts of the servants—men & women, the "girls," Papa and myself, in a few hours the carpet was removed, floor washed up, chairs put to rights and "Richard was himself" again! But the inroads of the waters did not stop with us. In the course of the day, sundry of our neighbours stepped in to utter the lamentations of Jeremiah over the doings of the storm of the night previous and each one had something to relate of their mishaps of the night, but as they were nothing that a little industry, good judgment and time could not remedy they served for something to talk about and laugh over. The roads as you will readily imagine are in a shocking condition, which just now I very much regret as a letter rec'd from Aunt Louisa yesterday informs us that she is in Washington and will be in Baltimore by the ten o'clock train of Monday, consequently I shall be obliged to go to the city tomorrow for her. The girls you know are still with me, whether Aunt Louisa intends taking them home with her I do not know. I think however they prefer remaining with us. . . . They both desire a great deal of love to you. Theodosia says, tell May when I am once more in the mountains I shall have nothing scarcely to occupy my time, and then I will write her such long letters that she will weary of them before she comes to an end. . . .

. . . Oh I had almost forgotten a little episode in which Buck figured quite *largely*. Papa, thinking he ought to do his share towards the support of the farm and the comforts of the family, concluded to harness him in his little cart and let Johnny and the Pony go on a chip expedition. Buck, not satisfied to work after so long a spell of idleness or else being invigorated by the fresh air and the feeling of freedom excited by being once more released from the confinement of the stables, resolved on doing the business his own way. So instead of moving forward as was the intention of the driver, the little fellow concluded a backward movement most desirable, so back he went, with a shake and a snort, which he intended should be very terrific, but which to his good-natured admirers around him only produced a smile; seeing *that* not so very effective, he resorted to gymnastics of a *higher* order—head went up, heels flew in the air, tail and mane stood out, and the snort and the shake again was tried, but as we still took all this very patiently and instead of giving the little fellow a whipping as task masters generally do their poor brute slaves, we soothingly patted him on the back, gave him a nice lump of sugar, all of which treatment he seemed thoroughly to appreciate and to feel ashamed of his own bad conduct, so looking calmly around, he quietly stepped forward and in a short time, he and Johnny were off to the woods, where a load of good chips were put in the cart, and the boy & pony returned home, a good example that kind treatment is better than cruel, and that even a little pony can be made sensible of that fact. Papa sends his love to you. Good night God bless you my child

Mama

### Monday, April 18, 1864

*. . . Louisa & I [went to the city], did some shopping, saw "Abe" and his caval-cade drive up Charles Street, and then returned home.*[8] *. . .*

Pleasant Plains<br>April 22d 1864

My very dear child,

    I fear you will think I have been unmindful of you, during your Aunt Louisa's visit to us, as I have not written at length for more than a week. . . . She and myself went to the city on Monday, bidding Papa and the girls goodbye at Pleasant Plains. We desired to have a few days *to ourselves* in the city before she left this part of the country. On Tuesday we called on . . . dear old Father Hickey, whom we found at "Mount Daugherty"—a new institution near Green Mount Seminary under the direction of the Sisters of Charity. . . . We had a most delightful visit to the dear old Father. . . . The old gentleman was much pleased to know I had a daughter at St Joseph's, and said he would pray that *you might never leave that place!* I thanked him, and surprised him by saying that was my most ardent wish—that I would rather give you to our Lord, than resign you to anyone on earth!

Aunt Louisa left in the morning train for Gettysburg—and I hope reached Mountain View safely that same evening. I returned home on Wednesday afternoon. The girls are to remain with me to an indefinite period I believe. . . . Papa is not so well today, but we hope a few day's nursing will bring him all right again. As he sits by me just now he sends much love to you, as do also Kitty, Emily, and Ruthy. Yours lovingly

Mama

# 6

# The Troubling Nieces

IN LATE APRIL HARTMAN arrived to spend a day at Pleasant Plains. Preston, who had been so nervous over this contemplated visit, appeared to enjoy his company after all; and every member of the family was charmed by Hartman. His engrossing stories of the California gold rush kept them together in the sitting room till a very late hour.

But if Preston discovered that he had no occasion for jealousy in Hartman's visit, Madge found just the reverse in the continuing presence within her household of her two young nieces. Some of Madge's discomfort may be apparent in her miswriting in her diary entry for May 1. It also seems implied in a coded paragraph about the girls in her May 1 letter to May. In this letter Madge also engages her daughter in a small conspiracy regarding Kitty's religious development. This secret pact may in some small measure compensate in Madge's mind for a different kind of conspiracy that she feels developing against herself. Clearly Madge feels isolated within her own family, with Preston and the two girls positioned in consort against her. Madge's hostile silence, responding to his (which she records in her May 5 diary page)  about something so transparently obvious as the girls' failure to return from an outing in town—highlights the rift now developing between the pair.

Pleasant Plains
April 29th 1864

I had hoped my darling child to have announced in this letter that your "box" was wending its way to your distant home, but . . . I shall not have it in my power to send the box till next week. . . . Much to our great satisfaction our friend Mr Hartman came out this afternoon from Washington, to spend the evening and remain all night with us. We found him so very entertaining that we have trespassed considerably upon our hours of rest, and have remained up till quite a late hour. We have . . . just separated for the night. The girls—Mr H—and Papa, taking their lights, bidding me good night, and each and all, retiring to their own apartments. I alone remaining up, to have a little chat with you my dear child.

In a few weeks, Mr Hartman will pass through Gettysburg on his way to the far West. Should he do so, he says he will certainly call at St Joseph's for the purpose of seeing you; it is our wish that you be permitted to see him and if he wishes to take you out for a few hours, tell Sister Raphael we have not a friend in the world with whom we would more willingly trust you than with Mr Hartman. . . .

Last night Rose & Theodosia—together with the girls at Union Hall . . . were invited to Eudowood. The girls think from the attention of Mr T. Taylor lavished on Mary Lizzie and the evident pleasure with which they were received, that there must be some truth in the report of their engagement, but we had not heard anything of it till your letter gave us an inkling of the great event. . . .

Mary Lizzie has not been very well lately, she has been suffering with daily headaches, so violent as to make it necessary to lie down some part of each day—yet notwithstanding she is looking very beautifully. Alice is well and pleasant as usual and dear little Willie as sweet as ever.

We are all well at home, but Papa who still complains. . . .

Good night, God bless you—
Mama

## Sunday, May 1, 1864

*Rose & Mr Preston spent the morning out of doors and Thede & I took a long walk this afternoon. On our return from walking, I was pained to see an evident agitation and embarrassment about those whom we had left him [sic], which indicated something wrong! . . .*

Pleasant Plains
May 1st 1864

Do not be alarmed my darling child at this formidable sheet of paper,[1] but as it is Sunday, and my portfolio contains nothing smaller, I am forced to take it, or else let you do without your Sunday letter—which shall I do? write of course I hear you say, Mama. So I will—for I wish so much to tell you of a glorious walk, from which we have just returned this afternoon— . . . peach trees, cherry trees and plum trees are in their full bloom, and here and there in the orchard an apple tree was showing a few of its early blossoms and giving promise of an abundance of fruit. . . . The grass is becoming quite "velvety" under the foot, and the little wild violet throws a purple hue over many a grassy bank and shaded nook—even the wrens were chirping their spring songs as they flitted past us to their leafy nests. . . .

Truly is this a lovely May day, worthy of the Blessed Mother to whom her children have devoted it. I was wishing this morning I knew the hour of the day in which you offer up your May prayers, that I might in spirit meet you at that time and join my prayers with yours. You do not know my child how deeply I feel the privations of all those spiritual comforts with which you are so abundantly supplied. I fear when you return home you will find the pleasures of home but illy compensate for those greater losses.

It gave me great pleasure today to see with what satisfaction poor little Kitty brought her simple offering of fresh wild flowers to put on "Miss May's altar"—indeed the child scarcely ever sees a new or pretty flower that she does not gather it and arrange it tastefully for the altar—from all this I look forward to a happy change in the now darkened heart and feel that when it does come, she will be as ardent in good as she has hitherto been indifferent to it. I shall try and do as you suggest in one of your letters, prepare her heart & mind for good instruction, and when you return home this summer, we will endeavor to take her to Father Lyman. You need not mention this in your letters, as they are generally read aloud and there might be comments on it, which would pain me to hear.

You will perceive from my late letters the girls are still with us, and are likely to remain, perhaps till you return; they prefer the quiet of our country home to the still greater quiet of theirs, and as they are content of course we are pleased to have them: Now that the weather is becoming pleasant, they spend the greater part of their time out of doors walking about with their Uncle, to whom they are greatly attached, and you know from personal experience how much your papa appreciates that kind of attention. They were out of course today enjoying the walk with us, and both came home laden with wild flowers and blossoms. They reminded me of you, gathering these beauties and bringing them home to be thrown aside and wither for want of attention—do you recollect how often I have lectured you for so doing? Good night May, our dear Mother have you always in her holy keeping

Mama

### Tuesday, May 3, 1864

*. . . We were favored with another storm of wind rain & hail this afternoon. Rose & Mr Preston were out in the whole of it. Mr Hillen came out this*

*afternoon and spent an hour with us, wishing to see Mr Preston, who did not come while he was here.*

### Wednesday, May 4, 1864

*. . . I got up early to arrange for going to the city to take May's box containing her new dress and sundries; before Thede & I left we had as usual another squabble which ended in Mr Preston giving me an insignificant box which by the time I put a doz oranges in it, and some other little things, there was very little room for the dress. . . .*

### Thursday, May 5, 1864

*Another glorious day. This morning Mr Preston arranged to go to the city and the girls concluded to go with him, and to try to go to Fort McHenry, as we have heard recently that Major Goldsborough has been removed to that place. Mr Preston drove in the carriage and they went too. Mr Preston returned home about five o'clock without them, but as he is not very well pleased with me, he has thus far not informed of the cause. As soon as they left this morning I told Emily to finish her morning work as quickly as possible and come up stairs to assist me in overhauling the trunks and airing & putting away winter clothing and looking over & fixing up spring & summer articles. I can't tell why it is, but there is no household duty so painful to me as this; it makes me singularly sad but why I do not know.*

### Friday, May 6, 1864

*. . . It gives me great pleasure to record here that Emily is decidedly the best dairy maid I have had for a long time, and with the two cows we have had all winter I have had more satisfaction with milk & butter than when we kept half a dozen and they were not properly taken care of. Mr Preston & the girls returned this afternoon, but as yet they have not explained why they remained in town.*

### Saturday, May 7, 1864

*. . . Mr Preston & Rose drove to the city and did not return till after sundown. I rec'd a letter this evening from Aunt Louisa in which she says, "the girls had better come home!"*

**Sunday, May 8, 1864**

*. . . Mr Preston as usual has spent the day, "tinkering," with both the girls
helping. I can't help recording here that I certainly do not approve of these
strange doings, and I can't help showing it by my conduct. . . .*

Pleasant Plains
May 8th 1864

My dear child,

I am not insensible to the fact that . . . more than three weeks have elapsed
since you wrote. . . . Mrs Burns . . . laughingly suggested perhaps your silence was occasioned by "your having been punished and not permitted to
write home"! I hope that it is *not* the case—if it is, I am free to tell the good
Sister who inflicted *that* punishment, it is the mother more than the daughter
who suffers by it—however I am only joking now. . . .

Let me know . . . if your oranges reached you safely. I almost regretted
sending them fearing they might endanger your dress. Let me know about all
the things. . . . The Sozodont, or toothwash, is a very fine article, highly recommended by Mrs Bateman, who has used it for many years in her large
family. . . . You unscrew the top of the bottle and pour on your brush a few
drops of the liquid, which when applied to the teeth produces a thick foam
unlike soap in its agreeability, but equally cleansing. This I would like you to
use night and morning and the powder accompanying the bottle two or three
times a week. I hope you have taken care of your teeth. You know how necessary I think clean good teeth are to the requisites of a lady.

I fill my letters with a great deal of nothingness. . . .

Mama

The Vale. May 6th 1864

My dear Mama,

I suppose you are beginning to be anxious about me as I have not written to
you for some time. . . .

. . . I have received several letters from you. . . . When I came to that part
that I might never leave St. Joseph's, I had a good laugh, and as there were
only a few girls in the play-room I gave it out for their amusement; they all enjoyed it as much as I had but in a different manner, as they think the good
father's prayers will be heard, for you must know every one says I am going to
be a Sister for certain. What do you think of that? Tell Papa that he need not
be at all worried about me for I do not think that is . . . my vocation. . . .

For the last month we have been making in sewing class a suit of clothes for a little poor child on the first of May in honor of our Blessed Mother. She had more than a complete set from the stockings to the bonnet. I took the precaution some time ago to ask Sr. Raphael to let me help to dress her. So on Saturday when she was brought over to be prepared for Sunday, Sister very kindly sent for me and one of the young ladies and myself dressed her. Her toilette was so completed and you may imagine how delighted both the little child and her mother were. . . .

Just to think dear Mama when you see me again I will be fifteen years old! Am I not getting to be a big girl? . . .

Your loving *little*
May.

### Friday, May 13, 1864

*. . . Mr Preston and the girls [went] to the city to remain all night and visit the theatre to see Forrest play Othello.*[2] *They left about 12 o'clock in the market wagon. . . .*

Pleasant Plains
May 15th 1864

My darling child,

As the large sheet of paper met so decidedly with your approbation, I think in future I shall adopt them. . . .

Notwithstanding the quantity of rain that has fallen during the past week—we, as usual, took our ramble over the place this morning—gum shoes, hoods and pages[3] were brought into requisition, and when we felt ourselves sufficiently fortified against the dangers of muddy roads—wet grass, sprinklings from the trees and an occasional good heavy shower, we sallied forth. The garden of course was the first place visited—and truly it was a sight to see. One would have imagined Aladdin's lamp had been working miracles—peas which but a few days ago were just showing their little green heads above the ground are now running round looking for some friendly sticks on which to twine their slender arms and support themselves when their blossoms and pods become too heavy for their fragile frame to bear without other assistance. . . .

After looking in upon the chickens and feeding some dear little young ones, we gladdened our eyes with a sight of your flock of sheep—which I believe has increased to *forty*—*three* little lambs having been added to the number last week. We brought up at the dairy! When a quantity of good butter, a number of pans of rich milk, to say nothing of a crock of buttermilk, gave evidence of nice cows well taken care of and a good dairy maid—which I am sure you will be pleased to know I have in Emily—good as Lizzie used to be, Emily is decidedly better—indeed she is excellent in every way—so kind—so anxious to please and so appreciative of all we do for her and her little child. I went to the kitchen early the other morning or rather shortly after breakfast, and the little thing ran to meet me, but judge of my surprise on looking down to take hold of her, to find nearly half of her wool shaved off her head. I exclaimed—good gracious Emily what is the matter with the child. "Why Missus, Ruthy cut her hair, I beg pardon her wool, off herself." I could scarcely believe it, but on asking the child—she said she did it, and took the scissors and showed us how she did it. Of course the other side had to be cut to correspond and she now goes about with her head almost bare, presenting the most comical appearance you can imagine. Every day she asks me "Mitty Miss May toming (coming)[4] home today?" "No Ruthy not for many days yet." Then she goes away repeating to herself—"Miss May not toming home yet." —so pitiful that I am obliged at times to stop her. . . .

So you laugh at my asking Father Hickey to pray you may never leave St Joseph's! Do you know I think as your young companions do, that the day will come when I shall see you a Sister of Charity, and I freely acknowledge I would much more cheerfully give you to our dear Lord to love and serve him in that holy way, than to see you exalted to the highest position this world could give you. I look around in these days of strife and bloodshed, and ask myself, what is there in this world to live for?—and then I thank God that you are not with me to be pained continually with seeing and hearing all that we are obliged to see and hear; and as you are happy where you are, I pray to our dear Lord to keep you in that quiet retreat. Don't imagine that I wish you *now* to "adopt the habit and take the vows." You are quite too young to decide on so important a subject, but after your education has been completed—then, you may bid me goodbye, and I will answer "God bless you!" . . .

I am constantly with you in spirit my dear child, now that your examinations have commenced, and pray most earnestly that *you may feel satisfied with your own doings.* . . . Therefore keep yourself calm and collected, pray to our Blessed Mother to assist you, and all will be well.

Mama

---

The following is an undated fragment of a letter from Madge Preston to May, of which the beginning has been lost.

As I am alone this afternoon and writing to you is more agreeable than reading, I will fill another sheet to you. Rose has retired to her room suffering from a headache brought on, I rather expect, by walking too far this morning

in the warm sun. Papa and Theodosia are wandering about the grounds—
Emily & Kitty "by Missus permission" have gone down to Union Hall,[5] and
dear little *darco* is sleeping on the floor at my feet. The little thing seems
never so happy as when hanging about where I am or sitting on the ottoman at
my feet. "Missus you going walking" "Yes, Ruthy"—"Don't Missus want me
to take care of Missus?" Yes Ruthy. Then off she trots to get her bonnet and
returns, holding out her tiny little hand for mine and walks by my side with an
air which plainly says, "Without me, my Missus could not get along." It is astonishing how much she has wound herself round all our hearts; we look
quite longingly in the morning to see her run in the sitting room, with out-
stretched arms and smiling face. "dood morning Missus, dood morning Master Willie"—"You right well Missus this morning." She utters the prettiest little expression sometimes you ever heard—and her affectionate little nature
prompts her constantly to do a thousand little acts which in the aggregate contribute in no small degree to our comforts—for instance everything that falls
to the floor, spools of cotton, thimble, scissors &c &c she runs at once to give
them to the one to whom they belong, as her watchful observation enables
her to know and understand many things usually uncomprehensible to much
older children. Every flower she gets & everything almost that she sees me do,
she at once thinks Miss May is in some way connnected with it. By the way
before Emily & Kitty left me this afternoon they stood at the sitting room door
to ask me to please give their respects and love to Miss May—poor little Kitty
is really a strange child, bad as she is, and you know how very bad that is.
Every day of the world, since she could find a flower, has she brought a fresh
bunch and put them on the altar—Yesterday she really surprised me in the
beauty of the arrangement and the artistic taste with which she placed the colors of a cluster of flowers she had gathered and put on the altar after Emily
had fixed up the room. . . .

Goodbye Yours lovingly
Mama.

---

On May's birthday, May 19, Preston sat down at his writing desk to
finish a letter to his daughter which he had begun on the previous Christmas
Day. He had put it aside uncompleted, then resumed it on January 3, breaking off again when a caller interrupted him. More than four months later he
finally brought it to a close. Preston's style centers on lengthy descriptions of
the surrounding scene, with didactic digressions and erudite allusions. The
style is self-conscious. Preston himself, one feels, was always center stage. Yet
throughout the letter—which ran eventually to fifteen pages, one for each of
May's fifteen years—threads a theme of despair and deep depression.

Pleasant Plains<br>
25th December 1863

. . .To-day being the anniversary of the birth of Christ, the mind naturally recurs to his mission. It was *peaceful*—he was styled the "Prince of *Peace*" he taught *peace* and good will to men"—the whole of his divine doctrines are founded upon *peace* and harmony—until his coming, revenge was ranked among the virtues—yet what do we see, our country governed by men who while they profess to be followers of the *peaceful* Jesus use all their power to desolate the land with famine, fire, sword, and blood death. If the fiends of hell were let loose in mortal form, they could not with all the aid of an infernal education more completely disfigure the beautiful earth which a beneficent God has furnished for the use of man. My visit to the battlefields of Gettysburg fully demonstrated this to me—and this they say is done to preserve the Union! well may we exclaim with Madam Roland, "Oh Liberty! Liberty! how many crimes are committed in thy name." . . .[6]

19th May—1864—I laid down my pen & put my letter aside on the 3rd January—four months ago! More than four months!!—again and again, I essayed to finish it—I repeatedly said—well! tonight I will finish May's letter—the night arrived and found me fatigued, disheartened, sick—sad—and then I said—I cannot do it now—I will put it off till tomorrow—tomorrow came and the words of the previous evening, or some substantially the same were repeated.

> "And thus the native hue of resolution
> Was sicklied o'er with the pale cast of thought."[7]

Oh how truly has it been said—

> "Procrastination is the thief of time"[8]—

My dear child, never put off until tomorrow what may be done today—Tomorrow seldom or never comes—

At my last writing the landscape presented a woe-begone aspect, the horses' hoofs pattering over the frozen ground appeared to ring out the knell of Nature recently dead, and the voiceless unclad trees appeared to shiver in melancholy at her tomb. Now all is changed! the unbound earth and laughing streams joyfully give forth the perfumed blossom and rush with sparkling melody to the glad ocean. . . .

We have commemorated your birthday in various ways. Your mother and your cousins have visited the various little places about the farm of interest to you—and we all concluded, Kitty and Johnny included, to each plant a grapevine in token of your fifteenth year—Each selected a place for the vine according to their own taste; Johnny and I concluded to ornament the roof of Buck's new stable and in the presence of the others we planted in front of the building a thriving Catawba and Isabetta. I hope they may live and that we may all yet pick luscious grapes from the branches. In addition to these horticultural achievements, other ceremonies were performed indoors. Kit made a grand cake which was eaten as a dessert, and at the same time your mother produced a bottle of homemade currant wine from which we all drank your health and offered up a prayer for your happiness. . . .

And now my dear child having written *fifteen* pages, that is one for each year of your life—I am about to say goodbye. I may or may not write to you again before you return home—but I cherish the anticipation of hearing a good account of your intellectual progress as one of St. Joseph's girls. . . . Give my regards to the dear sisters.

Wm P. Preston

Pleasant Plains May 19th 64

My darling child—

I shall only send you a loving kiss and pray that God may bless you now and ever. Papa has said all that I *would wish* to say, so much better than I *could* say it, that I will not add another word to his most beautiful letter of *fifteen* pages.

Mama

**Thursday, May 19, 1864**

*. . . Tonight we have had quite an excitement, but I will not record the particulars!*

**Friday, May 20, 1864**

*. . . The girls have been amiable & attentive today, the result of last night's doings.*

Pleasant Plains<br>May 30th 1864

My very dear "Daughter,"

I have purposely delayed writing during the past week, thinking it would take all your spare time . . . to read over your father's most delightful long letter. Was it not a treat, *such* a letter? and does it not prove to you how much

Papa loves his big daughter. Of course we all read the letter and we were all pleased to know you had so great a treat in store for you. . . .

I have sympathized with you *all* during the time I knew you were sitting on the "anxious bench," and shall rejoice with you also when I know you have "got well through" as the Methodists say, when a new member "gets religion"! —as if we had not always religion, if we would only *practice it.* It was quite amusing to hear *we ladies* recounting our troubles and difficulties in relation to the Distribution uniform necessary to you girls. I, as the most independent of the faction, was wishing that Sister Raphael had put you all in your school dresses and dispensed altogether with the "extras." You can have no idea of the difficulties attending the *purchase* and *making* of anything just now—to begin with—everything in the drygoods line is double the former price, some articles treble—only think of gloves *two dollars*—ribbon from $1.25 pr to $2.00 pr yard—and everything in proportion; . . . the *making* of the dresses however is the great trouble—a dressmaker scarcely to be had at any price —in that particular . . . I am fortunate as I still adhere to my old habit of making all your clothing. I purchased the things you desired . . . and shall endeavour to have them ready . . . to send up in the wagon. . . .

Yours lovingly<br>Mama

**Saturday, June 4, 1864**

*. . . It gives me great pleasure to record here the uncommon goodness of Kitty during the entire week. I could scarcely have desired to have her better. . . .*

Pleasant Plains<br>June 5th 1864

My dear Daughter,

I have just returned from spending the day at Aigburth Vale, and though wearied and tired from walking and talking, I yet cannot be happy or comfortable without a little chat with you. . . . Papa, Rose & I, in compliance with an invitation from the Owens, went over early in the day and returned just as the sun was setting. Theodosia not feeling very well remained at home to keep house. Aigburth, just now, is looking beautifully. Mr Owens has displayed great taste and good judgment in some improvements he has made in the grounds around the house, which gives more space and adds much to its looks. . . .[9] Rose and Theodosia had expected to leave us the last of the coming week, but they do not like the idea of not seeing you, consequently they have concluded to remain till after your return and be here to remain with Papa during my absence to Emmitsburg—as I have determined to go up for you and be present at the Distribution. I had hoped Papa would have accompanied me, but he seems to think he cannot do so. . . .

Papa, Thede and Rose send love to you and the girls. . . devotedly Mama

### Wednesday, June 8, 1864

. . . John . . . went early for Emily [who had had a three-week holiday] as was arranged he should yesterday. . . . About 10 o'clock we were greatly alarmed by the mare flying into the enclosure with the empty cart; on rushing out to see what had happened, we found John coming after the runaway horse, and learned that she had run off, and threw Emily & the children out, hurting Emily about the head and shoulder and cutting John's head slightly. From the extent of the accident it is wonderful that they escaped as they did. They all reached here about noon, looking bruised; . . . with our troubles have been mingled a cup of sweetness—our friend Mr Hartman spent the greater part of the day with us. He told us the matrimonial project between him & Mrs Reynolds was broken off—for which I am rather glad. He read us some letters written by a niece of his which are as beautiful as any letters I have ever read either written or published. When we bade him "goodbye" we were all sad enough. . . .

### Friday, June 17, 1864

The weather being pleasant I concluded to go over to Aigburth Vale and spend the day and learn to operate on the sewing machine. . . . This afternoon I took a lesson on the sewing machine and got along admirably. I stitched the bosom of a shirt for Johnny. . . .

### Saturday, June 18, 1864

Another pleasant day. After breakfast and when Mrs Owens had completed her morning duties, we went to the machine again and today I have really done wonders. I feel as if with a little more practice I could operate almost as well as anyone. I shall now expect Mr Preston to fulfill his promise and buy me a sewing machine. . . . Mr Preston is quite pleased with my progress on the sewing machine.

### Thursday, June 23, 1864

. . . Emily has made me acquainted with a most unpleasant piece of information today—an occurrence that took place during my absence last week & which I partly suspected though not to the full extent of what she insinuated.

### Friday, June 24, 1864

. . . *Emily this morning managed to steal into the storeroom and get liquor. The consequence has been that I have had very little good of her this afternoon. . . .*

### Saturday, June 25, 1864

. . . *I have had a most trying time with Emily, she having been stealing & drinking liquor until she is in a dreadful condition—and as we have had so much to do today I have been obliged to exert myself in a great degree. . . .*

### Sunday, June 26, 1864

. . . *This day being Sunday of course it could not pass without a "scene." Things look around me very suspiciously—what am I to do to change all things? Poor May will be greatly grieved as she cannot help seeing and being conscious of the proceedings. I had a conversation with Rose this afternoon and at the conclusion told her it was the last I should ever have* on that subject. *I feel convinced I have not acted or spoken without sufficient cause. I trust when my child returns and we are once more alone that all will be well again.*

### Monday, June 27, 1864

. . . *We started to the city at 9 o'clock. . . . I called at Sanders' and there ascertained Mr Hillen was also going to Emmitsburg tomorrow. . . .*

### Tuesday, June 28, 1864

. . . *We had a pleasant ride up and on reaching Gettysburg, I was delighted with the sight of Dr Smith and Louisa, who were also on their way to Emmitsburg. . . . we . . . reached St Joseph's at six o'clock, and had the pleasure of seeing our children and then drove up to Mr Dielman's where the family were waiting anxiously for me. They were kind enough to invite Louisa to stay with them, an invitation she readily accepted. The Dr remained in Emmitsburg. I think May is looking very well and in good spirits, tho' rather sorry at the thought of leaving her dear good Sisters.*

### Wednesday, June 29, 1864

*I find the mountain air considerably cooler than near the city. It is . . . very pleasant to have it so, as the exercises for which we have come to witness would*

*be very oppressive in a hot day. A large party . . . attended the College com-*
*mencement.*[10] *. . . One of the speakers, a Mr McClellan, did admirably. Na-*
*ture made him an orator, and so I told him on being introduced to him after*
*the ceremonies were over. . . . then all hands went to St Joseph's to have a good*
*long time with the girls. We walked over the house and into the drawing room.*
*I had the pleasure of being attended by Sister Leopoldine, May's Sister. She is*
*a good unpretending Sister, very well calculated to take the fancy of just such a*
*girl as May. . . .*

### Thursday, June 30, 1864

*. . . We drove down to St Joseph's . . . and on reaching there we were all taken*
*at once to the Distribution room as the Sisters wished the parents of their girls*
*to secure good seats. . . . In the course of time—the music commenced and the*
*girls two and two came in. Certainly nothing could exceed their perfect propri-*
*ety & modest deportment. There were over fifty crowns given, a number of*
*badges and a quantity of premiums. May rec'd a pink crown and a number of*
*premiums, and stood* third *in the first division of the second class. I am happy*
*to say I am very well satisfied with her. After the ceremonies were over I found*
*May preferred remaining at St Joseph's to going with me and I was glad she did*
*so as I had no desire to have her mixed up with the boys from the college. Aunt*
*Louisa bid me goodbye at St Joseph's and gave me the arrangements she wished*
*the girls [Thede and Rose] to have. They are to return home on the 6th of*
*July—and when they leave I hope they will never return. . . .*

### Friday, July 1, 1864

*At 6 o'clock this morning I bade goodbye to the Dielmans & Mr Hillen and I*
*stopped at St Joseph's for May and the girls. The parting with the Sisters &*
*girls was very affecting, both sides seeming to feel the coming separation. We*
*drove to Gettysburg and took the cars for Baltimore. We had a long detention*
*on the way but as there were a large party of us we did not feel very much an-*
*noyed. We reached Baltimore at 8 o'clock and found Mr Preston waiting for*
*us. . . . I shall take up my sleep apartment with May during her stay at home.*

### Saturday, July 2, 1864

*May & I talked ourselves to sleep last night and we have almost talked our-*
*selves into a headache today, we have been together all day unpacking and*
*fixing up the things May brought home. Mr Preston has remained home today*
*still fixing at the room over the dairy. I am not very happy and shall not be till*
*I am once more alone.*

### Tuesday, July 5, 1864

*. . . Mr Preston brings news of the Confederates making a raid into Maryland & Pennsylvania yesterday.*

### Friday, July 8, 1864

*Mr Preston roused us up early this morning to enable him to leave for the city in the 7 o'clock train. He did not return till six o'clock and then as usual we had a row about the girls going home. . . .*

### Saturday, July 9, 1864

*The weather still continues pleasant, with prospects of fine weather tomorrow on which day Mr Preston has concluded to leave home for Penna, with the girls. I hope the weather will prove favourable as they have made all arrangements to leave and I should not like them to be disappointed; another thing May & I want once more to feel ourselves alone. Mr Stansbury came up this evening to tell us martial law is again proclaimed in Baltimore, and no one can leave without a pass &c &c. I hope this news will not frighten Mr Preston!*

---

Pleasant Plains was of course beyond the jurisdiction of Baltimore. But Preston and the girls would be heading northwest, through a section of the countryside where Confederate forces were just then most active. Madge's anxiousness to get rid of the annoying presence of the two nieces apparently overcame any dread she might have felt that the small party could be endangered by the movements of troops through the territory they would have to traverse. Early the next day the three departed—before word of the military maneuvers reached the household.

### Sunday, July 10, 1864

*We were all astir this morning by 4 o'clock, took breakfast a little after five, and Mr Preston and the girls left us at 7 o'clock. They went in the market wagon with Black Hawk and Peri; what their fate will be, is in the future! Mr Stewart came over here about ½ past eight o'clock evidently very much excited by the news of the Rebel raid into Maryland and the near approach of the army at Towsontown. There are all sorts of rumours today of the Rebs—some say they are in great force near Cockeysville, and there has been great skeddadling from Hagerstown & Frederick for the last day or two. I should not be surprised if Mr Preston & his party should come across either one or the other of the armies! . . .*

On July 9 Confederate General Bradley Johnson had made a raid into Maryland to cut off Baltimore and Washington from the north. His brigade roamed through the region around Cockeysville, within ten miles of the route that Preston would travel. On July 10 Johnson's men burned the North Central Railroad bridges at Cockeysville.

Meanwhile Colonel Harry Gilmor, a dashing horseman after the style of J.E.B. Stuart, led a party of twenty Confederates into Westminster. On the tenth he went on to strike against the Philadelphia, Wilmington, and Baltimore Railroad at the Gunpowder River. Gilmor, who was a native of Glen Ellen and member of a prominent Baltimore family, knew the country well. With about 135 cavalrymen, he then swept into Towsontown. He fully enjoyed his dramatic return. Further south, General Jubal Early was trying to cross the Potomac to reach Washington.[11]

Both Preston and Madge were affected by these events—he with his small party traveling north, she with her daughter and servants remaining at Pleasant Plains.

## Monday, July 11, 1864

. . . *As Mr Preston has not yet returned home, I take it for granted they have succeeded in getting on their journey. I hope they reach their destination in safety and remain there! Johnny Stansbury came over this morning and in passing the springhouse saw two Rebels drinking and fitting their canteens from the spring. It seems a force of about 100 men came through Towsontown and went to Gov Bradford's house on Charles Street Avenue and after removing the most valued articles in it set fire to it and burnt it to the ground. They are certainly not very far distant from Baltimore tonight. . . .*[12]

## Tuesday, July 12, 1864

. . . *The excitement about the Rebels still continues. Johnny Stansbury came over this morning to give us an account of a slight skirmish at Towsontown last night. A good many shots were fired but "nobody hurt!" I heard the firing from my porch. Caleb also spent the evening with us and told us some pleasant things about the Confederates. . . .*

## Wednesday, July 13, 1864

. . . *Mrs Owens kindly sent over to me this morning a nice basket of fresh ripe currants together with a pleasant note in which she says the papers announce a battle in progress near Washington.*[13] *God grant victory to the South!*

### Friday, July 15, 1864

*This has been quite an eventful day. Before I was fully dressed this morning I was surprised by a squad of Yankee soldiers surrounding the house and on my asking the officer in command what was their object in coming, I was informed they were ordered to search the premises and also the house if they thought it was necessary. Of course there was nothing to be done but quietly to submit. They made, as they said, a thorough search and finding nothing contraband, they came and told me so, and took their departure. Though it was unpleasant to have them about, they in every respect behaved as gentlemen. After they left, our neighbours came up to see if we were alarmed and the extent of their doings; they also told us our boy Jim was with them.*[14] *From that, I infer it was not to search the house & premises for arms, but for the purpose of taking Mr Preston if they had found him. We were glad enough that Mr Preston was not home. John & William being apprised of their approach to the house, succeeded in hiding themselves and have remained away till tonight. Poor William is fearfully frightened.*

### Sunday, July 17, 1864

*[About 5 o'clock] we heard the sound of wheels and on going to the door, saw the wagon & horses, with Mr Preston & Aunt Louisa. It was such a relief to find Mr Preston had not brought the girls with him that I met the party with real pleasure. It seems Mr Preston & the girls met with some strange adventures with the Confederates, at least so says Mr Preston! I did not believe all that was told me, but I did not say so! Mr Preston & Aunt Louisa seem greatly excited by the raid made on the place yesterday, and I believe Mr Preston has concluded to go back in a day or two. The fact is, it is my impression that was his intention before he came down, and when he comes home to remain, he will certainly bring the girls with him. . . . Mr Preston . . . on his retiring told us he had concluded to leave tomorrow for Mountain View!*

### Monday, July 18, 1864

*. . . Mr Preston had been preparing all the morning for his departure and being ready he and Aunt Louisa left about ½ past two o'clock for Pena. I record here for future reference that I have not advocated Mr Preston's going away but have requested him to act of his own judgement, and then he could hold no one responsible but himself. I asked him before he left* not to bring the girls home with him! *which request seemed to make him very angry. . . .*

### Monday, July 25, 1864

*. . . Capt Shanabrook came over this afternoon and surprised me very much by telling me he had not yet been to Dr Smith's.*[15] *I have been wondering why the*

*Capt had not come over to tell me something about Mr Preston. The Capt tells me he is going up tomorrow, and he also tells me he intends to advise Mr Preston not to bring the girls home with him, as he is convinced they are looked upon as suspected individuals, and their going away just as the Rebels came into the state, he thinks, was in some way the cause of Mr Preston's trouble with the soldiers.*

### Friday, July 29, 1864

*I had quite an unpleasant episode this morning. Johnny, who was importunate last night about his clothes, came this morning to tell me he was going to Mr Whiteford's as he was not going to stay where he could get no clothing. I told him if he went he must remember he could not come back again. He did go and I let him. . . .*

### Sunday, July 31, 1864

*Surely we know not what a day or an hour may bring. May and I went quietly to bed last night little dreaming we were to be roused in the night by Mr Preston coming home, which he did about 3 o'clock this morning. I made no inquiry of him then as he was fatigued and went at once to bed. This morning he tells Crick and he came down from Gettysburg in the cars and came out in the Towsontown car and walked over. Mr Preston tells me a great many things that seems strange to me. At one time he thought of coming down in his wagon, but he changed his mind and came in the cars &c &c. The most astonishing thing of all is that Mr Preston is going back again to Mountain View in a day or two. The infatuation of that man is truly wonderful! What will be the end of it—God only knows. In our conversations today we have as usual been most unhappy. Mr Preston does not convince of the truth of half he says.*

### Monday, August 1, 1864

*. . . In our conversations yesterday Mr Preston insisted that May & I should make our visit to New York. Of course I understand why that is; it enables him to carry out his views with regard to the girls. Well so let it be!*

### Tuesday, August 2, 1864

*. . . Mr Preston went to the city, stopping on the way at Whitefords and sending Johnny home. The boy came to me this afternoon and made an apology and seemed quite penitent. Of course he is once more reinstated in his duties. . . .*

### Wednesday, August 3, 1864

. . . *Mr Preston has made arrangements . . . to go tomorrow morning early as far as Parkton (?) and meet the cars there and take them and go to Gettysburg. Mr Preston seems to have changed his mind about his doings in Penna. My own impression is he will bring the girls home with him, and I think that has been his intention all the time.*

### Thursday, August 4, 1864

*I rose at ¼ past 3 this morning and wakened Mr Preston; he got up at once and prepared for his departure. Mr P. is evidently ill at ease — the why and the wherefore I leave his own conscience to tell him. Mr P. left the house exactly at four o'clock, and I went to bed again — not however to sleep but to think. The servants are wondering very much at his sudden departure. . . .*

### Tuesday, August 9, 1864

. . . *Emily, who has been in a terrible spree for several days past, took it into her wise head to go away and remain all day without saying any [thing] to me beforehand. . . . Emily came home about [9 o'clock] and brought with her an old Aunty to remain all night. After a long chatter she cooled down and concluded to remain with us. . . .*

Pleasant Plains
August 10th 1864

Dear Mr Preston,

Had I not so fully calculated on seeing you at P. Plains before the tenth of this month, as was arranged . . . you would have had a letter from me by yesterday's mail. I regret now, I did not write, as it would have relieved you of any anxiety you might feel on account of your home and family. . . .

William, John and Johnny, by what they conceived a most Herculean effort, succeeded yesterday in finishing harvesting the oats — just think, they have been 7 days in cutting and taking in the oats of that small field. It did no good to "complain" of their tardiness, so I followed your example and let them get along their own way. . . .

You recollect Johnny was quite sick when you left here; for several days he was really very poorly. I found it necessary to ply him well with Aconite before I could in the least subdue the fever, then I alternated *that* and some other little pills for a day or two, and kept him without eating, much to Mrs Pent's horror and alarm and thus I cured him; yesterday morning he went to his milking for the first time. I think Emily said, The boy looks much better than he has for sometime past. Caleb Taylor, May and I drove to the city on Saturday; we had a pleasant visit to Father Foley and an unexpected interview with the new Archbishop, whom we found kind, pleasant and affable. The Archbishop asked me if my husband was of the "Preston family of the South." I said I believed there was some slight connection. . . . He said, I know them well in Kentucky—they are all great politicians and *worldly people*! Why don't you make a Catholic of your husband? I shrugged my shoulder for answer, and changed the subject.

I forgot to mention on Saturday coming home we found the wheels of the carriage so unsound as to be entirely unsafe; consequently, from this time I am a fixture at P. Plains, till you return. May joins in love to you and all the family.

Madge

### Wednesday, August 10, 1864

*. . . About five o'clock we heard carriage wheels and on looking out, we found it was our own wagon & horses, with Mr Preston and Louisa Mulgrew.*[16] *It was most gratifying to May & myself that the latter had come instead of the girls and we showed our pleasure accordingly. It seems Mr Preston must have had a terrible journey up the country with Mr Roder, and then he was obliged to remain over night at Hanover Junction. . . . Let me record here my thanks to God for this great deliverance from the presence of the girls.*

# 7

## The Sewing Machine

WITH LOUISA MULGREW SETTLED in as head of the household staff, Madge and May left for the planned visit in Brooklyn with the Greppos. Madge went with real pleasure, no longer worried that Rose and Thede would be spending this time with Preston at Pleasant Plains. During her absence the Emmitsburg music teacher, Mr. Dielman, planned to join the group at the farm for a few days' visit with Preston.

The travelers' journey took them by way of Philadelphia, where they spent a few days both coming and going with Mrs. Simmons. On the return trip they remained several days beyond their projected departure, shut in by a violent storm. When at last they reached Baltimore, sad news awaited both of them.

---

### Tuesday, September 6, 1864

*. . . On awaking this morning it was still raining, but after breakfast the rain ceased and we concluded we might as well start for home. The carriage came for us . . . and bidding goodbye to our kind friends, we turned our faces towards Balt . . . and found Mr. Preston awaiting us. On our way home Mr Preston informed us of the sudden death of Dr Joseph M. Smith and the consequent return home of Louisa last Saturday. This is terrible news to me, as I fear I will [find] myself encumbered with one member of the family that will render me unhappy. May also read a letter from her dear Sr Leopoldine saying she was on Mission in Baltimore;[1] we went up at once to see her, and on our return poor dear May has almost cried herself to sleep. Poor child! This is her first great sorrow!*

## Wednesday, September 7, 1864

*After the storm of the last few days, the sun rose bright and beautiful. . . . As soon as May dressed herself after breakfast, she went up to see Father Foley, and from there to Sanders. . . . May spent an hour with Sister Leopoldine & on her return to the office, Mr Preston was there and we started for home, which place we reached at dark. All well!*

## Thursday, September 8, 1864

*. . . I had a great deal to overlook today, as I found things in terrible disorder, particularly those things which Kitty had charge of. . . . Emily told me this morning that she intended to leave the last of this week.*

## Friday, September 9, 1864

*It was dull & cloudy this morning but notwithstanding, as Mr Preston was going to the city . . . to take Louisa's trunk to the Express office, I concluded to go with him . . . as I wanted yarn to knit stockings for Mr Preston. It cleared off before we reached the city. Mr Preston and I rec'd letters from Louisa in which she seems greatly distressed at the death of the Dr. Mr Preston answered it, I hope to her satisfaction.*

---

It seems curious that Madge did not add a personal note of condolence to her bereaved sister, with whose family she had lived during her own youthful years. When Madge's close friends had suffered similar losses, she had offered special, and instant, support; and of all of Madge's siblings, she had always had the strongest ties with Louisa. Perhaps now Madge felt some constraint because of discomfort over Preston's relationship with Louisa's young daughter Rose.

## Saturday, September 10, 1864

*. . . Emily fixed up her things this morning and after being paid her wages took, as she said, the day to herself—consequently May & I had to exert ourselves in housekeeping. We went to the pear trees and found some very nice pears, which we gathered and baked. We took dinner and tea together and thus arranged our doings. . . . Hearing there was a quantity of fine mushrooms in our fields we went out and gathered a long kettle full which we have skinned and prepared for breakfast. . . . During the night Emily came home and this morning she was "all right"—much to our satisfaction. . . .*

### Sunday, September 11, 1864

. . . *Mr Preston wrote a letter today to my sister, requesting her to come down to see him respecting her business. I also wrote to her a short letter, the first one I have written since the Dr's death. . . .*

### Tuesday, September 13, 1864

. . . *This morning Mr Preston and May went to the city, but before they went we all went to the orchard and gathered a wagon of apples to make some fresh cider, as May wished to take some to Sr Leopoldine. We also gathered a bag of fine apples for the same purpose. . . . When May & her father stopped at the Sister's, Sr Gertrude made her remain and spend the day. Of course May was delighted. . . . May rec'd her carte-de-visites today and we all think they are excellent. . . .*

### Wednesday, September 14, 1864

. . . *Mr Preston & Mrs Beer rose early & went in search of mushrooms; they returned to breakfast but had not been very fortunate. . . . Mr Preston remained home till noon superintending the cider operation, but he went to the city after that to meet my sister and remain in town all night. It is a singular fact, whenever Mr Preston brings Mrs Beer out, he always finds it necessary to remain in town over night. . . .*

### Friday, September 16, 1864

. . . *As May is to go to town tomorrow and remain till she goes away, I have been very busy fixing up and arranging her things. Part of the morning was not so very pleasantly spent—but no matter!*

*. . . This is the last night of my darling child at her home. Will she ever spend another one here? Thy will be done oh God in this, as in all things. If she never returns, take her to thyself. I have to pack her trunk yet.*

### Saturday, September 17, 1864

*Rose early expecting to start to town, but Mr Preston was not ready till near ten o'clock. It was almost twelve when we reached the city. . . . When we reached the house, we found Aunt Louisa there. . . . It was most painful to hear her account of the suffering of Dr Smith, his death however was most quiet, and evidently without pain. Poor little May had a hard struggle to keep from weeping today when she bade farewell to those at home and left it for her school. It is decided that May goes up with Aunt Louisa on Monday. She is spending the night with Sister Leopoldine.*

### Monday, September 19, 1864

*Rose early this morning to enable May to go to communion at Father Foley's Mass. Good child, to begin her journey with God's blessing upon her. Mr Preston & Aunt Louisa came in by eight o'clock, having left P. Plains a little after six o'clock. I had very little opportunity to say anything to Louisa but I said what I thought I ought to say, yet I fear it will have no effect upon her. At the right time, we started for the depot. . . . Dear little May bade us goodbye, evidently under much feeling, but well controlled. I feel so thankful to think to-night my dear child sleeps once more at St Joseph's! We remained in town till four o'clock . . . Mrs Beer coming with us. All right!*

### Thursday, September 22, 1864

*. . . Mr Preston came home this evening quite sick, but I soon discovered it was more nervousness than sickness. After tea we went to our room & then Mr Preston showed me a bundle of letters rec'd while in the city. One was from Louisa requesting Mr Preston to come up to consult with him. I am convinced that letter was the cause of the nervousness. One letter was from Theodosia to me; in it she asks me not to show the letter to anyone—of course I did not.*

### Friday, September 23, 1864

*. . . I wrote a long letter to Thede today, and one to May. I asked Thede to make us a visit this winter, but that part of the letter was dictated by Mr Preston. We are all going to the city in the morning, Mrs Beer to remain, Mr Preston to go to Mountain View. . . .*

### Saturday, September 24, 1864

*We rose early this morning to prepare for going to the city, in time to allow Mr Preston to go in the cars for Gettysburg. . . . What is to be the end of all this? For years Mr Preston seemed to studiously avoid my sister & her family, but within the last year, nay within the last few months, he has visited their home some four or five times and has had two of her daughters spending months with him, and not yet satisfied, has, through me, written to invite one of them to spend the winter with him. Again I say, what is to be the result of all this? . . .*

## Monday, September 26, 1864

*. . . I spent the morning looking over "old letters." Alas! alas! what changes a few years bring about. The writers of most are absent, estranged, almost forgotten. Those strange to say are best remembered, who are dead. It has made me sad to know the long, fervent, affectionate letters written by \_\_\_\_\_ can never be written again, neither can I, in return, send such answers as I once did! N'import! . . .*

## Wednesday, September 28, 1864

*. . . I had designed going to the city this morning, but I concluded to send Johnny on horseback. He . . . reached home . . . bringing with him a letter from May. . . . several of her young companions are yet at St Joseph's whom she thought would not be there this session. I am glad of it, as not having "her Sister" there, she would feel very lonely without her old companions. I thought possibly I might receive a letter from Mr Preston today, but I did not. Ah! me, I fear Mr Preston is tempting his fate too far. . . .*

## Thursday, September 29, 1864

*. . . Mr Preston came . . . down yesterday from Gettysburg and out this afternoon in the car & walked over. Mr Preston seems in good spirits & quite happy; he says the family were glad to see him. Theodosia wrote a short letter to me, saying she would come down soon &c &c.*

*Emily went off this morning chestnut hunting, and did not return till one o'clock, causing thereby a great deal of uneasiness, as we feared she had gone off on a frolic.*

## Sunday, October 2, 1864

*This afternoon Mr Preston and I went down to May's room; it was the first time either of us had been there since May left us. I do not know why I should have been so much affected, but I have not yet recovered of the sadness produced thereby. Mr Preston & I have passed the day alone, reading & talking.*

## Wednesday, October 5, 1864

*. . . Mr Preston and I had a search among his old clothes, and in a trunk in which he keeps them, we found some of them almost eaten up with moths. Some of them however were articles that have been in the house long before I came here. . . . They were terribly destroyed, but that was to be expected. It*

*caused as usual a great outburst of anger, and ugly words. Three pairs of pan-*
*taloons I cut up for carpet rags.*[2] *. . . This day last year I left Mountain View*
*with Aunt Louisa for Gettysburg. Alas! what changes have taken place there*
*since then.*

### Friday, October 7, 1864

*. . . Emily was busy ironing today; consequently Kitty and I were obliged to do*
*the cleaning of the house. As usual Kitty was very slow! Mr Preston and Wil-*
*liam drove to the city this morning, and came out again this evening . . .*
*bringing with them Theodosia. . . . Thede looks thin, but she seems pleased at*
*being with us again. . . .*

### Monday, October 10, 1864

*. . . Emily annoyed me this morning by again indulging in her foolish habit of*
*talking about "going away" and "hunting up a new home." I at once told her,*
*if she continued to talk in this way, she would certainly have to leave me, for I*
*would not be thus annoyed. Since then she has been quiet on the subject. . . .*

### Tuesday, October 11, 1864

*. . . Mr Preston remained home today, and, as I expected when Thede was with*
*us, he has had her pottering with him all day. They have been engaged at the*
*carriage which they had so long on hand, when the girls were here before. I have*
*been pained to perceive the same condition of things going on as I witnessed*
*last winter & summer. Mr Preston has been more unkind to me today than all*
*the time that we were alone. Mr Preston cannot have a second person about*
*him, without showing his "cloven foot"!*

### Wednesday, October 12, 1864

*. . . Kitty is still very ill, the poor thing has certainly taken the smallpox, and I*
*fear will have it badly. Emily has been wonderfully good for the last few days.*

### Sunday, October 16, 1864

*. . . We have spent [the day] alone Thede and I out in the woods this morning*
*and this afternoon at home, having as usual an unpleasant [scene] at the din-*
*ner table. Mr Preston seems nervous and uncomfortable, therefore I overlook*
*it. . . .*

Pleasant Plains
Octr 17th 1864

Rejoice with me, my dear child, in the good fortune that has just befallen me—Behold me the possessor of a sewing machine!—Yes! there it stands in all its beauty and all its usefulness, the very personification of all my wishes with regard to good little household fairies, who are to sit cheerfully working and toiling for me, while I enjoy the delights of a book—a good bracing walk over the green fields, or a hunt in the dear old woods for chestnuts, or the more quiet pleasure of social conversation with a friend. The good kind gentle little sprite . . . made its welcome appearance at Pleasant Plains . . . this beautiful October afternoon. . . .

Thede is almost as much pleased with the little Fairy as I am. You would be amused to see us looking over it, examining all its simple yet wonderful machinery, and touching each different ingenious and useful little adjustment, as though they were the wings of the beautiful creature and must not be handled too roughly! We count on doing wonders. There are to be no more complainings of want of good comfortable clothing—no untidy looking rent in anyone's particulars—no buttons off of shirts or stockings that need darning; our kind little friend will see that all these things are done & done well, and *we* are only to supply the articles with which all is to be done.

You are curious no doubt to learn how this great pleasure came about. . . . On Saturday Papa took Thede and I . . . to attend the Maryland Institute Fair.[3] While there we saw a lady operating on a sewing machine of Wheeler & Wilson's make. Papa was pleased and said to me, "If you want a machine I will give you one." I looked to see if he were in earnest and finding he was so, I at once said, "Indeed I do, Papa," so off we all started to the saloon in Baltimore St. And there I selected one of the best kind with all the modern improvements . . . the key was handed to me and I found myself the owner of a sewing machine. . . .

Thede & I made up a very nice basket of chestnuts & grapes which we carried to the city and Johnny left, *for your friends.* . . .

The "dinkeys" are well.[4] Good night God bless you

Mama. . . .

### Tuesday, October 18, 1864

*. . . Kitty being again about the house I could at once sit down to try my skill with the machine, but alas! not a bit could I move it. Thede and Mr Preston being in the orchard gathering apples, I flew out to tell them of my grievances. Mr Preston came in & then Thede and we all poured over it more than an hour without success. As John was going in this afternoon for Mrs Pent, I concluded*

*to go also and take another lesson, which I did, and was able to operate with-*
*out any trouble. We reached home just at dark and after tea, I sat down again*
*to the machine, but it would not work right; we all tried, but we find we have*
*not skill enough. . . .*

### Wednesday, October 19, 1864

*. . . This morning I again tried the machine but with as little success as before.*
*Mr Preston says he will take it to the city . . . and take a lesson on it himself. I*
*am greatly disappointed but not all discouraged. . . .*

### Thursday, October 20, 1864

*. . . Mr Preston took the Fairy with him and brought it home this afternoon. It*
*seems there was nothing wrong about it only the needle was not quite long*
*enough. It is all right now and I have been operating on it this evening. . . .*

### Saturday, October 22, 1864

*. . . as Mr Preston was obliged to go to the city, Thede concluded to go with*
*him and visit the Yankee and take a lesson on the sewing machine. . . . Thede*
*thought she had learned the art of the machine but on attempting to run it this*
*evening she found it would go wrong. It is very certain one must practice to be-*
*come perfect in any thing.*

Pleasant Plains
Octr 24th 1864

My darling child,
 Papa not going to the city today, I am disappointed at not receiving the letter I feel sure awaits me. . . .
 Thede and I live out of doors. . . . We have such jolly times in the woods
gathering nuts. . . . We were out a day or two since for a few hours, and . . .
we were so laden with chestnuts we concluded to measure them and to our astonishment we found we had *thirteen quarts.* . . .
 I am in hopes to be able to send your winter dresses soon; indeed, but for
my desire to make a Garibaldi body for you on our wonderful "Fairy," you
would have had your box this week. Now this same "Fairy," let me tell you, is
a most wonderful little sprite, subject to all the vagaries, ill humours, per-
verseness, and at times amiability, gentleness, sweet temper and willingness to
oblige that Mortals are, consequently you cannot always count upon her doings. You sit down to spend an hour or two in her company—at first you find

her sweet and clever, working to a charm, making the most perfect little stitches and the most dainty looking sewing imaginable. You are delighted, and in your enthusiasm you call the family around you to see the wonders —when lo! and behold! as the charmed and eager faces around are looking on in great expectations, the little creature begins to flutter about, shaking her wings, stamping her sandaled feet, hissing through her teeth as though a dozen serpents were encased in the box, flinging her band here, and there, pricking about with her little string sharp as a *needle* and frightening all around her by the evident fury she is in. Of course, *we keep our tempers!* getting angry would spoil everything; we try kindly doings, pouring *oil* upon her chafened limbs, loosening her leather girdle, tightening her relaxed muscles, surrounding the delicate nerves, wiping off the fair and polished face, and then letting the ruffled little sprite rest for a while, and then we again approach her; perhaps the troubled spirit is calmed down, and all is right again. You will perceive . . . that either the Fairy is not at all times to be calculated upon, or . . . that we have not yet learned to manage her properly. . . . In the meantime I enclose you a piece of Papa's handiwork. Papa . . . is greatly delighted with the Fairy; he sits by us, watching us operate, and when a screw needs loosening or tightening, a band to be readjusted, he is always willing to give us assistance. We have some of the funniest scenes imaginable; the other night the Fairy was in great glee, flying along with her bright needle and sewing all before her; Papa said let me see whether I can manage it. We fixed a piece of muslin in her hands, resigned our seat to Papa and gave him instructions how to paddle his feet, move the cloth along & *to hold on to* the end of the thread till the machine got well underway. When the wheel began to whirl round and the muslin fly before his eyes with the beautiful sewing upon it, Papa looked up at Thede and I, with the most astonished look and *jumping* to his feet and *holding on* to the end of the thread was the very personification of Phaethon, the ambitious youth, when he seized the reins of the fiery steeds and springing in his father's solar chariot, vainly endeavoured to guide it for a day, but unable to do so, set fire to the world; some such fate might have befallen Papa had Thede and I not been present to render assistance and stop the speed of the Fairy.

Thede & I have jolly times over the machine, indeed in many other ways do we spend gay and pleasant hours. I am *more than pleased* that Thede is with me this winter. She is a dear good girl, and I think I can with great safety calculate on much satisfaction with our pleasant little family. Papa also seems gratified, and has not at any one time expressed the least desire to have the parties changed & the other one brought in her place. With a kind of mutual consent, the name of the objectionable person is scarcely ever mentioned by any of us.[5]

I had like to have forgotten to tell you of the wonderful delight the "little monkeys" take in the sewing machine. Every available chair, stool, table &c &c is converted into a machine by them, and such a shaking of feet, ticking of mouths, sewing of scraps you never saw: it is really too funny. Ruthy is as amusing as ever and Milly grows better every day. She came to me the other day, and kneeling by my side; which by the way is her favorite position, said, "Missy how is Miss May? Missy I dont want Miss May to come home and live here all de time." "Why not Milly" I said. "Oh Missy Miss May love to be at her oder home, and I want Miss May to live all de time where she likes best to be." Now was that not sweetly unselfish?

Kitty has been quite sick, with that ugly poison on her face. She is well now, and poor Mrs Pent has taken her place. The poor old creature seems to have an attack of chills and fevers. . . . Emily is as good as ever, and William and Johnny as usual. . . .

Good night. Your loving Mama. When you write again direct your letter to your Papa *instead* of to me. I think Papa likes to receive letters direct from his little daughter.

### Saturday, October 29, 1864

. . . *I proposed going to the city with Mr Preston this morning to purchase some things for May's box; as usual it was the cause of a terrible outbreak and a painful wounding of my feelings! In a little while, however, Mr Preston repented of his exhibition of temper and became quite amiable. We drove to the city . . . saw Mrs Sanders and the girls, who by the way did not go to St Joseph's. The girls tell me they heard . . . that May was quite indisposed: that, together with May's own letter to me telling of her cough, makes me feel uneasy about the dear child. Mr Preston says he will write to Sr Raphael and if it is necessary either he or I will go up to see her. . . .*

Pleasant Plains Novr 1st 1864

My darling child,

I plead guilty to an apparent negligence in not writing sooner . . . not thinking any opportunity would offer itself to have a letter taken to the city. . . .

I hear with great pain my dear child of your continued suffering with that cough. I shall write today to Sister Raphael, and ask her to tell me exactly what she thinks of your condition. . . . I shall pack up this morning some things in a box which will be sent to you by tomorrow's wagon. . . . Have it opened and see to its contents at once, as it contains a potato pudding, apple pudding and jelly cake, sent you by your Cousin Eudocia . . . which articles came from a grand dinner party she gave last Thursday. . . .

A large party of gentlemen assembled at Eudowood early in the morning and started on a fox hunt. . . . The hunters returned about four o'clock in the afternoon and at five sat down to a magnificent dinner. Papa was there at the dinner and evening entertainment, but of course did not join in the hunt. Thede and I went over in the morning to assist . . . in arranging the table and dressing the fruits and vases with flowers &c &c. Everything was done in Cousin Eudocia's very best style and that, you know, is saying a great deal. The best of the affair was a violent storm of wind and rain came on about seven o'clock in the evening, fortunately not till after everybody was in the house, horses were well stabled and all out of doors work comfortably done up. The whole party were obliged to remain all night, Papa, Thede and myself among the number. Every room and bed were occupied, but in that fine, capacious house all were made comfortable and easy. . . . The next morning we all assembled at the hospitable breakfast table . . . and everyone were loud in their expressions of satisfaction and pleasure. All declaring they had rarely passed twenty-four hours more pleasantly. By eleven o'clock Thede and I, being the last of the party, bade them goodbye . . . Phil coming along with us bearing a basket laden with the "Spoils" of the feast. . . .

I hope you will be pleased with the way I have fixed your brown skirt. Mamie tried the body on, and it fit her beautifully. Your merino dress has only been cleaned and freshly plaited in the skirt. Your Christmas dress of course will come in due time. . . . Thede has picked out a few sweet apples which she thinks particularly good and wishes your opinion about them. To me they always seem slightly bitter, but Thede thinks them the very perfection of an apple. . . .

The sewing maching continues to be a wonder, and "tell it not in Gath, publish it not in the streets of Ascylon"[6] but the truth must be told to you, it is also at times an annoyance; it will though, I am sure (in time), become a comfort and satisfaction when we understand it better. Don't think I am discouraged—I bear up manfully. (I beg pardon) womanly with the breaking of threads, stopping of wheels gathering up of work and the thousand and one little kinks and twists to which sewing machines . . . are subject. . . . Examine your blue Garibaldi; it has some of my handiwork upon it, or rather my sewing machine work. . . .

. . . I hope my dear child this letter will find you restored to your usual good health and free from that ugly cough. Among the little packet of candies you will find a clear look article[7] which is manufactured of Icelan[d] Moss and thought to be beneficial to the breast & throat. I have also sent you a little vial of Aconite and one of Belladonna; take two or three drops of Aconite in half a cup of water and whenever you cough take a teaspoonful. If the Aconite does not relieve, take a few pills of Belladonna night and morning, always making the intervals longer as you feel relieved, and stopping altogether as soon as the cough ceases. . . . If you think I had better come up to you, say so at once and I will come.

Goodbye yours lovingly
Mama.

# 8

# Changes for Kitty

NOVEMBER 1, 1864. THIS DAY should have marked a turning point for one member of the Preston household—Kitty. For on this day all slaves in the nation were finally freed. (The earlier Emancipation Proclamation—of January 1, 1863—had referred only to slaves in the rebel states.) Madge knew the event was significant; for at the top of the page in her diary, she wrote these words: "This is a day memorable in this State. Today the Emancipation of the Slaves takes place!" She did not mention Kitty.

In the sixteen months since the flight of Lizzie and Jim, Madge had found dealing with servants a perpetual concern—from the unskilled Lucy, who had to be taught how to churn; to old Aunt Harriet, who stayed till her limbs got "too painy"; to Mrs. Newberger, coming in by the day for an occasional heavy cleaning. Finally Emily, whose toddler, Ruthy, enchanted the family, came to take over the kitchen and dairy.

During this period Kitty appears in the diary pages sometimes as a responsible and contributing personage, sometimes as a burden and liability. From the time that she joined the family as a child of three, she had been a special responsibility for Madge. The child's insecurity seemed intense, uprooted as she was from whatever environment she had known before. To six-year-old May, Kitty would have seemed at first like a living doll. But May's upbringing of privilege must have intensified for Kitty her own relative disadvantage. In a home where education held the highest value, Kitty had never been taught to read or write. We know her only through oblique glimpses provided in Madge's diary entries and letters. One senses a personality so fragile that the least change within the household is a major threat. But all of her outbursts are defined by others, of course, as signs that she is "bad." Because Preston found her annoying, Madge and May took pains to protect her; yet their solution—to bring her to "goodness" through the ministrations of their church—could put Kitty and themselves in jeopardy through Preston's ridicule.

In Kitty's new state of freedom, her life seems not to have changed at all. While ledger book entries, signed with Emily's X, show she was paid her monthly wages of four dollars, no such entries appear for Kitty. To the Prestons, of course, Kitty was still a child; after all, she was only twelve. Yet more and more responsibilities devolved upon Kitty. As Emily found her way into the stock of whisky, Kitty's name appears in a more positive light: "Thede was obliged to assist Kitty in putting [Emily] to bed tonight."

As Emily's deportment deteriorated, Kitty's seemed to improve. Daily she was bringing fresh flowers for May's pretty altar—an act especially pleasing to the older girl's mother. Madge looked ahead "to a happy change in the now darkened heart." Kitty must have been getting the favorable attention from her mistress which in earlier years would have gone to May. So marked was the change in Kitty's demeanor that Madge made a formal note of it. "It gives me great pleasure to record here the uncommon goodness of Kitty during the entire week." Perhaps she was trying to find her place in this new world of freedom, but no one seems to have shown her how.

---

### Friday, November 4, 1864

. . . *Last night just before going to bed, I was called by Emily to come down to see little Ruthy who was suffering with an attack of croup. I gave her Aconite, and petted her for a few minutes, and told Emily if she got worse in the night to call me. . . .*

### Monday, November 7, 1864

. . . *two letters from May . . . dear child she seems so happy to think I am satisfied with Thede's being with me. Her letters are most excellent indeed. God bless her she is a dear good child. . . . I am sorry to have to record that the little Fairy got out of order today and I was not able to sew with it. I very much fear an important spring is broken.*

### Tuesday, November 8, 1864

*After dinner, [Mr Preston] and John drove down to the polls to vote: On Mr Preston's return he represents things there as alarming in a great degree. Men with pistols intimidating those whom they knew would vote for McClellan. John voted, but Mr Preston did [not]. . . .*

### Wednesday, November 9, 1864

*. . . Poor Emily has not been able to put her clothes out this week, but like a good industrious woman as she is, she has occupied the time whitewashing and cleaning the lower part of the house . . . and things look very nicely indeed.*

### Saturday, November 12, 1864

*. . . I have had a conversation this evening with Emily about her going away, she seems decided on the subject, therefore it is better to let her have a trial. It seems she leaves on Monday—poor little children I wonder what will become of them.*

### Sunday, November 13, 1864

*. . . Thede, Mr Preston and I walked over to the fields to see the fifteen hundred head of cattle Mr Potee has grazing on the field. It is a wonderful sight indeed: I could not help thinking if the Confederates had the chance of running them off it would be a clever thing. . . .*

### Monday, November 14, 1864

*We rose early this morning and were glad to find I should have a fine day for my journey [to visit Mrs Stout in Dover, Delaware]. Emily, poor thing, looked sad when she came up to bid me goodbye. The children of course were gay and happy at the prospect of a change. . . .*

### Tuesday, November 15, 1864

*. . . I have had several talks with Mrs Stout and am surprised at many things she tells me of her sufferings during her married life. In the expose of her private life in court, the people of Dover must have been wonderfully astonished. . . .*

Dover, Del. Nov 16th 1864

My darling child,

I can readily imagine your surprise, on receiving this letter, postmarked as it will be, from Dover. I came down to this place on Monday at the earnest request of my friend Mrs Stout. . . .

I reached Dover on Monday evening . . . and . . . the first person to meet me was Mrs Stout, who had been awaiting my arrival for an hour (the cars having been detained that length of time in consequence of extra trains running with soldiers). . . .

I was grieved to find both the boys suffering with chills & fevers. Henry is now in bed with it. . . . Dear little Emmanuel had his "spell" yesterday, and today is able to be up. I wish my dear May you could see this child. To me, he is the loveliest boy I have ever known—bright, smart, loving, affectionate and intelligent to a wonderful degree. When I began writing, he came to me and said he wanted to write a letter to you also. . . . The dear child has just finished a short German letter to you and unfortunately, while we were still talking & laughing about it, the chill came upon him, and we were obliged to put him to bed with hot bricks to his feet &c &c, and there he lies shivering and shaking. You must bear in mind this boy is only eight years old; he speaks perfectly the English and German languages and is able to speak and understand the French language also, but he is not able to write it well enough to send you a letter. . . .

Goodbye love to my young friend Anna[1]

Yours devotedly
Mama.

### Friday, November 18, 1864

. . . *After a pleasant ride or rather a safe one, as car riding can never be very pleasant, we reached the city at one o'clock. . . . While at the house Mr Macgruder told me a niece of mine was in the city. I waited several hours to see who it was, but as she did not make her appearance, I am inclined to think it was Rose, and not Louisa, as Mr Preston says.*

### Sunday, November 20, 1864

. . . *Not having Emily, of course I was obliged to exert myself in the kitchen, but Kitty was tolerably good, and things went on nicely. . . .*

### Thursday, November 24, 1864

. . . *We had quite a scene today in consequence of a stove difficulty. We have for several years been annoyed by having to use an old stove in our kitchen, which being greatly broken consumed a vast amount of wood and gave great trouble. Mr Preston from some cause or another would not get another and thus we have gone on till at last we could not cook without a fearful annoyance. This morning I rebelled and hence our difficulty. It has ended however in another stove being put in its place, but as we have not tried it yet, I cannot tell how good it will be. Owing to a certain cause we had an accident happen to a lamp, the lamp was broken and the oil spilled over the marble under the stove but fortunately none went on the carpet.*

Pleasant Plains
Novr 25th 1864

My very dear child,

The last letter I addressed to you was dated Dover, Delaware. You will be pleased to learn, I am sure, that my visit there was attended with great pleasure to myself, and I am convinced it gave great comfort and satisfaction to my friend, Mrs Stout, and her two interesting children. . . .

I am sorry, my dear child, to learn you are so badly off for chemises. I ought to have thought that two would not be enough. I have just finished today one for you, which I made altogether on the machine; as it is the *first article* entirely made by the Fairy I feel quite proud of it. . . .

Papa and Thede are sitting by me deeply immersed in a "Game of Chess," and ever and anon, I hear one and the other cry out "Check." Just now they called me to look at a very pretty "Check mate"—pretty, no doubt to the winner, but not so nice to the loser. . . . Remember me to Sister Raphael, Sister Genevieve and Sister Lucia. Good night my child, and may the Angels have you in their holy keeping.

Mama.

### Friday, November 25, 1864

. . . *Mr Preston finished putting up the stove in the kitchen and we think it will do admirably. I feel quite provoked to think that stove has been on the place for years and yet we have been using that old burnt out thing.* . . .

### Saturday, November 26, 1864

. . . *I have been making the body of a dress for Kitty, the dress formerly belonged to Aunt Nancy,*[2] *but she only wore it once, consequently it is almost as good as new.* . . .

### Sunday, November 27, 1864

. . . *I made an unpleasant discovery today. It seems Kitty has been committing depredations on the things in my green chest. I can't tell how far her thievery has gone, but I fear she has not stopped at the one article.*[3]

### Monday, November 28, 1864

. . . *Emily & her children have gone to live at Mr Chew's, consequently I was not able to get her to wash for me today.* . . .

## Tuesday, November 29, 1864

. . . *Thede took a long ride on horseback today and seemed to have enjoyed it greatly. She hunted me up a washwoman in the shape of a little Irish body. She is to come tomorrow. I hope she will please me in the washing.* . . .

## Wednesday, November 30, 1864

*Another delightful day. I rose early to be ready for the woman, who came according to promise and has done a good day's washing. She comes again tomorrow to iron. Thus far I am much pleased with her. I went down to Stansburys' today & employed a man to come up soon and kill a steer for us.* . . .

## Friday, December 2, 1864

. . . *Our little woman came this morning to iron, and after leaving us this evening she returned, having been wandering through the woods an hour, quite bewildered and not able to find her way home. Notwithstanding the bad night, Mr Preston took his lantern and walked home with the poor woman.* . . .

## Saturday, December 3, 1864

. . . *We have had an extremely busy day, and to me an unprofitable one. Thede's churning and taking charge of the dairy is such a farce that I feel as if I should be obliged to stop it. Kitty & Johnny were all the morning fussing about and accomplishing nothing. I operated on the machine a little this afternoon, sewing up the seams of May's body. Mr Preston has been tinkering about all day and like the rest of us has accomplished nothing.* . . .

## Wednesday, December 7, 1864

. . . *The Irish woman came to finish her ironing.* . . . *Thede tells me the woman refused to take the 1.50 cts I left for her demanding 2.50!*

## Thursday, December 8, 1864

. . . *I am fixing up May's red "Garibaldi" for Kitty.* . . .

Pleasant Plains
Decr 8th 1864

I hope my darling child you do not allow yourself to be made unhappy when your letters from home do not come at the time you might reasonably expect them? . . . Sunday, which is my usual letter writing day, happened unfortunately . . . to be also one of our visiting days. Half our friends of the neighbourhood called at different times during the day and evening, thus preventing my accomplishing what I so much desired to do, till it became too late and I too wearied. . . .

Thede says, "tell May my letter will come some of these days." . . . She desires much love to you, as does poor little Kitty, who, when she knew I was writing to you, asked me to give her love to you and to tell you that she was going to wash and iron your new chemises, which I have just finished and which *as a great favour*, I have promised she should "do up" for you. By the way, these same chemises I made on the sewing machine and I think them quite a success. The one marked No. 2 is the last one made. Now I want you to give it your particular attention and tell me if you do not think I have made considerable progress in my work. You must know it generally takes a good long time to learn to operate on a machine (well); for this reason the work done on them is put together entirely different from sewing by hand, and as we were in the country we were obliged to find all out by experience and had not the advantage of being taught. You are right in saying we still look upon the machine as a "novelty" but were it otherwise my dear child, my sewing, on the machine or by hand, or anything else done for you would always be a pleasure. . . .

Papa comes in for his letter. I must leave

Yours lovingly
Mama. . . .

### Sunday, December 11, 1864

. . . *John Kaniff came over this afternoon to see us. He looks the effect I suppose of confinement. Poor little Kitty trigged herself out in her new finery this afternoon and went visiting in the neighbourhood to show it off. Indeed it was worth exhibiting. Mr Preston and I played chess tonight and I beat him the first game and had almost beat him the second when he became annoyed and so frightened me that I let him be victor in the other games.*

### Saturday, December 17, 1864

. . . *Kitty & Johnny cleaned up the kitchen very nicely and have been very good children and to reward them I made a "turn over pie" for their Sunday dinner. . . .*

Pleasant Plains
Decr 18th 1864

My very dear child,

We sent off to you on last Thursday . . . a trunk, of which I should liked to have apprised you before this. . . . Papa wished to send some articles to Mr

Dielman and concluded to make the one box contain the things for both you and Mr Dielman, the trunk to be first sent to Mr Dielman and he to take from it such things as were for him and then he was requested to send the trunk to you. . . .

The dress I am sure you will like. . . . You will understand *why* I trimmed your dress with "green" and be gratified accordingly! . . .[4]

With regard to the little articles you sent for—you may be well assured my child that you could make no request I would not wish to gratify, but my child, that cannot always be. I went to Kelly Hedien & Piel's Bookstore to see about the book of which you wrote, the "Vade Mecum." What do you think they asked for the first copy I laid my hands on?—*twenty dollars*—of course you know that was out of the question—other prayer books ranged from four to twelve dollars—even the lowest of these prices I thought too high in these hard times to indulge in; I therefore contented myself by purchasing you a dozen little pictures with which you can gratify your wish for presents to your young companions in these festive times. I wanted to have your old prayer book bound, but even for that they wanted three dollars and a half! You can judge from these prices how difficult it is to purchase all other articles; consequently we will for the present be obliged to deny ourselves the luxuries of life and be content with just the necessaries and be thankful we are able to have them.

I have sent the shirt you are making for Papa, without having it washed, for this reason; if it had been washed, the edges would have frayed so much as to render the sewing of it very unpleasant and it would be almost impossible for you even to make your sewing look as neat as you would desire it. . . .

. . . Yours devotedly

Mama. . . .


## Thursday, December 22, 1864

. . . *This evening Thede and I played a trick on Mr Preston, by dressing our-selves in his clothes & seating ourselves at the table while he was asleep. We looked very funny and amused Mr Preston and Kitty very much.* . . .


## Saturday, December 24, 1864

. . . *How many varied recollections crowd upon my mind this night, and how my thoughts wander back to days long past and friends of other times. I believe I can almost recall every Christmas Eve for many years; those that give me most pleasure are filled with the memory of my darling child; who when she was younger took such delight in the merry doings of Christmas, and now that she is old has equal happiness in the pious & holy nights of this season. Dear child,*

*I trust she is in the enjoyments of all this blessing tonight and will awaken tomorrow to the full happiness of all our holy religion can give her. God bless her now and ever.*

### Sunday, December 25, 1864

*. . . Thede and [I] gave Kitty and Johnny holiday and set about to get the turkey cooked. Mr Preston according to promise took Kitty & Johnny down to church in the sleigh for ten o'clock Mass. . . . The children say Mr Preston went to church and observed the forms of the church, crossing himself and kneeling with the rest of the congregation. What will May say to this? . . . Kitty & Johnny and the boys from Stansburys' were sliding on the pond, and poor Kitty, as usual being the Jonah of the party, must needs get a fall which almost broke her head and laid her up for the rest of the day and evening. . . .*

### Wednesday, December 28, 1864

*. . . Mr Preston and Thede went to the city this morning to see Louisa McGrew, who left a note at the house saying she was in the city &c &c. On Mr Preston's return tonight he seemed very nervous and before he had been in the house ten minutes he began to scold and in the midst of it, went off to bed!*

### Friday, December 30, 1864

*. . . Mr Preston and Johnny took up the carpet in the parlour today, intending to have it cleaned and taken to the city for the house there. Mr Preston thinks of going to the city for the remainder of the winter; we shall take some few things with us and make ourselves comfortable. I hope it will result favourable for Mr Preston.*

### Saturday, December 31, 1864

*. . . Mr Preston as usual is in an ill humour and has gone to bed, leaving Thede and I alone. Kitty is sitting with us as a favour, it being the last night of the year. . . .*

### Sunday, January 1, 1865

*I was awakened this New Year's morning by a kiss from my husband, — the most acceptable present I could possibly receive. On getting up in a few moments after, the sun rose bright and beautifully, shedding its red glare on the surrounding landscape, which, together with the trees being covered with snow, presented the most glorious sight. It froze very hard during the night and today has been a fine bracing winter's day. This is the first day of the New Year, and happy indeed would I be, if I might take this day and its doings as a prototype of all the rest of the year. Mr Preston and I took a sleighride. . . . It was near dark when we returned. This evening Thede & I played 27 games of backgammon, I winning 16—Mr Preston & I played chess. Mr Preston beat me 2 games, and retired from the third. It is near twelve o'clock. [in the left-hand margin] Mr Preston & Thede cooked the turkey for dinner.*

### Monday, January 2, 1865

*A bright beautiful sunrise this morning, and very cold. . . . Mr Preston drove over to Towsontown this morning in the sleigh and sent it back by Johnny, designing to go to Baltimore when he got through his business. . . . Our little Kitty has come out today in the character of washwoman. She gathered up the soiled clothes herself and took them to the kitchen, where she has washed and boiled the fine clothes and has got the coarse ones ready for the same operation tomorrow morning. Mr Preston did not return this evening, consequently we are alone.*

### Tuesday, January 3, 1865

*Thede slept with me last night and according to arrangement we rose early and set to work to clean our sitting room, as Mr Preston was not here to annoy us; we took the chinking out of the window and door, and made a thorough cleaning, finishing all the operation before Johnny went over to Towsontown for Mr Preston, who together with Johnny reached home about 12 o'clock in good spirits and all right. Kitty got at her washing quite early this morning and by noon, with my assistance in starching, she had them all on the line. They dried this afternoon and she took them in. We are all greatly pleased with this her first effort, and her Master has promised her a hood as a reward. . . .*

### Wednesday, January 4, 1865

*It snowed again last night about two inches, this morning for half an hour "the old woman" picked her geese terribly, she then ceased and the sun shone out clear and bright; a high wind blowing all day has drifted the snow, Mr Preston tells me, as high as the fence on the Hillen Road. . . . Mr Preston Thede & Johnny went to the city this morning in the wagon. Thede remained in tonight with her sister Louisa, who is visiting at Mr Riddlemoser's. . . .*

### Saturday, January 7, 1865

*I have been very busy today pie making—bread baking and butter churning—Kitty and John have worked nicely today and Johnny as a reward goes to church tomorrow and I shall let Kitty visit at Stansburys—Thede and Mr Preston are playing chess.*

### Monday, January 9, 1865

*The sun rose bright & beautiful this morning and we also rose in much better mood. . . . After breakfast Mr Preston packed the stove & buffet in the wagon and he & William drove to the city and while there put the above articles in their places in the parlour. Thede and I have passed an agreeable day working & sewing. I made three linen collars for Johnny on the machine today. . . .*

Pleasant Plains
Jan the 10th 1865

My darling child,

I have put off to the very last moment writing to you today, hoping this terrible weather would brighten up and thereby cheer my spirits a little, but alas! for such pleasant expectations each hour has only darkened the day and now the mist is so dense that we are scarcely able to see a foot from the window —and my gloom is correspondingly dense. I see there is nothing left for me but as little Ruthy used to say—"pitch into it" at once and by talking a little while with you gladden my heart a little. Don't think my baby I am low spirited in consequence of any *real* trouble, just now I ought to be happy, as the weather is my only solitary annoyance—but that to me, is dreadful. The roads you know become so shocking that they confine us or rather *me* to the house almost entirely. Thede is more of a philosopher and braves the storms whenever Papa will take her with him. . . .

Thede is treading away at the dear little sewing machine, and ever and anon apostrophizing over it in the most amusing manner. You can't imagine how much we love the little pet and how much we improve upon it. I look forward to your being as much pleased with it as we are.

By the way I must not forget to tell you of a wonderful achievement of Kitty's last week . . . since Emily left us, we are at times a little troubled to get a good laundress in the neighbourhood. . . . So Kitty came to me the other day, and said "Missy, I think if you will let me try, I can do it better than the last woman that did it." "Well," I replied, "Kitty you may make the effort"—and so she did and I assure you she did it very nicely indeed. She washed and ironed four shirts for Papa, together with the other articles of an ordinary wash—now don't you think that was doing very well? . . .

Kitty . . . desires me to give her "respects to Miss May" and please Missy tell Miss May I did the washing and ironing last week. Johnny also sends his respects. Can't you send Kitty an Agnus Dei in one of your letters, she would be so much pleased. Good bye, love to all my dear girls. Yours lovingly

Mama

## Wednesday, January 11, 1865

. . . Mr Preston & William went to the city with another load of furniture and on their return Mr Preston brought out the parlour stove with the intention of taking the coal stove in as we shall like it better than wood. Kitty finished her washing today and got her clothes nicely dried. . . .

## Friday, January 13, 1865

Thede and I slept together last night, and awakened this morning refreshed and gratified with each other for a bed-fellow—As Mr Preston was not at home, we resolved to make the most of his absence. Thede gathered her clothes together and she and Kitty washed them, but being so many they were not able to hang them all but they were left the remainder of the day in soak water. I have been engaged for an hour or two, looking after a poor old sheep and a little young lamb—which through the neglect of the boy William was brought to death's door and while I was working with it, passed through its portals and will be seen no more. Mr Preston and Johnny returned about 6 o'clock. . . . Mr Preston brought me Sr Raphael's report of May's doings during the past session. Dear child she has gone far beyond my most sanguine expectations, and Sister in a letter attached to the report, tells me they have all been very much gratified by May's conduct & attention to her studies. Mr Preston brings the news of Rose being at Mr Herant [handwriting unclear] in Baltimore.

## Saturday, January 14, 1865

It was dull & cloudy this morning, with a slight sprinkle of rain, about 8 o'clock, at which hour Mr Preston, Thede and William left for the city. Thede going in to see Rose, and Mr Preston doing the same! sub rose! Johnny & Kitty have been very good children today. About 6 o'clock this evening the wagon returned, bringing Mr Preston, Thede & Rose as I had feared! Rose looks badly—Thede is suffering with headache! and Mr Preston is very nervous! tonight. . . .

## Wednesday, January 18, 1865

*. . . Thede, Rose and I have passed a pleasant day. We, teaching Rose to oper-ate the sewing machine and she giving us lessons in telegraphing.⁵ This eve-ning we have amused ourselves with chess and backgammon—I am disap-pointed tonight by not receiving a letter from May as I had hoped—Kitty commenced her week's wash today but of course did not finish it. . . .*

## Thursday, January 19, 1865

*. . . Mr Preston and William drove again to the city this morning and while there succeeded in putting up the stove and on making a fire in it, was pleased to find it operated admirably. The girls and myself have spent another pleasant day. When Mr Preston returned this evening he brought with him a "Key for Telegraphing," which he had made after Rose's model. Thede had a terrible accident this evening with the molasses syrup.*

Pleasant Plains
January 20th, 1865

My dear child,

Each day that Papa has gone to the city this week, I have looked for a letter from you, but thus far, each day has brought its disappointment. . . .

We have had quite a pleasant week at home. Rose came down to the city to make a visit at the Alexanders'. At the conclusion of her visit there, of course she came out to see us and remain a day or two. I found her so very much im-proved and evidently anxious to please me in all she did that I invited her to remain longer with us. She made the week out, which was all the time she had and left us yesterday. You will be pleased to hear this, and also pleased to know that I have had none of my former troubles with *any one*, everything in that respect is going on just as I could wish. . . . Love to all my dear children and love to all the dear Sisters. Papa, Thede, and Rose are in the city so I can-not send messages from them, but I know they would have a great deal of love for you. Kitty and Johnny always wish to be remembered. Yours lovingly,

Mama

## Friday, January 20, 1865

*Early this morning the weather was intensely cold, but as the sun shone out it moderated and became a fine pleasant winter's day. Mr Preston, Thede, Rose and William left P. Plains after being well packed in the wagon about 11 o'clock. . . . I busied myself in "cleaning up" and in the afternoon, Kitty and I ironed the clothes; this evening I had a fire made in "our" room up stairs, and Johnny and Kitty came up with me and assisted me to pack the clothing I was to take to the city and such as I would leave at home. . . .*

St. Joseph's. Jan 19th/ 65

My dear little Kitty,

You know I have for a long time promised to write to you when I should hear a good account of you, and as Mama's last letter contained so much that was to your credit, I thought I could not do better than fulfill my promise. . . .

I was delighted to hear that you and Johnny accompanied dear Papa to Mass on Christmas morning; nothing could have given me more pleasure. That morning when I went to Holy Communion, I made as one of my particular wishes an intention that some of my family might go to Mass on that Holy day, and dear Mama's letter, soon after, assured me that there is nothing like prayer and faith.

Now that you have accomplished so much (for you know, to hear Mass is a very great blessing), I hope soon to hear that you have been able to go to confession, as you so much desired. Believe me, my dear little child, I shall pray most earnestly for you; indeed I think I seldom make a petition without your being included in some way.

If you see Father Foley you must tell him all you think I would like to say were I able to visit him myself, particularly that I hope he will make a very good little girl of you. . . .

Now my dear Kitty hoping that you will be the *very best* of children I remain

Your most affectionate
Mother.[6]

### Monday, January 23, 1865

*. . . Mr Preston remained home today superintending the packing of the mirror which is to go to town tomorrow. I have been operating the sewing machine, and it did admirably. I cut the skirt of a . . . frock for Kitty which I should like to make before we go to the city. This evening Mr Preston and I played chess; we played 3 games and Mr Preston won all of them, after which we had one of our "interesting confabs"!*

### Tuesday, January 24, 1865

*. . . Mr Preston and William drove to the city this morning taking with them one of the large glasses and the large picture of the "Mother & Child." The*

*heavy sleet on the ground made it very unpleasant for them, but William re-*
*turned about 3 o'clock bringing word that all things went safely. Mr Preston*
*remained in the city—and will I hope stay there now till the house is fixed. . . .*
*Kitty has provoked me greatly today by her bad doings.*

### Wednesday, January 25, 1865

*As Mr Preston was in the city last night Thede and I slept together; on awaking*
*this morning we were pleased to find the weather clear. . . . It is however in-*
*tensely cold, perhaps the coldest day of the winter thus far. William & Thede*
*left P. Plains about eleven o'clock this morning for the city—Thede will re-*
*main in, perhaps, till we go "for good!" William came home this evening and*
*will go again in the morning, taking with him wood, an article which it seems*
*they are entirely without in town. Mr Preston wrote me a letter quite like olden*
*times. I am all alone tonight, no one in the house but Kitty & myself—Kitty*
*by the way, has been a very good girl today.*

### Thursday, January 26, 1865

*Still intensely cold weather. The men, according to orders, rose early this morn-*
*ing and at once went for wood, which they sawed & split and packed in the*
*wagon before they ate their breakfast. I wrote a long letter to Mr Preston, and*
*William started for the city about 9 o'clock. Shortly after Willie Stansbury &*
*his mother drove up in the sleigh, she remaining with me while Willie took the*
*horse to be "roughed."⁷ . . . Kitty put out her washing this morning without*
*my assistance. We had a fearful fright this evening. The horses started off at the*
*gate while Wm was out of the wagon, and came up to the house, round the cir-*
*cle & past the door in a fearful gallup. Brave little Johnny seized hold of the*
*back of the wagon and held on while they were running; the horses eyed around*
*to go to their stable, but they became entangled in the wood and Johnny seized*
*them by their bridles and held them till William came to his assistance. The*
*night being quite dark, the roads terribly slippery and the weather so fearfully*
*cold, I think it was the most wonderful escape I ever heard of. Neither horses*
*nor wagon was in the least injured. Mr Preston wrote me a very pleasant letter*
*in reply to mine of this morning.*

> Pleasant Plains [n.d.]
> "Peep o' the Morn"

Dear Mr Preston
    It was almost six o'clock yesterday evening when William reached P. Plains
too late entirely to get wood. I therefore made arrangements with "all hands"

to be up early this morning and at once bring a load and prepare it for you . . . before breakfast. The boys cheerfully assented and this morning long before the usual time, the old bell rung out a merry peal to call them to their work. Kitty and I, not disposed to be behind in the good work, rose too, and here I am while the "Stars are in the quiet skies" (where do they go when they are *not* in the sky?) writing you an account of our industrious proceedings. The boys have already gone for the wood and I listen momentarily for the sound of the wheels over the frozen ground telling me with the mournful plaint of an ice harp (not Irish, remember) that they come laden with the crooked and broken limbs of some dear giant of the forest.

If William should be later than you expect him, don't scold, for thus far he has done as well as you could desire. I have sent you a bag of shavings and chips, which judging you by myself, will be acceptable this cold morning and hasten up the burning of that fire you must so much stand in need of. Bad management! Bad management!—Wood should have been there *the very first thing taken to town*!!! Perhaps you are not aware of the fact that the weather is intensely cold—fearing you might be in ignorance of information so necessary to know, I have thought it right & proper to tell you. Again let me impress it upon your mind & *feelings* too—as Mollie did about the pudding—the weather is awfully cold! All joking aside, I really did feel very much for you last night and poor Thede too, who by the way neglected to take her brick out of the wagon—Well if people will be so forgetful and so negligent they must suffer. Remember you can't always have your Aunty with you, to see to your comforts.____

Just as I finished the last sentence, Kitty brought the breakfast in and insisted on my "stopping the writing" and taking my breakfast while it was hot —said breakfast, consisting of nice *thick* corn cakes, cold butter and molasses—hot tea—and (but don't mention it to Johnny the dairy maid) rich cream—making a breakfast a queen might envy, and taken in state too, all alone by myself. Kitty, standing in solemn dignity by my chair, going through all the ceremony of waiting on the table! waiting forsooth—"Misses I can stay up and wait on you I have baked all the cakes." Well there she stood, talking more than waiting—I rather think it was for *that* she desired to stay —"I *guess* Master wonders what we are doing this morning" "Yes Kitty. Your Master I *reckon* thinks we indulge ourselves in bed when he is not here" —Then a broad grin came over her darkey face and she muttered—"Master don't know how much better we get along when we are alone—Master keeps everybody waiting most of the time on him!"—I found Kitty's penetration was equal to my own, as she had made the same discovery I had, long long ago—

Tell Thede, as yesterday was washing day I was too busy to attend to any of the extraies (is that a correct plural of that word?) consequently have nothing nice to send her—will try however to have something when the wagon goes in again. . . .

I send you the whiskey[8] and would have packed up some preserves &c &c at the same time, but the wood I guess is heavy enough.

Love to Thede, Mrs Beer &c &c &c

Madge. . . .

# 9

## A Stormy Winter in Town

THESE LAST FEW WEEKS had been very happy. The bantering tone of Madge's last letter suggests how truly relieved she felt. Rose's return to Pleasant Plains, so threatening a prospect for Madge, had turned out to be no threat at all. Somehow, from the moment the sewing machine came into their lives, new pleasures had seemed to dominate family life—much laughing, excitement, mutual explorations of all the machine could be put to do. Even Preston had shared in learning to master this new device. Then close evenings of backgammon and chess filled the dark hours, as winter hemmed them in. Even the deplorable kitchen range, an annoyance for years to those who dealt with the cooking, had been replaced.

As January ended, Madge was looking forward to spending the rest of the winter in town. No longer would she be cut off by weather from all her friends. Preston was also resuming his law practice. Why he had stopped and for how long a period are not explained in the family papers; but Madge found his decision a cause for optimism.

Since January 24, Preston had been spending most of his time at the house in town, leaving Madge with responsibility for packing up whatever household furniture and goods they would need for comfortable living in the city. Preston seems rather good-humoredly to have set up housekeeping in Baltimore—even without a good wood supply to keep fires blazing through the icy January days. Thus the hauling of wood to Baltimore became the highest priority; for a while it had to take precedence over transporting the household items that would be needed there by the family. But at last the sewing machine—Madge's "good Fairy"—was sent for; and then the whole family moved off to join Preston in the city: Madge, Thede, and the faithful Kitty. Only John, the orphan boy, was left at the farm home at Pleasant Plains to look after the dairy and feed the animals.

Pleasant Plains
January 26th, 1865

So the little girl has come to the wise conclusion that Mama has forgotten her, because she happened to be one whole day behind the time of writing! . . . I plead guilty my child to a paucity of letters of late, but not to your accusation of forgetfulness, as neither a day nor hour passes without your dear little self being present to my mind. . . . By the way . . . if you could have seen poor little Kitty, when I handed your letter to her and told her you had actually written to her from St Joseph's, you would have felt yourself amply repaid for any trouble you might have had in the writing of it. I read Kitty's letter to her and she was more than delighted; she asked me to put a string to her Agnus Dei at once, that she might put it on. Tonight she came to me and said —"Missy, in your letter to Miss May please tell her I have said two 'Our Fathers' every day since she sent me the Agnus Dei." Again she said—"Don't you think Missy, Miss May will be pleased to know I have said that prayer?" . . . Love to my dear children from your devoted Mama

### Tuesday, January 31, 1865

*The weather still continues mild. . . . Tomorrow being the day fixed by Mr Preston to resume his professional duties in the city, I should be very sorry if the weather should be bad. I shall feel it a bad omen, and I am so anxious that Mr Preston should be successful. Mr Preston has not returned tonight. Kitty and I together have ironed the clothes we had washed yesterday and they look very well. I have repaired a pair of corsets with the sewing machine and they look beautifully.*

### Wednesday, February 1, 1865

*. . . It has thawed considerably today, consequently the roads & the walking round the house is very bad. I sent for Mrs Newberger to come and wash a large linen rug and some few other articles, which she did very nicely. Kitty has been uncommonly good today and the consequence is I have been able to do a good day's work myself. I have remodeled an old frock of Kitty's and made it almost as good as new. About 4 o'clock this afternoon Mr Preston came home, having come out to Towsontown & walked over. This being Mr Preston's day of commencing anew his professional duties, we were quite glad to see him, and to hear him tell of the clients who had come to see him today. Another thing he told me has made me quite sad. Our friends the Sanders have broken up their establishment in Baltimore and have gone to New York to live. . . . I regret it very much as, of all my acquaintances, I prefer them most!*

Pleasant Plains
Feby 9th 1865

My very sweet child,

I was so fortunate as to receive your dear favour of the 4th immediately after it reached the Baltimore p. office. . . . I believe your letters are to me the greatest comfort and pleasure of my life. . . .

I have been intending for some time past to tell you of a juvenile addition we have to our family and whose affectionate and playful doings about the house contribute hourly to our pleasure & amusement. Our little pet . . . by her love and pleasant ways, amply repays us for our trouble or responsibility we have taken. Some three or four weeks ago, Papa, Thede and Rose had gone down to Glen May to take a survey of the premises after the Roders left there . . . and on approaching the house, they heard a plaintive little moan as of something in distress, which upon searching out, they soon found proceeded from this poor little thing, whether left there designedly by the Roders, or put there by some unfeeling person in hopes that it would be discovered by some member of the family and taken care of, at that time we were not able to tell. . . . It was at once picked up and brought to the house, where warm and nourishing food and a comfortable bed were at once provided and we soon had the pleasure of seeing our little foundling, or rather our Eureka, open its eyes, stretch its white and beautiful limbs, spread out its soft arm as if to embrace and thank us for our kindness, and look its love and then fall off to sleep again. And thus the little thing has been living with us since that time, and now it only depends upon you to say whether it shall for the future be considered as one of the household, share in its comforts, pleasures and prosperities, or be given to some other person who will adopt it and do for it as Papa, Thede and I are willing to do, if we have your consent.

Reflect on the above and when you write again, let me know your decision on this important subject, as we are anxious to settle the position Puss is to occupy about the house!!! . . .

Kitty desires her "best respects to Miss May's." Poor Kitty is like the little girl at St. Joseph's that was crowned for "trying to be good"—we praise her all we can, for "trying to be good"! . . .

Yours lovingly,
Mama

## Sunday, February 12, 1865

*On awaking this morning we were horrified to find it snowing quite fast. And it continued the entire day with a high wind blowing and drifting the snow in a blinding manner. Mr Preston was obliged to go to the city this afternoon; William & Johnny drove him to the toll gate in the sleigh and he walked in to his office. The boys were nearly perished with the cold when they reached home. This we all think is the most unpleasant storm of the winter. I begin to have some superstitious dread of going to the city; every time I set a day to go in, something occurs to prevent our doing so. This evening I brought Johnny up in our room and made him read for me. I am greatly surprised to find he is able to read as well as he does. I have told him he must come constantly till I go away. . . .*

Baltimore 15 Feb 1865
12-30 P.M.

Dear Madge,

The boys have just arrived in the most miserable condition that can be conceived of—wet to the skin and covered with ice and snow. In addition they have to carry the wood, which is equally wet, in by the armful—no trifling job—When I look at them, their horse, and their load, my heart trembles. It is really paying too dear for the whistle. I have taken off Johnny's coat and cloak, made a large fire and shall attempt to dry them. The poor boy however in the meantime has to stand in the wagon in the freezing rain and hand out the wet wood to John, who carries it in. Hereafter a sounder judgment must be used in relation to the weather and to journey made from P. P. to Balto. unless the weather is propitious. I have directed Mrs Beer to make some good warm coffee &c &c to give the boys as soon as they get through the carrying in of the wood. To make the scene more affecting, just as the boys got to the door, 1000 unhappy half-clad, weary, haggard looking men (southern prisoners) were marching under escort of squads of well-fed, well-clad government soldiers through our street. It was certainly a most distressing sight. Painful in the extreme to see under civilization poor human nature thus reduced. The men, scarcely able to drag themselves along, had to carry in addition the weight of sleet and frozen rain attached to their battered garments—and this is called Christian life under what is called the refinement and blessing of civilization!!!

As soon as the boys get home, see that Wm instantly turns out to give them all the aid in his power. Cold and wet, they will be but poorly able to give the horses the care they will really need. . . .

Say to William as soon as you call him that I told you to say "All right"; he will understand.

Affect. W. P. P.

St. Joseph's. Feb. 13th/ 65

My dear Mama,

How shall I begin to tell you the state of excitement your last letter has thrown me into! Did you mean that we have a real child at Pleasant Plains? I could not tell from the way your letter was worded whether you were talking about a human being or a cat, and Sr. Raphael has not been able to decide either. If it is a *real child by all means take it.* You know that for many years I have prayed earnestly for a little Sister, and lately I began to despair of a Sister, and have begged our Lord for some person's child when I should be old enough to take care of one. May I hope that my prayer has been heard. Write immediately so that I may know for certain. If you have no objections I would like her to occupy the place of my sister at our house. As you have so far honored me by asking my consent I hope that you will answer this request, and also one of more importance, which is that it may be *baptized.* I want you to have it called *Maud* you know that is my favorite name. On Friday I will write more on this subject at present I have but a few moments, and then I do not know whether I am talking about a person or an animal. Oh! Mama please never write that way again, be sure and let me know what you mean.

Forgive all mistakes as I am not exactly able to write a sensible letter since the news yours contained.

Love to dear Papa and Thede.
Please write soon.
Yours lovingly
May.

### Wednesday, February 15, 1865

*Let me record this as one of the most unhappy & miserable days of my life, yet nothing of importance has occurred to me neither have I done anything to seriously regret. It is the contemplation of the wretchedness around me and the terrible state of the weather that has affected me so. On awaking this morning I found it was hailing, yet as the boys had made arrangements to go to the city with wood, I sent them off. The clouds looked as if they would break away and the weather become clear every minute. After they had started, it began to rain, to hail, to snow and to blow, such a day one rarely sees. I suffered greatly on account of the poor boys. But thank fortune, they came home about ½ past 4 singing and shouting, and in good spirits. I had a good supper prepared for them and they were soon made comfortable. Mr Preston sent me a letter from May, in which the dear child seems to be greatly excited at the idea of my having adopted a little child, as I foolishly joked in my last letter about the finding of a little cat. I am too much distressed to have caused her so much anxiety. I am suffering dreadfully with headache from the excitement of the day.*

Pleasant Plains
Feby 16th, 1865

My dear, generous, noble hearted little child! How can I ever forgive myself for the pain and anxiety my thoughtless folly has caused you! In my foolish desire of writing something to please and amuse you I forgot, that that very "something" might produce a contrary effect, as witness the very thing I did write—I thought, my dear child, the last sentence in my silly remarks about our little foundling would have explained to you that it was a poor little cat the Roders had left at Glen May and we had brought it home to cheer us with its gambols.

I cannot tell you how much your letter has distressed me. I hope however, long before this reaches you, your Father's letter explaining my nonsense will have been received and your mind set at rest. It is very generous and unselfish in you to be willing to share the comforts of your home and the affections of your parents with another, and your goodness *almost* tempts me to wish our foundling was indeed a real child. . . .

. . . Goodbye, yours lovingly

Mama

Baltimore, Feby /65

My dear child,

On Saturday the 18th we made our long contemplated move to the city. We had hoped to have been here long before, but the many storms of this most stormy winter, the intense cold, and the bad roads till that time prevented us; at last human patience could endure it no longer, and I resolved to brave anything and everything, and come on the above day—as if Our Blessed Mother smiled upon the undertaking, after a snowy night, the sun rose bright and beautiful on the morning of our departure from P. Plains and in a short time its warm and springlike rays had melted the snow of the previous night, and our drive to the city was really delightful. . . .

And now I suppose you would like to know what we are doing in the city. Well, I believe we are tired of the country and have come to rest ourselves for a while in the city. We furnished our parlour, a bedroom for ourselves, one for Theodosia and one for Kitty. Our cooking and washing is to be done by Mrs Beer and her servant, so you see we are pleasantly and comfortably situated. . . .[1]

## Sunday, February 19, 1865

*Slept till ½ past 7 this morning and then rose, and by the time I was dressed it was too late for early Mass. We rose and took our first breakfast under our new housekeeping—pleasantly and comfortably. After breakfast, Sunday as it was, Thede and I fixed up our cupboards, buffets &c &c and got things to our satisfaction; we have not been out today but have been quiet & content at home. Poor Kitty wanders about, trying to be pleased, but she does not seem very satisfied.*

## Monday, February 20, 1865

*It was clear and pleasant today but it froze quite hard during the night and thawed all day. I rose early this morning and went to church, thinking it right and proper to ask God's blessing upon our present undertaking, I heard the Bishop [say] Mass and returned home happy and hopeful, but Alas! alas! for all my good intentions and pleasant anticipations. I returned home to find Mr Preston in one of his most shocking tempers, which in a short time became so violent as to be frightful, after heaping all the abuse upon me possible, he cooled down and wished me to forgive. I treated him as he deserved, which was forgiving but cool! Thus we have been all day. This evening he dressed himself nicely and went to a dinner party at Mr. Abell's and returned after 12 o'clock, all right, but unforgiving to me. . . .*

## Thursday, February 23, 1865

*On awaking this morning I was sorry to find it raining and it has continued all day, at times raining quite hard. As Mr Preston was annoyed by our not getting up this morning as early as he desired us, we were greeted by another of those "scenes" to which I have of late been so much accustomed; the scene of this morning was one of peculiar violence, poor Kitty being the victim. The entire day has passed in the same manner, till I have almost made up my mind to re-port Mr Preston as insane, and a dangerous person to be living with, either that or to leave the house!*

---

That evening Madge began a letter to May which, in a continuation the next afternoon, she says she broke off in order to give a full account of a visit with Sister Leopoldine. None of the section written on the twenty-third survives except the following sentence: "This winter has been a trying and wearisome one, without good servants; consequently I look forward to a few months rest in the city with a wonderful degree of satisfaction." The passage must have been composed between Preston's early-morning rage and Madge's diary comment on his probable insanity.

Her very extended account of the visit to the Sisters in the next day's installment contains also a passage on the war and the fall of Charleston. Then, thinking of some of May's companions at the school, Madge wrote: "Alas! Alas! for our dear Southern friends. Don't mention this to the Southern girls if they do not know it already."

Whether the war news, disappointing to Southern sympathizers, compounded Preston's violence we do not know, though doubtless resumption of his law practice in some way increased his stress. The family were too often hostages to his angry outbursts; and Madge's long visit with the Sisters (though

she does not say so to May) was an effort to seek shelter from emotional storms
at home. On the same afternoon she tried also to call on Father Elder but did
not find him in. No hint of these pressures occurs, of course, in the letter to
May, except a brief postscript disguising the problem: "I am very nervous from
walking please excuse the writing."

### Friday, February 24, 1865

*Clear but somewhat colder than yesterday—Of course our breakfast table
must again be a scene of contention and anger. After the morning duties were
over, I started out to make a visit to Father Elder, but unfortunately he was
not to be seen. From there I went in the car to St. John's Academy,² to see Sister Leopoldine; there I was greeted with great kindness as the mother of little
May, whom the Sisters said was as well known there as one of their own children. On my return, I finished a long letter to May telling her all about my
visit &c &c. During this afternoon we have all been as unhappy as well could
be owing to Mr Preston's humour which unfortunately for me, fulminated this
evening and ended by Mr Preston striking [me] to the floor almost senseless. I
record this fact, that it may, if necessary, be known to others in the future.
Theodosia was sitting by, but of course said nothing!*

### Saturday, February 25, 1865

*I had some fears for my personal safety last night but notwithstanding, I slept
in the bed with Mr Preston. . . . Things have gone on a little better tonight
than usual. Mr Preston seems to be suffering with headache, but somewhat
amiable. . . .*

### Sunday, February 26, 1865

*. . . After breakfast, Mr Preston left us to go by the cars to Towsontown & from
thence to P. Plains. Kitty dressed herself very nicely and went up the cathedral
to High Mass, returned after one o'clock greatly pleased with the church. This
afternoon she went again to the cathedral to Vespers and after Vespers the poor
child went to Father Foley's confessional and went to Confession—on her return she was very much affected and told me where she had been. The Grace of
God must have been strong within her to have enabled her to have done so
painful a thing. How she accomplished an act about which she knew so little
and in which she had never been instructed I cannot imagine. I shall try & see
Mr Foley and explain all things to him. . . .*

**Monday, February 27, 1865**

. . . *Mr Preston & William reached here this morning, about 11 o'clock with a wagonload of things from the country. It was not long after he came upstairs before we had another scene almost as violent as some of last week. . . . During the afternoon, I went up to see Father Elder, had a long conversation with him, which made me feel much happier than I have done for sometime past. On reaching home, I found three letters awaiting me. . . . —one from Mrs Stout. The letter announcing the death of Mr Stout.³ Mr Preston intends sending Thede down to Dover tomorrow to see Mrs Stout as I have declined to go.*

**Tuesday, February 28, 1865**

. . . *Thede left here for Dover this morning and I wrote a letter to Mrs Stout by her. John & William brough[t] in a load of wood today. Kitty went to Confession again this afternoon and this evening for a wonder has been spent quietly.*

**Wednesday, March 1, 1865**

. . . *This evening I made up a flannel petticoat on the machine and it looks beautifully. This is the first of my sewing in the city and the machine worked like a charm. We had quite a fright about Kitty—before going to bed Mr Preston went over to see if she was in bed, but she was not to be found about the house. After a while she came in the front door, having been out to see some negroes in the neighbourhood.*

---

Ten days elapsed before Madge wrote again to May. May's godmother had come to the city for a few days' visit, and she and Madge had gone shopping together. Madge had also demonstrated the wonders of the sewing machine by doing up a pile of mending for the old lady. During most of this time Preston had been at Pleasant Plains.

Baltimore, March 6th [1865]

My dear child,

I have no doubt you thought when Mama came to the city, she would have so much time . . . but alas! . . . it seems to me—thus far—I have been so constantly engaged that letter writing has been almost out of the question. . . .

At least Wednesday was the beginning of Lent. . . . I made a visit to Father

Elder on Saturday afternoon, as I wished to begin the holy season of Lent with the right dispositions. I then went to Father Foley's early Mass at the cathedral on Sunday morning. After which—I walked over to Sister Leopoldine's and went to High Mass at ½ past 10 o'clock at St. John's Church, and much to my surprise and very greatly to my satisfaction, I had the pleasure of seeing the Archbishop & Mr Foley at the Sisters' and also of hearing the Archbishop open the Jubilee by one of his beautiful sermons. So you see I was very much favoured. Sister Leopoldine and the other Sisters were well and gave me a kind invitation to come up at any time and attend church with them. You will perceive from the enclosed paper a mission is to be given at St. John's Church this present week. The Rev'd Fathers whose names are mentioned in the paper said Mass. You can't imagine how strange it looked to see them walking about the sanctuary in sandals—and *no* stockings on their feet—now—not to say anything disrespectful of the good Fathers, who indeed looked very holy—their feet did not look any too nice. . . .

Papa spent yesterday at Pleasant Plains and says . . . poor little Johnny . . . misses us very much. Kitty has been up each Sunday since we have been in town to church at the cathedral and seems to like going very much. Thede says—Give my love to May, and Mrs Beer says the same thing. Poor Louis is still confined in Fort McHenry, though there seems to be a prospect of the prisoners finally being released. . . .

Goodnight my dear child. Yours lovingly

Mama.

---

The Jubilee of which Madge wrote drew many people from the countryside, including Aunt Christie Monk, an old friend from Eudowood. She stayed for several days with the Prestons in town in order to attend the services. Perhaps because of the presence of such visitors, Preston's rages had been suppressed. But he found other ways to nettle Madge. Poor little Kitty, trying literally to carry out May's wish that she go to Confession, was now slipping out regularly to go to church. She thus became a target for Preston's ridicule.

But so also did the absent May. In a letter of March 3 May had sent a copy of original verse, "Autumn Gifts to Our Mother," a fairly satisfactory piece of amateur schoolgirl verse. In a better mood Preston would doubtless have cherished it. Now he seems to have found fault with it, using his daughter's effort at verse as a vehicle to hurt and disappoint his wife. Madge's letter acknowledging the poem conspicuously omits Preston's name from the list of the author's admirers, though the absence of his name is wholly disguised in the tactful phrase, "we all read it with pleasure."

But on the issue of Kitty's religious commitment, Madge had to abandon her secret conspiracy with May when Father Foley also ridiculed the black girl's attempt at piety. Too much was at stake for Madge herself in continuing her good relations with her church. Throughout the whole period of the Jubilee, a two-week mission held by the Redemptionist Fathers, Madge found spiritual confirmation and emotional support in the words of the sermons and the shared attendance with Catholic friends. Her letters and diary pages are full of it.

### Wednesday, March 8, 1865

. . . *I had another painful conversation with Mr Preston this morning about my dear child, and the simple little piece of poetry she wrote.*

### Friday, March 10, 1865

. . . *Mr Preston has been in his office as usual and Thede & I have had great satisfaction with the machine. I am engaged making the bosoms of shirts for Mr Preston. . . . a large number of Confederate prisoners passed and Thede Christie & myself went out to meet them in the street. . . .*

### Sunday, March 12, 1865

*Did not rise early enough to go to early Mass, but we all assembled to a good comfortable breakfast, after which Christie and myself dressed for church & Mr Grindle & Eliza called for us and took us to High Mass at the cathedral. . . . I . . . then returned home. I found Thede and Mr Preston just finishing a letter to Mr Owens. In the afternoon I again went to the cathedral to Vespers, and did not return till 6 o'clock. Thede and Mr Preston had evidently spent the time of my absence together; during the whole of the evening neither of them have mentioned anything about their doings in the afternoon. Rather suspicious! . . .*

Baltimore March 12th 1865

My darling child

I feel certain that everything of interest to me is equally so to you; I come then at once to tell you how happy I have been today and how bright my prospects are for the same kind of enjoyment during the present holy season. Do you know, my child, that I take great pleasure in believing these blessings come to me through your innocent & pious prayers, else, how should it happen that after long and weary years in the country, away from church and all its blessed privileges, I should, *just now*, at this most wonderful time, when the church, by her Jubilee, is pouring its abundant graces upon her youthful followers. Does it not seem very strange to you that I should be in the city now?—with the opportunities of going to church daily? . . . Thus today I attended the cathedral at High Mass in company with Aunt Christie, and Mary Eliza Grindle—both of whom ought to be Catholics—and whom I shall try hard to bring to their duties during this holy season. I say *I* shall try—for the good Father who opened the "mission" at the cathedral this morning said, we "Each and all had a 'mission' to fill as well as he had—if we knew a friend luke-warm or astray plead with them to come to the fountain while it was overflowing"; on coming out of the church, I told the girls I would take it upon myself to see they attended church very often during the time of the mission; whereupon Mr Grindle who was with us—said—"I wish you would, Mrs Preston, it would give me so much pleasure to have Millie a good Catholic." It seems Mr Grindle is a most pious excellent, practical Catholic, but unfortunately, his wife is not; consequently the children have been allowed to grow up without "belonging" to any church. . . .

This afternoon the girls and myself again attended at the cathedral, at short Vespers when we heard another of the good Father's explanatory of the mission, &c &c. . . . How much I wish you could be with me now, though I know you also enjoy the happiness of religious privileges. Still it would be a great consolation and pleasure to attend and join in this mission together —but though separated, we can be and are united in spirit! . . .

I have so many things to say to you that I scarcely know where to begin particularly when they are of an unpleasant character—for instance in reply to your remarks about poor little Kitty. I am greatly exercised about the poor creature; it is no use to attempt anything like religious instruction with her. —I will relate a circumstance and then you will understand me. Two Sundays ago I sent her to High Mass at the cathedral—in the afternoon she stole out of the house and did not come home till dark—when she came to my room her face was bathed in tears and she had evidently been very much excited. "Missus," she said, "I have been to confession to Father Foley"—"Why Kitty!" "I could not help it, I felt so anxious I finished in the confessional and told Father Foley who I was *and then went to Confession!*" I was as you may suppose greatly delighted—talked to her as best I could—soothed her excited feelings and then put her quietly to bed. Fortunately your father was in the country and I had no *ridicule* to contend with. I intended to see Father Foley and talk to him about her, but repeated efforts to that effect failed, and I did not see him till the Sunday I saw him at the Sisters of which I told you. In a few words he laughingly told me of Kitty's visit. Of course I understood there has been nothing of a Confession. In the meantime I had been sending her to church, &c &c—but to no purpose—not any of her former bad habits were corrected—indeed she seemed worse from the liberty given her to go out, till at last her master forbade me to permit it anymore, and I had to suffer the mortification of hearing very unpleasant remarks. . . .

I reserve for the last, because most pleasing, subject my comments on your sweet little effort at writing poetry. Indeed my child I think it does you credit. It is a pretty innocent subject and sweetly and lovingly handled, and the dear Sisters must have been as well pleased with it as myself else it had not been read at the concert. We all read it at home, and some of your friends who called and asked after you—and we all read it with pleasure & satisfaction —Laura, Walter—Miss Mary—Mrs Beer &c &c and each one desires to be affectionately remembered to you. But most of all, was dear Aunt Christie delighted: "Dear little May do give my love and kisses to her." . . .

And now my dear child, I fear my long letter will weary you—but think of the love which guides the pen and will not let it stop at times. God bless you and may our Blessed Mother have you always in her keeping.

Mama. . . .

### Sunday, March 19, 1865

*Did not rise very early this morning as I was not going to church till ten o'clock. I was unfortunate enough to make comparison between Mr Preston & Mr Owens this morning, thereby calling down on me a terrible fierce philippic, so much so that I could scarcely eat any breakfast. I was so nervous from it. After doing my work I dressed and went to High Mass at the cathedral, heard a beautiful discourse from Father Henniger . . . came home and heard that Mr Hartman had spent the morning with Mr Preston; this afternoon Mr Preston and I have had one of our unpleasant conversations but it did not end violently. . . .*

### Tuesday, March 21, 1865

*Rose early and made arrangements for going in the country after breakfast. Mr Preston walked down with me to the car and bidding me goodbye left me. . . . I got out at Govanstown and shortly after the wagon came in sight, Thede & Kitty in it. I got in and we drove home. . . . I took William & Thede and we went to work with a will and we trimmed the grape vines, the rose bushes, &c &c round the house; in the meantime Johnny had cleaned the dairy, took his crocks &c and put it in good order for the milk which Johnny put there this evening. Just before dark it began to rain . . . in the midst of the rain Mr Preston came in having walked from Owens'. . . .*

### Friday, March 24, 1865

*Still cloudy, windy cold and unpleasant; we made preparations to leave for the city by 12 o'clock. . . . Mr Preston met with a strange adventure today which has ended by his bringing to the house a poor unfortunate woman large in the "family way." What is to be the end of all this I know not. . : .*

### Saturday, March 25, 1865

*Still cold cloudy & windy. It being the "Annunciation of the Blessed Virgin," I went to High Mass this morning. . . . The Yankee woman is still with us. I made six mince pies this afternoon, which made me feel quite like being at home.*

Baltimore March 26 1864 [misdated for 1865]

Dear child,

Since I last wrote to you, Theodosia, Kitty and I have spent a few days at Pleasant Plains. . . . The grass is beginning to grow—the buds are swelling and even some dear little birds were chirping a welcome to the coming spring—but pleasant as it all seemed, I felt no disposition to remain there. I became so heartily wearied of the country this winter, that nothing less than your presence will ever make it agreeable to me again. I was glad too to return to the city to enjoy the happy privilege of attending the mission; you can have no idea my child, how much true happiness and comfort I have had in that way.

We came in on Friday the 24th—my first visit was one of great pain to me, and which I am sure will give you pain also. Our friend Adolphus Schaeffer met with quite a severe accident last Monday. Going out to his farm in his buggy, he foolishly attempted to shoot a bird. The gun (it is supposed from an overload) burst the barrel, and in doing so, shattered poor Adolphus' left hand, so terribly that to save his life the physicians found it necessary to amputate his hand. The operation I am told was a very severe one owing to the lacerated condition of his arm, but he bore it with great fortitude, and spared his mother the pain of seeing him suffer as much as he could. When I called on him, he was doing as well as could be expected, but you cannot know how sad it made me feel to see the poor boy lying there maimed for life. He said to me, "Mrs Preston—I am unfortunate. This time last year I was near dying with small pox and now I am suffering with this accident." I did not tell him so, but I could not help thinking, that our dear Lord suffered all these things to come upon him, to bring him to a knowledge of the worthlessness of the things of this world, and the greater happiness he would have in living for higher and holier purposes. . . .

All the family join most lovingly in sending good wishes &c &c to you

Mama.

### Tuesday, March 28, 1865

*A glorious shining day. I went to church this morning at ½ past 7—Saw Priests offering Mass at the three altars in the cathedral. Father Wayrich preached a sermon and announced that the mission would close tonight . . . and this evening I went to the close of the mission. And here from the depths of my heart let me Thank God for the great privilege of doing so. The services were of the most solemn character. The whole congregation together with the Archbishop, Priests & mission Fathers renewed their Baptism vows in a loud voice in the church. The congregation rec'd the Papal Benediction and thus ended the mission. And after all this happiness I came home to what!*

### Thursday, March 30, 1865

*. . . I was unfortunte enough this morning to sprain my ring finger, since when it has swelled greatly and is very painful. Our little Yankee woman rec'd a letter from her husband today which was quite satisfactory to all parties. I have finished my shirt all to the button holes. . . .*

The Vale
March 30th, 1865

My dear Mama,

It seems to me that I have more to tell you to-day than I ever have had in all my letters since my first written from St. Joseph's. . . .

We had a delightful Retreat—kept by Father Guistiniani. At first as he was a stranger, there were only seven of us going to Confession to him, but we were so much pleased with him (I think he must have resembled your dear old Father) that many more went to him, each time a band went to church his number of penitents increased. . . .

But while we were yet enjoying the many pleasant things connected with our Retreat, sorrow as is usually the case came to blight our happiness. Last Sunday morning Mrs Ryan, the sister of our dear little Anna Northrop, arrived at St. Joseph's, not as she had left it for then she was a school girl, but as a refugee from a Southern home that had been burnt before them, and without the next article of clothing to wear. Nor was she alone, she has a little baby only five months old, her mother[4] also a St. Joseph's girl, and two little children, one two and a half years, the other four months old. They say that when left without a place to shelter them, they prayed God to direct them, and they thought of their *old home*, St. Joseph's. A Mr. Gordon of the federal army with several other gentlemen kindly assisted them in reaching Maryland, which they were a month in doing; during all that time they slept but once on a bed, and that was the night they stayed at Barnam's,[5] where they were treated very kindly. If you could know all the circumstances of their journey and all that they have suffered I am sure it would almost break your heart. But four years ago these ladies were happy school girls. Since then they have been married and are now the mothers of the little children I mentioned. Mr Northrop has died, from all accounts, a most violent death; you know he was a very influential man in the South; and poor little Emily's husband is a captain in the Southern army. When she married him, Mrs. Northrop wrote to St. Joseph's saying she never knew a finer young man. His young wife is but nineteen years old, but could you see the fortitude with which she bears her troubles and the consolation she affords her little sister, I am sure you would admire her as much as you could a much older person. Dear little Anna, too, bears with the greatest resignation the death of her father, to whom she was devotedly attached, and said when I met her for the first time after the knowledge of her loss, "Don't let Sister Emmie see my crying." The Sisters have been like so many mothers to them, and have done everything they could for them. I think they have indeed come to their "old home" and found it the same as when they left. I am sure it would make you happy to see how pleased the Sisters look when they speak of it in this way.

Now dear mama, I have something to ask of you that I think will gratify both yourself and Papa; would you please to get two little baby caps for the youngest of the three children and send them to me so that I might give them to the little things?

Sr. Raphael says she does not think they would feel hurt at my doing so. You know Anna and I are such good friends that it would look like a present that any school-mates as much together as ourselves might make. I think those little soft merino ones would be pretty and comfortable. Poor young lady! only a short time since, Mrs. Ryan laid out two thousand dollars for her wedding things and now she has lost everything. I should except two faithful servant girls (negros) who through all their troubles have remained as respectful and attentive as when on their plantation, and they burst into tears when their master is mentioned. It looks very strange to see babies and colored people at St. Joseph's. . . .

When you send my dress please send me some letter paper about the size of this. I forgot to tell you that one of the baby caps would have to be larger than the other. Forgive all mistakes as the latter part of my letter has been written in a dreadful hurry. Tell Sister I will try to write soon.

Yours devotedly,<br>
May

## Saturday, April 1, 1865

*. . . I spent an hour this afternoon with Adolphus and fear he is not so well as we could desire him to be. Kitty cut her thumb quite badly today. Poor miserable child, she gives me so much trouble, I scarcely know how to get along with her.*

## Sunday, April 2, 1865

*This has been a glorious day. The weather is very fine for the early spring. Mr Preston & I came out in the car this morning as far as Govanstown, where William awaited us. We stopped at the mill property, which place Mr Preston bought yesterday, and remained there an hour or two walking over it and looking through the house & mill. I think it a dear purchase, but as Mr Preston is pleased, I have no right to find fault with it. We reached home about 1 o'clock, found Johnny waiting for us and everything in good order. After our little dinner I walked out with Johnny to look after the "doings" since I was last here. I don't think as much has been done as would have been done if I had been here but I did not say so. . . .*

## Monday, April 3, 1865

*Mr Preston and I left P. Plains about 3 o'clock, William driving, stopped at the mill property and then came to the city, where we found bells ringing, colors flying, drums beating and boys shouting for joy that "Richmond was taken!" Of course, we are all sad enough tonight knowing the terrible amount of suffering there is in the South at this time!*

## Tuesday, April 4, 1865

*. . . I went out this morning to do some shopping on a very small scale for my dear little daughter . . . to buy her two baby caps to make a present of them to two young mothers at St. Joseph's who are refugees from the South. Dear child she has no idea of the expense of such articles, else she never would have asked for them, and I cannot refuse them to her! Mr Preston & William were pot-*

*tering about all day till 4 o'clock, at which time they and Kitty went out to P. Plains. It was very evident to me that Mr Preston did not like the idea of going out without company and yet he had not the courage to ask for Thede! . . .*

### Wednesday, April 5, 1865

*. . . Mr Preston sent William in with the horses to take out the wagon, and sent me a lugubrious note about Kitty; consequently, Thede went out to remain with him. I suppose he is now satisfied & happy. Thede & I went out this morning and purchased a Balmoral for May & this afternoon Mrs Beer & I have been together, have been making it, and May's frock. It is almost 12 o'clock and yet I sit here unable to go to bed, thinking of my unfortunate fate!*

### Thursday, April 6, 1865

*. . . This evening the city is illuminated to celebrate the taking of Richmond by the Federals. Mr Preston & I walked out to see the sight and the crowds in the streets; we came to the conclusion it was a very meager affair, and very little enthusiasm evidenced by the people. . . .*

### Sunday, April 9, 1865

*. . . Mr Preston wanting to go to the mill property gave me permission to accompany him & Theodosia that far and then with Johnny to go to Father Lyman's church; we did so. It being Palm Sunday, we found the ceremonies very beautiful, and the sermon good and very much to the purpose and enjoyed the church and its duties greatly. But alas! alas! for all my pleasures and enjoyments—they soon take wings and flee away. On reaching the mill, Mr Preston and Theodosia were ready for us. On getting into the carriage she had some rubbish (as I thought) in her hand, and I asked her to throw it away. It proved to be an old umbrella frame she picked up for me—consequently a mortal offence to my lady and her uncle! and such a shocking outbreak as I received surpassed anything of the kind I have listened to for a long time. It did not end here; on sitting down to the table it broke out afresh, and was worse than ever. As Mr Preston continued eating all the time most heartily, I really thought he would bring on an apoplectic fit and was frightened in consequence as he filled his stomach; however, the vials of his wrath became emptied and he, quiet! I walked round the place this afternoon and spent a quiet but sad hour in May's little nook. Mr Preston & Theodosia retired early & I have sat up alone! . . .*

What really happened we will never know. Probably Madge spoke curtly to Theodosia. Probably Theodosia, thinking to do Madge a favor by retrieving an object she thought usable, felt truly hurt. One element in Madge's story, however, is unambiguous—to which of these women Preston showed the greater loyalty. In this matter, Madge had clearly lost.

### Monday, April 10th, 1865

. . . *On going to the breakfast table this morning, Theodosia told Mr Preston she wished to go home, whereupon Mr P—broke out afresh and in his remarks said, he did not wish her to go home, and continued by saying "If you do go home, I will bring a woman in the house, who will make her know what she is about." Evidently intending to threaten me with a woman. Mr Preston also told me I could not go to town this week and May could not have her box for Easter. This, he said, was done to* spite *me! "Spite me"—a beautiful expression for a husband to make, in the presence of another woman, whom he is at the same time treatening[6] with the greatest respect and affection. Before Mr Preston went to town, he struck me over the eye with his cane, which has blackened it in the most terrible manner. Since then I have been in bed sick & miserable. Mr Preston came home this evening and has been more brutal than ever. [in the margin] I record here an expression made by Mr Preston, threatening me with the kind of woman he was going to bring to the house when Theodosia should leave.*

# 10

# When Lincoln Died

"I RECORD THIS FACT, that it may, if necessary, be known to others in the future." With these words Madge signaled that her volume had taken on a new purpose. The day before, February 23, she had written of her inclination to report her husband as insane "and a dangerous person to be living with." Clearly she feared for her life.

When Preston struck her again on April 10, she set down another entry as a formal record of their warring relationship: "I record here an expression made by Mr Preston, threatening me with the kind of woman he was going to bring to the house when Theodosia should leave." Perhaps Madge believed the notation would someday confirm her husband's insanity. But its real purpose seems clearly different—to immortalize, as if chiseled in granite, the range of his iniquity and the depths of her outrage. Madge's anger explodes in the furious underlinings of key words on that page—even more in the Freudian slip of the coalesced *treating* and *threatening*—"in the presence of another woman, whom he is at the same time treatening with the greatest respect and affection." Preston's perhaps exaggerated deference and courtesy to Thede is clearly a "threat" to Madge, who must cope also with verbal and physical assaults from her husband.

Preston may or may not have had a sexual relationship with Thede. He may or may not have had a sexual relationship earlier with her sister Rose. But clearly Madge was suspicious that he had. Clearly also she was angry about the presence in her home of the younger woman, whom she had herself invited by a letter she was forced to write. Yet on Madge's better days—when Preston himself was away from Pleasant Plains—she also enjoyed the companionship of Thede.

The April 10 passage tells much about Preston, who conspicuously and outrageously taunts Madge with his actual, or threatened, resort to prostitutes.

Madge no longer holds back from her private journal disclosures concerning her husband's disloyalty.

It is not certain when the relationship between this formerly happy couple began to go so seriously awry. The precipitating event was surely the aggravated assault Preston sustained in the November 1859 election. But when Preston began to turn his own rage as victim against his wife is not clearly marked. In the first few months after the assault, the violence that he directed toward Madge seems to have been merely verbal. Yet overt violence was all around them—encouraged openly in Know-Nothing rallies, erupting in mob outbreaks over the war issues, flaring up in enforced impressment of individual men into unwilling military service. In 1861 the newly elected President Lincoln, for fear of mob action, had had to be sneaked through Baltimore in the middle of the night on the train trip to his inauguration. Passions were further heated by the open hostilities of the Civil War. The sense of frustration among Confederate sympathizers, such as the Prestons, was aggravated by the staggering losses sustained by the Southern people; and perhaps even more by the inability of these sympathizers, in this Northern enclave, to offer assistance or to speak out openly about their true feelings. The defection of many slaves and then the final freeing of all those whose labor had supported the plantation economy brought further dislocations in a settled way of life. The country was ripe for further violence—in public hall and in the home.

---

### Tuesday, April 11, 1865

*Still cloudy this morning. Sophia came up and put out the clothes. Mr Preston it seems has relented with regard to our poor child and this morning when he went to the city, he took with him a memorandum of the articles I wish sent to her in the box and said he would send them by the wagon today. Of course I thanked him! Thanked him for attending to his own child! . . .*

### Wednesday, April 12, 1865

*. . . Sophia came up this morning and ironed the shirts and collars and left at noon, making in all a day and a half, for which I paid her $.12 cts. . . . On Mr Preston's return, he appeared to be in a most amiable mood but finding no corresponding emotion in me, he took fright and went to bed. . . .*

### Saturday, April 15, 1865

*. . . Not having Mr Preston home this morning we were able to get along quietly and quickly with our work. I made pies for Easter. Thede cleaned up the*

*sitting room & Kitty scrubbed the kitchen, and all was done by 2 o'clock. At eleven I sent Thede & Johnny to the city to bring Mr Preston home, but owing to a joyful circumstance for this country, they were not able to get in, consequently returned bringing me the good news. It seems President Lincoln was assassinated last night at the theatre in Washington and as poor Baltimore must be punished and suspected of doing all the wrong that is done the government, the authorities placed a guard round the city and will not let anyone in or out of the city without a pass. Of course Thede & Johnny came home and either owing to the rain or the troubles in the city, Mr Preston has not come home tonight. Thede & I played chess—both beat.*

## Sunday, April 16, 1865

*Easter Sunday was ushered in by a bright beautiful sun and the entire day has been glorious. I sent Thede & Johnny down to Govanstown to meet the nine o'clock car but when they reached there, it seems there was no car come up. Johnny went on to church and Thede came home, bringing yesterday's paper with her; we then drove over to Eudowood and spent the day there, and a pleasant and happy one it was. The news of Lincoln's assassination was confirmed, together with that of Seward and his son. The secretary is not dead, but it is thought he cannot live long. There seems to be a wonderful excitement in the city and elsewhere—I fear it will lead to great troubles and misery—Thede and I reached home just at sundown. Thede and I played chess. I beat.*

## Monday, April 17, 1865

*A glorious day. . . . I gave Johnny holiday as it was Easter and fixed him off to have a picnic party with some of the little boys in the neighbourhood. He came home in good time after having enjoyed himself. Kitty also had holiday given her, but as usual she violated the terms. Mr Preston came home, reaching here about 11 o'clock; he seemed very happy and was quite affectionate, but not meeting with a response of feeling, he has shown the cloven foot again. Mr Preston says the city is still in great excitement and people have to be careful of their remarks.*

## Tuesday, April 18, 1865

*Another glorious day, and vegetation is improving accordingly. Cherry trees are now in full bloom, peaches and pears also. . . . John called us up this morning to tell us that Kate the mare had twins. Thede and I went down to look after the colts, and found one lively & well and the other weak and poorly. We nursed it up all day, giving it the bottle &c Mr Preston went to the city today, by the way of the mill, taking Johnny with him to do some work. . . . Mr Preston retired early in consequence of pain in all his bones.*

### Wednesday, April 19, 1865

*. . . Thede, Johnny and myself drove to the city to see the great show or pageant or whatever you would call it. The whole city was hung in black and has been for several days mourning over Lincoln's death. The people of the city looked melancholy & sad, and indeed it was enough to make one feel so, the sombre appearance of the city, the tolling of the bells and the firing of the minute guns—all inspired a feeling of sadness. . . .*

Pleasant Plains
April 24th, 1865

My darling child,

I have been suffering with the worst cold I have ever had for the last week or two, and of course its accompanying headache. Each day I have put off writing, hoping the next day would find me better. . . . I still feel badly, tho' today my hand seems firm enough to hold my pen. . . .

Since the dreadful crime of the assassination of the president of which you have doubtless heard, scarcely any business has been done in the city, stores have been closed, the whole city was draped in mourning and for several days the post office was only opened for an hour each day; consequently, those persons who could not force their way through the crowd were obliged to do without their letters. As Papa remained in the country nearly all the week —in fact till Saturday—your letter also remained quietly in the post office box till that day. I am glad to know the articles pleased you. . . . You ask if you shall get a body for your brilliant skirt;[1] not if you can do without it. The sending of the skirt was a mistake of poor, kind, good Papa. You recollect I told you Papa packed the box as I could not go to town—seeing that skirt among the other articles he of course concluded it was to go also. . . . When I was fixing your things, I could not buy a yard of brilliant for less than 75 cts per yd. Of course that was too much to think of giving, and I got in place of the body the calico frock with which you seem to be so well pleased; enclosed in this letter you will receive a net—it is your white one colored. . . .

While I am in town today I shall attend to having your baby caps made. I suppose you were the most delighted girl in all the school, when the dear little baby fell asleep on your shoulder. You would be quite amused to see how much interested we all are in your babies. When you play with them occasionally, give them a loving embrace and kiss and tell them your Mama sent them. . . .

You ask me how I spent my Easter; as I never deceive you in anything, I must tell you I was not well enough to leave home. Now I hope you have too much good sense to be alarmed at what I have written—even if I *have* suffered, you must perceive that I am better, and I trust in a few days will be quite well. . . .

Yours lovingly,<br>Mama

### Tuesday, April 25, 1865

. . . *Mr Preston having to go to the city today, Thede went with him, to see the mourning condition of the Exchange and the way it was arranged for the reception of the president's body. They reached home just at sundown. . . . I am suffering dreadfully with earache tonight. . . .*

### Wednesday, April 26, 1865

. . . *I have to record that I suffered the most agonizing night of pain last night that I have ever endured. I had not one moment of intermission from such pain as I had never imagined in all my life. Mr Preston was patient & kind all the time, and this morning he and Thede together with poor Kitty have done everything that the most loving kindness could suggest. I rose about ten o'clock and with Thede's assistance got Mr Preston some shirts ironed and his clothes ready for his little trip to New York. . . .*

Baltimore<br>April 28th /65

My dear child,

I have this instant sent off by Adams Express a box containing the little caps for which you sent some weeks ago. Sundry things prevented me sending them sooner, but perhaps it is just as well they were not sent sooner, as by the delay I have been enabled to have made an article of the latest and most approved fashion. I went to the "little milliner Mrs Camper" as you suggested, and she, being one of the friends of the South in the city, took great pleasure in making them. . . . I do hope they may be worthy [of] the acceptance of your little pets, and that you will be pleased with the effect of them on their infant heads! . . .

I send by tomorrow mail a beautiful piece of music called "An Answer to the Maiden's Prayer"—or rather "The Maiden's Prayer *Granted.*"[2] If you can, I wish you would learn it before you come home. . . .

Your devoted

Mama

St. Joseph's. May [incorrect for April] 1865.

My dear Mama,

I received your letter . . . and was pained more than I can tell you at hearing of the sufferings you have lately undergone with such a bad cold. How could you have taken it? As you are so seldom sick, my dear Mama, I know that a sleight illness has more effect upon you than on one enjoying less better health. I have asked several of the Sisters and girls to pray for you as well as my self and trust that by this time you fell so much better that you will amost have forgotten that you were indisposed at all. Write as soon as you can a[nd] let me know how you are. Do not think though that I am unhappy on your account—I am not for I believe you when you say that you are so much better; still knowing how anxious you are that I should not feel worried about you unnecessarily I hasten to relieve your fears on that point. Although it was not a letter day Sister Raphael very kindly gave me permission to write. . . .

Now good by my, dear Mama, Write often to me and pray for

May.

### Tuesday, May 2, 1865

*Nothing could be more delightful than this day: but I have not been able to enjoy being out of doors, owing to an intolerable earache with which I suffered all night and the greater part of the day. Thede slept with me, and was obliged to make a fire in the night and was up the greater part of the night nursing me. If I am well enough I will go to the city in the morning and see the doctor. . . .*

### Wednesday, May 3, 1865

*Was glad to find the sun shining brightly . . . this morning, as Thede & I arranged to go to the city. After attending to the household duties and giving Kitty work for the day, we left P. P. . . . I had suffered greatly during the night, but had not called Thede as I thought it not necessary to do so. Mr Preston was not in, and after waiting till near two o'clock, I left Thede to inform Mr Preston of our coming and went up to see Dr. Haywel. On telling him of my symptoms, the old Dr said I had no cold but was suffering with an ulceration in my forehead caused by some violent concussion, and if I was not careful, I would be very ill. I had thought the same thing myself knowing the fearful blows I had rec'd on my face during the last two months could not pass away without some bad result. The Dr gave me medicine, I came home, went to bed, and about five o'clock Mr Preston and Thede went home, and I have remained with Mrs Beer. . . .*

### Thursday, May 4, 1865

*. . . About 8 o'clock Mr Preston came in bringing Thede with him in the carriage; he came up to see me for a few moments & then he & Thede drove to the Fish House, Mr Preston saying he had business there but all the business they accomplished that I could hear of was the eating of a good fish dinner! . . .*

### Friday, May 5, 1865

*. . . I did not feel quite so well this morning, having had a restless night. About 9 o'clock Mr Preston came in. . . . Mr Preston both yesterday and today has exhibited such a strange kind of nervousness that I am convinced it could only result from a consciousness of wrong doings. It is all folly for me to say anything to Mr Preston; it does not stop & only brings trouble and something worse on me. Before Mr Preston went away this afternoon, we had a most unpleasant scene owing to my not wishing to kiss Mr Preston, who offered me a kiss before leaving, but I so detest a Judas kiss that I could not receive it. . . . I am very sad tonight!*

St. Joseph's
May 5th/65

My dear Mama,

You must by this time have received my note . . . to acquaint you with the arrival of my box containing the baby caps. . . .

I told you in my last letter that the Archbishop was here on a visit some time ago. . . . we had been expecting him for some time as he promised last fall to visit St. Joseph's in the spring. . . . He spent Friday the 22d with us, and gave us holiday. We received him in the Distribution room; at first we kept the places that had been assigned to us, and which were at some distance from him; but in a few moments the ice of ceremony was broken, and we gathered around our Father as if we had known him always. He seemed to be very much pleased with our doing so, and in return told us ever so many stories. After dinner he returned to our part of the house and kept us laughing . . . at the numerous anecdotes he related to us. He told us a Dutch, a French and an Irish story; the last you may be sure was the funniest. . . .

Now after telling you some of our pleasures, I must let you know something of our sorrows, and thus give you a true picture of life in our miniature world. The dear little baby who afforded me so much pleasure by falling asleep on my shoulder has gone to rest on God's bosom for all eternity. The dear little child was only sick three days before he died, and suffered during that time with the most dreadful convulsions. His poor mother seemed at first unable to sustain this fresh trouble, but somehow before he died she became perfectly resigned. I would scarcely believe if had not seen it, that a mother just twenty-three years old could bear as she does so many trials. The little Alfred was buried last Friday at the College, and the simple yet touching ceremonies of his interment were related to us by Sr. Ann Scholastica who accompanied Mrs Northrop to the funeral. To Mrs. Northrop his death is of course a dreadful blow, but when we think how much trouble lay before them we must consider it a mercy from God. . . .

. . . Dear Aunt Louisa, with Crick and Cousin Rose were over here yesterday, and spent the greater part of the afternoon with me. We went to the grave yard and saw Mother Rose's grave after whom Cousin Rose is named, then around the grounds and to the old house of Mother Seton. We had a delightful time. . . . Rose is house-keeper now and says she makes excellent butter. Is not that well.

Beg dear Papa to write to me at least on my birth-day, which you know is fast approaching. . . .

Pray our Blessed Lady, Pray for my dear Father and Mother and protect your little

May

Baltimore May 7th /65

My darling child,

It was quite thoughtful and considerate in you to send so promptly as you did your note . . . announcing the safe arrival of the little box and its contents. . . .

I can't tell you my child how pained I have been with your account of the many trials and troubles those poor young mothers have endured. "God tempers the wind to the Shorn lamb," and he also "loveth those whom he chaseneth." Surely then he must in an especial manner have folded his loving arms around these his suffering children. The very resignation which you tell me came upon this loving mother in that terrible hour of parting with her idolized child speaks of the abundant graces which God in his mercy bestowed even while the fountain of affliction was still showering over her.

I rejoice to feel your thoughtfulness with regard to the little caps has made them also useful, and I now regret that a false delicacy on my part prevented me sending an abundance of beautiful articles, some of them never worn and others but slightly, but which in the hasty journeys these ladies have been obliged to make would have been so very useful to their babies. If you ever see them again, remember me in all kindness and tell them it required but a slight stretch of the imagination with so sympathetic a nature as mine, to feel the soft arms and warm kisses of their sweet children round my neck and on my cheek. . . .

Your letters have become exceedingly interesting to me of late. I do not mean my child that they have not always been interesting; every line coming from you is more precious to me—but the style of your letters and the pleasant and satisfactory manner in which you relate the incidents that transpire around you causes me to look forward to Saturday afternoon *and three o'clock* (the time I always receive your letters when in the city) with the utmost eagerness. Yesterday I was not very well, but I watched the clock, and as soon as the hand indicated the right hour, I sent an order to the office—and there lay May's letter! Though the letter, like our lives, mingled light with darkness —joy with sorrow, and pain with pleasure, yet, as by a happy provision of nature light predominates over darkness, so did happiness in your letter have the ascendant—but even there, the gloom of the grave was ringed with the brightness of Heaven, for it was the body of a little child you had lain there, and we know its spirit was already with the God who gave it. . . .

I was greatly surprised last night by Mrs Beer coming to my room and giving me a letter to read from Louis, at the same time handing me a little packet which on opening proved to be one of the most beautiful black gutta percha[3] necklaces and watch guard I have ever seen. Suspended from the necklace is a cross also cut out of gutta percha, inlaid beautifully with mother of pearl —workmanship is wonderful, and the whole article reflects great credit upon the table and skill of the workman. You will be pleased . . . to know this beautiful necklace and chain was made by Louis himself, while confined a state prisoner at the fort, and is a present *to you*, as a memento of the dark days that opened on Louis' young life, and as a token of the kind feelings he has always entertained for his young playmate. We are hoping that Louis' long and painful captivity may now soon come to an end. . . . God bless you my child.

Yours lovingly Mama

### Thursday, May 11, 1865

*. . . Mr Preston came in this morning reaching here about 11—he remained till after six o'clock, leaving here in all the storm. I could not see the necessity of his doing so—but I suppose there was a strong attraction at Pleasant Plains. The lightning & thunder have been terrible this evening & the rain frightful. Poor Mr Preston.*

## Friday, May 12, 1865

*It thundered, lightened & rained in the most frightful manner the greater part of the night. The paper states this morning the storm of yesterday & last night has rarely been equalled. . . . Mr Preston reached the city about noon, tho' he was out in the storm last night and it was 9 o'clock when he reached home, yet he insists in saying it was* not *very unpleasant.* I suppose not! . . .

## Monday, May 15, 1865

*[Pleasant Plains.] Another delightful day, we all rose early this morning to enable Mr Preston & Thede to make an early start for town. . . . After they left, I found it necessary to make an inspection of the house & kitchen. I found many things that needed my attention. I have been annoyed with Kitty cutting up and destroying a frock for the purpose of making herself a jozey! I finished my alpaca dress today—mended my sun bonnet and one of Kitty's, and dressed a calf's head for Mr Preston's supper which he and Thede pronounced delicious. . . .*

---

On May's birthday as he had the year before, Preston sat down to write a letter to his daughter. He would build on the tradition he had then begun —to write one page for each year of her life. Still his theme was his own depressed mood, though he gave some attention to the "cold" that disguised Madge's true indisposition.

> Pleasant Plains
> 19 May 1865

My Dear May—

For more than a week past, I had intended to write you a letter, but chiefly deferred it, because of my feeling scarcely able to do it. I have been for a long time past suffering with a severe pain in my left side, —I have often wondered that it did not disappear or kill me. How it could remain so long without being better or worse I cannot conceive. Lately it has increased in violence, and at this time I am also afflicted with a sore throat, the consequence as I suppose of being out in a shower which wet me through, some'eight or ten days ago. In the midst of these troubles as to my physical condition, I have been obliged to be in court and try cases—a very long and very dry case relative to the paving and grading of the Northern Avenue has been in progress at Towsontown for four days past. I am one of the counsel and although I am sick enough to be in bed, I am obliged to aid in the trial of the cause. People see me in court, listen attentively to my arguments or laugh at my smart sayings—alas! how little do they dream of the pain which at the same time is gnawing at my vitals. But such is life! The stream may glide along smoothly and many objects of beauty and interest be clamly mirrored in its placid surface—the rocks of disappointment—the shifting sands of vexation are all below—down in the depths, where the eye of God alone can penetrate. On this subject a very good poet has said—

> "If ev'ry man's *internal* care,
> Was stamp'd upon his *brow*,
> How many whom our *envy* share
> Would claim our *pity* now."

I quote from memory and do not think the above quotation is verbally correct, but the verse contains the *sentiment*, which after all is the marrow of the poetic bone.

For several weeks past your mother has been—like myself—but poorly. In the early part of Lent she took cold—I think she took cold in the cathedral. She does not agree with me in opinion—but I remember well observing the first symptoms of it, one day shortly after her being at Mass. At all events . . . it has been very troublesome to her, a short severe cough and violent pains in the face. It gives me great pleasure to be able to assure you that she is now much better, the pains and the cough have almost left her, and I am no longer uneasy on her account.

I have read with great satisfaction your several letters addressed to your mother and myself—the current course of your thoughts as manifested in your writing pleases me. Your ideas follow one another in smooth and consecutive order—the best evidence of a well-balanced undisturbed mind—in addition to this, your sentiments are such as I approve of—they are sound and wholesome and a vein of charity runs through them. In many of the wonderful works of God bright and beautiful veins are visible—in the quartz of California, the marbles of Egypt and the precious stones of the East. In the morning's dawn—and the rose twilight—and when fleecy clouds float lazily between us and the bright full moon. In all these the graceful veins of a god-like tracery are perceptible, and so my child it should be with our sentiments and our feelings—a vein of charity should run through the whole. . . .

. . . I perceive I am at the *sixteenth* page—a page for every year, as this is the sixteenth anniversary of your birth—with us the landscape is fresh and beautiful—graceful leaves and promising blossoms surround us and awaken gratitude and hope. This is the spring of Nature. With you my dear child it is the springtime of life. May a beneficent God deck the prospect before you with flowers of beauty and loveliness. Your cousin Theo joins your Mother and myself in love to you—the girls, and the pious Sisters. May the Lord protect you all

W. P. Preston

---

Preston's elaborations in his letter to May on how Madge caught her "cold" seem to confirm his feelings of guilt, an example in writing of that "strange kind of nervousness" that Madge earlier had attributed to "consciousness of wrong doings." Outside May's knowledge he was also making arrangements that would bring together two troubled families. One was that of his sister-in-law, Louisa Smith, who since her husband's death had need of some source of income. The other was that of his friend John Owens.

When Owens left Maryland for an extended tour in England with his acting company, he turned over to William Preston, his friend and neighbor, responsibility for handling the Owens's business and personal affairs. These included a small settlement for support of his mother-in-law, a Mrs. Stevens, who was an alcoholic. For a long time her behavior had embarrassed Mrs. Owens, who did her best to keep her mother out of sight. Preston's suggestion was to send Mrs. Stevens away from the influences and temptations of city life; and to this end he had written Louisa, hoping she could take in Mrs. Stevens as a paying guest. Madge knew of the proposal.

### Saturday, May 20, 1865

. . . *Mr Preston drove to the city this morning and did not return till 8 o'clock this evening, somewhat wrong and out of sorts. Mr Preston rec'd a dispatch from Louisa saying "Proposition accepted," which means she will take Mrs Stevens to board at Mountain View. This thing does not meet with my approbation at all. . . .*

### Sunday, May 21, 1865

. . . *Mr Preston goes to Phila tomorrow morning, consequently was obliged to go to the city this afternoon. As he wanted to see Mrs Owens before he went away, Mr Preston & I drove over there to dinner. . . . I was not pleased with Mr Preston's conduct and by my manners let him and the ladies see it.*

### Monday, May 22, 1865

. . . *With Thede & Kitty's assistance I ripped up my black & white plaid dress, washed & ironed it and have nearly put it together. . . . I hunted up a black*

*dress of mine . . . and gave it to Thede, I also gave Kitty my striped thin dress,*
*which I think fits her nicely and will make her a good dress for the summer. . . .*

Pleasant Plains
May 29th, 1865

My dear child,

Your . . . reply to dear Papa's sixteen pages and yours to me . . . have been
received. I am sure, my dear May, you have reason to feel greatly obliged to
the kind Sisters for their indulgence in this letting you write twice out of time.
I myself am so much obliged to dear Sister Raphael—you know Papa does
not understand the rules of the school as well as *we* do [and] consequently
would have felt, *perhaps*, a little neglected if a speedy answer had not come to
his birthday letter . . . Papa was evidently *very much pleased* and so expressed
himself. . . .

You will readily believe, my child, that both Papa and I fully appreciate the
many little pleasant attentions and affectionate acts of kindness shown you by
the Sisters and your young companions, and were much pleased to know you
spent so happy a birthday. God grant that all you spend in future may be
equally happy and with a like pure and innocent surroundings. . . .

. . . You say, "You are sorry to say you have not grown much."—then my
little May, or rather my big daughter, there must be some mistake in the measure you sent me. On placing the piece of thread you enclosed in your letter
on the white skirt you wore last Distribution, the thread is several inches
*longer* than the skirt—surely it cannot be so! Have you worn your new calico
dress and is it a good length? I wish, my child, you would be particular in the
measuring of the dress, as it would be most unfortunate a thing if I should
send your dress and it would be too long for you to wear it. . . .

I must tell you of a delightful drive Papa and I had this morning. Papa was
obliged to go to Westminster this morning on professional business, and to
meet the morning train, he had to drive over to the Relay House,[4] which . . .
is situated just by the side of Swan Lake, . . . we started from Pleasant Plains
after an early breakfast and travelled through the most beautiful country I
have ever seen in all Maryland. The lake is perfection, and so charmed were
both Papa & myself that we planned a pic nic to come off as soon after your
return home as we can make it suit you. Theodosia, Kitty, Papa and myself
will constitute the party and . . . "we will make a day of it." I am sure you will
be delighted. Papa thinks, and I *believe* I do also, that the lake and its surroundings are infinitely more beautiful than the famed Central Park of New
York.

Theodosia has been staying at Aigburth Vale for the last week. Our friend
Mr Owens having sailed for Europe last Saturday, Mrs Owens & Delia ac-

companied him to New York to bid goodbye and say a *prayer for him,* which strange to say, I wrote for them on the very day that you wrote your "Remember" for Papa. Is not that a singular coincidence? Mrs Owens and Delia have promised to say the "Remember &c" daily during Mr Owens's absence, and I shall also say it, and beg our Blessed Mother to make them all good Catholics by the time Mr Owens returns, which perhaps will not be for six months or more.

Poor Kitty, as usual at this season, *has the poison on her*! or rather she *had* it last week. Yesterday and today she is better, but her two teeth which I think I told you she was cutting pain her very much. She is quite anxious you should know all about her sickness to have your sympathy I suppose.

And now, my dear child, let me assure you that I am getting quite well, indeed I can scarcely believe that I was so recently so very sick! I could not see the necessity of alarming you or causing you anxiety, when you could do me no good and it might have proved of serious disadvantage to you in your studies. When I became *very* sick, I made them take me to the city, for the twofold advantage of being near medical attendance and the sending for you, if it became necessary. Of course you will believe I was not unmindful of the still greater advantage of spiritual counsel.[5] Through the kindness of our merciful Father I soon felt the benefit of the medicines my old doctor administered and I felt all danger for the present was over. I then returned to our country home, where I have improved so rapidly that my friends say I look as "well as ever."

And now I have a request to make. Do not, my child, mention my sickness again; it is all over, and there is no necessity of recalling the painful and anxious time. Papa was unnecessarily anxious; and I do not like him to be reminded of it.

When I commenced writing this evening, I expected to be alone, but about nine o'clock who should walk in but Papa. . . . After a hastily gotten cup of tea, Papa has retired, Kitty also has "gone to roost" as she poetically expresses retiring, each leaving their love for you, and I also will follow their good example. . . .

Mama . . .

### Thursday, June 1, 1865

*A warm clear pleasant day. As it was the president's fast day for poor Lincoln, our men came this morning to inform me there was a fine of ten dollars for anyone found working; of course there was nothing to do, but give them holiday. . . .*

# 11

## A Time of Change

As THE NATION AT last put off the crape it had worn during the period of mourning for Lincoln, Madge too recovered from physical effects of the brutal beatings she had received and from her accompanying depression. With the calendar turning again to June, she had many things to think of concerning the Distribution ceremony at St. Joseph's. She was hoping to travel north for the occasion—perhaps to bring others along to share her pride in May's accomplishments and in the institution both mother and daughter so greatly cherished. Preston was away at Westminster, involved in a long and complicated lawsuit.

Friday, June 2, 1865

. . . *Johnny was so unfortunate as to lose the dairy key this morning and after searching for it nearly all day and every one of us worried about it, I found it in a spot where we had all looked a dozen times, but as Kitty had just passed that spot we knew that she must have laid it there. . . . Johnny Stansbury brought me over two shirts to make, for the Confederate prisoners who pass through the city daily. Thede & I will make them. . . .*

Sunday, June 4, 1865

. . . *Thede & I have spent the day alone quietly. As the shirts Christie sent us were intended for the poor ragged Southern prisoners, we thought it was no harm to make them on a Sunday; we consequently set to work and finished them. . . .*

**Monday, June 5, 1865**

*The evil spirit of our family seems at play just now; everything relating to Mr Preston and his cases seems to go wrong. This morning about eleven o'clock Theodore came out from the city bringing with him a note from Mr Preston which should have been rec'd on Saturday; in it, Mr Preston sends for books which he required for his argument in the case he is trying in Westminster. I at once packed up and went to the city, took the package to the baggage man on the train and he said he would see that it went safe as far as he could do so. I am in hopes he will still receive them in time for his argument. I returned here about 7 o'clock and found Thede in high dudgeon, where she has remained all the evening. . . .*

Pleasant Plains
June 12th 1865

My dear child,

I wrote you a hurried letter some days ago, intending to follow it up immediately . . . but alas! as I have often had occasion to say before, for "good intentions." . . .

Lately, Papa has been unusually pressed by professional duties, and you know, when that is the case I am very apt to feel the effects of such pressure —for more than three weeks past Papa has been oscillating as it were, almost daily—having several important cases on hand in each place at the same time; the consequence was that it kept Theodosia and I in a constant trot with Johnny accompanying us—backwards and forwards from Towsontown to P. Plains from P. Plains to the Relay House to catch the cars for Westminster, leaving Papa . . . at these different stations. Saturday completed these runs, but this week a new state of affairs begins in the city, where Papa is again engaged with business. I tell you this to account to you for your not receiving your box by the next trip the wagon . . . shall make to Emmitsburg. Dear Papa takes such pleasure in superintending the packing up and sending off of any little thing going in your direction that I could not have it in my heart to let a box be forwarded to you without Papa having a "finger in the pie." . . .

I am very much in hopes your father will accompany me to Emmitsburg when I come up for you. . . . When you write again, don't say I told you he was coming, but ask him yourself to do so, and say to dear Sister Raphael that I said, if she would be so kind, as to write a few lines to Papa by way of *invitation* and enclose the note in your letter, I thought it would surely bring him to St. Joseph's, and I am so anxious to have him go up. . . .

I made a pleasant visit to Union Hall this morning. . . . Each and all send much love to you. I have not seen Mamie since before Christmas and I was astonished at the change these six months had made in her. I think she is as tall as I am and beautifully proportioned in her figure and her face is really beautiful. She has also become much more animated and talks with ease and fluency. Altogether she is one of the most attractive young girls I know. Alice I have seen more frequently. She is still the pleasant, piquant, pretty little fairy of former days. I forgot whether I mentioned a visit Adolphus and our young friend Clara Cox made by some two days ago. . . . Poor Adolphus I fear just begins to realize the terrible loss he has sustained by his late painful accident; he is cheerful however & resigned. . . .

Yours lovingly<br>
Mama

Pleasant Plains<br>
June 16th, 1865

My dear child,

Papa and I have just finished packing your box. . . . I send you a white dress—a fine skirt to be worn under the dress. . . . I have just a draw string around the waist to give you the fullness of a hoop or the appearance of one. When drawing the string, be careful to have the gathers placed right; one pair of corsets—which if they do not fit you, be careful not to soil as they can be changed for others; one pair of gaiters . . . a net, which as they are fashionable I suppose must be considered pretty, tho' it will take me some time to become reconciled to the Indian look of the beads, hdkf, gloves, ribbon, toothbrush & powder and hair tonic. I have also sent you a piece of fine oil silk which I wish you to have put under the sleeves of your pink dress, and with what is left over your scapulars—as the warm weather is apt to make them discolor your underclothing . . . if there is anything else you desire, write for it and if possible you shall have it.

In a letter written a few days ago, I told you I should be with you at the Distribution. Papa also wishes to go up and nothing but business will prevent his doing so. . . . If I go up alone, I shall . . . make Aunt Louisa a visit at Gettysburg. . . .

I suppose the news of dear Hillen's return from the South has already reached you through the girls. . . . Of course he has gone to New York to his family. Louis has not yet been liberated, though his mother hopes each day to have him restored to her. . . . Each and all send love to you, *particularly* Papa & Thede, who are sitting by me playing chess.

Love to the girls<br>
Mama

**Sunday, June 18, 1865**

*. . . Mr. Preston remained home today till 2 o'clock. . . . After Mr Preston left, Thede & I went upstairs; just as we fixed ourselves comfortably in her room a carriage drove up, containing as we thought Mr Scharf & his wife; not wishing to see them, we remained quiet, and old Mrs Pent almost banged the doors down trying to find us; at last she gave up & when we heard the carriage drive off, we came down and heard, much to our dismay, that it was Mrs Owens, who wanted to see me particularly. When William came home, Thede & I got in the carriage and drove over to Aigburth, and explained matters to Mrs Owens, who laughed heartily. While there, Mrs Owens told me Mr Preston had proposed to her to go up to see her mother with him & Thede sometime this summer, but understanding all things, she will decline! ! . . .*

------

What is Madge insinuating? The passage suggests that she had been sharing with Mrs. Owens at least some of her worries about Preston and her nieces. Since this kind of intimacy seems uncharacteristic in a woman whose oft-repeated theme is reticence, the admission here may herald Madge's developing alienation from Preston as her anger continues to grow.

Pleasant Plains
June 21st 1865

My dear May,

Your welcome . . . letter of the 14th came to me just after I had sent my last one to the post office . . . your long and interesting letter . . . gave great pleasure, together with the "wee one" congratulating me and wishing me happiness on my birthday. The little thing caused much amusement and pleasure, and gratified me to find my darling child had remembered what everyone at home had forgotten. . . .

Papa, as I feared, will not be able to accompany me; I shall therefore leave Baltimore on the morning of the 26th and go by the way of Gettysburg, reaching there by one o'clock, when I hope to meet Aunt Louisa. . . . We will . . . go over to Emmitsburg Tuesday morning . . . to see a certain little girl called "Little May." . . . I do not wish you to go with me to the hotel . . . neither do I suppose you desire so to do. I would not, for any consideration, have a young daughter of mine doing as I heard of some of the St. Joseph's girls last summer; . . . some of the young ladies from the Vale and some of the young gentlemen of the Mountain were seen walking the public roads *after* twelve o'clock the night after the Distribution. It distressed me to know the quiet discipline and modest propriety of conduct during a year at dear St Joseph's should so soon have been forgotten. . . .

. . . I think it would be well for . . . you to say to the Sister who has charge of your "goods and chattels" in packing your things to come home, *not* to pack anything that will be useful the coming year—for instance your books and table furniture. If nothing happens more than we know at present, you will certainly return to St. Joseph's next session—*to graduate I hope!* Papa has freely given his consent, nay, I believe he is equally desirous with myself to have you remain at St Joseph's and put a "finishing touch" to your education! Though dear Papa satirizes the idea of an "ornamental education," he nevertheless appreciates to the full extent pious, solid, good instruction of the mind and heart, such as he feels convinced you are receiving at your present home. Of course, you will bring with you your music, as you will need that, and your clothing, as it will be necessary to remodel, repatch and make anew a goodly portion of it. . . .

Mingled with the good, kind wishes of your friends, believe me my dear child, your Mother's prayers and love are closely woven.

God bless you,
Mama

### Monday, June 26, 1865

*On awaking this morning I was somewhat sorry to find it raining, but as I had concluded not to start to St Joseph's today, I did not very much regret it. Mr Preston put Johnny and William to fixing up the old house for the use of an old Virginia Negro—Jim, who is expected to occupy it on the first of July. . . . Thede washed and did up Nannie's clothes today and then dressed her this evening and I shall take her with me to St. Joseph's. . . .*[1]

Mountain View
June 30th 1865

Dear Mr Preston,

As I have often heard you say "no news, is good news" I have acted upon it, and hence you see me dating my letter from Thede's old home. . . .

Of course our dear Theodosia told you how comfortably and snugly she saw me seated in the cars and off for Gettysburg. . . . Judge how agreeable the surprise that awaited me when I tell you the first person that met me on the platform was my sister Louisa—then Dr Tate, and then my nephew George —each and all giving me a warm and hearty welcome. Dr Tate (of whom I can scarcely speak sufficiently grateful) at once took me in charge and we walked round to his pleasant little domicile, where his good little wife and my dear little niece met me with open arms and kind greetings. It seems they had expected me the day before and the Dr waited the arrival of the cars in all the storm with a close carriage to take me to his home without a ducking.

I had purchased a through ticket to Emmitsburg . . . , which when the Dr saw, and heard of, he laughingly said—"Aunty this is of no further use to you, as I intend from this hour to take charge of you and see you safely to Emmitsburg and back again myself." I . . . told him his offer was so gracefully tendered that I accepted it thankfully and while here would be perfectly submissive to all his movements. . . . After a good dinner—with a nice cup of tea as an accompaniment, the Dr brought his carriage and two fine horses to the door. . . .

While on our way—the whole party *concluded* it an impossibility that May and I should so soon return to Baltimore, as I had expected to do. The world and the "rest of mankind," you know, are to be in Gettysburg on the fourth of July. Of course dear Aunt Louisa and her family are to swell the number, and she and Dr Tate and Mary would not hear of my passing through the town at *this time* and not tarrying for a few days. As the Dr said, "Aunty, I will take you and Ma and May to Mountain View as soon as we return from Emmitsburg, and bring you back to Gettysburg whenever you wish to come"; I concluded to remain, provided I could hear from you saying I might do so. As it was impossible to get a letter to the post office from Mr Dielman's in time for the mail of the next morning, Dr Tate very kindly offered to write to you from Emmitsburg. . . . Well, on reaching Gettysburg last evening and finding no telegram from you, we felt satisfied you gave your permission for us to remain till after the 4th! . . .

May acquitted herself much to the Sisters' satisfaction and mine also, and is looking very well and though most anxious to see you and be at home again, is nevertheless greatly pleased at the present arrangement. . . . Mrs Stevens is looking well and tells me to say she feels as though among old friends and hopes to express to you personally soon how grateful she feels. . . . Say a thousand kind things to dear Theodosia and tell her I hope she will forgive the apparent selfishness of my leaving her so long, but really I could not resist the pleasure of this little trip. May sends love & kisses to you and Thede and love to all the rest of the family. . . .

> Affectionately,
> Madge

## Thursday, July 6, 1865

*The day has been a delightful one, and gaily & pleasantly spent. Visitors began to come to the house from early dawn till noon. A strange circumstance* occurred, a young gentleman, a Mr Baugher, came from Gettysburg, was here, and when he saw me he recognized me as having been the lady at whose house he came together with a party of soldiers to search the premises. May & I knew him as one of the party who were here last summer during Harry Gilmore's raid in Maryland. This party came out for the purpose of gunning and left before dark. . . .

### Friday, July 7, 1865

. . . Dr Tate & family came out yesterday and today they took May & I in to Gettysburg and . . . we left in the car for Baltimore. Louisa McGrew went with us as far as Hanover and Mr Baugher left us at the junction. We reached the city in good time and walked to the office. . . .

### Saturday, July 8, 1865

. . . This morning May & I walked out to do some shopping and to call on Sister Frances and [Sister] Leopoldine; they were pleased to see us and invited May to come and spend some time with them. We also called on Father Foley and the Archbishop, and had a most delightful & satisfactory visit. While out May purchased a beautiful set of studs as a present for her father, and to be worn in the shirt she made him at St Joseph's. About 4 o'clock Papa came to town & May saw him for the first time. The meeting was a very affectionate one. . . .

### Sunday, July 9, 1865

. . . Everybody was cheerful and alive this morning. While at breakfast Mary Lizzie & Alice came up to see May. . . . This afternoon May dressed herself as she was dressed at the Distribution & went down to her father, showed him her honors and gave him the shirt she made. Papa seemed greatly pleased and told May to keep her rigging on during the evening. We walked out and May saw for the first time Peri and her little colt. . . .

### Friday, July 14, 1865

. . . Mr. Preston . . . and Thede spent the greater part of the day measuring points of land &c &c to enable Mr Preston to draw up a proper agreement with Mr Scharf, who wishes to rent the farm for a term of years. Kitty washed a quantity of May's clothes today and did them nicely. . . .

Aside from sketchy references in Madge's diary to the Scharfs as future tenants of Pleasant Plains, the Prestons' papers offer no information on the couple's decision to leave the farm residence where they had spent so many years. Madge's aversion to the isolation imposed by wintry weather, implicit in her relief when they moved to town in January, must have played its role. With May away, and servants so hard to obtain and keep, the farm and its large house may have seemed increasingly a burden. Preston's law practice, which appeared to be flourishing, may also have required his almost daily presence in the city.

The first reference to the Scharfs (and Madge's effort to avoid them) occurs in her diary entry of June 18. By the time negotiations had moved toward a decision, May was no doubt at home and the flow of letters that might have reported these events, discontinued. The diarist, writing to and for herself, assumes her own motivation and that of her husband in this momentous change.

### Sunday, July 16, 1865

. . . *Mr Preston and I were engaged the greater part of the morning writing an agreement between Mr Preston and Mr Scharf relative to the renting of Pleasant Plains for a term of years. This afternoon Mr Preston & Mr Scharf surveyed the premises and Mr Scharf approved the form of agreement and will come next Tuesday and execute it. . . . It is quite pleasant to see how nicely Thede & May get along together. They are very fond of each other and enjoy themselves nicely.*

### Tuesday, July 18, 1865

. . . *Sophia & Kitty finished their ironing today and did it beautifully. I made a dotted linen body for myself on the machine, which I think looks very well indeed. . . . May & I will . . . leave on Thursday for Philadelphia to spend two weeks with Mrs Simmons. Mr Scharf came today, and he and Mr Preston executed the agreement which give Mr Scharf control of the farm for six years. It was a very painful thing to do—to give up a home of so many years standing. Mr Preston seems quite sad tonight. . . .*

### Sunday, July 23, 1865

*[Philadelphia.] We went to High Mass at St John's Church this morning & May saw for the first time the place where her parents were married. I always*

*feel sad when I think of the great changes that have taken place, and the holy vows that had been broken. . . .*

Leaving Old Point Va
23d July 1865 6. A.M.

Dear Madge,

I dare say you will be very much surprised at the heading of this letter—but in the age in which we live we have perhaps no right to be surprised at any-thing. You may remember that when we parted at the depot Captain Russell joined me in bidding you and May goodbye. On our way up town the Captain cordially invited me to accompany him on his next trip to Norfolk. I told him . . . that I scarcely felt justified in leaving my niece at home. His ready answer was, bring her with you. . . . Acting on the moment, I at once resolved to ac-cept the Captain's invitation—. . . and on reaching home informed Theo-dosia of my determination. Of course it was a great surprise. . . . Accordingly 6 P.M. of Saturday found Theodosia, Kitty and myself on board of the Louisi-ana. . . .

It would take a volume and more time than I have just now to give even a faint inkling of the many remarks—expressions of delight &c which were made by both. When the boat started (that is *our* boat, the Louisiana) another boat, a brag boat of a Northern line lately gotten up in our now Yankeeized city, also started, and went ahead of us with a flourish of trumpets—a boat called the Dictator. I happened to express to one of the Negro deck men my apprehension that she would be at Norfolk before us. The Ethiopian replied "No sar—you see when we gets into the deep water—we leave her sar as de fish leave de frog"—and we did so—a few miles below Annapolis; the Dicta-tor no longer dictated to us, she was in our wake. . . .

We found on reaching this place that the boat would remain some time before she resumed her trip to Norfolk. No sooner could we do so than The. and I hastened on shore and in a few minutes walked over the ruins of what was in former days the promenade ground of the Hygea Hotel—all changed —ashes, burnt stones—rude buildings filled with sutlers' stores or offices for military officials; but there we stood—only a hundred feet and a moat filled with water between us and the "Case Mate" in which is confined the South-ern Chief.[2] Poor The. strained her eyes full of tears at the aperture, hoping she might catch a glimpse of the veteran whose renown and pending fate at this time fills so much of the world's speculation, and who in his hapless ad-versity awakens so much of fanatical malice or envy. . . .

I am interrupted. We are put about to arrive at Norfolk where I intend this letter shall be mailed.

Love to all—God bless you

W. P. Preston

Pleasant Plains
25th July 1865 5 A.M.

Dear Madge

My last written while the boat was on her course between Fortress Monroe and Norfolk was necessarily abrupt and probably incoherent. The centre table of a crowded steamboat cabin—surrounded by all ages and sexes—all hands gabbling and a majority of the crowd slab-sided hungry-looking Yankees uttering detestable sentiments, originating in fanaticism—cupidity and religious (Q)³ bloodthirstiness—is but a poor place to write a letter. Fancy a long-legged, heavy-jawed lout with a chunk of bread baked in Massachusetts and the nether end of a ham-bone raised heaven knows where sputtering with his mouth full, "Heere Nan, luke heere! Why don't ye luke?—Heere's the place where *Our* men whipped the rebs; and sunk that thundrin big ship —Zac Cummins was along and gin me an account of the hull out." A rat-eyed, lank-haired girl—with a cockle shell hat, trimmed red, white, and blue—stretched her neck out of the cabin window, gaped a minute or so, and as she drew her frontispiece back, grinned satisfaction, and drawlingly responded to her companion, "Dun't say!—Well neow! how I should a liked to heern Zac's account on't." Alas the day! . . . As soon as we reached Norfolk and got rid of the great crowd of voyageurs, Captain Russell and I took a ramble through the ancient city. In many places *painful* evidences of Vandalic destruction awakened distressing emotions. When I was last there, it might truly be said to be a gem of floral beauty—now, many residences which at that time might well be regarded as the houses of persons of affluence and taste are either deserted—in ruins or appropriated by the government to official uses. Theodosia joined a Mr Anderson (known as Genl Anderson before the war) and his wife—very clever persons residents of Baltimore, and whom we met on board of the boat on our way down. . . .

Kitty in the meantime had been put under the charge of Drucilla, a matronly looking American of African descent. Whether Kit went ashore or not at Norfolk I am unable to say. On the way up she approached me and said, "Master if you'll let me stay in this boat—I'll be very good. You shan't hear any bad of me." I told her I would have to see the Captain about it—I did see the Captain, he consented and Kit is No. 3 in command of the staterooms of the good ship Louisiana. We go from Kitty to Katherine this day. Heaven send the change may be for the better. . . . All well here. God protect you. W. P. P.

## Thursday, July 27, 1865

*. . . The postman brought me another long letter today from Mr Preston written in his old, kind elaborate manner, which makes me hope all is right at*

*home at present. God grant it may so continue. . . . Kitty has . . . left us and is now on the Steamer Louisiana as one of the stewardesses!*

Pleasant Plains
26 July 1865 5 A.M.

Dear Madge,

Before this reaches you I suppose you will have received my letter of yesterday. . . . As intimated in that . . . despatch, Crick wended his way to Pleasant Plains last evening. The boy looks very well and has grown astonishingly. I sent him out in the 6 P.M. Towsontown Train, inasmuch as I had to bring Catherine with me in the buggy and therefore had no room for Crick. . . .

The Bear[4] was as furious as a scorpion surrounded by fire because I took Catherine away. I said nothing but left the poor reptile to sting herself to death if she chose. In addition to any interest I might personally have in Catherine's removal, I felt it to be my duty not to let Catherine remain with the Bear any longer. The poor girl was mercilessly worked almost to death—in addition to considerable brushing, rubbing scrubbing &c through the house she had to do the washing for Mr & Mrs S.[5] and Madame and le jeune gentilhomme. I thought this looked like adding pomatum to imprisonment if not insult to injury. . . .

The poor girl, [who] was never in the country before, told us last evening she had never seen a blackberry growing—did not know whether they grew upon trees or upon bushes. . . . How she may answer I cannot tell. I think she is kind-hearted and honest and I hear her already pottering in the kitchen. I am to take Mrs Pent into Baltimore with me this morning to afford her an opportunity of arranging her rooms preparatory to her moving from P. Plains on Tuesday next. The absence of Kit creates quite a void but I can assure you an agreeable vacuum. A source of great torment has been got rid of. It is not easy to tell how great a relief it is to no longer feel a tremulous apprehension of mean peculation. It is true we suffer some inconvenience from lack of her services, but this is small in comparison with her numerous and scarcely to be endured annoyances. She appeared to be very cheerful on board of the boat and very active—stirring briskly through the various staterooms—loaded with a basket of napkins—distributing them, waiting on the ladies, &c &c. It is more than probable she will do very well. At all events she appeared to be greatly pleased. Captain Russell's new boat—the *Kelso*—is to be ready by the 15th of September next. It is said she will be the most magnificent boat ever put upon the Chesapeake. The captain says that by that time Kit will be "broke in" to the routine of stateroom duty—and if she realizes what from her movements at present he anticipates, she shall be installed under regular pay as second stewardess of the *Kelso* so that it may be poor Kit has found her vocation at last. . . .

I have not yet heard of the Bear being provided with rooms, but my impressions are that she will tear herself away about the first of August. . . . Well with Kit gone—the bears gone—the Pents gone—and about to go ourselves, I certainly have food for reflection[6]—and other food too; thank God, for Theo has just announced breakfast ready. . . .

We are all well here. Jewell and the cats included. We have however one drawback on the health list—old Jim's wife Alice. I fear she will not last long. I made some physic for her last night but it seems she is no better. Love to you and May

W. P. Preston

Pleasant Plains
27th July 1865 5 A.M.

Dear Madge,

. . . I stated in my last that I had an engagement with a man from California in relation to the mill property. On my way to town accompanying Mrs Pent, according to my engagement I met my friend at the mill. Everything was examined and great deal of incidental talk took place, first as to my selling him the "mill lot" with its improvements for $7000. . . .

During the mill discussion—occupying a couple of hours, old dame Pent waddled about and poked into everything. . . . In her peregrinations she made an effort at being romantic and walked over the rocks in the brook—suddenly I heard a piercing sound like "Oh! My !!" and turning round saw the old woman's pedal extremities cutting fandangos in the air. I feared she was hurt and ran to her assistance, but found she had only scratched her elbow and splashed her bonnet in the crystal stream she was bending to admire. Another incident to prove romance, and rocks, and stones, and streams are only for the young—not for pussy old ladies whose comfortable rotundity needs level ground. . . .

12 o'clock found me at the house in town. The Bear had installed Theodore as doorkeeper—but walked up herself to give me an account of visitors &c; at the close of her narrative she volunteered a remark evidently to invite an unpleasant discourse—she said, "Mr Preston, I hope you do not think that I care about your having taken Catherine away—She was not here for by[7] [sic] benefit and I have had a great deal of trouble with her"—I quietly responded by saying, "Mrs Beer, I am surprised that a person of your age and shrewdness should attempt to foist so gross a falsehood on one of my observation and judgment. Your crying sin appears to be ungrateful[ness] in appreciation of every service and kindness rendered you—I had no desire to speak of Catherine—and I do believe that nothing short of a guilty conscience induces you to mention her name. You feel that you behaved brutally towards the poor girl—made her work like a slave rubbing scrubbing and washing for

your own family—(while you played the lady). . . . Now you have the auda-
cious impudence to seek to cover up your harsh unfeeling conduct by a lie.
Your own sense might have taught you that such an attempt would only
render you more despicable in my eyes, and awaken in my recollection your
heartless cruelty in exposing poor Georgy half clad to the bitterest storm of the
winter." At this state of the entertainment, a gentleman whom Theodore had
let in walked up stairs and the discourse abruptly terminated. . . .

I left Dame Pent in town & arrived home about 7 P.M. and found every
thing moving along well. Catherine is slow but Theo. says she is willing to
learn and is quiet and we believe honest. Crick amuses himself in various
ways and manifests a willingness to be useful. Old Alice is still very poorly
—so much so, that Jim has to stay at home and attend to her.

Yours truly

W. P. Preston

---

How did Madge feel about all these changes in household staffing? She
must have written back, expressing a sense of loss at least in Kitty's departure.
Her letter is missing, but one from Preston on July 29 seems to refer to it when
he insists that "Kit . . . is at best a poor subject for emotion." His characteriza-
tion of Kitty which follows is abusive, though perhaps to comfort Madge and
May, he acknowledges that he has given Kitty a small sum to start her out. As
to Mrs. Beer and Mrs. Pent, Preston continues in the sarcastic vein he has
earlier adopted. Mrs. Beer, he reports, would be housekeeper for a boarding
school to be opened soon by a group of educated Germans.

Pleasant Plains

1st August 1865, 5 A.M.

Dear Madge

Your pleasant letter . . . and May's . . . were both received yesterday. That
you should dub my letters bright scintillations of the morning while you
characterise your own as dull and prosy is rather wicked. If our respective
merits as letter writers are to be determined upon, I hesitate not to affirm the
decision will be in your favor. Thede says and insists upon it that you are "the
best letter writer that ever lived." I said "except Lady Mary Wortley Montagu
—Madame de Staël and Corinne."[8] She says she "never received any letters
from these persons but she has no doubt they couldn't hold a candle to
Aunty"—Be this as it may your letters have been very interesting and very acceptable. I am much gratified to know that you and May . . . are enjoying
yourselves. . . .

When I arrived in town yesterday and drove into our yard, I found a deuce of a turmoil—half a dozen of various ages and sexes gabbering Dutch and an inconceivable amount of all sorts of queer things—carpets, tables, chairs, boxes, pots, pans and heaven knows what besides—the various figures were brushing & scrubbing, washing, folding, tying &c. In a word everything indicated a flitting and all the Stung's[9] and all the Bears were as busy as a bear at a bee tree. Black Hawk pricked up his ears and I wondered how so many odd things could have got into my house without my knowledge. The chattels literally represented two hemispheres. In the house the scene was equally lively; three or four noisy Dutchmen were carrying down heavy articles of furniture and everything was life and motion. . . .

I am better in health this morning and the weather is cooler—in my next you shall have the sequel—in the meantime our love to you all. This is with me a busy day. W. P. Preston

Pleasant Plains
2nd August 1865 5 A.M.

Dear Madge

At the close of my hastily written letter of yesterday I suggested the opinion in relation to the Bear that probably your prophecy respecting the goods and chattels would not be realized, that opinion has since been affirmed in the high court of events, for verily she hath departed. At about 12 M [eridian] of yesterday—the immortal 1st of August!!! the great bear solemnly entered my parlor and with elevated chin, uplifted nose and visage which Mrs Gobble the wife of the magistrate in Sir Launcelot Greaves might have envied—said "Sir—as I am about to leave—I come to hand you my card." At the moment of this important announcement I happened to be cosily seated in the arm chair with my reading glass in one hand and the newspaper in the other —both digits being thus employed, I replied in a tone of suppressed grief suited to the occasion, "Mrs Beer put it down," and accordingly she placed the precious autograph monogram, or whatever you may call it, upon the table and away she waddled with a pigeon-toed wriggle out of the room. I sat in silence and mused—I could not say like Manager Crumbles, "Wonderful woman! the first time I saw that woman she was standing on the head of a spear in the midst of a shower of fireworks!"; on the contrary I had to look through the varying vista of more than thirty years to see her with upturned skirts upon her knees surrounded by tubs and slops and floor cloths—and now delectable to say, she hands me her card!! Strange inconsistency of nature, no sooner did the heavy slamming of the door below proclaim her departure and interrupt my reverie than I sprang to my feet, looked at the card and relieved my melancholy by a burst of laughter—and I now enclose to you the veritable missive which occasioned my uproarious unholy mirth. Thus endeth the chapter on bears!—And last writing, to wit at 5 o'clock of the morning of the said immortal 1st of August, and while writing as "aforesaid," sundry bustling and unusual sounds were discovered to proceed from the Penthouse thereof, and on looking out of my window I discovered a wagon and two horses and various beds and bedsteads and tables and chairs and pots and pans, and every article of the said chattels looked melancholy and had an expression of a sad goodbye upon the shapes thereof—and while thoughtfully contemplating the same a tremulous tinkling of the bell broke forth, sounding like the death knell of the ringer. Alas! for sentiment and romance! "Villiam! Villiam! come do yourn breakfasd—de meat will be cold"; the person addressed suddenly let fall a sheet iron dripping pan, which fell with a ringing sound and said as plainly as a pan could talk, "the devil it will!"—and the said "Villiam" wheeling to the rightabout, disappeared for the purpose as I supposed of making an onslaught on "de meat" aforesaid—A change came o'er the spirit of my dream—seven o'clock declared itself, and the wagon aforesaid with one William Pent perched upon a Dutch chest painted red, the crowning figure of a load of household stuff, wended its rumbling way towards the iron gate of P. Plains; very shortly afterwards, I found myself seated in a vehicle commonly known as a buggy with a prosy little Dutch woman by my side. Theodosia was standing near as a tear seemed to moisten the wrinkled cheek of the little Dutch woman. "Goot bye! Goot bye!" I suddenly pulled up and Theodosia came running when Mrs Pent all smiles expressively nodded and nodded her head, and said to Theodosia as a last remark "You finds de bredt and the coffee in the pig tin bucked" "Good Heavens" I exclaimed "Mrs Pent I thought you had forgotten something" "I dit—I dit" was her animated reply —as I continued our journey, I found myself whistling or singing in spite of all I could do, a new song to an old tune "Her heart's in her belly—her heart's in her belly. No! No!"—. . . .

William's departure at this time greatly incommodes me. He would have been *very* useful for the next two months, but so it is—and as usual I shall make the best of it—and the best of it cheerfully—I agree with you that it is just as well that May is not here just now. It takes the experience of age to blunt the sensibilities of childhood. In my next I hope to be in a practical humor. . . . with my love to you all I am affectionately

yours

Wm P. Preston

## Friday, August 4, 1865

*Fearfully warm today, indeed there never was so warm a spell of weather. On going down the street today, I met our friend Mr Stewart, and strange to say, he was on his way to Baltimore, intending to be in the 1 o'clock train. May & I left Phila after bidding our friends goodbye in the same train and found Mr Stewart at the depot. We had a pleasant trip & on reaching the house found Crick awaiting our arrival. It seems Crick has remained in town since Mrs Beer's departure. . . .*

## Saturday, August 5, 1865.

*Rose early to dress for breakfast at Barnam's, where Mrs Emory & Walsh, Crick May and myself took breakfast, for which to our great astonishment we were obliged to pay 1.25 per breakfast or 3.75 for the 3 breakfasts. May took her little box which she purchased for Sister and went up to spend the day with her. Crick & I went home, and about ten o'clock Mr Preston came in. He seemed quite glad to know we had come home. . . . About four o'clock we left the city in the wagon with Jeff & Black in harness. Crick came with us to spend Sunday in the country. On reaching home Thede met us and was very glad to see us home again but it was quite painful to not see poor Kitty, and the Pentz, all having left the house during our absence. Catherine has taken Kitty's place and Thede seems to like her very well.*

## Sunday, August 6, 1865

*. . . This morning Papa and I wandered over the place and stopped at Uncle Jim's. I saw poor Alice, whom I fear will not live very long. Poor thing, she would be better in Heaven! Johnny went away this morning and did not return till after the storm; it was too late for him to see his cows, consequently they were not milked. I have been rather annoyed with Mr Preston tonight. I brought him from the city a pair of sleeve buttons & cuffs and he received them so ungracefully that I took them back and said I could use them myself.*

## Tuesday, August 8, 1865

*. . . Sophie was here to wash the largest wash she had had for a long time. Catherine helped, but very imperfectly; poor thing she tries hard to do as she is told but her mind is very weak. . . .*

## Thursday, August 10, 1865

*. . . Mr Preston and Thede went to the city, and as usual did not reach home till late. It seems they stopped at Aigburth Vale and took tea. On their return, I happened to make a remark about wishing to have been there myself; that was a plea for a terrible scold on Mr Preston's part which convinced me he was not satisfied with himself!*

### Friday, August 11, 1865

. . . Mr Preston remained home today and he and Crick has been cleaning Mrs Pentz's house, much to my annoyance. I have been busy in the kitchen today, making pies. This afternoon I operated on the sewing machine a little. Thede has made up her mind to go to Mountain View for a little while and leaves tomorrow. . . . I hope she will not return till after May leaves for school.

### Saturday, August 12, 1865

. . . On going to see Mr Preston this morning, I met a warm and pleasant reception from him and a reminding that it was the anniversary of our wedding day! Mr Preston & Thede left this morning for the city and from there, Thede started for Mountain View. . . . May & I were busy fixing up the house and cleaning it all to our own satisfaction. Catherine assisted and now we have really got things in good clean order and I hope we will be able to keep them so. . . .

### Wednesday, August 16, 1865

. . . Mr Preston remained home working at the storehouse or pic nic spot, as I shall call it in future, till three o'clock—at which time he drove to the city to meet Mr Dielman and bring him home with him. I prepared everything for a nice supper and waited till ½ past eight o'clock and then we gave them up, thinking they would remain in the city all night; so Crick & I took our tea and just as we rose from the table, the carriage drove to the door and Mr Preston and Mr Dielman got out. They enjoyed what was left of the supper. Mr Dielman played for us and we retired about eleven o'clock. Papa sleeping upstairs in our room as May was not home. . . .

### Thursday, August 17, 1865

. . . May came home while we were at breakfast and was delighted to see Mr Dielman. After breakfast Mr Dielman took May to the parlour and gave her some very fine lessons and instructions on the piano. After a late dinner, Mr Preston & Mr Dielman drove down to Mr Hillen's & Mr Abell's and returned about nine o'clock, after which Mr Dielman played for us till eleven and then we retired—first eating a nice watermelon.

### Friday, August 18, 1865

. . . Mr Preston & Mr Dielman drove to the city this morning . . . as Mr Dielman returns home tomorrow. May & I have been . . . making pies which I *intend sending in to Sister tomorrow when May goes in to spend those few days she has been talking of doing. . . . We have spent a quiet day and as May is suffering with a bad headache we intend to retire early. Catherine is improving vastly in the cleaning line tho' she will never do anything in the cooking department.*

### Thursday, August 24, 1865

*Well the long agony is over and the pic nic too! And a great success and a great affair it was. A more glorious day never was witnessed and if we had asked of our good Lord the weather we had wanted, we could not have anything more delightful. By twelve o'clock the greater part of the company had assembled and dancing had taken place. The grounds were admirably adapted for the purpose, and by universal consent the pic nic was pronounced the best affair of the kind ever gotten up in this neighbourhood. Mrs Owens was there in all her glory and accompanied by five ladies and two young gentlemen as satellites revolving around their sun. The two Miss Waters, three Miss Pinkney, Mrs Brown, Mrs Pinkney & Mrs Zecorskey. The county was splendidly represented, and everything passed off satisfactorily with one exception. There was too much liquor afloat! Mr Preston returned home after it closed, and went to bed. Crick, May and I did the same, and by ten o'clock, all was quiet & at rest.*

### Sunday, September 3, 1865

*Somewhat cloudy all day and showery occasionally. Mr Preston was engaged all the morning writing a letter for Mrs Owens to send to Mrs Stevens.*[10] *Mrs Owens came over and spent the day with us and left about six o'clock. We heard this afternoon that the Abells were not going up to Emmitsburg for several days, consequently May cannot go tomorrow as we expected she would. . . .*

### Monday, September 4, 1865

*. . . May and I . . . intend going to the city in the morning for the purpose of seeing if any of the Sisters are going to St. Joseph's, that May can accompany them. . . .*

# 12

# Moving Away from Pleasant Plains

As MADGE HAD HOPED, one of the Baltimore group of the Sisters of Charity was indeed planning to leave for St. Joseph's—Sister Ambrosine, whom Madge and May located during May's farewell visit to Sister Leopoldine. On this third year of May's leave-taking for school, it was easier for Madge to part with her beloved daughter. Still her diary page closes: "Our last night together."

On the morning of September 6, Madge rose at five o'clock—to purchase fresh fruit for May's journey and to buy a beefsteak for her breakfast. "I did not think it prudent," Madge wrote, "to send her traveling on a light breakfast." At nine o'clock both Madge and May were at the depot, where they joined Sister Ambrosine and Sister Ursula, who had come to see off her colleague. "I bade the dear child and Sister 'goodbye,'" wrote Madge that night, "and with a sad heart, saw the car move off with my treasure." This sentence was written neither in Baltimore nor at Pleasant Plains. For after calling on friends in the city, Madge decided to stay the night with the Owens at Aigburth Vale. Preston and Crick were at home in the country, and Catherine, the girl Preston had rescued from the exploitative supervision of Mrs. Beer, would look after the household chores.

If Madge was later disappointed in Catherine's work, it was not perhaps the girl's fault. "I have been quite annoyed with Catherine. . . . she having neglected to do, or rather badly done the work I left her. I find myself each day more and more troubled with her, and yet poor thing, I think sometimes she tries to do her best." Under Madge's supervision, they put things to rights —baking, washing, ironing, and moving ahead on the chores for the morrow, when Madge expected the Owens women to return her visit.

Pleasant Plains
Sept 11th, 1865

My darling child,

I have only time this morning to acknowledge the reception of your welcome favour of the 7th inst[ance], stating your safe arrival. . . .

I am glad to know your return was a cause of pleasure to the Sisters and your young companions, as it speaks well for the estimation in which my little girl is held among them. I had hoped to have written a letter to dear Sr Raphael before this in regard to your doings the coming year, but indeed my time is so constantly occupied with the contemplated change in our domestic movements that thus far I have not been able to find a spare moment. . . . I wish you to pay as much attention as possible to your music—both Papa and I have come to the conclusion that your *voice is worth cultivating* and it will gratify us to know that Sr Raphael places you under the best instruction the institution affords for both vocal & instrumental instruction. I am also anxious about your French, and do hope you will avail yourself of every opportunity in your power to perfect yourself in that study. . . .

I will write you an account of our doings since you left in a day or two . . . everything has gone on quietly & pleasantly. With the exception that Papa still complains of his side. Papa, Crick and'all the family send

their loves to you
Mama


## Tuesday, September 12, 1865

. . . *Crick and the men had quite an excitement this morning in their efforts to catch the little colt Lee and lead him down to pasture at the mill. They were obliged at length to ride down Kate & Jack. Lee & Kate's colt followed without any trouble. . . . Mr Preston . . . and Crick spent the day at the mill tinkering. Catherine is suffering with a painful boil on her arm, and I am not able to get Sophia to put out the clothes and do the ironing till Friday.*


## Thursday, September 14, 1865

. . . *It was intensely warm all day . . . as to make us fear for the comfort of those to be at the picnic. Mr Preston . . . and I went over to Eudowood where the picnic was held. . . . Mrs Stansbury's park was well adapted for the purpose and everything was nicely arranged, the ladies looked pretty and were well dressed. . . .*

### Saturday, September 16, 1865

*. . . This has been one of my busy days. I have been making new garments out of old ones by the aid of the little Fairy, on which I am beginning to operate very nicely. Mr Preston went to the city this morning, regretting apparently that he had to go. I thought at the time there was something under all these regrets but was not able to make it out, but when the night came and no Mr Preston, then I was certain something peculiar was to occur. Nine o'clock came, and then came Mr Preston and with him Rose Smith. The mystery was explained! and the nervous condition of the gentleman accounted for as usual; when she is about Mr Preston's conduct is unaccountable!*

Pleasant Plains Septr 17th 1865

My dear May,

. . . I cannot deny my sweet child, that I turned with a sad heart from the depot after saying "goodbye" to you and Sister, knowing that for many a long and weary month, the bright, glad smile and cheerful voice of my loving little girl would not greet me; just as I passed through the door, I met George Abell, who told me it had been decided the night before that the boys would not return to St Mary's College, and consequently the girls could not go back to St Joseph's as they could not be separated. They are all going to Georgetown. I am really glad the poor boys are not to return to a place for which they seem to have so great a dislike. I have never thought it politic to insist on children remaining at a school when they have once become dissatisfied with the teachers, the rules, the studies, or whatever it may be. I expressed myself so to George at the same time, saying I regretted the necessity for the removal of the girls, as I thought it a serious disadvantage to change a school . . . when children were happy & satisfied—to all of which George acquiesced. . . . I went directly home and there found Mrs Emory, who, I suspect, seeing I was somewhat depressed, remained sometime with me, chatting and making herself quite agreeable. Finding Papa did not come in, I arranged affairs about the house, and as I told you I would do, started in the Towsontown cars for Aigburth Vale, at which place I met a warm and loving welcome from Mrs Owens and the girls. . . . You will be surprised to hear I remained there till Friday. . . . Papa knowing where I was, very kindly encouraged my remaining, knowing I would feel less your departure by being with our kind & cheerful friends. It was quite amusing to hear how they had kept Bachelor's Hall—poor Catherine being less than nobody! Catherine hailed my return home with the greatest apparent delight and tried to do everything to gratify and please me, fearing I suppose, I would go away again and leave her the responsibility of housekeeping. When Mrs Owens left me, it was with the understanding that she and the girls should spend Sunday with us. Consequently bright and early on Sunday morning the carriage drove to the door and I welcomed our friends of the Vale to Pleasant Plains. . . . Our friends did not leave us till evening, and when they did, they promised to give me another day during the coming week. I was over to Eudowood this afternoon and when I returned home, I brought with me a basket of nice peaches, the gift of Mrs Stansbury. Of course the kindest inquiries were made about you . . . by all the family. . . .

Papa has remained in town all night superintending during the day the fixing up of the back buildings, which Papa thinks are not in habitable condition. I send however Papa's love, together with Crick's, Johnny's and Catherine's.

Good night

Yours devotedly Mama

---

Madge's letter to May omitted all mention of another visit of that afternoon—this one to the William Stansburys. Some comment on May's close childhood friends Alice and Mamie would have been natural. But Madge's diary page for the same day reveals why news of this later visit had been suppressed. If the girls behaved unaccountably in Madge's view, perhaps they had information concerning Preston and Rose which had been withheld from Madge. Possibly the behavior of this pair had become so blatant that they were subjects of gossip around the neighborhood. But a likelier explanation is that Madge's own earlier confidence to Mrs. Owens had been shared with these other near-neighbors. When Madge explained "all things" to Mrs. Owens in dissuading her from the trip to visit her mother at Mountain View in Preston's company, Madge appeared in some way to implicate Rose. Madge herself may have let the secret out.

## Sunday, September 17, 1865

*The nervous condition of the said gentleman still continues as does also his brutality.*[1] *I must exonerate Rose from any companionship in it: as far as I can observe, I think she is behaving correct in her conduct. This afternoon she and I drove over to see Mrs Owens & the girls but they had gone to church; we then drove to Eudowood and made a visit, saw the family, and on our way home stopped at Wm Stansbury's and there I felt quite insulted by the conduct of the girls. What the cause of their conduct I cannot divine—Alice scarcely spoke to Rose and Mary Lizzie was little better. We have spent a tolerable pleasant evening.*

### Monday, September 18, 1865

*We . . . rose early to enable Mr Preston and Rose to go to Baltimore [in] time for the ½ past 9 train. Just before they left, Mr Preston said, If I had expressed to him a wish to go to the Mountain I might have gone, and I might go tomorrow if I wished; so acting on that, I have been getting ready all day—I remodelled my bonnet, done some washing and ironing &c &c—but unfortunately this afternoon a storm came up. . . . I shall not be able therefore to go. Mr Preston came home by 5 o'clock! this afternoon, not having to wait for anyone!*[2]

### Tuesday, September 19, 1865

*The sun rose clear & bright . . . and Mr Preston seeming so strangely anxious that I should go up to the Mountain, I considered and made my arrangements hurriedly, and we were off by 7 o'clock; we reached the city in good time, and drove to the office, but Mr Preston having his own reasons for not letting me go in, I was obliged to let him pack my dress in the valise and then go to the depot. There I met 2 Sr of Charity, who were going to St Joseph's. I also saw Mother Ann Simeon & Sr Matilda, to whom I introduced Mr Preston—we then bade them goodbye and started for G——g [Gettysburg], on arriving there Theodore was waiting to meet me and took me at once to his house. To my surprise I found Mary had been confined on Saturday and had a nice little girl. As it was not well for Theodore to leave Mary, we remained all night and will start early in the morning.*

### Wednesday, September 20, 1865

*We left G——g about 8 o'clock and reached M. View at 10, saw Aunt Louisa and some of the family; the rest having gone to the fair, we soon started also, and when we arrived at the grounds found many of our friends there and much surprised to see me. The articles at the fair on exhibition were very creditable to those who had made and raised them, and altogether I have been very much pleased. Theodore has a fine ham on exhibition, which we hope will take the premium. . . .*

### Friday, September 22, 1865

*. . . Thede drove me over to St Joseph's this morning, where I saw May; and to my surprise the child has had her hair cut off and wears a cap, which looks childlike & pretty. I took May to Emmitsburg, and after a little pleasant conversation alone we went to a store and I spent two dollars for her in confection-*

*ary, we then took our dinner and walked out to St Joseph's, where I had the satisfaction of seeing a number of May's schoolgirls, who have taken a great fancy to me; we spent an hour in pleasant recreation & talk in the Infirmary. I bade the dear children goodbye, and . . . I drove to Emmitsburg with Dr Tate. . . . We drove to Gettysburg and soon after Louisa & Theodore came in and we are all together for the night.*

### Saturday, September 23, 1865

*. . . At 8 o'clock we left Gettysburg and Thede was to meet us in the noon train at Hanover Junction. . . . We had a pleasant trip to the city and on reaching the depot we found Mr Preston awaiting our arrival. We went to the office, and to our surprise found Kitty there. . . . Mr Preston concluded to go out to P.P. with the horse & buggy and the Dr & Thede were to go in the car as far as Towsontown and walk over. We all reached P. P. nearly at the same time and found the family in bed, they having thought it not necessary to wait our coming, as Mr Preston said, "possibly under certain circumstances he would not come home this evening, but remain all night." For what reason I know not! Theodore seems quite pleased with Mr Preston's attentions. Mr Preston is in one of his most unpleasant humours, complaining terribly of ill health and sufferings!!!*

### Sunday, September 24, 1865

*We have had a delightful day. . . . All hands wandered over the place showing Theodore & Thede the things to be seen. . . . Christie came over this afternoon with a letter from Mrs Owens to Mr Preston; poor thing, I fear she is still in trouble with her mother. During my absence Catherine has not done as I requested; today however she is trying to do better. Mr Preston is complaining more than ever, and for some reason, scarcely speaks to Theodosia!*

Pleasant Plains
Septr 25th 1865

My darling child,

I steal a moment from one of the busiest of days, just to tell you I am again at Pleasant Plains. . . .

You will be amused when I tell you Kitty was there and had prepared a nice little supper for us. . . . Kitty was looking very well and asked a thousand questions about you and really seemed to regret not having seen you before you again returned to St. Joseph's. Yesterday Theodore spent with us, apparently much pleased with all he saw, particularly the horses and your little pony. . . .

. . . I must bring my letter to an abrupt termination as Mr Preston calls me. Goodbye. Give my love to all the kind Sisters who care to have any and love to the dear children, particularly my nieces Emma and Anna.[3] Keep any amount for yourself and believe me always

your devoted
Mama

Pleasant Plains
Octr 1st 1865

My dear child,

It really seems as if I should never have time again to sit down and write quietly and deliberately to you. . . .

Aunty Brent, quite unexpectedly, came out last Thursday to spend a week or two with us. She has just returned from "Nyack," on the Hudson river about thirty miles above New York, where she placed Minnie Sommers at that institute. I think Aunty Brent's preference would have been for St Joseph's, but as Mr Sommers (Minnie's uncle), who has adopted her and educates her at his own expense, selected this particular place, of course she was obliged to yield to his choice. The place seems on all accounts to be beautifully situated . . . and as well as I can understand from all I hear, is a school of high standard, and where a young lady would have all the opportunities of receiving a thorough classical education. . . .

Aunt Louisa came down yesterday to remain some time with us. The evening train is due in Baltimore at half past five; of course we were there at that time with the carriage—Papa, Crick and I, owing to an accident some distance up the road, the cars did not reach the depot till near nine o'clock —judge of our annoyance at being obliged to wait all that time in such a situation. . . . Late as it was, we drove out to P. P., reaching there near eleven o'clock . . . and there on our arrival, the kind welcome awarded us and the good supper already prepared for us, made us soon forget the discomforts to which we had so recently been subject. . . .

Yesterday I went to the city and while there purchased for you a shawl, which I think you will find more comfortable and convenient than a sack or jacket. . . . I had the pleasure of seeing Sister Matilda, who told me she was going up on Tuesday and would cheerfully be the bearer of the bundle to you. . . . Dear Papa was kind enough to carry it up for me, as he wished to have an interview with Sister before she left the city. I must tell you what Papa says of our dear Sister. "Of all the ladies I have ever met, Sister Matilda stands preeminent in conversational powers." I recalled what you had told me about Sister's powers in spiritual instruction and could readily believe Papa was correct in his judgment. I also saw Sister Leopoldine and was pleased to see her looking so well. . . .

. . . Give my love to Emma & Anna. . . . Papa & every one send lots of love to you.

Mama

## Monday, October 2, 1865

*The weather has been quite pleasant all day, but internal disquietudes have made it very unpleasant to me. Mr Preston was annoyed by Thede not going to the mill with the pic nic party. Consequently the thing fell through and Mr Preston has been in a pet all day. . . .*

## Wednesday, October 4, 1865

*. . . Aunty Brent went to the city with Mr Preston this morning and left in the three o'clock train for Washington. Aunty Brent wants Mr Preston to send the articles to her which she left here years ago; they consist of chamber furniture and will be sent to her as soon as convenient. Catherine put out the clothes today and ironed some of them and they really look very well. Mr Preston returned early and all seems well. Made a jar of tomato pickle.*

## Thursday, October 5, 1865

*. . . Mr Preston, Thede & Crick went to the mill this morning and it was dark when they reached home. The men also spent the day down there. I was so unfortunate as to run a needle down my thumbnail last night, and it has been so painful all day as to prevent my sewing any or attending to my household duties without great pain. Mr Kidd came out this afternoon and purchased all our sheep, 48 in number, but leaving us a pair of very fine English sheep. We rec'd $4.75 cts per sheep making in all $218. I am delighted they are gone. . . .*

## Friday, October 6, 1865

*No rain tho' we are praying constantly for it. Mr Preston & Thede drove to the city this morning, taking in with them the wool. They did not reach home till long after dark, and when they did they had a wonderful story to tell us about a "grand, splendid procession" the Negroes had in Baltimore.[4] Mr Preston sold the wool and rec'd for it (one hundred & forty four lbs) $85.05 cts., so dear little May has not lost on her wool. . . .*

## Sunday, October 8, 1865

*Mr. Preston was quite sick during the night, but I was not uneasy as I knew it was a sickness caused by seeing his friends! This morning he is much better and cheerful. . . .*

Baltimore<br>
Octr 13th 1865

My darling child,

You will perceive by the date . . . that I am in the city tonight. Papa brought me in this morning together with Catherine & Johnny for the purpose of overlooking the cleaning up and fixing the house preparatory to our moving in. Don't suppose, however, that desirable end is to be consummated . . . with the celerity we would desire. On the contrary it is one of those events that admits of much delay and I fear will be particularly so, in dear Papa's hands, as it is very evident, now that we approach the time for leaving dear old Pleasant Plains, Papa lingers round the spot, hallowed by so many pleasant memories to him particularly, as if he loathed to leave it. I am not surprised . . . the best years of Papa's life, and let us hope the happiest also, have been passed amidst its peaceful & quiet shades, and it is hardly in human nature to uproot the habits and associations of half a lifetime without a feeling of sadness and many regrets. Still with all these feelings keenly alive, I think Papa looks forward to the contemplated change. . . . The care and anxiety of our country home, since we have been deprived of our "own people" by the result of the late war, together with Papa's duties in town, are becoming too arduous for him, and almost any change that would relieve him would be hailed with pleasure by both of us.

A strange circumstance occurred at P. Plains today; when the carriage drove from the gate containing that party for the city, there was not left on the farm *one individual* actually belonging to the Pleasant Plains family. The men had gone to the mill property with a load of furniture not wanted for the house in town, and the rest were with us. Aunt Louisa, Thede and Crick remained in full possession of the entire establishment! Catherine and I have remained in tonight, while Papa & Johnny returned home. You will perceive . . . that we are making use of the new place Papa recently purchased. Of course there are many things in our present large establishment not needed in our city house . . . such articles we are storing in the mill property; consequently . . . we have really two movings going on at the one time; but we take all very quietly and hope to vacate our old premises by the time "Rufus" wishes to take possession. You will be pleased to know Rufus' cornfield, notwithstanding the drought, yielded a wonderful crop. For more than two weeks, they took on market days two hundred dozen ears! . . .

I have just completed a little cap, which I will try and send up in a day or two and which I think will be pretty for you to wear on Sundays and when you go to Holy Communion. The black one, of course, is very suitable for every-day use, but if Sister does not object, I think I should be better pleased to know you flourished on high days and holidays in something nice. If the cap I send you suits you, I will keep you supplied with such as long as you need any; if it does not fit and you suggest any improvements I will cheerfully make them. You can write on a slip of paper enclosed in your letter and Papa need not see it, or anyone else whom you do not wish to be made acquainted with the interesting fact of your having lost your hair! While on this subject, let me tell you that I do not wish under any persuasion to have oil or tonics of any kind put on your hair and I am perfectly convinced that good health is the best tonic for the hair and, thank God, that you have, when the hair begins to grow. Keep it clean by good brushing and occasionally sponging your head in water *without* soap; this is all that will be necessary, I think, to ensure you a fine suit of hair. What do you do for night caps? I think it would hardly do to sleep without any! . . . Remember me always to Sister Raphael, Sister Lucia, Sister Ann Scholastica and dear kind Sister Genevieve. Papa always makes the kindest inquiry after Genevieve, remembering her kind attentions to the poor soldiers after the battle at Gettysburg. . . .

Love from Papa and every member of the family, with any amount of it,

from your devoted
Mama

### Monday, October 16, 1865

. . . *Crick & Johnny took down to the mill this afternoon one of the par-lour buffets, and Mr Preston met them there and assisted them in removing it from the wagon and placing it in the house; when they reached home it was not dark. I saw at once that Mr Preston was extremely nervous, and it was not long till I felt the full force of it. I happened to ask how Louise⁵ reached her home, and from the answer I rec'd, I knew full well what had been going on in town!* . . .

### Tuesday, October 17, 1865

. . . *Mr Preston & Crick did not reach home till after nine, owing to Mr Preston forgetting his keys and Crick had to go back to the city for them. Some-*

*thing must be dreadfully wrong with Mr Preston, he seems not to be able to at-*
*tend to anything! and is in a very ill humour! . . .*

St. Joseph's. Oct. 15th, 1865

My dearest Mama,

. . . By this time I suppose you have received my letter . . . in which I told you that we would have our celebration of Mother's feast-day last Monday. . . . I wish, dear Mother, you could have participated in our pleasures. The night before when we were arranging the dresses for those who were to take an active part in the grand doings, we concurred in thinking that the beautiful ornaments intended for *Ceres,* who was to present the fruits, were of such a nature that they would not show to any advantage on the very little girl who had been chosen for the occasion. . . . I proposed Miss Fannie Kenedy, a young lady from the west, and a scholar of this year. As what I say of her here cannot make her vain, I will tell you that . . . she is one of the finest looking young ladies I ever saw. Very tall, light brown bordering-on-auburn hair, clear beautiful complexion, and easy graceful manners. Sister Raphael approved. I darted down to the play-room and in a few minutes returned triumphantly leading Miss Fannie. It is needless to say that she was chosen. The next thing to be done was to curl her and Kate Parr's hair. Already the silence bell had rung and this was to be done before we went to bed. "Oh!" said Fannie, "if we only had some *tea* it could be done so nicely." This was the first time that any of us had ever heard of such a thing, but *here* when anything is to be done, so that it can be done *well* the trouble is not thought much of. Sister immediately dispatched someone to the kitchen for the tea! But alas! tea leaves and coffee grounds were so thoroughly blended that neither could have been procured without the other. Sister Raphael sent us into a little side room by the dormitory occupied by two of the young ladies, and when she came to view our exertions in the hair dressing line, she was astonished and amused when I held up the candle snuffers and said, "See Sister necessity is the mother of invention! and then proceeded to heat them over the light and show her how I used them for *curling tongs.* . . .

The next morning . . . our preparations began. Fannie's hair curled beautifully. Kate's was just nicely frizzed. About half past eight we went in ranks over to the Community-room, and entered it singing a gay, pretty song in honor of the day; then Miss Mary Burke read an address of her own composition. . . . Then Kate Parr read the verses that I have enclosed (which I am ashamed to own I composed) and our beautiful Ceres presented her basket of fruit. . . .

Our dinner was truly a grand one. With the *ect* we had nine dishes at the first course, and three kinds of desert. Now let any one say that we don't live well!!! I can also assure you that we did ample justice to our good things.

In the evening we gave Mother a serenade. Nine particular singers and several choruses. You will be amused when I tell you that I sang a duet with Emily. We did not brake down. . . .

> With much love to dear Papa. . . .
> I remain
> Your most loving little
> May. . . .

## Wednesday, October 18, 1865

*All hands were up early again this morning, Mr Preston being obliged to meet a carpenter at the mill this morning; after attending to him, Mr Preston returned to P Plains and he, Thede & Crick went to the city together. I am unwilling to think this move has been premeditated, and yet it looks very strange. Crick was sent home and Mr Preston, Aunt Louise & Thede are in the city together tonight! As it is a very stormy night it will not be possible to enjoy themselves away from home. Alas! Alas! is this deception never to end. Sophia finished a large ironing today but owing to the rain was not able to put the curtains out. They are still in water and she will have to come another day and finish them. . . . I feel very sad tonight.*

## Thursday, October 19, 1865

*. . . The men went to the mill this morning to assist in laying the foundation of the barn. . . . Catherine has been pottering about today, doing very little for herself or me. I have been packing up trunks and chests for the last two days occasionally. . . . I rec'd a letter from Mr Preston, handed me by Ensor the carpenter, telling me to send Crick down to the mill to remain all night. I did not do so, as I thought it ill advised.*

## Friday, October 20, 1865

*. . . Crick drove to the city this morning, and this evening Mr Preston & Thede came home, Crick remaining in the city. It seems they have been in the house together each night for what purpose I know not, but I cannot help thinking it was premeditated. They both seemed ashamed of themselves!*

Pleasant Plains
Oct 22 / 1865

My dear child

I trust my letter written to you from Baltimore . . . has relieved you of your affectionate anxiety on my account. . . .

I told you in my former letter that we had commenced "moving," and that it was by no means the easiest or quickest thing to do. Papa, of course, wishes to superintend the packing up and sending off most of the articles, and as he has his professional duties also to perform, it is only occasionally Papa can give a day for "flitting" purposes.

. . . The mechanics finished their work at the house in town and now we can begin in earnest to send the furniture there. I . . . find I shall be obliged to take much more to the city than I had contemplated. Thede and Crick will in all probability be with us the entire winter; consequently two more rooms will be needed, with their complement of furniture. I do not however regret the extra trouble or expense, as they both . . . contribute greatly to our pleasure and satisfaction. Thede continues to be the good affectionate girl I told you she was . . . and makes herself as useful as my own child could be. Crick is Papa's right-hand man in all things. . . . Poor boy!! I pity him at times; until his going to school at the Mountain, I suppose he had never been taught to control himself in the least; the consequences are easily to be seen in a very violent temper and inclination to have his own way. The boy is perfectly conscious in this he cannot be indulged, and has made wonderful advance in the suppressing and controlling of his feelings and emotions. I am satisfied his being with his uncle will be of great advantage to him. . . .

And now my child let me acknowledge the reception of your pleasant letter. . . . Your efforts in the "hair dressing" line were very funny. I laughed and told Papa, if he continued to let his locks grow till you came home, I would certainly insist on your exercising your skill on his head. Your "Ceres" must have been a very lovely object to look upon. . . . the character of Ceres, of all the goddesses, I believe has had most of my sympathies. I recollect in my younger days, and when I thought the history of the gods and goddesses very wonderful and perhaps believed in them a good deal more than I would now be willing to acknowledge, thinking of all fates hers was the saddest. I pictured to myself with great vividness that poor mother, frantically seeking her only child throughout the world, and when she found her, having discovered to her great distress that her daughter Proserpine had eaten while in Pluto's dominions a few pomegranite seeds and thereby rendering it necessary for her to return occasionally to the "lower regions". . . .

. . . If there are any . . . articles you need to make you comfortable, I hope you will not hesitate to let me know what they are . . . and whether there is anything else you require for that poor head of yours which, like Uncle Ned's, has no hair on its head.[6] Uncle Ned reminds me of Uncle Jim; the dear good old soul asks about once a week when we heard from "little Missy," "whar she well" and many other questions indicative of the great interest—delight, with which the poor old man regards you. Catherine & Johnny ask also very kindly about you. Johnny has come quite frequently of late with beautiful rose buds from the bushes round the dairy, "to put on Miss May's altar." Strange to say . . . in every instance the bud, no matter how closed up when broken from the bush, has expanded and grown to a full blown rose. Some of them have been perfectly beautiful. Good night, my dear child, and in future if you do not hear from me the days you think I ought to write just remember Mama feels almost too tired to write—not from *doing* so much as *thinking* so much; you know, in this packing business I have to think for everybody. Remember me lovingly to all my sweet children, and give my affectionate regards to the dear Sisters.

Mama. . . .

### Tuesday, October 24, 1865

. . . *Mr Preston remained home this morning and all hands were engaged in moving the grand piano from the parlour to the library. It was of course very troublesome, but we got along admirably and it now stands ready for the piano men.* . . .

### Thursday, October 26, 1865

. . . *Mr Preston desired me to go to the city this morning, as he said to see that all was right at the home in town, but I know it was for some other motive! Johnny and I drove to the city . . . we took with us the green carpet from our room and intended for the spare room in town.* . . .

### Saturday, October 28, 1865

. . . *Mr Preston concluded to take another load to the city and as usual became so nervous as to make everyone unpleasant and unhappy about him. After a hard struggle the large wagon and market wagon were loaded and they all started off. Sophia did her ironing very nicely and I finished Johnny's shirt and fixed up the house and got everything comfortable for the return of the family. I cooked a nice quantity of mushrooms which Johnny gathered, and then sat down and waited for the wagon. During the afternoon it began to blow and by night a perfect gale was raging. Mr Preston did not reach home till ½ past eight, and because I complained of his coming late Mr Preston became very much irritated and refused to eat supper. The consequence was we were all unhappy. After the difficulty was adjusted, Mr Preston told us the Fabers had arrived from S. Carolina and would be in the city in the morning. Thede & Catherine came with him.*

### Sunday, October 29, 1865

*Mr Preston rose at four this morning and he & Johnny drove to Baltimore to meet the Fabers. . . . They will take possession of the mill tomorrow and remain till April. . . . This is our Sabbath of the year and perhaps the last one we shall spend at Pleasant Plains—Strange that after a lapse of so many years I should leave the place with so little regret. . . .*

Pleasant Plains
Oct 29th 1865

My dear child,

In all probability this is the last Sunday night we shall be at Pleasant Plains! Notwithstanding my great satisfaction at the move we are making and my firm conviction that it will prove beneficial to dear Papa and pleasant to the rest of the family, yet, now as the time approaches for us to leave the dear old place, hallowed as it is by so many happy associations, I find myself growing sad and my steps lingering over the dear familiar spots, hoping thereby to prolong even for a short time the parting hour. . . . I have wished a thousand times for you during the past week; you could have been of such great assistance to me. I believe it occupied me one whole day gathering together and packing up the little articles belonging exclusively to you. . . . Your little bureau of course will go to the city with us, as also Nannie's bedstead and Nannie & Daisy also.[7] When the men were taking down the bedsteads & removing the heavy articles of furniture from the upper rooms, I said to Uncle Jim, "Uncle Jim, there is a bedstead in the large room that I fear you and Father will scarcely be able to handle, and yet I shall expect you to lift it with great care notwithstanding its weight and size." "O Missus, just you let me get my hands on it, I s'peck I am quite able to lift it." "Well come and see it, Uncle Jim." The old man followed, and when I pointed to the wee thing, he stood in perfect amazement. "The Lor bless me, did ever anybody see the like of this? Well, I knows that belongs to the young Missy. Just you tells young Missy when you writes again, that Uncle Jim looks arter all her fixins." And suiting the action to the word, he picked the little bedstead in his great arms and carried it down the stairs as carefully as though you had been sleeping in it.

We have had a most strangely divided household for some days. Thede with Catherine has been in town, receiving the furniture as it was sent in. Crick has remained at the mill, superintending the men at work there, and seeing that the corn, grain and fodder sent there is properly disposed of, and Papa and I have remained at P. Plains packing and sending off articles to their respective destinations. All this seems very trifling, but when you consider —one wagon load goes eight miles to the city and another goes four miles in the country and but one load can be made by each wagon these short days, you can readily understand this moving is somewhat of an undertaking. . . . Papa has complained less this last month than I have known him for years, and I think thrives on his labours. I could not help remarking this very day how well he was looking.

I sent word over yesterday to Mrs Owens that we still had a few chairs left to sit on and a dinner table with the etceteras, at which we would like to see herself and Delia seated. Of course they came, fearing, as Mrs Owens very feelingly remarked, that this might be her last dinner at P. Plains. We had a right jolly party. Mrs Owens & Delia—Papa, Thede, Crick and myself.

. . . Your last very pleasant letter Papa brought to me Monday evening. . . . Papa after reading your letter and Farewell to Pleasant Plains, said, "Well I think May's poetry is not bad," and then continued, "I am much pleased with her style of writing and think *the child is not without talent* and under the instruction she receives, it will be well developed."

I assure you, my darling child, I was greatly delighted to witness the evident pleasure and gratification Papa felt in his little daughter's improvement. Sister Lucia was right in thinking I would be pleased to read your poetical efforts. . . .

God bless my child. Mama

Pleasant Plains<br>Octr 31st 1865

My Dear Child,

I wrote you a long letter Sunday evening, which doubtless you are reading at *this very time*! I thought then, I was in all probability writing you for the last time from Pleasant Plains. I counted however "without my host," as you will perceive by this very letter. Papa was yesterday invited by Capt Russell to accompany him, together with a party of gentlemen, all friends of Papa, in the trial trip around the Cape from the Delaware river to our own beautiful Chesapeake. The party left Baltimore this morning in the car for Chester, where the fine new steamer of which the Capt is commander was built, and from which place they start at twelve tonight, expecting if all things go well to reach Baltimore by Thursday noon. . . .

This little arrangement has been in contemplation for sometime past, and the party would not have been complete without Papa, at least, so thought our good friend the Capt; indeed I think so myself as few persons are possessed of the fine convivial qualities that our own Papa is favoured with; so yesterday when a dispatch announced that all was ready with the steamer and the party would leave Baltimore today and Papa was expected to be one of the number, I would not listen to any reason Papa was trying to urge why he should not go, but insisted that moving operations should be laid aside for a few days and Papa should cease his labours for awhile, forget his cares and anxieties about the comforts of his family and go with them and enjoy himself. My *persuasive eloquence* was too powerful to be resisted. . . .

Anxious as I am to finish moving "and to be at rest," I yet most cheerfully linger over it, even a week longer if necessary, for the sake of giving Papa this enjoyment. These nautical proceedings are just in Papa's line. You know how fond he is of a vessel, and of the water, and in fact of anything pertaining to sea life. Oh! I do hope and pray all may go well in this adventure. I have just been thinking how strangely we are all separated tonight. Papa is at Chester. Thede is in Baltimore—Crick at the mill, May at St Joseph's and Mama at Pleasant Plains! Shall we ever be together again? . . .

The other day I was packing up some things in the store room & Uncle Jim was helping me; while doing so I came across some of your little toys, and gave a few to Uncle Jim and told him they were yours. "Thank you Madam; Uncle Jim'll keep them kareful all his long life and whenever he looks at them he'll think of young missus, God Bless de child, everybody *has to love her*." Poor old soul nothing pleases him so much as to work under my instruction and talk about you. Goodnight, Love to all who ask after you.

Mama

65 Fayette St.<br>2nd Novr 1865<br>11 A.M.

Dear Madge—

I have just arrived and find John—Tommy, the horses and wagon and wood. I avail myself of the opportunity to drop you a line; although I am scarcely in a condition to put two ideas together. I . . . left for Chester Pa where we arrived at about 5 P.M. We were there met by Cap. Russell and spent a delightful evening . . . at 11 P.M. we all bid our host good bye and departed for the steamer. In a short time we reached the "Thomas Kelso"[8] —and at about ½ past 11 got underweigh. She is certainly a magnificent boat. . . . On board of the steamer there was no sleeping—nor did any of us think of "turning in." The Philadelphians joined the Balto. party and what with story, song and mischief there was, to say the least of it, a considerable racket. . . .

As day broke on Wednesday morning, the sun rose out of the sea looking as fierce as if he had been at the battle of Solferino[9] and scattering strips of blood stained laurel over the thousand foaming crests of the ocean. . . . There had been what the sailors call "dirty weather" outside and although the gale had abated, the "ground swell" was literally awful. Before long there was what the naval novelists would designate a "tremendous short sea"—the ocean in fact looked like a man who had been in a passion—the noisy storm over, but the face still full of wrathy lines. The steamer being a new one, and this her first experimental trip—she was without cargo or ballast, and therefore rolled like a tub in the swash of Niagara. Frolic and fun were soon at a discount and gentlemen who began to "cast up" their accounts found a balance against them. Eight o'clock arrived and the unsteady steward wobbled on deck and announced breakfast . . . in company with a half a dozen I clutched my way down stairs, where the smoking viands on a most abundant table mixed their delicious odors with the smell of the new stoves, the freshly varnished paint &c &c. . . .

Captain Russell in his blandest manner said "let me help you to a piece of this steak—you will find it delicious"—I was about offering him my plate, when an inward monitor caused me to spring to my feet. "Bless me what is the matter," ejaculated the Captain—before I turned round and took to my heels, I vociferated, "I'm sick—send for McManus"—the old sea captains seated at the table roared out their hoarse laughter, but while I hastily clambered up the cabin steps I found I was running a race with several gentlemen, to see who would first reach the vessel's side. . . . While the ship pitched and strained, the passengers strained and pitched.

. . . Captain Rollins, who is somewhat of a wag, came up behind me—and tapping me on the back, said in a tone of mock sympathy, "My dear sir, how is with you? What do you think of it?"—"Think of it," I replied, "Why sir I think the ship's drunk or she would never stagger so." . . . Cap Russell admitted it was the sickest ship's crew he had ever seen—in addition to the wonderful roll of the sea, I think the fresh paint, varnish &c had something to do with it. Certain it is I never was as sick before. I ate not a morsel of food from breakfast on Wednesday until breakfast on Thursday. . . . I still stagger like the ship at sea, and whenever I close my eyes the only color visible is a beautiful pea green. The whole party will never forget the first trip of the Thomas Kelso. . . .

Dear Madge either come or send for me any time tomorrow.

Affectionately<br>Preston

Pleasant Plains Nov 3d 1865

Dear Papa,[10]

With all the sympathy in the world for your suffering from the "Mal de mer," which seems to have been the principal thing on board the Thomas Kelso, I nevertheless have laughed myself almost sore with your ludicrous account of its effects upon you all. I would not for any consideration withhold the perusal of your letter from May. It will afford amusement for a month to come to she and her young companions, nor would I put it past the good sisters to have a hearty laugh over it also.

When I found the weather so unpropitious after you left, I feared you would have an unpleasant time rounding the Capes, but now that it is over, I do not regret the cleaning out your system has had. I feel satisfied it will be beneficial to you. No wonder you were sea sick; with such an accumulation of bile as you must have had in your stomach, I can account for the frequent and unnatural ebullitions of temper of late. But now—it is really refreshing to think what an amiable, gentle, good-natured Papa will return to us. I shall be shocked and unwilling to forgive if I see the least show of ill temper for a month to come. I hope, dear Papa, by this time you are entirely recovered and your stomach in a condition to relish the simple goods we shall be able to give you in our country home when we hope to see you tomorrow.

I am glad you sent Thede out today. I think after the confinement of the past week the run in the country today will do her good. . . .

. . . Goodnight.

Yours truly Madge

## Sunday, November 5, 1865

. . . Thede & I rose early and prepared a good breakfast, thinking Mr Preston & Crick would be out to eat it, but they did not reach here till one o'clock and then they brought Mr Faber with them. Mr Preston was in a fearfully nervous condition and so cross there was no living with him. This afternoon Mr Preston sent Thede & Crick to the city, Thede to remain & Crick to come home. Crick reached home about 7 o'clock, and as soon as he came in he gave the information that "Rose was at the house." It was all made plain to me why Mr Preston was in such a strange humour! . . .

## Saturday, November 11, 1865

. . . John took a load of wood and the safes[11] from the store room to the city and returned about dark. Crick & Johnny took a load in their wagon similar to *the one of yesterday. Thede baked pies today and Matilda*[12] *did sundry things about the house. We are beginning to like Matilda very much; she is not a very good house servant, but for the hard work of a country house she is excellent. It was past 7 when Mr Preston & Johnny reached home; consequently I was annoyed and Mr Preston was angry. Mr Preston told us this evening that "Skipp Sanders," Matilda's husband, came to the office this morning from Virginia. Matilda has been looking for him anxiously, & I doubt not will be glad to see him.*

Pleasant Plains
Novr 14th 1865

My darling child,

Thede and I have just returned from spending the evening at Eudowood, where we went for the purpose of saying goodbye; having, as dear Papa would say "So nearly come to the end of our ropes," as to feel that any day now may see us turning our backs upon our country house, and wending our way to the city. As I have told you before, this moving business often has to give way to professional duties. Papa has been engaged for nearly the past week at court in Baltimore . . . but as the weather has been so gloriously fine, we have rather been glad than otherwise at being able to enjoy this beautiful season of Indian summer in the country. . . .

And now daughter how comes on "the little bald head"?—When you write, tell me something about it. You can do so in such a style that I will understand you, though the rest of the family cannot. Tell me how long you will be obliged to wear your cap; and when the time comes to lay it aside, I hope you will be careful not to take cold. Is there any prospect of *wavy* locks or are they be of the smooth order? . . .

In one of your letters you ask if "Skipp Saunders has been heard from." I have carried on quite a correspondence with the said gentleman—or rather by proxy, as I am inclined to think the said individual is as guiltless of the power of writing as his wife Matilda. A few days ago, a knock at Papa's office door, elicited from Papa the quick, "Come in," so characteristic of our Papa, the door opened and a short, stout solid looking old negro walked in, and quietly but respectfully taking off his hat, asked if that was Master Preston? On being answered in the affirmative, he bowed and scraped, and smiled, and said I am "Skipp," the husband of Matilda that lives on your place. So you see that Skipp has not only been heard from, but has been seen also. Our surprise was great on seeing an individual like the one I have described, instead of the gay, dandified, pompous-looking darkey his *name* would seem to imply. Uncle Jim is still as attentive and careful as ever of all your things, and inspects the packing of them with great interest. Nannie's bedstead went in yesterday, and now I think "all your treasures have reached the city." . . .

Yours most lovingly Mama

### Thursday, November 16, 1865

*. . . Crick and Johnny took in the market wagon my fine dinner service. They reached home early, but without Mr Preston. I cannot account for this absenting from home. I feel very certain someone from a distance has been with Mr Preston during the week. Uncle Skipp came up this morning with a fine large pumpkin and a few apples, begging me to accept them. They came from Virginia and are very nice. . . .*

### Friday, November 17, 1865

*. . . Mr Preston sent me a note saying he was obliged to go to Westminster in the morning and would not be home till Sunday. I think this staying in the city all the week looks very suspicious to say the least of it. . . .*

### Sunday, November 19, 1865

*. . . This is the first day for one week Mr Preston has been home. I can't tell why it is, but I feel a great repugnance to being with _____ today. I don't put faith in what he says about his absence. . . .*

### Monday, November 20, 1865

*. . . Mr Preston . . . has been engaged taking his liquors to the mill, having made two loads today. We thought this would have been our last day at P. Plains, but not so, we are likely to be here some days longer. Mr Preston has business in Philadelphia on Wednesday and talks of sending me there in his place. I wish he would do so. I should like to spend a day or two there just now. . . .*

Pleasant Plains<br>Novr 21st 1865

You will perceive my dear child, that I still date from Pleasant Plains, but in all probability this is the *very last act* before I leave the dear old spot. . . . There is literally "big box, little box, band box, and bundle" in masses high enough to frighten a less capacious vehicle than ours or stouter horses than the willing and gentle animals that have been doing duty for the last two months by way of moving Pleasant Plains to 65 Fayette Street Baltimore.

I am sorry I have not been able to keep you constantly informed of all the doings about us for weeks past—"The brave, the gay, the gentle and severe" —to say nothing of the ludicrous, would have interested you. . . . The family . . . has been divided between P. Plains and Baltimore, but for the past week Thede has been staying with me. . . . Oh! So often and often, my darling little one, we have wished for you, and the other dear children that you might all have a good run in our grand old woods before we should leave and the "place that has known us so long shall know us no more forever!" . . .

Last Saturday I found it necessary to go to the city and on my passing by the market, not having a full sense of the poverty to which we had reduced ourselves, and being tempted by the profusion of "good things" with which the market abounded, I stopped and purchased a generous supply, intending to have, as you used to say when a very little child—"dood meat for Sunny (Sunday) dinner." But alas! I had indeed counted without my host, chicken and beef—sweet potatoes and irish—stewed pumpkin and apple sauce— cold slaw, pickles &c &c, what a dinner for three plates—two dishes, nothing like a vegetable dish, and only. . . .[13]

## Tuesday, November 21, 1865

*Baltimore 65 Fayette*

*Well here we are at last, having left Pleasant Plains at ¼ before five o'clock. Mr Preston drove in to the city in the market wagon, Thede & myself with a dozen and one bundles, Johnny came in with us, and he and Crick returned to Pleasant Plains this evening, Mr Preston remaining in town with us. Before leaving today Mr Preston made two trips to the mill, taking down with him his demijohns of liquor; there were thirty-three of them and they all reached there safely. I find so much to fix up I scarcely know where to begin. . . .*

## Wednesday, November 22, 1865

*. . . After a frugal breakfast we set to work in earnest. We concluded to turn the room lately occupied as a bedroom into a sitting room. We took the bed down and put it up in the 3d story front room, and in a short time we had Thede's bedroom & mine fixed up, and also the sitting room. . . . Mr Preston seems much pleased with our arrangement of things.*

---

Though the moving process occurred during May's absence, May followed its progress through her mother's letters. In one of her rare diary entries, she tried to record this time of transition in all their lives. But she could not seem to summon the emotion she apparently thought appropriate. For whatever reason, the entry trails off without closure.

### Nov. 23d 1865

*I received a letter from my dear Mama to-night dated really for the last time from dear old Pleasant Plains. It is all over now and I how do I feel not at all it seems to me. I am like*

# 13

## The Mount Hope Case

MADGE HAD BEEN HOPING Preston would send her to Philadelphia in his place, as he sometimes did, to see to the recurring business responsibilities of the Simmons estate. After the anxieties and stresses of the move to town, she was looking forward to a change of scene. When he acquiesced, she left joyfully, turning her back on the unsettled condition of the house in town. She was gone for four happy days. During this time Madge called on her Aunt Eliza, visited with Mrs. Simmons and her two small boys, and also renewed acquaintance with Preston's business partner William Swain. The latter was gravely ill, in an advanced stage of alcoholism. "Poor man," wrote Madge in her diary, "what a wreck was there! I think he would like to have had me remain, but as my doing so was not seconded by Mrs Swain, I could not do so."

While Madge was away, Preston spoke at a ceremony aboard the Thomas Kelso. Captain Russell's friends—that group of gentlemen who had suffered together during the ship's maiden voyage—were making a formal presentation to their host of an elaborate silver service. Preston's remarks, in his heavily metaphorical style, were later printed in full in a front-page story in the *Baltimore Sun* of November 29. Preston was "frequently interrupted by outbursts of applause," the *Sun* reported.

Then on December 12 he spoke again. This time the occasion was the inaugural lecture of a series to be offered at the Maryland Institute. Preston's topic was the city of Baltimore. The *Sun's* notice on the day of the lecture was full of promise: "From this gentleman's thorough knowledge of the prominent actors and events connected with the various epochs of the city's history, a literary entertainment of unusual excellence is expected."

At home, however, the lecture carried a totally different psychic meaning.

### Thursday, December 7, 1865

*. . . Mr Preston has at last been interested in his lecture & began to write it today, but unfortunately I broke the looking glass in Mr Preston's escritoire and it had the effect of making Mr Preston very angry and an unpleasant scene took place which ended in the lecture being thrown aside and I being made very miserable. While the rest of mankind were enjoying Thanksgiving we have been simply remaining at home.*

### Sunday, December 10, 1865

*After the storm of yesterday it cleared off quite pleasantly today, but having Mr Preston to assist in his lecture I did not go to church today. Mr Preston wrote the greater part of the day, and I copied. About two o'clock Sister Matilda and another Sister called to see Mr Preston and remained with us some time. The Sisters are beginning to feel some considerable anxiety about their case, which comes off on Wednesday next. . . . Mr Preston & I wrote till near twelve tonight. . . .*

---

Six months earlier Preston had written to the Sisters of Charity, offering his services on the defense team in a law suit concerning their operation of the Mount Hope Insane Asylum in Baltimore. When Sisters Matilda and Euphemia visited Preston, they brought a letter from May describing with what solemn prayers the girls and the Sisters prepared for this stressful event. May also sent her father a medal depicting the holy family that she enjoined him to wear at the hearing and "then wear it constantly." The trial was scheduled for the thirteenth, the day after Preston's lecture.

### Tuesday, December 12, 1865

*—Well at last the long agony is over and Mr Preston has finished his lecture and has just gone down to deliver it. I have been made so nervous and miserable by Mr Preston and his lecture that I could not go to hear him. Rose came down and Crick came in & Thede and they have gone down to hear Mr Preston. Catherine also went, and I am home alone. . . . I sincerely hope Mr Preston will succeed in his lecture tonight.*

### Wednesday, December 13, 1865

*The sun rose bright & beautiful this morning, auspicious I hope of the good ending to the Sisters' cases which were to have been tried today. Mr Preston*

*rose like the sun bright & fresh after his lecturing last evening. Crick & Mr*
*Preston went to Towsontown in the cars, Crick to go to P. Plains and Mr*
*Preston to attend court. Rose & I walked out this morning and she made some*
*purchases and I got my bonnet, which I think is very pretty. I finished the skirt*
*of May's dress and this evening have cut out the waist and fitted it. Rose went*
*home in the 3-½ o'clock train. Mr Preston did not reach home till near eight. It*
*seems the prosecuting attorney abandoned all the cases but one and that is to*
*be tried next month. The Sisters' lawyers think this a great triumph. . . .*

---

Madge took that word—triumph—from conversations swirling around
the courtroom that day in Towsontown. Doubtless it was her husband's word.
The defense team had been elated when, after a two-hour discussion with the
prosecution lawyers, the state's attorney, John T. Ensor, agreed not to prosecute except for one indictment. Ensor consented, he said, to save the time of
the court, since the other indictments had not been "framed with [as] strict
observance of technicalities as [he] would wish." The case was flimsy, the indictments sloppily drawn. Such was the conclusion of all who rallied to defend the Sisters.

The dismissed cases involved charges of assault and false imprisonment,
which had been brought against Dr. William Stokes, physician at Mount
Hope for more than twenty years; Mary Blenkinsop (Sister Euphemia), recently its chief administrator; and several other Sisters of Charity who had
helped to operate the facility. Left still to be tried was the indictment against
Sister Euphemia and Dr. Stokes: "a conspiracy to deceive and cheat such inhabitants of the State as have the control and disposal of insane persons, by
means of false representations as to the conduct of an insane asylum."

For the third time within the last two and a half weeks, Preston received
complimentary attention in the *Baltimore Sun*. His presentation speech
honoring Captain Russell had been printed in full, his Maryland Institute
address, which had cost Madge such tedious hours of copying and those
frightening outbursts from her tense and nervous spouse, was prominently ad-
vertised; and now, only two days later, the propitious events of the preceding
day's trial hearing received detailed attention. Again Preston's name was on
display.

Although the family papers do not say so, Preston must have found re-
warding this chain of successes. What Madge's diaries and the exchanges of
letters among the family do record is a brief time of happy activity.

**Thursday, December 14, 1865**

*The roofs of the houses were covered with snow this morning. . . . Mr Preston*
*has remained in today, arranging the stoves. We have the sitting room stove*

*put up and the old stove has been taken . . . to be repaired. I was out awhile this morning shopping, and this afternoon I have cut the sleeves & body of May's dress. Sister Matilda and Sister Anne Aloysia were here this afternoon.[1] They came to thank Mr Preston for the interest manifested in their case yesterday. They remained some time and seemed quite cheerful. We like our stove in the sitting room very much. . . . It is very cold tonight, the water froze in our tin bucket on the rack. . . .*

Baltimore Decr 17th 1865

My dear child,

The nice, long and satisfactory letter written by Papa this week to his little girl, I am sure more than compensated for mine. . . .

It must have given you great pleasure to learn the "Mount Hope cases" had been so admirably disposed of. It is regarded by all . . . as a great triumph, and . . . I think will have a most beneficial effect on the solitary case left for trial. So you see, my dear child, "the prayers of the righteous availeth much."

In Papa's letter he told you that . . . I attached the medal you sent him to the one he already wears together with the Agnus Dei, and now they all rested on his bosom to be worn there I hope for all time. I must tell you something in connection with the medal that will amuse you as well as please you. The night before the Sisters' trial came off, Papa was to deliver a lecture at the Maryland Institute. . . . Of course we were all very anxious about Papa and desirous that he should acquit himself with satisfaction to the public and credit to himself. Just before the committee called to take him to the institute, I said, "Oh Papa, let me put May's medal round your neck, perhaps it may inspire you to do something clever tonight." "Oh no, Papa replied—You must not put it on till tomorrow (Wednesday). You know May said I must wear it for her particular intention."—The medal, of course, was not worn till the day you stated—but has been religiously worn ever since.

The dear Sisters have been obliged to make repeated visits to Papa during the pending of these cases, and generally I have had the pleasure and satisfaction of being present. On each occasion after they have left, Papa has expressed himself as being greatly impressed with the beauty and simplicity of their manners and their refined and highly cultivated minds.

I am pleased to know this feeling is entertained by the good Sisters in a great measure for Papa also. Sister Matilda in an interview I had with her the day after the "triumph" said in speaking of Papa, "I am sure our dear Lord will not let so good a man as Mr Preston die without first becoming a Catholic." Oh my child if such happiness is in store for us, I feel that all the trials of his life could cheerfully be born. I think Papa's health and spirits have been greatly improved since we are settled in the city—or rather since we are in the city, for we are by no means *settled* yet. We are sufficiently fixed however to be comfortable and begin to feel quite at home. Though I must say—this dark, dismal, dingy looking house is a poor compensation for the light, cheerful pleasant house in the country. Yet if it were ten times as gloomy, I would rather be here than at PPlains during the winter. . . .

Your loving Mama.

**Wednesday, December 20, 1865**

*Another very disagreeable day. I have been engaged the greater part of the day making up a bonnet for myself. It is made out of a sleeve of an old black silk basque and trimmed with some purple velvet ripped off an old black bonnet Miss Stuart made me years ago. . . . Thede and Mr Preston say it looks very well. I went out this afternoon and purchased the articles for May's Christmas box. It has cost me altogether over five dollars—but . . . I would cheerfully have given five times that much money, to gratify so good a child. . . .*

Baltimore Dec 21st 1865

My dear child,

We have just sent off by Adams Express a Christmas box for you. It will reach you a day after the box containing your dress. . . . When you write to acknowledge the safe arrival of the boxes—mention them in such a way that I will understand you have rec'd *two*—but the "rest of mankind" will only know of one. . . .

I was just thinking how clever it would be if Sister Raphael would indulge you girls during the holidays by allowing you to wear your hoops. Your nice full dresses would show to so much greater advantage. . . .

May our Blessed Mother have you now and always under her protecting wing.

Mama

Baltimore Decr 22d 1865

My dear child,

Papa is just directing a box to be sent . . . to you . . . containing a *small oyster supper*. . . . The oysters are some of a barrel which Captain Russell sent as a present to Papa, and being so very fine we thought it would be selfish to enjoy them without giving you a taste. . . . Catherine opened them—Thede ground the crackers, and Mama superintended the frying of them and Papa packed them; thus you see we have all had a finger in this pie. The other little etceteras each gathered up as we thought of them. The wine is some made at

Pleasant Plains, the jelly also. The pickle, unfortunately, comes as most precious articles on a *very* small scale, the reason why—we could not find a jar sufficiently small to pack in the box. . . . The crackers we fear you will consider a failure, but if you had seen poor Catherine running round the streets this cold night to procure them for you, you would welcome them though even plainer than they are. The *good* stores were closed when she went for them and she was obliged to buy them at some little out of the way place of her own knowing. . . .

Papa, Thede, Crick, Johnny, Catherine and Mama unite in wishing you all the happiness and pleasure of the coming season.

Mama

### Sunday, December 24, 1865

*After the bright beautiful night, we were horrified this morning to find everything covered with snow, which soon turned to rain & hail and a more shocking day could not be imagined. I was disappointed in not being able to go to church this morning; to compensate for my disappointment, I fixed up May's altar, and put it in a corner of our room; it looks very well and gives a Christian appearance to the house. Mr Preston as usual has been engaged tinkering all day. I wish I could see from here to St Joseph's, I am so anxious to know if May rec'd her boxes, particularly the one containing her dress. And this is Christmas Eve, alas! alas!*

### Monday, December 25, 1865

*Well, nothing could be much worse than the effects of the weather on everything today—one could scarcely believe this was Christmas. The sun shone out occasionally, but that only made the streets the more horrible: On awaking this morning, instead of being greeted with a pleasant smile & sweet words on this holy day—all was anger & unpleasantness. I therefore remained quiet, and perhaps might have appeared perverse. Of course I had to get breakfast, and while thus engaged the boys, Crick and Johnny, came in, having left Pleasant Plains a little after five o'clock. I tried to be as cheerful as I could and made them feel happy & pleasant. Notwithstanding the bad walking, Thede & I went to church and were delighted with the beautiful ceremonies of the day. On reaching home, we found the boys had returned from church & Catherine had been trying to cook the turkey. We soon had dinner & Mr Preston coming in, we sat down & enjoyed it. After dinner the boys left for P. Plains. I gave them all the good eatables I could find and they went away rejoicing. I wish I knew how my darling child was getting along today and if she rec'd all the things we sent her for this day.*

Baltimore Decr 28th 1865

It is consoling to know, my darling child, that this dark, dull, dreary, dismal, dirty and unChristmas-like weather in no wise militates against the pleasures and comforts of the dear inmates at St Joseph's. However stormy and threatening the outside world, there at least all is calm, serene, harmonious and sunshine. When Christmas morn broke upon us, and Thede and I waded through three inches of snowy water to the cathedral, and as I met friend after friend, each and all looking sadly disappointed at the gloomy prospects the weather held out to them of anything like social greetings, my thoughts constantly turned to dear old St Joseph's and I smiled inwardly as the happy consciousness came over me that the weather made no sad hearts among my happy children, and I mentally thanked God for the present bright and happy home you were all enjoying and prayed Oh so fervently that the storms & clouds of this life might never be felt by any of you—and I am *almost* afraid you will think Mama was not kind when she tells you, she prayed with equal fervor that you might know no other home.

Ah! my child, you must never think Mama does not love you because she feels and writes thus. It is my very love for you that makes me willing to give you up to our dear Lord and thus shield you from the trials and troubles—nay at times the wretchedness and misery—of the denizens of this world.

Forgive me, my little girl! I did not mean when I sat down to write to you to sadden the present happy and cheerful season with a homily upon the miseries of mankind, in the delights of a recluse. I wished to tell you how we spent our Christmas, and to express our wishes to you that your boxes, &c &c had reached you safely.

On Saturday evening, Papa, Thede, and Catherine and myself promenaded the streets till after ten o'clock, as children do, looking at the pretty things. There was not however much evidence of the Christmas gaieties that we used to see. On our return home we expressed ourselves pleased at the prospect there was of fine weather for the holidays. Judge then of our great disappointment on awaking Sunday morning to find everything covered with snow, and in a short time to find the snow turn to rain & hail and on such a day—of course church was out of the question on Christmas morning. Crick & Johnny came in to spend the day with us; perhaps you do not know that we have not altogether left P. Plains and that the boys are keeping Bachelors Hall together at the little cottage; this week however will end that too, as Papa gives up the place on the first of the year. . . .

Papa, Thede & Crick send much love to you. I also desire to be most affectionately remembered to all the dear Sisters, particularly Sr Raphael, Sr Lucia, Sr Ann Scholastica, Sr Germaine and my own dear young friends—

Yours lovingly,
Mama.

## Sunday, December 31, 1865

. . . *Mr Preston & the boys finished the shelves in the storeroom today. This afternoon much to our surprise Rose Smith came down from York to spend a few days with us. This is the last day of the year, and a time for meditation, but my reflections must not be put on paper. I will confine them to my own breast. We begin tomorrow our city life with all our family. God only knows what is to be to [sic] result of our movement.* [2]

Baltimore Jany 2d 1866

A Happy New Year, my darling child, even though it comes a day later than the usual greeting; still I hope you will consider it none the less sincere & loving—

Does it ever seem to you, when you bid "goodbye" to a grand old year and lay it quietly away among the years that have gone before it, as if a dear friend had passed away and been gathered to the tomb and was lost to you forever? Thus it always seems to me, and the same sadness and heartaches that I feel for the departed friend are experienced for the dying year. It is well to greet those we love at this season with the sweet expression—"A Happy New Year". For there it lies all unknown and untraveled before us—and whether our paths through the intricacies and vicissitudes of its twelve months be strewn with flowers—lighted by the sunshine of prosperity, and gladdened by the sweet smiles, loving words and affectionate caresses of loved ones—or whether the storms and clouds of adversity—the chilling winds of unkindness—and the rough and stormy ways of misfortune are to be our lot, God alone knows! Therefore the greeting comes timely and appropriate.

Your loving though hasty letter . . . was duly rec'd, and I could not but smile at the coincidence of the letters, yours & mine, having been written on the same day and in all probability at the very same hour. . . .

I can't tell you my child how delighted I am to know your dress pleases you so well and the "fit" is so exact. It is rather strange that a tall, slender Mama should have a figure so much like a short full-bodied little girl—but I rejoice that in future I need be dependent upon no outsider when "fixing up" for my dear child. . . .

And you enjoyed your oyster supper. It gives us all great pleasure to know our little efforts to gratify you are rewarded by so much success. . . .

Your pleasant and graphic descriptions of your holiday sports were very gratifying. . . . So you represented the queen—please tell me how you wore your crown on that little bald head of yours? I am quite curious to know how the "curls" are growing—please send me a specimen of the crop. . . .

In relation to your taking lessons in silk embroidering, our father desires me to say if you can conscientiously feel that this embellishment will be worth the time and money it will cost, you may incur the expense. Father thinks the most valuable part of education is that which conduces in afterlife to the promotion of comfort and utility. . . . Not that he is entirely averse to that which is generally regarded as ornamental, but that he is of opinion that time ought only to be devoted to it, when time cannot be occupied in acquiring something more truly serviceable. With these remarks on his part, he leaves you to the exercise of your own good judgment. . . . With love from each member of the family to you and loving regards to all my children.

Your
Mama

Baltimore Jany 5th 1866

My dear child

Accompanying this note you will find a little hood, which I think may possibly be comfortable on your poor little bald head—if it should prove so—wear it, and while doing so you can have the satisfaction of knowing Mama wears one of the same pattern but different colors—mine being the loveliest shade of blue and white. . . . We hope you will like it as we all think they are the prettiest things of the kind we have seen.

I am going to take *this* up to the asylum and ask the Sister Superior if she can send it to St Joseph's for me. Of course I shall see Sister Leopoldine—Don't you envy me? . . .

Yours lovingly
Mama

Baltimore 1866 Jany 12th

My dear child,

I am so sleepy I can scarcely see to write and yet I am unwilling to let the week pass without sending you a letter. . . . Last Friday your Cousin Thede and myself called on *your* Sister and Sister Louisa at the asylum. . . .

Sister Leopoldine, I thought was looking very well. . . . She was kind enough to give me a beautiful picture and three Agnus Deis, the latter made, so Sister told us, by a certain little girl at St Joseph's. They were beautifully made, and in good taste. I hesitated to take them, but I found Sister had laid them aside for me before I went up, consequently I rec'd them, and really felt grateful to Sister for her pretty gift. Thede was delighted with her visit, and charmed by the quiet dignity and simplicity of the Sisters' manners. I intend soon to take her to see Father Foley, and then I trust she will visit him for instruction &c &c. Don't mention this in your letters, as it would have a bad effect upon her, if she thought I was *managing* her! . . .

The family all unite with me in love to our dear little absent darling.

Mama

Baltimore Feby 1st 1866

My darling child

I have just turned from the family circle to write you that which I know will please you to hear. I was fortunate enough to see and speak to your dear Father Foley yesterday afternoon. . . . Father Foley was pleased to hear of you and says he will with great pleasure say the Mass you requested of him. On looking over his engagements, he found he would not be able to say the Mass till Tuesday the 6th of February—on which day, at six in the morning, the Mass will be offered. I am thus particular thinking perhaps you would like to unite in spirit with us. I say with *us*, as I desire also to offer my communion on that day with the same intention as you do.

I must tell you a singular circumstance that occurred to me this afternoon. Tomorrow being the Feast of the Purification &c, and also the anniversary of my first communion, I wished to go to confession this afternoon, and to receive Holy Communion in the morning. About three o'clock . . . I went up to the seminary to see Father Elder, but to my great disappointment and sorrow I learned that Father Elder was ill and not able to see anyone. I was too anxious to carry out my wish to go to Confession to be easily discouraged, consequently walked down to St Alphonsus Church and went in, hoping to find a priest to whom I might make my Confession. The penitents about the confessionals looked so "very Dutch" that I began to fear my American tongue would find no ready listener. At length I mustered courage to ask a lady in a pew near, "If the Revd gentlemen spoke English?" The lady looked up and replied, yes, she was going to the one by whose confessional we were kneeling. We smiled on recognizing each other. It was Rose Abell. At the same time she rose and went in, I—designing to go in after she came out—while waiting, the door of the next confessional opened and a priest came out whom I recognized as my good Father Warick, with whom I was so much pleased and to whom I made my general Confession the time of the mission and jubilee last spring. As he passed down the aisle, I rose up and asked him if he could spare the time to hear me. With the most benign smile you can imagine, the good Father entered again the confessional, &c &c &c.

On meeting Rose afterwards she was greatly surprised to learn that Father Warick was in the city and regretted *so very much* she had not gone to him. Father Warick, it seems, has been absent sometime, and I believe *this* was about the first time that he had been in the church since his return. Was it not singular that I should have met him just at this particular time—when in all probability I shall be obliged to select another director, as my dear old Father Elder may never hear Confession again. I regard this meeting as an especial act of Providence and really feel that our Blessed Mother has guided me to Father Warick. . . .

By the way, do you know I begin to have great hopes of Thede's becoming a Catholic? She goes every Sunday morning to church with me, and from her conversations I find she must give the subject very considerable reflection. Do pray for her my dear child and say something to her on the subject in your letters, but *not* as if I had written to you about it. . . .

Yours most lovingly,
Mama

Baltimore Feby 3d 1866

My darling child,

I am more willing to believe that some detention of the trains or mails has deprived us of the pleasure and satisfaction of receiving your Friday letter, than to think you had not written on that day. . . .

Yesterday was quite an eventful day with us. Johnny came to the city bright and early, and after making a grand toilet, Mr Preston took him over to the College and introduced him to Father Clark, who received him kindly and at once ushered him into the schoolroom. He underwent some little examination and a list of books such as he will require for the present given him, and he was then dismissed with the rest of the boys and he came home rejoicing. As he commenced on one of the feasts of our Blessed Mother, I told him he must put himself under her especial protection, and beg her prayers and intercession for his well doing. The boy promised he would do so, and I feel certain he will. You know he has always been more or less piously inclined. Father Clark came over one evening to see Mr Preston and had some quite interesting conversation with him. Father told me he invited Mr Preston to come and see him and said, although you are a very learned man, I think I could *instruct* you in some things it would be well for you to know! Papa was much pleased with the interview and on bidding the good Father good night, said, Father Clark, your words and manner are very persuasive. I was not present during the interview, but was told the *important* part of it by Father Clark. Don't mention it in your letter. Papa might think we were *inveigling* him!

Thede has not yet made her promised visit to Father: when you write, do urge her to do so. . . .

lovingly your Mama

St. Joseph's Jan 30th /66

My dear Mama,

I have as usual to begin with many thanks for your kind letter. . . .

I know, dear Mama, that you would soon have to cease hinting and ask me plainly what was the extent of hair my unfortunate head could boast. Sr. Raphael said that in reply . . . I must tell you what I told her the other day when she wanted to tease me a little about it. She said, "Well May what do you think your hair is going to be, curly or straight?" "Indeed Sister," I replied, "I do not think anything about it except that it stands on end all the time that I am not brushing or combing it." If you can straighten out this answer into anything, well then I suppose it is a sign that my locks will be straight, but if the more you think of it the more tangled it gets, well then I will leave you to think what you like about it.

Sr. Raphael very kindly showed me the notice in the "Mirror" about the Mount Hope case. We are looking anxiously forword to Monday and praying for those engaged in the trial. Tell my dear Papa that he must say his little prayers with particular devotion at that time, and to beg the Holy Family and St. Anthony to help him.

Since I began this letter we have done ample justice to the good things contained in the little box you sent. I often think and say, "Oh! if our friends could only see how much enjoyment they give us by their kind presents how pleased they would be." Your children send much love and I mine to dear Papa, Cousins Thede and Crick with all the family, though for the life of me I cannot find out who they are. Devotedly, May.

St. Joseph's. Feb. 2d 1866

My dear Mama,

Although you will receive my letter of the 30th at the same time you do this, you must not be surprised. . . . I will tell you in this of our celebration of Father Burlando's feast-day. . . .

All during last week our remote preparations engaged our leisure moments. In our culinary department we were occupied in making the cakes and other good things that annually prove to our dear Father how we are succeeding in domestic economy . . . I must tell you of something particularly funny about our doings. There is a most beautiful barn and stable being built in place of the old one that for a long time has been out of keeping with its surroundings. It is a splendid building of the Swiss style of architecture and we always call it Le Chateau des Vaches. As Father Burlando drew up the plan for it and of course takes a great deal of interest in it, the Sisters thought it would be pleasant and amusing for us to make a Chateau of good things in opposition to

Father's. I was charged with writing the piece to be read on its presentation to Father. . . .

The truly beautiful and poetical part of our celebration was entrusted to dear Sr. Caroline. Her piece, which I will try to send you, supposes St. Francis (Father's patron) to have left on earth the lyre whose strains had enchanted us during his life. To represent this we had a beautiful lyre of some twenty-six or eight inches in height made. The strings were gilt and the framework most exquisitely ornamented with geranium leaves, moss, fern and delicate flowers. The lower part was so formed that a music box could be introduced and surprise us by its unexpected harmony. When the reader came to the line "Hark etc," a few cords were to be drawn of the guitar and at the end of the piece the little music box, which had been previously wound up, was to be placed in the frame of the harp and renew for us the music of St. Francis' lyre.

. . . We had our celebration in the study-room where we met about eight o'clock. Our Chateau built entirely of cake, candy, conserved fruits, and all the good things that could be thought of was placed in the middle of a prettily arranged table on which the lyre and our cakes were also to be placed. Anna Northrop read Sr. Caroline's poetical piece, Mary Burke read mine, and one of the other girls read the prose address composed by Miss Mary Burke. . . . Indeed we have not had such a fine time for a long while.

Good bye dear Mama there is the bell.

May.

Baltimore 1866 Feby 5th

My darling child,

Your charming and satisfactory letters . . . were rec'd in due time on Saturday. Dear Crick has learned the hour the mail reaches the city on Saturday and punctual at the hour the boy finds himself at the p. office awaiting the letter which he knows so many anxious hearts are expecting. . . .

Your letters last week gave unusual pleasure—they were so well and so cleverly written—so cheerful and so content and happy the frame of mind in which they were indited I could not help repeating your own gratifying expressions. "If our children only knew what heartfelt pleasure their attention to their duties and their efforts to be good gave their parents, I am sure there would be very few naughty ones." We all took so much pleasure in reading your letters that I was foolish enough to believe the dear Sisters, yours especially, would derive some satisfaction in their perusal, so yesterday morning, when going up to High Mass, I put your letter in my pocket with the intention of giving it to Sister Leo—if I should meet her. After church I stood on the steps waiting for the orphans to pass out, when to my great satisfaction Sisters

Louisa & Leopoldine came last. I at once joined them and walked home with them. I handed them your letter and told them I had brought it up for them to read and the other Sisters that desire to do so, as it contained a good deal about St. Joseph's that would be interesting to them. You can't imagine how really pleased the dear Sisters were with what they were pleased to call my kind attentions to them. They both desired their best love to you. . . .

Papa says—"Why May is getting to be quite clever—really this little poem is very creditable—very indeed—"! My child, can it be possible that pleasures in after years will be relished with the same zest that these simple ones that you are now enjoying? Ah! treasure the remembrance of them my dear children, for the day will come when you will look back upon these times as the bright spots of your existence. . . .

Sister Matilda and Sister Euphemia had a long interview with Papa this evening after Sister Matilda had had that long ride from St Joseph's—Dear Sister looked weak and wearied, but you know the Sisters never complain. It was really beautiful to see with what anxious care and tenderness Papa saw the Sisters in their carriage, and the charges he gave the driver to be cautious in driving—to go slowly and carefully over the frozen ground, &c &c. Each day, I am convinced, increases Papa's admiration and interest in all that concerns the Sisters and their institutions. I do believe, May, that the scales have fallen from Papa's eyes, and a strange and new emotion has entered his heart and I *feel* that he will soon be what we have so ardently and so long prayed for, a good Catholic! But dear child say nothing of this in your letters, only continue your prayers for both of us.

Papa, Mr Schley & Mr Gittings went out to Towsontown this morning and a number of the witnesses on both sides—but they did not begin the case owing to another case already on hand which was not finished till sometime during the day. It comes on however tomorrow "for certain." I am just as sanguine about the result as ever. I have not now and never have had the least doubt of the result. I believe the verdict will be an acquittal and I believe the Sisters and their institutions will come out like refined gold from the fire, brighter and better appreciated than they ever have been. You will smile when I tell you, of all the lawyers in this community, I think Papa the one best calculated for this particular case. The very enthusiasm and ardency of his nature enable him to grasp at with a wonderful tenacity all that which is favourable for his own side; and to see and feel the base and unworthy motives that actuate the prosecuting party. If I thought the Sisters would desire it, I would cut out of the papers each day the report of the case and enclose it to you. I think I will do so anyhow and if Sr Raphael does not approve of your reading it, why of course she must withhold it from you.

Now you saucy little rogue, I would like to know how I am to untangle your tangled description of that cross of yours. One thing I am sure I ought to congratulate myself, that the poor little head is no longer under my care, else my patience would be greatly exercised in straightening the curls if they are as twistificated as your answer to my queries. Goodnight, love to all my child,

Mama. . . .

———————

The newspaper clippings sent up to May on the Mount Hope case were substantial. During each of the trial's seven days, the *Baltimore Sun* ran at the least a full column of front-page coverage—on the last day more than two. No one in the reading public of Baltimore (and through Madge's thoughtful packet of daily clippings, the anxious Sisters at St. Joseph's) could fail to know of defense and prosecution strategies, of witnesses' testimony, or of the dramatic rhetorical flourishes that governed the style of lawyers on both sides of the case.

On that first morning, February 6, the court room was crowded. The early cars of the York line to Towsontown—the horse-drawn street railway in which Preston had been an original stockholder—were packed with the curious. They had come out from the city to watch the proceedings at the county courthouse. Some, like Madge, were devoted partisans of the Sisters of Charity; others shared anti-Catholic, anti-immigrant prejudices that had given rise to the Know-Nothing party, powerful in Baltimore before the Civil War. The political ambitions of a similar group, in fact, were thought to have motivated the prosecution in the first place. Still others in the crowd may have been titillated by an event concerning so intriguing an institution as an insane asylum and the dramatic charge of its blatant mismanagement. Maybe they hoped to see some of the crazy people who were said to be among the witnesses. Among the crowd also, but arriving more comfortably in private carriages and hired hacks, were the "ladies and medical gentlemen"—the phrase was the *Sun* reporter's—who had been summoned as witnesses.

The trial would be heard without jury by the Honorable D. C. H. Emory, judge of the Baltimore County Circuit Court, in whose impartiality and justice the defense team claimed absolute confidence. But they were distressed, they said, by the vagueness of the indictment. "It had ever been conceded," said Preston, "that where there was a charge of conspiracy, vagueness would not do. . . . Dr. Stokes and Mary Blenkinsop had been charged with fraudulently receiving sums of money from certain parties. Now, what were the sums of money and who were the persons? They were charged with printing certain false and malicious matter. . . . [W]hat was the nature of this printed matter?"[3]

To the latter question the prosecutor gestured to a pile of volumes—the 23-year accumulation of the institution's formal annual reports. These had been regularly prepared by Mount Hope's physician in charge, and the printer testified that all his negotiations had been handled by Sister Euphemia. He did not know her by the name under which she was being tried. Holding up the latest booklet—that for 1865—attorney Alexander H. Rogers began to read. The report's description, he summarized, of "the excellent condition of the institution, and the mild and humane treatment to patients" was in fact the fraud charged. Not only were the Sisters, as women, inadequate to operate the institution, but their lower-class status told against them. "In a majority of cases," the attorney deplored, "these Sisters were illiterate, and cruel in their treatment of the insane inmates . . . some . . . had recently been but a short time connected with the Sisterhood, and had recently been domestics in families, others sold in market, and one had been employed in a factory in the neighborhood, and in almost all cases unfit for their positions. . . . All the wrongs perpetrated, and outrages committed, by ignorant Irish girls at Mount Hope" went "uncorrected" by Dr. Stokes and Mary Blenkinsop. Herein lay the conspiracy.[4]

Of the emotions felt by the little band of Sisters, conspicuous by their distinctive habits among the other persons in the crowded room, no record remains. But Madge's indignation is not hard to imagine as she listened to the patronizing and sneering portrait of that pious sisterhood from whose association she had drawn so much personal strength. That her husband was seated among the attorneys who were to defend this maligned group of women must have brought to the forefront her enduring hope—her persistent belief that if she prayed strongly enough and often enough, her wayward, tempestuous spouse would somehow become again the kindly, thoughtful man she once had known.

On the eighth of February Preston at last swung into his defense. His bent was literary, his style emotional. The prosecutors had provided the theme and issue; he could supply the drama. Heatedly he flailed at the prosecution charge that sought to "involve in the disgraceful ruin a numerous band of noble ladies, whose unobtrusive piety and self-sacrificing actions are themes of admiration and praise throughout the world. . . . Are we blind? Have we lost all sense? Are we dead to every emotion of human feeling?" Gathering himself, throwing out his arm in a gesture that showed how strongly he was moved, he cried: "Strike down the Sisters of Charity! Cover with infamy and disgrace an order of women, who, in the midst of every privation, in the midst of every suffering, without limit to endurance, have invariably been found wherever human woe was deemed most bitter."

Preston had not far to reach within his own memory for such an example of human woe. "Within the sound of my voice," he continued, "and within this court-room, is one whom upon the bloody field of Gettysburgh I saw bending over the dying and the dead—binding up with her own hands the prostrate soldier's wounds, or commending, with her earnest prayers, his departing spirit to the mercy of his God. . . . "[5] Not for nothing had Preston and Hillen made their visit as sightseers to that dismal field two and a half years earlier.

Attacking the weakness of the indictment, Preston played with the potentialities of the context. "It *looks* more like the work of one demented," he pounced, "than of a lawyer. . . . [N]ot a single name is upon this indictment except those of two crazy women, one of whom is under a committee—the other . . . supported by the Sisters of Charity, at Mount Hope, for several years as a pauper. Whom then has been defrauded—upon whom has been made an attempt to defraud?—who is complaining? . . . . *It is not only an insane case but an insane indictment.*"[6]

For three and a half hours Preston held center stage. Even the prosecuting attorney, Daniel Radcliffe, who spoke in rebuttal the next morning, had to concede the spellbinding quality of his adversary's presentation: "one of the most classic and beautiful displays of eloquence I have listened to for many a year past."[7]

For three more days the case dragged along—with prosecution charges of stories told by the Sisters at the asylum to alarm the insane: of secret homicides, "of a boy beaten to death" and secretly buried. The prosecution witness Miss Fleming was objected to by the defense attorneys on grounds that she was not competent because insane. The prosecution's patronizing criticism of Miss Peggy Mahoney, one of the Sisters, as an ignorant Irish woman was ridiculed by the "astonished" Preston, who referred to her distinguished family's 200-year history in Maryland's Charles County.

At last, on the fourteenth, the case collapsed. The state's attorney filed a plea of *nol pros*, the defense arguing the greater appropriateness of a "not guilty" verdict. And thus ended the Mount Hope case. The Sisters of Charity were vindicated. Editorials ran in all the local papers—the *Sun*, the *Gazette*, the *Evening Transcript*, the *Baltimore American*—unanimously expressing outrage that the trial had even taken place.[8] And Preston, now a celebrity, could bask in the nearly universal acclaim.

Baltimore Feby 16th 1866

My darling child,

You and the Sisters will really think I have Mount Hope on the brain. I believe I have been a good deal excited on the subject but it is, I hope, all over, and these enclosed "slips" are the last I shall trouble you with. Indeed they will have to be, as my stock of stamps is well nigh exhausted with the repeated duplicates put upon my budgets of late to St Joseph's. I have enclosed two "Editorials," taken from the two leading papers of this city. The *Sun* and the *Gazette*—the remarks of the *Gazette* particularly, are very severe and evidently, as Papa says, written by one who thoroughly understands the subject.

We know a popular newspaper generally expresses the feelings and views of the public. You can judge then by these editorials the pervading sentiment of the populace; I never doubted, myself, that the opinions of all right-minded persons—as well Protestants as Catholics—would eventually turn in favour of the Sisters and their institution, and so it is; as Papa says, nearly every person who met him yesterday and today congratulated him on the happy result of his case. Sisters Matilda & Euphemia have just left us, having called as they said to thank Mr Preston for his great kindness and attention &c &c. Papa was not home, so I had the pleasure of listening to all the good things they said about him. I told Sisters I was only too happy to know they were gratified and that I thought our dear Lord had been especially kind to Papa in granting him the privilege of being thus useful. You will perceive I am writing in great haste—indeed all my letters of late have been written in a whirl. I hope however soon to be more quiet and then I can write at my leisure. . . . Papa of course always unites with me in love to his little daughter—

Yours lovingly
Mama

St. Joseph's Feby 16th 1866

My dear Mrs Preston,

As you have entered so intensely into our feelings of anxiety in the case, & I may say were almost as much identified with it as Mr Preston, you can well imagine how jubilant we were when the good news reached us. Father Burlando & your most welcome letter journied together. May has given you an account of the manner in which the joyful tidings were received & our thanks for the success. The Sisters enjoyed your letter, which was read aloud in our Community Room that evening. Our lawyers cannot be too much extolled for the manner in which they carried the case through. We may justly feel *proud* in styling them our *champions*. They certainly had to struggle for their laurels but won them. What guerdon shall be theirs? Indeed they merit one that will not fade with time. I am sure you must be doubly rejoiced. I read the different speeches with deep interest. Mr. Preston is a powerful & glowing orator. I wish you could have seen dear little May, how deeply interested she was, & how modest she was when her father was spoken of in praiseworthy terms! There is one thing certain—the Sisters will not fail to make a daily memento of Mr. Preston before the holy altar. I will *not* say we *will enter* into a crusade for his benefit; of course you will join us. I am very thankful for your kindness in furnishing us with the clippings; they were eagerly read.

May is doing well. The Sisters unite in kind regards. Yours affectionately

Sister M Raphael

Baltimore Feby 22d /66

My dear child,

I made a visit to the asylum this morning and had a delightful interview with dear Sister Euphemia, Sr Matilda and Sr Louise. Sister Euphemia said she expected to go to St Joseph's tomorrow and would be the bearer of any thing I desired to send to you. . . .

I shall . . . content myself with a letter. . . .

I did not see Sister Leopoldine as it was during school hours that I was at the asylum; but I was told by Sister Louisa she was quite well. I saw Sr L——on Sunday last, and she told me she had rec'd a letter from you a few days before, was much pleased and sent in my next letter her love to you. . . .

My dear child, I wish you to thank dear Sr Raphael for a delightful letter she wrote me, and for the kind and clever remarks made of our good Papa. The dear, grateful Sisters overrate Papa's efforts, at least Papa says so, for he was so ably assisted by Mr Schley and Mr Gittings, and I am sure Papa feels it was a great privilege to be permitted to labour in so good a cause. Papa is now reviewing the manuscript previous to the publication of the pamphlet containing the whole of the trial, speeches &c &c. It all having been taken down by an excellent stenographer. It is said the other party are also getting up a book, which of course will be as false as all their other doings. We rec'd your letter also, and were quite of your opinion that it was better to have withheld the subject from the girls till it was finally settled. I hope my dear child you appreciate the kindness of dear Sister Raphael in permitting you to have the "slips"; it is very gratifying to me in as much as it convinces me the Sisters knew they might confide in your prudence and discretion and that you were true to your trust.

I have reserved for the last page a little piece of information that I hope will give you some pleasure. I have rec'd a kind and cordial invitation from Sister Euphemia to spend holy week at St Joseph's, as Sister says "by way of penance." Now this is a penance to which I most cheerfully submit, and if you and Sister Raphael only give me a slight intimation that my presence will be welcome, I shall accept the invitation and accompany Sister Matilda when she goes up to St Joseph's. . . . Tell Sister Raphael and Sister Genevieve I say I can't come unless they second the invitation—as I know I shall be billeted in their quarters and give them the trouble of my being there. Only think of Mama and her little girl sleeping under St Joseph's roof together!—I shall begin to count the days till the time comes. . . . When you write tell me exactly what you think of my coming—if you wish it, or if you would rather I would defer my visit till Distribution. Goodnight my darling. Remember me to all the Sisters whom I know and kiss my dear children—

Mama. . . .

St. Joseph's. Feb. 24th/66

Dearest Mama,

Imagine if you can what a happiness I enjoy in being able to say that dear Sr. Raphael and Sr. Genevieve join most cordially in Sr. Euphemia's kind invitation to you to pay our valley a visit. Oh! my precious Mama, it makes me so very happy to think of seeing you in a few weeks, and to feel that you will be so kindly welcomed by our dear Sisters. . . . If you had seen me when Sister told me that Sr. Euphemia had invited you to St. Joseph's, I think you would have laughed heartily at my look of surprise and delight. I think it was so beautiful of dear Sister to ask you to come up. I tried to say how much I felt her kindness; from the bottom of my heart I say to our dear Lord and everybody who has anything to do with you coming, "I thank you."

When I spoke to Sister Genevieve about your wish to have her especial approbation on the subject, she drew me in her kind motherly way close to her and said "Tell your Mama, yes indeed, and that she must make my part of the house her own while she is with you"; so you see you are truly to have the pleasure of sleeping under dear old St. Joseph's hospitable roof as in times gone by. She seems as fond of Papa as I could possibly wish, and bids me tell him for her that he must have changed greatly since she met him on the battlefield at Gettysburg, for he did not seem to be such a terrible person then as his friend Rogers appears to think him now.[9] But if I were to attempt to deliver half the messages and kind words dear Sister sent you I should fill pages, and that must not be as dear Sr. Raphael also intends writing to you. Suffice it to say that I feel that you will be truly welcome, or as Sr. Genevieve herself expressed it, that you will not be a bit more so by our own little daughter than by the Sisters. . . .

With love to my dear Papa,
Cousins Thede and Crick
I am your little
May.

My dear Mrs. Preston,

Most heartily do I second good Sister Euphemia's invitation to pay us a visit & enjoy May's company at St. Joseph's. We are delighted at Sister's thoughtfulness & wish that Mr Preston could accompany you. But I propose his coming in May or June; it will be a delightful time of year to walk over the grounds, & I am sure he will find St. Joseph's a pleasant spot to rusticate for awhile. The Sisters unite in kind regards to yourself & Mr. Preston.

Yours affectionately
Sister M Raphael

Baltimore March 11th 1866

My dear child

If I do not write you as long a letter as you wish, you must scold Papa for making himself so agreeable to Thede and I tonight—I have actually been trying to tear myself away from the little circle ever since tea time, but each time I moved away, something pleasant and agreeable was said to call me back again. At last I jumped up, saying I would talk to no one for the next hour, or at least till after a short chat with my little daughter. Of course my move was a signal for a general dispersing—Thede took a book and seated herself at one end of the table and Papa surrounded himself with piles of manuscript of the Mount Hope trial, which he has taken upon himself to correct before going to the press. This, of course, is entre nous, as the supposed editors would not, I think, wish it known. —I have come over to my own little desk to make you a short visit in spirit and tell you such things as would be pleasant for you to know of the past week's doings. . . .

. . . Papa, Thede & Crick join me in an abundance of love to you. Remember me to all *my* Sisters, and give my love to my children.

Yours most lovingly
Mama

Papa says tell May I am pleased to see by her last letter a great improvement in her handwriting! Always be careful in your writing. Papa is so anxious you should write well.

Baltimore March 19th 1866

My dear child,

You will be somewhat surprised when I tell you that I came very near being with you this evening. Early last week Sisters Matilda and Theresa came to see Papa on business; after which they came up to see me and Sr Matilda told me she intended to go to St Joseph's on Friday the 16th and expected me to go with her. Upon reflecting, however, I thought just now I could not be spared from home two weeks . . . as I particularly wished to be at St Joseph's during holy week. . . .

Thede and I went to the depot on Friday and Saturday to see Sister Matilda off, but each day we were disappointed, so we suppose the rain one day and the high wind the next frightened Sister from going. Saturday being St Patrick's day, you may be sure I did not forget to pay your respects to your good Sister. Aunt Louisa, who by the way reached the city on Friday to pay us a visit of a week or two, together with Thede, accompanied me; on our way we stopped at Feast's and I selected a new variety of carnation, which Mr Feast said would bloom about Easter and had it taken to the asylum[10] for Sr Leopoldine. Dear Sister seemed so much pleased with our little attentions—of course she asked most kindly after you, sent lots of love, and expressed herself as greatly pleased that I was going to see you. . . .

You will be pleased to know your cousin Anne is also on a visit to the city; she only arrived today and staying with us. Thus you see we have Aunt Louisa, Thede, Anne and Crick. Louisa McGrew is also in the city but not with us. She is stopping at Mrs Beer's, who by the way has succeeded admirably in her boarding house. . . .

. . . Papa and Aunt Louisa have just gone to a "spiritual meeting" when some fooleries are to be practiced. . . . I, hoping soon to see you, close my short letter, with affectionate regards to the Sisters and all my children.

Mama

St Joseph's March 26 1866

[To William Preston]

Well, here I am safe and happy at dear old St Joseph's and such a welcome as was awarded I had not dared to dream of. My letter to Sr Raphael did not reach here till the day after I did . . . consequently there was much disappointment and surprise at my nonappearance. May and my *other* children had prepared themselves to receive me grandly, having donned their best apparel, brushed up their curls and put on their sweetest smiles; even the dear good Sisters were looking a welcome to the cumbersome old rickety stage that was to bring the long looked-for guest, and when it loomed in sight, approached the house and deposited a young girl from Lowell, Massachusetts, "come to be a Sister," the Sisters turned away, quite disappointed, so Sr Raphael, kindly informed me. Nevertheless, when I did come on Saturday, though the best dress was wanting & the curls not quite so artistically arranged, the sweet smiles and the loving caresses, and the affectionate greetings were there in all the warmth of girlhood. Mrs Parr's coming being altogether unlooked for was a great delight to her daughter and niece. And dear Mother Euphemia,[11] I verily believe, out of compliment to me invited Mrs Parr to remain with the girls at St Joseph's, so here we have been having the most charming times. We laughingly said yesterday was our grand levee day—as nearly every Sister in the community as well as Father Burlando and Father Gandolfo have called on us. Father Burlando, Mother, Sisters Raphael, Genevieve, Matilda, Camilla, in fact every Sister who has spoken to me, have desired me to give you their "grateful and heartfelt regards." Sister Genevieve says, "Mrs Preston, we have a perpetual prayer for Mr Preston; in this community he can never be forgotten"; you can't imagine the great pleasure and satisfaction the picture I brought up has given.[12] It went the rounds of the community yesterday, and a little while ago Sr Raphael came in to see me and to say Mother Euphemia says you cannot have the picture again, as we think we are fairly entitled to keep it as our champion! The book also was hailed with great satisfaction. I gave it to Mother as coming from you, immediately after my arrival. She was much pleased; the Sisters, it seems, are looking forward to Sr Matilda reading your speech to them as a great treat. I am told she imitates you even better than Sr Louisa. I shall try and remember all the clever & funny things said while I am here to amuse you all on my return.

And now let me say something about May. She is looking "fresh as a rose," as Mrs Parr says, and the picture of good health, but I think by no means a *pretty picture*; indeed she is less pretty than I have ever known her, but then she is *so good*! Everyone, Sisters as well as girls, are loud in her praise—"so honorable—so upright—so thoughtful—so disinterested—so kind to the "little tacks"—so careful and attentive to *lame girls*, and so affectionately respectful to all the Sisters!" Now is not that character more to be desired than beauty?—I really believe May is the most popular child in the school. She asked so much about you and her Cousin Theodosia & Crick, and sends so much love to you and her cousins; she says tell Papa I am going to write a long letter to him by you. I am to say such things as I do not wish everybody to see—I suppose a confidential letter! . . .

I regret so much I did not bring two or three copies of the trial with me. I know Sister Raphael and Sr Genevieve and May also would like to read your speech, but it will be a long time before they get through with the book among the Sisters. . . .

> I must close
> Goodbye love to all
> Madge

Baltimore 27 Mar 1866

Dear Madge,

About an hour ago I received your interesting letter. I am gratified to know . . . that you received on your arrival a hearty welcome. At this however I am not at all surprised, for in addition to any special kindly feeling the good Sisters may entertain for me and mine, their own good pious hearts would induce them to make a guest perfectly at home, especially at this Holy Season. It is very pleasing to me to hear that May is so much beloved. My experience through life has taught me that whatever flattery, prompted by interest, may be accorded to individuals—affectionate regard is never extended unless it is really merited. . . .

Yesterday I had an interesting interview with Archbishop Spaulding. He told me that he had carefully read the whole of my speech in the Mount Hope case and I was gratified by hearing him express not only his approbation but his admiration. I told him that in my opinion, as a mere forensic effort, it had little to recommend it. Like a very plain vase freighted with precious odours —it could only be considered valuable as the vehicle of a deserved tribute to virtue, piety and charity. The Rev.d father expressed himself as pleased with our interview, and cordially invited me to visit him. I am as you know but a very poor visitor yet I think I shall manifest my appreciation of the old gentle-man's kindness by calling on him—of one thing I am certain, his urbanity, learned intelligence, and Christian liberality of sentiment will amply repay any momentary indisposition of mine to depart from my general rule as to visiting—in a word I was much pleased with him. I have been pretty busy since you left, engaged in an affair in which I felt a deep interest —although not a profitable one—I think I can say I saved an excellent man, an amiable woman, and a large family of interesting children from unmerited disgrace and utter ruin—the family know it—I know it, and God knows it. When we meet I will fully explain the matter to you. . . .

Present to the Mother and the Sisters my best respects. I hope to have the pleasure of seeing them in June. . . .

Love to you and May,
W. P. Preston

# 14

## A Case of Measles

MADGE RETURNED, ELATED BY her visit to St. Joseph's. She was flattered to have been offered a room in the Sisters' residence, and the Sisters' pleasure over the happy outcome of the lawsuit colored all the exchanges of conversation between themselves and Madge. Madge was pleased to see her husband in his new character: the Sisters' "champion." Her hope began to grow that his conversion to Catholicism—her dearest dream—might finally come about. Doubtless she imagined that such an event would dispel forever the wild rages that had been directed against her so frequently in these last years, that as he found spiritual comfort, he would renounce his sins of the flesh. It must have been pleasant to feel, too, that she and May, who had profited so greatly from the kindness and nurturance provided by the Sisters at St. Joseph's, had been able to repay that debt in this spectacular rescue, with their own husband and father playing the major role.

---

Baltimore April 6th 1866

My dear child,

This is the first hour since my return that I felt I could quietly sit down and devote to you and dear old St Joseph's! Papa "took me in tow" immediately on my reaching home, and I have been busily engaged with him ever since; so you see my little darling, I came home just in the nick of time. . . . As soon as the car reached the depot, I looked around, hoping to see some member of my family, as I despatched from Gettysburg that I was on my way. I soon saw through the crowd Papa's long hair floating in the breeze and an instant after his dear, kind face was visible, and by his side stood Crick, each of them peering through the windows in search of Mama. . . . Of course everyone was glad to see me, but I gave no one a chance to talk for about two hours, taking that privilege altogether to myself. How delighted they were with all I told them and how grateful Papa was for the kindness extended to me by the dear Mother and kind Sisters during my visit was very apparent by the flushed cheeks and moistened eye as he earnestly listened to my recitals. And I too! How shall I express, in what words convey, the intense happiness and enjoyment I experienced during my "week at St Joseph's." Of all my life, it was truly the happiest, and I wish you so to tell Mother and Sisters! . . .

You will perceive I have written in haste, but hope soon to write more at leisure, when I will tell you about the fair, as I am going with Papa there to-night. Love from Papa, Thede, Crick and Mama.

---

The fair Madge referred to was the Southern Relief Fair, held at the Maryland Institute from April 2 to April 13. On its last day Father Burlando, Mother Euphemia, and May's classmate from Charleston, Anna Northrop, joined Madge to mingle among the crowd of patrons.

Baltimore April 18th 1866

My darling child,

. . . The Great Southern Relief Fair has been a grand success. The ladies having realized upwards of one hundred and thirty thousand dollars. There is also to be held at the Front St Theatre a grand Soiree on Monday the 23d of April, which it is hoped will swell the amount to nearly ten thousand dollars more. I am sure I wish it would be ten times that much if the Southern people were sure of getting it. It is said there is a fearful amount of suffering through the Southern states, and from what we know ourselves from private sources, I fear the accounts are only too true. The more I see of the Southern character the more I find to admire in them—warm-hearted, generous noble, and with the kindest impulses.[1]

You know I told you of Papa's Southern friends residing temporarily at the "mill"? well a few weeks ago they were fortunate enough to receive from Charlestown, where the most of their property is located, a remittance of some hundred dollars—a day or two afterwards the lady came to the city and purchased a large quantity of dry goods and groceries—which she sent by express to some friends of hers in the South whom she knew to be in a suffering condition. Although she was scarcely above want herself, she could yet feel so deeply and substantially for others. When you write, don't mention the particulars of this in your letter; our friends in reading the letter would know whom you mean, and we do not let the neighbours know their condition, as few people sympathize with poverty. While at a good distance from them, from here to South Carolina for instance, they are willing to hold out their hands and act with great friendship; but when it comes to be a next door neighbour, they are very apt to turn their backs upon those who are so unfortunate as to be poor.

I called on Sister Leopoldine and gave your message and little packet, with which she was much pleased. . . . Just as I finished the last sentence, Kitty came in with her face all aglow and looking as pleased and happy as she could look—to tell me she had just come from catechism to Father Foley and that she knew every question Father Foley asked her and he was very much pleased with her. Poor Kitty I really think she is trying to be a good little girl. She sends lots of love to Miss May, and says "Please Missus tell Miss May, I go to church regularly every Sunday."[2] . . .

By the way . . . Father Burlando told Papa he would expect him to be his guest during his stay in Emmitsburg and he and Father Gandolfo would do all in their power to make him comfortable and happy. Was not that sweet and beautiful in dear Father Burlando? and your Mama is again to be a guest at dear old St Joseph's, so says our good, kind Mother. But here I am arranging about a time that I may never see—two whole months and where may we be?[3] . . .

Yours lovingly Mama

Baltimore April 24th 1866

My darling child,

It is possible I may send my letter by two of your young companions who leave the city in the morning for St Joseph's. . . . As your letter informed me that Emily would be in the city on Tuesday, of course I called at the asylum in due time on the afternoon of that day, but found no Emily there. Dear Sr Louisa however, on hearing me say I wished to go up to St Joseph's House of Industry,[4] very kindly suggested that Sister Leopoldine should accompany. Imagine with what pleasure we started off, to have, as I laughingly said to Sr Louisa, a "regular jollification." On reaching the "House," we were very cordially met by Sr Marianna and Sr Josephine, who both seemed to take real pleasure in showing me over their quiet and unassuming establishment. It is wonderful how everything prospers and thrives that the dear Sisters have anything to do with—no, it is *not* wonderful, for the grace of God is certainly over all! There were fifteen (I think) young girls, from the ages of ten to twenty—neat, clean and happy, evidently, from their smiling faces. Sister was kind enough to take me to their sewing room, and the Sisters who superintended their work showed me the work of each child. I saw some of the finest linen undergarments most beautifully embroidered by these young girls, who have only had the instruction of a few months as this establishment only went into operation last October. You who know my fondness for this kind of needlework can well imagine with what gratification I looked upon all I saw and how fully I appreciated the good Sisters' efforts in behalf of these orphan children. . . .

. . . I must not forget to tell you, Papa took the "Egg" to your old friend Mr Hopkins, and that dear old gentleman was wonderfully pleased at your attentions. Mr Hopkins was kind enough to say some very pretty things about you, which though I do not repeat to you, I shall take great pleasure in remembering.[5] . . .

. . . Goodnight. Papa, Thede, Crick & Johnny send much love to you.

Mama

Baltimore May 3d 1866

My dear Baby

I regret I could not have a letter yesterday for our kind friend Mr Parr, to carry with him for you to St Joseph's. . . .

I am sure you will be pleased to learn that Mrs Parr intends giving our dear Kate her full consent to the dear child becoming a Catholic *at once*. I had a long conversation a few days since with Mrs Parr and told her all that Kate had communicated to me on the subject while at St Joseph's. Mrs Parr, like a true good mother as she is, desires her daughter's happiness above all things, and as she is convinced it will be best promoted by attaching herself to that church from which the dear child *sees* and *feels* "all graces flow," she told me she would write to Kate by her Papa, giving her permission to Kate to become a Catholic before she leaves St Joseph's—Dear Kate! my heart yearns to her with a love stronger than to any other child I know—perhaps it is because I can so fully sympathize with all her feelings and emotions on this great and all-important subject that now fills her young and guileless heart. Give my best to her, and tell her I say I will be with her in spirit on the day of her happy first communion and shall *almost* regard her as my God child!

I need not ask you, because I know your kind and loving little heart will prompt you to the performance of such sympathizing acts as may be desired and agreeable to Kate at this particular time. None but a *convert* can know how much a convert has to *overcome* and to *learn*: though I acknowledge, to a child living three years under a Catholic roof, there would not be so much to learn as under other circumstances—yet I am sure a young and loving friend of Kate's own age to whom she could speak freely would be most acceptable. . . .

Your Papa, Thede, Crick & Johnny went directly after breakfast to the "mill" to spend the day with the Fabers, Catherine & I remaining in the city to go to church. Rose came in a few minutes ago, and while I am finishing my letter she is reading the "Mirror" by my side.

. . . I had several things I wished to mention, but Rose's chatter has put them entirely out of my mind, and I "guess" you have had enough in this long letter so I will bring it to a close, asking you first to give my love to dear Sr Raphael . . . to Sr Genevieve, Sr Lucia, Sr Ann Scholastica, Sr Caroline, Sr Loretta, Sr Juliana and each and all of my children. . . .

Yours lovingly
Mama

May 17th 1866

My darling child,

You will regret to learn that our gifted friend Mrs McMullen, formerly Mary Genan, is dead! The sweet voice that has so often charmed not only her many friends but strangers also is hushed and silent, and the bride of one short year has just been consigned to the tomb. . . .

. . . Mary's death was most sudden and unexpected, she having been sick but a few hours. . . . The congregation of the cathedral felt her death most sensibly, remembering as they did how long and how often they had been charmed with her sweet singing. Father Foley officiated at the Requium Mass, and when it was over and he addressed her relatives and friends and the immense concourse of persons who had assembled to pay the last mark of love and respect to her poor remains, he was so deeply affected, she having been, as he said his penitent from girlhood, as to be at times almost unable to utter the words of loving praise to which he thought her so fully entitled. Mrs Hillen, Miss Sally Keen and myself rode out to the cathedral graveyard together. . . . While standing beside her grave, we were most fully impressed with the one great truth—death comes to us all sooner or later; it were well with us, if we were at all times prepared to meet it. . . .

We have remembered all this week that Saturday will be your birthday and that you have reached the mature age of seventeen years! Alas! alas! I shall soon have to cease writing *my child*, and shall be forced to look upon you as a young lady and no longer as the little May so willing to be careful and loved as our "wee one." I think you may expect Papa's "long letter" without any fear of disappointment. I believe he anticipates the pleasure of writing *that* letter with as much satisfaction as you do in receiving it. . . .

As Papa will write to you tomorrow, I shall say nothing of him. Except that he is as well as usual, complaining *of course* of his side. Thede and Crick . . . unite in love & good wishes to you I also my precious child send love & blessings to you.

Mama

---

Preston's euphoria after the Mount Hope case seems to have waned as he subsequently sank into another deep depression. However inappropriate to the occasion, his seventeen-page letter for May's third birthday at St. Joseph's is intensely lugubrious, an apostrophe to human mortality. In one section he attempts to amuse by relating a patronizing anecdote concerning a black woman and misses her message about white injustice. Instead he turns her story into a homily on death. Although Preston's depression probably spilled over on to the family as it had in the past, the disappearance of Madge's diary has expunged whatever unambiguous record she herself might have set down.

Baltimore 19 May 1866

I congratulate you my dear child on this the seventeenth anniversary of your birth! It seems but as yesterday since I first heard the plaintive wail of your tiny voice rising and falling like the faint murmurs of an aeolian harp; and yet seventeen years have passed away!—Seventeen years!! . . . How many upon whom the dawn of 19th May 1849 beamed life and health have passed away for ever or are now lingering in the agony of disease. In our own circle as in that of others the record is a sad one. I look around in vain for many of my former friends. I no longer hear the cheerful sweet, inspiring voice of my dear devoted friend Mrs Friese borne upon the wings of the heaven-born harmony which God permitted to be the companion of her life; her spirit, as you may remember, left its tenement almost at her beloved instrument.[6] To me she was a dear friend—in happy hours, she made them happier and when trouble came she cheered and consoled me. Peace to her ashes!—and her fine manly noble son! poor Henry, he who so often dandled you upon his knee or led you around to view with him the mysterious beauties of the flowers and plants he loved so well, he too, is gone!—You were his last companion here on earth, for when we least expected it his delicate spirit . . . passed away for ever! and the queer old gentleman—"old Mr. Friese"—whose quaint and almost stolid look, covered so much good sense, and such a kind heart, is also among the absent; and we must add to the list the dear old Captain—he whose immeasurable love for you death alone could chill—he has found a resting place with God, and old Judge Stump and the gallant, bright eyed brave hearted Judge Legrand—and Aunty Carlon, Mrs. Adler and Mrs. Thelon—all all gone—and what my dear child do their departures teach—only what Longfellow has so well expressed that—

"Life is short, and time is fleeting
And our hearts though stout and brave
Still like muffled drums are beating
Funeral marches to the grave"—

. . . During my life I have often wondered at the different impression made by death on different persons. I remember and will relate to you a rather amusing instance—One fine summer's day many years ago, an overgrown lump of African obesity ycleped[7] Ann Coates—waddled into my office. She was interested in a petition for freedom then pending before one of our courts. My office chairs being armchairs, were really too small to accommodate so large a lump of ebony, and there she stood before me puffing and blowing like a porpoise. "Well," I said, "Ann what is the matter with you—You appear to be disturbed"—She twisted about in the queerest way; her great fat cheeks shaking with mirth as she replied—"Ise happy—happy, Master. It is so good to know dat dey can't cheat death—no dey *can't* and I knows it"—"Cheat who" I inquired. "Death Sir—Death!" the old woman emphatically responded—"Why Ann what in the world has Death to do with our freedom suit—Have you lost your senses"? "No Master—no I'se sensible to de last —just'fore I comed in to your office I heard the rich Mrs Gordon was dead. Ah Master its 'soling to know de rich must die, well as de poor" and then she laughed outright. "Ann" I continued, "you certainly are not glad because Mrs Gordon is dead—I thought you were a kind hearted woman. You are too fat to be ill natured."—"I *is* good natured Sir! werry good natured, but Sir if de rich didn't die as well as de poor, we Niggers would be in a bad way—I tells you Sar, in a werry short time dere wouldn't be one on us left—dere'd be no use for abolitionists I tell you." "Ann I do not understand you—what *do* you mean"?—"Mean Sir" responded the philosophic Ann "I means sar de trufe —de bressed Lord's trufe and it is dis—the moment Master Death called on Mrs Gordon sh'd put her hand in her pocket and pulled out $20,000 and said Mr. Death, you let me go—go ater dat ole Nigger—Bress de Lor' Sir —if he'd had a pocket to put de money in he'd a cotched me in no time dat he would—fat as I am—but sir dey can't bribe death—if dey could it wouldn't be long before dere wouldn't be a Nigger in dis country—so you sees Sir de Lor be praised de rich must die as well as de poor." I could not help smiling at Ann's moral philosophy, but queer as it is there is something in it perhaps worth reflecting upon. . . .

My dear child at the commencement of this letter I stated that the last seventeen years had many pleasing and painful recollections, and I have specifically referred to some of the *painful* ones. Allow me to assure you, that the most *pleasing* one—and one which to the hour of my death I shall believe was most approved and most favored of God—was my defense of the Sisters of Charity to whom through you I now send my most affectionate regards.

Wm P. Preston

Baltimore May 27th 1866

My precious child,

A visit from your Cousin Rose today and a long letter of a business character I have just finished to our little friend in Phila will prevent me from writing the folio I had hoped to have despatched to you by tomorrow's mail. . . .

Ever since my return from St Joseph's I have wanted to be invested with the Scapulars,[8] that dear Sister Bibliana gave me while there. On that day I felt particularly desirous, and concluded to call on Sr Leo and ask her to go with me to Father Giustiniana's church for that purpose. Everything seemed propitious—Sister and some other Sisters were going there to Vespers, and I accompanied them after Vespers. I spoke to the good Father on the subject, and he at once blessed my scapulars and invested me; at the close Father asked my name—on leaving the church Father Giustiniana came up to me and asked me if I had a daughter at St Joseph's, to which I gladly answered "Yes Father." The dear good Father then told me he had recently seen you at St Joseph's and had had a long conversation with you in which you had expressed a wish to him that we should live in the neighbourhood of his church and belong to his parish &c &c. . . . Now I think this was another singular circumstance that I should have had such an ardent desire to receive the scapulars from the Father with whom you had so recently had the conversation about your parents. When you come home we will sometimes attend Father Giustiniana's church.

Your Papa made his accustomed visit to Phila the first part of this week. The little woman was, as she always is, delighted to see him. You know she looks upon Papa as the best friend she has in the world, and I really do think she has reason to think so, for ever since the death of Mr Simmons Papa has watched over and protected her interests as faithfully, nay much more so, than he does his own.

While there, nothing would do but Papa must go up and see "May's room," which she has gone to the expense of recarpeting and refurnishing in beautiful style and calls it altogether "May's room." She looks forward to our annual visit with as much pleasure and satisfaction, I really think, as we do to yours. She has very kindly expressed a wish to have Theodosia make her a visit, which Thede intends to do. . . . You will find Thede the most improved person you ever saw, indeed I cannot tell you how pleasant she is to me at all times— so kind—so affectionate and so anxious to please me in everything. . . .

Rose also is becoming perfectly charming—so much so, that I have laid it down as a rule that she spends every Sunday with us. The poor child is confined during the week so constantly that the coming to us on a Sunday is looked forward to during the whole week as the most delightful event that can possibly occur to her. We have had our bathroom very nicely fitted up, with warm and cold water, shower bath &c, and whenever Rose comes down, the first thing she does is to "fly for a bath" as she says.

. . . Good night May God bless you and may our Blessed Mother have you always under her protecting wing

Mama. . . .

St. Joseph's May 28th 1866

My dear Mrs Preston

I promised to inform you of any indisposition of your dear little May when you were here, & I must be as good as my word & tell you of a singular *freak* of Dame Nature to purify her system. On Sunday May complained of head-ache & preferred taking a nap instead of coming to the dinner-table. In the evening about 6 o'clock her face & neck were completely covered with measles. Dr Patterson said they were finely marked & *beautifully developed*. As soon as they made their appearance, the head-ache passed off & she felt relieved. Sister Genevieve soon brought in the aid of saffron tea. May declares she is perfectly [well] & pleads strenuously against the *tisans*[9] & low diet. Her appetite has been improved by the restraint & Sister Genny promises to make amends in a few days. Lelia Duffell is keeping her company. Of course they are not lonesome, the room is kept dark for fear their eyes will suffer. I will take care that she will not resume her studies too soon. . . .

Now my dear Mrs Preston do not give yourself the least uneasiness, you know that measles is a disease of children & we *old ladies* know how to manage it without much medicine. . . .

May sends her love to Mama & Papa.

My kind regards to Mr. Preston.

Yours affectionately S M Raphael

[no date, no heading]

My precious little darling,

I find I cannot let my letter to Sr Raphael be sent off without a line or two to you, to assure you of our deep solicitude in your behalf, our sympathy in your sufferings and our hopes and prayers for your speedy restoration to your usual good health. . . .

. . . I am happy to assure you that I approve of all that has been done for you. Dear Sister Genny, knowing my peculiar views on the medical subject, has adopted the plan of all others most agreeable to me. Simple teas and low diet—with these harmless auxiliaries Dame Nature can work out her own salvation.

I need scarcely tell you, my child, to yield your own inclinations entirely to your kind nurses—be amiable and patient with any privations they may see proper to put upon you, and be assured their better judgment sees the propriety of it. Submit to the lowest possible diet, for in that is your greatest safety—tea and crackers will sustain life a long time, and yet it is no food for disease to thrive upon. Keep in bed quiet and calmly as long as Sr Genny thinks it advisable, and do not desire a light room while Sister wishes you to be in a dark one—but above all, submit to any loneliness rather than by going among your young companions too soon, running the risk of disseminating that ugly disease that has shown itself on you and Lelia, among the other children. Only think what a dreadful thing it would be if it should prevail as an epidemic in the school at this particular time! I hope and pray our dear Lord will keep that chosen spot from such a calamity. I shall not mention to anyone who has children at St Joseph's the nature of your sickness, as parents are so easily alarmed. I shall request Sr Raphael to be kind enough to read this to you as I do not wish to try your eyes by attempting its perusal. . . .

Goodnight with a prayer that our Blessed Mother will watch over you,

Mama

St. Joseph's May 29th 1866

My dear Mrs Preston

Fearing you may be anxious, I write to assure you that May, whom I have just left discussing a chicken bone & bowl of broth, is doing remarkably well. The Dr. allows her & Lelia to sit up & enjoy a little sunlight. They are both in excellent spirits and highly amused to find themselves the isolated victims of this ill-timed accident, but they are turning it to the best advantage by improving their conversational powers. May afforded Sister Genny some recreation last evening by requesting the clock in the Infirmary to be stopped as it disturbed her, & she also found fault with her sheet, because it had a seam in it! These little symptoms speak well for her convalescence; before this reaches you, she will be pretty nearly herself again. . . .

May sends her love & will send you a few lines herself on Friday.

Mother & Sister Genny unite in kind remembrance.

Yours sincerely
Sr M Raphael

St. Joseph's Infirmary
June 1st 1866.

Dearest Mama,

Sr. Raphael's daily letters have doubtless kept you informed as to the state of *our* health. I say *our* as I cannot think of the measles and myself, without including dear little Lelia, my faithful companion in all the stages of the past week's sickness. . . . This is my first exertion with the exception of a fine dance that Lelia and I had this morning while left to ourselves for a while. I wish you could have seen us. Sr. Genevieve says that she always thought it customary to take up the carpets when people had balls, but that we were wearing out hers at a fine rate "without leave or license."

It is rather late after all this nonsense to begin to thank you for your nice long letters to dear Sr. Raphael and myself. But you know I have been so completely turned up side down that you need not have been surprised if you had found my letter commenced Yours affectionately.

May—and the envelope folded neatly up in the letter. Now I do not want you to think that because I can laugh & cut up now that there was nothing the matter with me and that we only wanted to frighten you a little, Not at all. We have had our full share of as the Doctor expressed it—"Real old fashioned Measles" but thanks to our dear Sr. Genevieve's efficacious prayers and good nursing, and the kindness of every one about us we are able to be up and are doing remarkably well. . . . We have everything in the world done for us, every indulgence granted us. . . .

I am glad you saw Father Giustiniana and received the scapular from him. The way that conversation came up between us was this. To begin with we St. Joseph's girls are very fond of F. Giustiniana and I think he is of us. So when he was up of course he came over to see us. While in the play-room he asked for me as I happened at that time to be absent. When I came in and got to talking to him he asked me where I lived I told him that would be a rather hard question for me to answer then we laughed & talked about it for some minuets [sic] and at last it was decided that if ever I settled down in the city I was to live in F. G-'s parish. I being anxious to have him know my dear Papa as he had been instrumental in the conversion of the father of one of my companions. Sr. Genevieve has just come in & is giving me fits for . . . daring to elude her vigilance and write such a long letter when she only gave me permission to write a few lines. She says she has been in church with our dear Lord and he never told her a thing about my disobedience. . . .

With love to my dearest Papa and a thousand thanks for your delightful birthday letter which I had hoped to answer long before this I am

Your own little
May.


Baltimore June 4th /66

It is impossible to tell you, my precious child, with what joy we rec'd and read your letter of the 1st. Its cheerful, healthful tone told us full well that the disease . . . had at length succumbed to Dr Patterson's professional skill and dear, kind Sister Genevieve's tender, gentle, and affectionate nursing. . . . Thank dear Sister for me in your very best manner for taking you under her care and not giving you up to the dr. —I should have been dreadfully annoyed to know you were dosed by his vile drugs! . . .

Theodosia leaves us tomorrow to spend two weeks with Mrs Simmons, by special invitation; she will then return home to remain with the servants during our absence to Emmitsburg. I say *our* absence, as I think Papa is . . . to go up with me a few days before the Distribution. When dear Mother and Father Burlando were here, Father Burlando very kindly invited Papa to remain with him during his visit to St Joseph's, and Mother at the same time turned to me and said, "*we* will take charge of Mrs Preston." Now my child, I really hesitate to accept so much kindness from the dear Sisters. . . .

It is quite late, and I am sitting alone, Papa having gone out . . . to spend the evening with the late Admiral Semmes of the Confederate Navy. As he is one of my great heroes of the late rebellion I was most anxious to have Papa go, that I might know what he looked like and if he really was the wonderful man I have imagined him. . . .

Make my affectionate regards to dear Sr Raphael, Sr Genevieve and Sr Juliana. . . .

Yours
Mama

Baltimore June 11th 1866

My precious little Baby—

Sister Camilla (with whom I had a delightful interview) kindly promised to be the bearer of anything to you that I might wish to send; I therefore avail myself of this opportunity and have hastily prepared a box. . . . Of course you must be guided entirely by Sister Genevieve in the eating of the oranges, and the drinking of the lemonade, which you must concoct yourselves with the sugar I also send; and not trouble Sister. . . . I had it in my heart to send sundry "sweet things" but Papa vetoed the proceeding, as "injurious to sick stomachs." . . .

I hope by the time the box reaches you, "Richard will be himself again!"[10] and all the other little Richards, who have been your sharers in measles and misery. . . .

I am sitting in full view of your altar. I wish you could see the beautiful flowers that *everybody* sends me for "May's altar"—two of the most beautiful pink peonies I ever saw, from Pleasant Plains, together with a cluster of the Belle of Baltimore—brought yesterday by Johnny—who went out to see if "cherries were ripe." . . . The little image of our dear Blessed Mother smiles down upon it seeming to say, I will bear in affectionate remembrance all those who have been in any wise instrumental in gathering these sweet flowers in my honor. I always say a Hail Mary for everyone who brings me a flower for the altar. . . .

Give my love to dear Sr Raphael and tell her I hope the girls will be well, as *I do want to stay at St Joseph's!* Love to everybody

Mama. . . .

# 15

## Happier Days

FOR THE FIRST TIME since May's enrollment at St. Joseph's, Preston went north in June to attend the Distribution ceremony. He was to give the commencement address on June 27 at Mount St. Mary's, the boys' school on the hill above St. Joseph's.[1] No doubt he seemed the inevitable choice: the Sisters' champion and acclaimed orator of the Mount Hope trial. Father Burlando, who had sat through the week-long court proceedings in Towsontown, had already shown his appreciation by inviting Preston to remain as his houseguest. As at Easter, Madge occupied a room readied for her in the Sisters' residence.

Because Madge's 1866 diary is missing, no record remains of her own emotions during this festive period. But she must have been proud. The program for the Distribution ceremony at St. Joseph's shows that May performed two piano numbers, and the certificate awarded to her indicates that May took "First Degree" awards in Christian Doctrine, Writing, Composition, Rhetoric, Chemistry, Geography of the Heavens, Profane History, Use of Globes, and Piano; and for the rest—French, Improvement on the Piano, and Domestic Economy—she received a creditable "Second Degree" recognition. No doubt her father was pleased. He had always prized neat handwriting and serious studies above embroidery.

One can see her, smiling and excited, marching forward with her peers, all in their white dresses sashed with blue, the Virgin's colors. With her white-gloved hand she would have received from Sister Raphael the decorative certificate so carefully and—in the words of the document—"Affectionately" inscribed. The date was June 28, 1866.

All that remains, however, of this happy time, beyond the inscribed certificate and printed program, is a letter from Preston, recording his return alone from the sojourn at St. Joseph's. Madge and May had gone on with the widowed Aunt Louisa to spend a holiday at Mountain View. From this farm home, Madge answered Preston's letter.

———————————

Mountain View July 2d 1866

You will perceive my dear Mr Preston, that to keep my temper, I am obliged to resort to a pencil letter. Dear Aunt Louisa supplied herself lately with a bottle of ink, which *she* thinks excellent, but which I believe to have come from the same fountain as that which has so long tried my patience in 65 Fayette St. and as I do not wish to disedify May, who is sitting by my side with ebullitions of ill temper, I fear I shall try your temper with the reading of this scrawl. . . . Mountain View never looked so grand as at this present time. Every hill & vale, every field and meadow, every spring & stream seem to be in their full perfection of beauty—from the magnificent old trees of the forest, with their heavy foliage, down to the little creeping plant, trodden unheedingly beneath the feet—all, all are in their glory—and dear Aunt Louisa, not to be outdone by Dame Nature, has brought her artistic skill to work to complete its beauty. A new porch the entire breadth of the house—extra steps on the back porch—replastering of ceilings, plastering of rooms—white washing—but above all, a "splendid" new bathroom finishes the place. . . . In every turn I make, and in everything I enjoy, I wish you and the girls were with us. I take an extra dip or plunge in the bath every day for you, Rose & Thede, and eat an extra bunch of cherries. . . .

Not satisfied with "fixing up"—good crops—fine garden—nice chickens &c &c, we have the greatest little baby in all the country. Tell Thede, Sade's baby is a trump! I have never heard it cry since I have been here. It is a fine healthy little fellow, and well deserves the name destined for it—*Marine Wickham*.[2] Sade is doing very well, and wears her maternal honors quite gracefully. Writing of Sade reminds me to tell you I have some idea of bringing home with me a girl who is now nursing Mrs Smith, and whom the family recommend very highly as a good working girl. If she consents to come, do you not think I had better secure her at once? I should like to have a person with us who is a stranger to the city & its ways. Aunt Louisa sends lots of love to you & Thede. . . . Crick is very well, and Peri looks beautifully.

Good night
Madge

Baltimore 2nd July 1866
9.45 P.M.

Dear Madge

I have just returned from the Archbishop,[3] where I have passed a most delightful evening. I went to the house for the purpose of seeing Father Gibbons, who happened not to be in his room. . . . Disposed to wait, I took a seat in the parlor. . . . when the Archbishop walked in and said—"I have only this minute heard of your being here—and of your having been here some time. Why did you not send up your name?"—"Father," I replied, "for some time past I have intended to pay you a visit—but such was not my intention to-night. I called to see Father Gibbons. I am happy however that the occasion has brought us again together."—He sat down and commenced a conversation which lasted until half past 9—during which we discussed pretty freely the social and religious condition of Europe. I found the old gentleman full of learning, facts and anecdote. At the end of our chat he said, "From the views you have expressed I think it would interest you to read my History of the Protestant Reformation—if you will accept it. I will present you a copy"—I thanked him and he went upstairs, obtained the book and gave it to me. He then made me promise to call and see him again and bade me good-night. . . .

All about as well as usual here. With my love to you and May and kind re-gards to others,

Papa


Mountain View July 4th 1866

My dear Mr Preston,

I suppose you all know this is the fourth of July. The knowledge came to us, not by the booming of cannons . . . but by the reunion of a happy family who have assembled under the Old Homestead roof to enjoy together a long & pleasant summer day. Aunt Louisa has with her today every member of her family, grandchildren and all, with the exception of Thede and Rose, whom I told Aunt Louisa did not in reality belong altogether to her any more. . . .

I am glad you did not spend the day at Aigburth Vale, but remained home to receive Rose and give her an account of your doings at the "Happy Valley." And also to give Thede & Rose an opportunity of fixing May's little altar, and as I know the girls are interested in the doing of it. . . . Give my love to the girls, and tell them, I saw them in my mind's eye flitting about the Blessed Mother and arranging to the best advantage the winged and wingless angels and the little ornaments pertaining to the oratory. I wished many times you were all with us, but not having an Aladdin's lamp or a charmed carpet, I could not accomplish the desired event. . . .

. . . We shall leave here Saturday morning, and be with you Saturday evening. . . .

Each and all the family send love to you and the girls.

Affectionately    Madge

Balto. 4 July 1866

Dear Madge

I remember when the 4th of July brought gladness to my heart—when I regarded it as the anniversary of an event inaugurating freedom and brotherly love among men—Alas! I do no longer so consider it. Time has proven that it was in reality the inauguration of a power which has given strength to fanaticism—bloodshed and misery. It now in my judgment commemorates a murderous, cold-blooded thieving puritanism which for the purpose of gain would burn at the stake an aged woman or an infant. The day however opened here with a most infernal noise, the ringing of bells and the explosion of every conceivable kind of villainous saltpeter compound. Thus Yankee patriotism passes away in noise and smoke. . . .

I have had a number of interviews with various persons in relation to the ground rent[4] of which we spoke but up to this time nothing has been accomplished. Everyone appears desirous of making a little too much—perhaps it is also my own fault. I cannot wonder at it—the very air is Yankeeized—and selfishness and gain are now the dominant moral diseases. Truth, simplicity and disinterested friendships have given place to falsehood—artifice and hypocrisy. I find I am out of humor and snappish—well, I can't help it—the snuffling bells and other unharmonious sounds which at this moment are clanging in my ears are the cause of it. I wish I was at Mountain View where the lowing of a cow or the cackling of a goose would be far more musical and where above all I could feast my eyes on the glorious mountain scenery—and where I would [not] smell the stench of Yankee fireworks. I fear you will not thank me for this splenetic acrimonious scrawl. I sat down to write you three cents' worth of pleasant matters—but the cursed Yankees prevented it. I wish with all my heart they were all in New England hemmed in by a wall of everlasting fire or some other wall which would prevent them getting out. It is consoling just now to have an opportunity of sending my love to you all. Theo is not up or I know she would join me.

Papa

---

The next day Preston wrote again. He apologized this time for his "grumbling effusion" and described grumpily the "Saturnalia" of Baltimore's celebration of the Fourth. The evening, however, had been spent more pleasantly, as Madge's old classmate Mr. Hartman appeared, then later Father Gandolfo from Emmitsburg. "I showed Gandolfo May's altar," Preston wrote, "and the old gentleman in the presence of Mr. Hartman, Theodosia, and myself—knelt down and blessed or consecrated it. . . ."

As to Madge's inquiry about bringing back a servant girl, Preston opined that "it is often 'better to bear the ills we have than fly to others that we know not of.'" He did not, however, object if Madge felt otherwise. But apparently Madge and May returned alone.

How they spent the rest of the summer is illuminated only on those occasions when separations prompted letter writing. No doubt they settled into a routine at 65 Fayette Street after the first pleasures of showing May how they had fixed up the place for comfortable living. She would have exclaimed over the new bedroom with all of her familiar childhood belongings. May's altar would have been freshly bedecked with flowers, and the family would all have commented on her particular good fortune to have her private altar blessed by Father Gandolfo.

As the summer's heat bore down on Baltimore, leaving them all out of sorts, May must have welcomed an invitation by old Mr. Johns Hopkins and his kindly sister to visit them at Clifton. The elderly couple had always taken a special interest in the Prestons' young daughter.

Baltimore August 4th 1866

My darling child,

I rejoice to think how charmed you will be on awaking this morning to find yourself in the midst of the beautiful scenery surrounding "Clifton," the princely mansion of your kind friend Mr Hopkins.

I hope you saw the sun rise over those grand old woods and shed his first bright rays on hill and vale this cool and lovely morning. You would prove yourself false to all your early teachings if you wasted in needless slumber the calm, sweet and refreshing hours of the early day. Think how much you would miss if you did not hear the little birds sing their morning carol to the Creator of . . . this beautiful work, and if the sweet buds opened their bright eyes and smiled their thankfulness to God for the refreshing dews and gentle winds of the past night. I trust my little girl has been mindful of all these pleasures and was early enough abroad to enjoy them, and will have *industry* enough to write me all about it!

We spent a comparatively quiet evening; that is, we had no little chatterer to amuse us with her nonsense, but then we had the delightful music of our friend Mr Dielman, who played for us till near ten o'clock, at which hour we bade each other goodnight and prepared for rest; but alas! just before putting out the gas, we heard the alarm bell, which indicated the fiery element was doing mischief, and immediately we saw over the houses thick volumes of livid flame, and sparks of fire which made us think the fire alarmingly near. Papa dressed himself quickly and went down the street. On returning sometime after, papa told us the fire was in McClellan's Alley, just where Mr

Shepherd's stables used to be. Considerable destruction occurred among the carpenter shops located there, and several good energetic clever men will find themselves almost ruined this morning.[5]

I hope you will let us hear from you occasionally and that you are giving and receiving pleasure. Make our kind regards acceptable to Mr Hopkins, Miss Hopkins and Mrs Tenney. . . .

Your loving
Mama

---

Preston also went away for a few days, on another voyage to Norfolk with Captain Russell. This time Preston was able to call on Jefferson Davis and his wife, with whom he exchanged words of admiration concerning the Sisters of Charity. Near the end of August Madge and May traveled to Philadelphia, no doubt to visit with Mrs. Simmons and the two boys. May would have stayed in the special room set aside in her name. Correspondence between Madge and May does not resume again until the month of October.

Why May did not return to St. Joseph's in the month of September, as she had in earlier years, is suggested in a reference in Madge's letter of October 4. Madge casually comments about returning to "Loyola" from a day spent at Pleasant Plains. Sometime in the early fall the Prestons had moved again.

With May at home for the summer and Thede still a member of the family, the quarters in the dark old townhouse on Fayette Street must have felt more and more cramped and inadequate. The new place, whose name reveals Madge's ever-strengthening commitment to her religion, was within a few steps of the church of St. Ignatius of Loyola. The address was 173 Calvert Street, about seven blocks north from the old place where Madge and Preston had begun their married life.

During the late-summer hiatus another change had also crept into their lives with the maturing of their daughter. Two young men—"Castle" and "Van"—had entered the Prestons' lives. Although the former was soon to recede—both his identity and connection with the Prestons still unexplained —Van (or "Vanity" as they liked to call him) became an important figure. He was Joshua Vansant McNeal, son of a prominent Catholic family of Baltimore, and named for a distinguished politician.[6] "Vanity" was later to marry May.

Baltimore Octr 4th 1866

My dear child,

Your welcome letter . . . reached us in good time, and gladdened our hearts with the assurance that you were safe at St Joseph's. . . . I could easily imagine your delight on entering the Infirmary, and seeing in their old familiar places Sisters Raphael and Genevieve! That part of your letter made me regret I had not gone back with you. . . .

I wrote to dear Sr Raphael on Monday and in my letter told Sister of the pleasure and happiness I had rec'd on Sunday, in having Papa accompany me to the cathedral. I can't tell you my child how much I wished for you, knowing what happiness you would have experienced in being present with your dear Papa at the Holy Sacrifice of the Mass. Tell Sister Jenny, I am sure the Sisters' prayers are working this great wonder and I look forward to the still greater wonder of seeing our dear Papa when we have so earnestly prayed to find him in the bosom of the Catholic church. I told Papa a day or two ago I had really regretted not having kept you home till after the sitting of the Council.[7] Papa thought it better you had gone, but I think it a pity you could not have remained to see what will be the most important, as well as the most imposing, gathering of the hierarchy that has taken place for more than two hundred years! If I thought Sister would not think it amiss I would cut [out] of the papers and send up to you the published proceedings of the Council: I will send in this letter the Archbishop's most able and beautiful sermon of last Sunday and if you let me know, if the other proceedings will be admissible, I send them also. . . .

We have not seen or heard any thing from "Castle" since you left, neither has "Van" condescended to look in upon us. Consequently we now know who was the attraction—Good night. Love from Papa, Cousin Eudocia, Thede and Crick. Give my love to Anna, Kate & Lizzie.

Lovingly your
Mama

St. Joseph's Oct. 10th 1866

My dear Friend,

In May's letter of last week I said a leisure moment was to afford me the pleasure of writing & speaking of our little girl, for she has become particularly interesting to me, since a new relationship has been established between us. Your few lines by Dr Dielman were handed to me this morning, just as May, Annie & myself were discussing very cozily the derivation of *words*, and enjoying the pleasant & witty style of our author. I did not recognize the hand & said—'a moment girls, this may require an immediate answer'—I opened it—then handed it to May saying, 'do you know this handwriting!' "Oh Sister, Mama's," was the immediate reply. Then I very *unwarily* said May let us read it together, it relates to the Council—When lo the secret was disclosed! —I only wish you could have seen May's countenance! I told her if I could only send you a *sheet of illustrated news* from St Joseph's on this occasion it would speak more than I could write to give you an idea of what she thought of your proposal.[8]

I consulted with Mother & we both think it would not interfere with May's success or studies to make the visit for such a sight. Oh! yes, willingly I agree for her to leave on *Saturday* & return on *Monday*. . . .

Now for a word of our dear child. She is doing admirably well, & she appears pleased with our arrangements for class. Indeed the hour & a half I spend with her & Annie every day is a most pleasant one. They enter into my plans for their improvement & study from the real relish & love of learning. May will enter into detail about her studies. She has come back so happy & bright, she is like a *sunbeam* in the house. What a grand triumph for Catholics, Baltimore is witnessing. I hope Mr. Preston attends the days the Bishops preach. I have made a compact with *My* Angel guardian to prompt Mr. Preston's Angel & urge him to act in accordance with his convictions. Never lose hope. . . .

Yours affectionately
S M Raphael

[no date, no heading]

My dear child,
    . . . Dear little Annie! how I wish she could be brought down too. If someone's pocket was capacious enough to hold her, I have plenty of room for both of you when you are here. With regard to your wardrobe, I think you had better wear your brown dress and scarlet sacque—that with some of your belts and ribbons is all you will require, as I can find enough things at home for you during the day or two you will be in the city. I hope you will be able to come down in the early train reaching here by noon, that you may see some of your friends on Saturday. . . .

Yours lovingly
Mama

---

On October 13 May and Anna Northrop, who had been permitted by Sister Raphael to accept Madge's tactfully oblique invitation, descended from the train. Sister Raphael was herself their chaperone. The girls were excited, of course, at this unexpected leave from school so soon after May's return to the north. They were among the crowds of the devout and the curious who convened in Baltimore to witness this extraordinary display of Catholic organization and power.

But the most spectacular event of the two-week Council was already over. On the previous Sunday seemingly all of Baltimore had gathered to watch the opening-day procession as all the highest church hierarchy of the United

States moved solemnly from the archepiscopal residence, where the bishops had gathered, to the cathedral. The bishops, in their red vestments, formed an impressive body as they moved slowly along the route.

Only the Sunday and Thursday sessions were open to the public. But even the closed sessions must have been impressive in numbers, since every Catholic province and diocese in the United States was represented. Immense throngs crowded the cathedral to hear the sermon by the Most Reverend Archbishop Purcell of Cincinnati, whose remarks were summarized in the Monday edition of the *Baltimore Sun*.

The Prestons and Anna were joined by Dielman, who had also come down from Emmitsburg; together they attended a gala band concert and reception on Thursday evening, October 18. Since leading Protestant citizens were among the 700 people who had been invited to attend, one could scarcely imagine that the defense attorney in the Mount Hope case or the Protestant music teacher for Mount St. Mary's would have been omitted from the guest list.

The episcopal procession for the final day of the Plenary Session was beyond compare. "It is no exaggeration to say," the *Sun* opined in an article of October 22,

> the splendor of the procession, the impressiveness of the ceremonies within the sacred edifice, the grandeur of the music and the exceedingly large attendance of people of all denominations, together made it an occasion which has never before been equalled, in its way, in church history in this country and rarely surpassed in Europe.

All the prelates wore vestments of white, "rich and costly" materials and "studded with jewels." About two thousand people gathered to watch the display; and even President Andrew Johnson came in from Washington for the event.

At this final service two of the Prestons' friends had prominent roles—Baltimore's Archbishop Spalding, attended by Madge's beloved Father Thomas Foley as a deacon of honor, among others. The archbishop's formal reply to an address from the archbishop of Cincinnati preceded the ceremonies closing the Council. What stories would the two excited schoolgirls have had to tell on that Monday night, back at St. Joseph's, as their admiring schoolmates and the patient Sisters gathered around!

Baltimore Octr 23 1866

My darling child,

On returning to your room, after our "goodbye" at the depot, much to my regret I saw your "beads" lying snugly under your pillow; knowing how pained you would be without them, I hung them round our Blessed Mother at the same time begging her to comfort you for their absence. Papa very kindly told me this morning to enclose them in an envelope and he would see them sent off safely to you. . . . we missed all day yesterday the cheerful chatter of you and our other little child and last evening we regretted Oh! much that you were not with us to enliven us with music and talk. . . . Our friend "Van" called last evening and enquired very kindly about the young ladies, and asked if they had got off comfortably in the morning! How different from the "Castle"? . . .

Lovingly<br>Mama

Baltimore Octr 28th 1866

My darling child,

I hope you will not think me lazy or over indulgent to self, when I tell you I have just awakened from a most refreshing sleep of nearly an hour's duration. I came to my room after dinner, intending at once to sit down and answer your last most welcome letter of the 26th inst[ance]—finding the room deliciously warm and comfortable, made so by the fire in the parlour below, I picked up "Fabiola," thinking to enjoy the comfort and quiet in a few moments reading, when lo! sleep came over me, and I was oblivious to everything but the delights of "Tired Nature's sweet restorer."[9] . . .

It is a constant source of congratulations to all of us that we sent for you; as we think by so doing we gave you a pleasure and satisfaction perhaps never again in the lives of any one of us to be enjoyed. Dear Sr Raphael, coming down with you and Anna, made the event complete and, as Papa said, "formed *to us* one of the most interesting features of the many pleasant things that occurred during the sitting of the Council." . . .

I am just thinking, my dear children, that perhaps of all the years of your life, the scholastic year upon which you have so recently entered will be the most interesting, the most profitable, the most attractive and the one longest to be remembered and perhaps the one to give the coloring to all your future lives! . . . I cannot imagine two children more pleasantly and happily circumstanced (you see, it is impossible, neither do I wish, to separate you and Anna in my thoughts), both with loving relatives willing and anxious to do all in their power to promote the welfare, success and happiness of each; placed while still very young with those best calculated to improve the intellect God in his goodness has given you and to watch over your comfort and health with almost more than motherly care & attention—then, loving each other so truly and sincerely as you do—in class together—not as rivals (dear Lord keep them from ever being such!) but as a stimulant to each other and with the dear Sister for instructress, whom of all persons in the world had you your choice, you would most have desired—located too in the loveliest spot on earth—surrounded by good and pious Sisters, teaching by example as well as precept all that is required to fit you for any sphere in life, in a word, to make you Christian women; and among your privileges and not the least of them, is your constant intercourse with young, loving, generous hearted companions of your own ages, whose cultivated minds give a relish to social intercourse, whose refinement of manners subdues the exuberant hilarity of youth and whose friendships formed now, while the heart is susceptible of the finest emotions, will I trust in many instances, be as lasting as life itself. Think! my precious children, of all these privileges and advantages, and then from the depth of your hearts pray God to give you grace to reap their full benefit. . . .

I must tell you of a pleasure I have given myself ever since you left me. I go over to the church at that most lovely of all parts of the day, the time between daylight and darkness when the busy hum of the day is hushed into silence but the gloom of the night has not yet come. The hour I think most suited for prayer and meditation. I usually spend a half hour there and one of the happiest moments I enjoy is while saying a "Remember &c" for "our trio" as we all call the little St Joseph's party. . . .

The family were all well and Papa, Aunt Louisa, Thede & Crick unite with me in love to "both the children"

Mama

Baltimore Novr 1st 1866

I am afraid, my dear child, that I make a great many rash promises. I think I said in my letter to you and Anne that I would "write soon." . . .

This has been a St Joseph's day with us in our early rising, Papa having accepted an invitation, from a committee appointed for that purpose, to attend a political meeting to be held at Bel Air[10] today; we were obliged to rise at four o'clock to give Papa his breakfast and enable him to start in the early train. . . .

I was stopped just now in my writing to welcome Papa, who returned rather unexpectedly about eight o'clock, bringing with him a whole armful of beautiful bouquets which the ladies presented him after making his speech. The piece of ribbon which I have enclosed was tied round the prettiest of them. I send it to you as one of Papa's trophies. . . . Papa has told me of more than a dozen gentlemen who begged him to come to their houses, each intending to have a grand jollification provided he would be their guest. It is complimentary and gratifying to know that Papa preferred coming home to going elsewhere. Papa is sitting by me nodding very comfortably and ever and anon rousing himself up and suggesting some pleasant little message to you and Anna—for instance he says, Tell the girls I wish I had had them with me today, that they might have come in for a share of the attention shown me and which I am sure would have been very gracefully and freely extended to them. Papa sends his love to both of you. . . .

I don't know whether I told you in my last letter that I spent a day since you left me at Aigburth? I had a pleasant visit and both Mrs Owens and Delia asked very kindly after you. They amused me much by their evident anxiety to know something about the "Castle" but I quietly avoided alluding to the subject as I did not wish them to know my *real* feelings about it. I have not seen any of that particular party since you left—but "Vanity" has been quite attentive, so much so as to call from Papa the remark one evening as "Vanity" left the house, "We shall at all times be pleased to see you." . . .

Your old friend Mr Hopkins asked very kindly after you the other day and was much pleased when Papa told him you had remembered him in your letter. When you write again, be sure you send some pleasant message to him . . . both Papa and I will be gratified to have you write to the old gentleman. . . .

Mama

More than a week went by before Madge wrote again, and the description of a kind of ennui with which her next letter begins suggests that she was wrestling with some form of depression. Her twice-daily visits to the church across the street, which she had noted in an earlier letter, suggest the same thing. She still kept a diary, as this letter makes clear, and doubtless confided there her darker thoughts.

Baltimore Novr 9th 1866

My dear child,

Though I have supplied myself with this large sheet of paper, I am afraid I shall scarcely find the energy to fill it, or as Thede would say the *industry*, as something like a lazy spell with regard to writing seems to come over me very often of late, and when the fit is on me, it is almost impossible to overcome it. On looking over my diary I find it was a week yesterday since I wrote to you. . . .

The great event at home of the past week is the all important one of Thede having had her hair cut off Novr 1st. All Saints Day is the ever memorable day on which she was first shorn of her locks: she asked me to cut them off, but not exactly believing in her sincerity to have it done, I declined; shortly after Thede came into my room looking very peculiar, and on my inspecting her more closely I soon discovered she was minus "a woman's crowning glory." . . . It was an inch or two long on her head for some days, we not thinking it prudent to have it shaved till she had become in some measure used to the loss of the large quantity she had lost. The weather being so pleasant today, Thede concluded all things were propitious for the final operation, the barber was called in, and the head shaved! Thus far, she has not permitted her Uncle and I to see her head without its natural covering, but in a day or two she will, I doubt not, be reconciled to our looking at it. She bids me tell you all about it, and to say, *nothing* could induce her to have it on her head *in the same condition.* . . . Thede says she has fully realized all the delight of having a clean head. She has adopted your practice of washing it daily with soap and water; and it is quite amusing to hear her descanting on the comfortable feeling she experiences. Thede has arranged quite a becoming little cap of black silk, with short curls round the face; upon the whole we think this decapitation has been quite a success.

I turn from this subject to one that has been of a painful and anxious character to all of us for days past. This day, one week ago, our young friend Mary Lizzie Stansbury was ill unto death. Of course I hastened out to the country at once, and when I entered the house, I met the most wretched family I ever saw. The poor girl was too ill to be seen by any one . . . as the doctor said the least undue excitement might cause her death at any moment. She has Dr Martin, a distinguished homeopathist. It seems she has disease of the heart, together with typhoid fever. I have no doubt she has always had an organic affection of the heart, and that accounts for the constant & fearful headaches with which the poor child has always been afflicted. . . . Each day we have feared almost to hear from the country . . . but thank God, today the welcome intelligence was brought that she is better and there are faint hopes of her ultimate recovery. It is impossible to give you an idea of the distress of that family . . . nothing could exceed the care and love bestowed upon her, and yet I could not but be painfully struck with the difference between a Catholic and Protestant family under similar circumstances. Here the poor girl would have been permitted to die without the slightest preparation for death "because it would not do to agitate her." When she herself thought she was dying—and perhaps felt the need of spiritual consolation. The thought was at once banished from her mind and "cheerful subjects alone discussed in her presence," so said the family and so it was. . . .

With love & affectionate regards to Sr Raphael and Sister Genevieve, and ever so much to the girls I am always yours most lovingly.

Mama


Baltimore Novr 18th 1866

My very dear child . . .

Your brief letter enclosing the French one was received yesterday and brought with it all the pleasure you could desire. As much as I like *long* letters, especially from you, I nevertheless forgo the pleasure of them in consideration of your many school duties; nay I would even give up *my* letter to have you devote one of your letter writing days to dear old Mr Hopkins. Do try to have the "Spirit move" you and send him a letter soon. The old gentleman asks so kindly about you, whenever he meets Papa.

By the way, that reminds me of Mrs McCoy, whom we met on the race grounds last Wednesday. These races you must know have been the most fashionable events of the season and Papa, wishing us to enjoy what everybody also seemed to take so much pleasure in, invited us to accompany him out there.[11] . . .

There were a large number of elegantly dressed ladies on the stand prepared for visitors and among them, conspicuous for dress as well as beauty, was your young friend Molly Banks, her mother and aunt. On taking our seat, I was glad to find myself seated next to Mrs McCoy and Mrs Bartlett. Mrs McCoy is a great favourite of mine; she possesses one trait in such an eminent degree that she has, in consequence, always commanded my admiration. — It is this, never to speak unkindly of anyone, and to throw oil upon the troubled waters flowing around her mutual friends. After exchanging the compliments of the day, talking about the beautiful girls around, admiring the horses, and eating a lunch, Mrs McCoy turned to a subject she thought at all times agreeable to me—yourself. She asked kindly about you . . . [and] ended by saying, I wish May was here this afternoon. I am sure she would enjoy the surroundings. I replied I wish so too; but though I might send for May to come down and be present at a sitting of the Council, Sister Raphael would think I had taken leave of my senses to send for one or both of her "Seniors" to attend a horse fair! The idea was so ridiculous, we had a hearty laugh on the strength of it. . . .

You would have laughed, "Ma chère petite Enfante," to have seen Papa and I gathering up our long since neglected knowledge of the French language to enable us to read your most welcome and interesting "lettre en français." We were greatly gratified, I assure you, at your evident improvements. . . .

We were like yourselves much disappointed that the great meteoric showers did not come off, at least, where we could see it. Poor Papa said he was glad the showers were not often expected, if his slumbers were to be so much disturbed. During the three or four nights of anticipation, I was jumping out of the bed every hour, fearing to lose the grand sight. Enclosed you will see where they *did* make their appearance and that the most favoured people were the English.[12]

. . . Good night, and may our Blessed Mother have you now and always under her protecting wing.

Mama. . . .

Philadelphia Nov 22d 1866

My dear Mr Preston,

I have never been more thoroughly convinced of my own folly and the superior wisdom of other people than I was in the cars this morning. Evidently no one travelled at the early hour I set forth on my journey than such poor wretches as a stern fate sent forth to brave the morning air, while more sensible and fortunate people kept to their good warm beds and sallied out for a pleasure trip at the proper and reasonable hours of nine or ten o'clock! Mem! —never appoint to go in the 7:20 train to Phila. Many reasons for not doing so—no one in the cars but fogy old politician, or still more old fogy ladies. Train stops every five minutes to "accommodate" passengers, taking them up and letting them down. Doors opening and shutting so constantly that it becomes a question whether it is not more agreeable outside than in, particularly to one who, as Dr Patterson said of May with the measles, had a most "beautiful development of cold." Tell Thede not to flatter herself, but she can take credit for being a first rate prophet. The cold, which her superior penetration discovered peeping out of my eyes, making itself visible by the underside of my nose, and showing itself by the stiffened condition of my back and limbs, fully presented itself by the time I reached 1320 Arch St. My left eye is a respectable rival of poor "Van's" . . . my sneezing capacities superior even to Aunt Louisa's, and if I get off without laying in a fresh supply of pocket handkerchiefs I shall think myself most fortunate. You can't imagine anything or anybody in a worse condition than I was when I reached our kind little friend's hospitable mansion, and yet the dear little thing was kind enough to say, "I was looking very well, and had *such a beautiful little bonnet.*" To the latter article of dress, I am sure I was indebted for the compliment about looks; she stopped there and did not let her eyes fall to my face.

But notwithstanding the discomforts of my cold, and the heavy shower of rain which poured upon me, when the train reached the city, I was in good spirits and received Mrs Simmons' warm and friendly greetings as freely as they were given. . . .

Goodbye truly yours
Madge[13]

Philadelphia Novr 26th 1866

My dear child,

You will be surprised to learn I have been in this good "City of Brotherly Love," since Thursday the 22d. . . .

Mrs Simmons has asked in the most affectionate manner about you and has given you for Christmas a beautiful new fashioned neck tie. . . .

We attended St John's Church yesterday both morning and afternoon; on each occasion I saw our friends Mr & Mrs Chandler. . . . Speaking of the Council, when I said, I wish they had been in Baltimore to witness it, Mr Chandler said—"You know, Madge, we have seen cardinals where you had bishops and for archbishops we had a Pope!" I said, "yes I know that, yet nevertheless it was a grand sight and one to make a Catholic feel proud." Father Dunn preached one of the most delightful sermons I ever heard. It was on the close of the Ecclesiastical year. The substance of it was that we should enter into the examination of ourselves, particularly of the "sins of omission"; those of commission, he said, were prominent and stood out boldly and were not readily forgotten or overlooked but the sins of omission seemed to fade away from our memory and it was so convenient and agreeable *not* to remember them. Father Dunn, by way of example, then began putting questions to parents, to children, to brothers, to sisters—indeed to all classes, and it was astonishing how they came home to the hearts of each individual. I never felt before how much I would have to answer for in that respect. *My* sins of omission loomed up so gigantic as to be almost appalling and I mentally resolved to hear Father Dunn's sermon in remembrance at all my future examinations of conscience. . . .

So you and Anna are curious to know the result of the contemplated visit, suggested by Mrs Owens' note, for last Tuesday. Well, the evening appointed came . . . and at the proper time came also Mrs Owens & Delia, sweet and pretty and fashionable as usual and with them also came the "Castle," evidently somewhat dubious of the reception which was to be awarded. "Between you and I and the Post" (tell Anna *she* is the "post" just now, I think), the "Castle" sought the shelter of the two female individuals instead of affording shelter, as castles usually do. As we were all cozily seated in the parlour when they came, the reception was so general that no one individual in particular could take any act or word to themselves; so I intended it should be. In due course of time, "tea" was announced, and as it was at my own table, I suppose I may be excused if I give you and Anna the bill of fare. "Tea" being the article to which they had particularly invited themselves, due care had been taken to provide the best and in a sufficiently generous quantity. As oysters were presumed to be the greatest rarity we could give our country guests, a steaming tureen of those dainties, at the foot of the table, sent forth their savory odors, testifying I hope to my skill in preparing them. In another dish, also prepared by Mama's fair hands (?) was some of the most delicious frizzled beef you ever ate. Plenty of good rich cream from the mill, and sweet butter together with other seasonings made it a dish fit to set before the king or his "Castle" either. . . . There now, have I made your mouths water? As the "Castle" was the "Stranger" at the table, I took it under my special care— Papa doing the honors to Mrs Owens & Delia. A jollier little party you can't imagine than we were; even Thede seemed to be inspired with unusual gaiety and poor Catherine on several occasions sought shelter in the pantry to in-dulge her feelings. On adjourning to the parlour, the "Castle" asked me in the most provokingly natural manner, "Mrs Preston, where is Miss May?" "At St Joseph's," I replied. "Ah indeed, then she really *did* get off?" "Yes." "I was told she went once before, but as she was flourishing at the concert, and conspicu-ous at the Council, I wondered if my information was correct." All this was said in the most demure manner imaginable, and I answered equally de-murely. Conversation then became general about you and in that way the "Castle" got all the information desired. The "Castle" seems not to have the same amount of gaiety that distinguished the building last summer. The "girls"—Mrs Owens & Delia—attribute that to being overtaxed with work, having within the last month undertaken to teach a Latin class for the old "professor." About ten o'clock we again sat down to some light refreshments and where we amused ourselves talking and eating till long after eleven o'clock, at which time Mrs Owens & Delia sprang up like two Cinderellas, to hasten to their home before the clock should strike twelve and they be locked out. Thus ended the "tea" drinking and that eventful visit. I believe the "Castle" left, feeling its foundation, though shaken, was pretty firmly settled again and very much happier in consequence. . . .

I am pleased to know my dear child that you are writing to dear old Mr Hopkins—write him a good, long, cheerful schoolgirl letter; take *my* time, if you can spare no other. I will cheerfully do without my letter to give due to him, for I know it would be so great a pleasure to him and his dear old Sister. . . .

Good morning. Don't forget to remember me affectionately *always* to dear Sister Raphael, Sr Genevieve, Sr Maria, Sr Aimee, Sr Juliana, Sr M. Ed-ward, not forgetting Sr Bibliana. . . . Love to all my dear children and kisses to Anne and *yourself.*

Lovingly your
Mama.

Baltimore Decr 10th 1866

Eight days, and no letter from Mama. Methinks I hear you utter the above exclamation in a wondering tone; and then, with my mind's eye, I see you and dear little Anna put your wise heads together, and say this, and that, and the other must be the reason for Mama not writing and then the little affec-tionate hearts, not satisfied with suggesting some *reasonable* cause for Mama's silence, give themselves all the unnecessary pain they can by coming to the conclusion that Mama is sick and can't write. Now if this has been the case, let me at once relieve you of any anxiety on that subject. For a few days after my return form Phila I had a good deal of my old-fashioned headache; but quite suddenly, one day much to my great satisfaction, the headache left me, and thank God, I have had no return of it. On the contrary, I am now, and have been for some days, unusually well. . . . You can readily imagine that after an absence of two weeks from home I would find sundry things on my return that would require my immediate attention during the day—then when night comes, reading the papers, talking with Papa over the events of the day, or entertaining a friend occasionally fills up the time, till ten o'clock—at which good and reasonable hour I begin to feel wearied and more like going to bed than sitting up to write letters. Don't imagine from this, that I do not *want* to write; on the contrary, if all things suited, I could write to you daily. . . .

You can scarcely imagine, my sweet child, how very much pleasure your delightfully long and satisfactory letter to Papa and your equally pleasant and affectionate letter to me, has given us. . . . Papa and I often talk of you and Anna, and wish we could peep in at you occasionally, when discussing, with dear Sr Raphael, the beauties of the *Iliad*, or enjoying with Sister a "ramble among words." Much as we wish you with us, we would not for any treasure that could be offered, deprive you of your present great advantages. . . .

You will be surprised to know that Theodosia has gone home to spend a few weeks. She expects to remain at Mountain View till after the holidays and will then return to us again. . . . Thede has had her head shaved three times, allowing it to grow two weeks between each time. I think I never saw anything so much improved as Thede's hair; of course it was very short, but still you could see that it was in a very healthy condition. Thede will try and come over to see you during her stay with her family. . . .

I went to St. Ignatius Church yesterday and heard a grand sermon from Father Clark, on the "Immaculate Conception." "Vanity all is vanity!" The best exemplification of that sentence is *myself*, for I really think with me, all is "Vanity." I like Vanity better than anyone I know. Vanity sent respects to Miss May and Miss Northrop. Tell Anna to have patience with me, and give her my love, also Kate, Stella & Lizzie.

Baltimore Decr 17th 1866

My dear child,

You will be pleased to know that I made a pleasant visit to *your* Sister this afternoon; she, as well as Sr Louisa, made the kindest inquiries after you, and desired me to send their loves to you when I should write. . . .

Papa and I shall spend this Christmas entirely alone. Thede you know is already at the mountain and Crick goes up on Thursday, consequently Catherine is the only one with us, Johnny remaining now altogether at the "mill." I am afraid you will think me the most selfish of mortals when I tell you this segregated life is *to me* the most delightful of anything I can imagine. When you come home, of course I shall feel differently but until you are with us, I greatly prefer being alone! Papa too seems perfectly contented and happy and I think as cheerful as I have ever known him.

Crick . . . will be the bearer of the box containing your Christmas dress &c &c. Those &c &c's are a little black silk apron made after a Parisienne one, which we—that is, Papa and I—think very pretty, and as you have had but one silk apron during school days at St Joseph's, we think you were fairly entitled to this one; and a necklace of large crystal beads, being very fashionable at present among young people, and which I think are pretty and dressy looking. The little blue necklace presented by Mrs Simmons, the bundle of linen scraps from "Mama's linen box," Anna's black silk basque, which I found in the closet after she left, your corsets (nicely done up), one new chemise and one of your nightgowns, which you must have left behind and which I fear you have wanted . . . also a pair of boots. . . .

I met Cousin Caleb in the Street on Saturday; he asked kindly about you and sent a quantity of "respects." Caleb tells me that Mary Elizabeth is able to walk about her room, and there is every prospect of her speedy restoration; her recovery is certainly one of the most wonderful I have ever known. Caleb says, they were all sent for one morning thinking she was dying. I believe I told you she had selected Dr Martin a homeopathic physician, much to the horror of the neighbourhood, who believed she must necessarily die under such treatment.

Yours lovingly,<br>Mama. . . .

Baltimore Decr 20th 1866

My darling child,

We have just finished packing your box. . . . Ah me! I wish I could have changed myself into some little Christmas fixing and been packed up along with those other articles in that self-same box, and resumed my identity when Sister and yourself were wondering over that "queer looking package!" As dear Kate would say, "would not that be jolly"—imagine the said queer looking package unrolling itself, opening its eyes, stretching out its arms and exclaiming "A Merry Christmas to you all." Now would you give me a welcome and would you let me share in your little frolics, join in your sports, partake of your Christmas good things—in other words, would you let me "be a child again"? Sister Louisa and I were discussing the delights of dear old St Joseph's the other day, and we both came to the conclusion that of all times in the year, Christmas was the most delightful and pleasant season at St Joseph's; dear Sister said it was her fortune to be there generally in summer, but she hoped some day to be there Christmas times. So she shall; whenever I become the Mother, I shall issue a proclamation to this effect, "That all sisters on mission wishing to spend Christmas at home are perfectly welcome to do so!" Tell dear Sister Genevieve the "queer looking package" will sleep *in spirit* in the "little room" so memorable for happy hours, and she must not forget to awaken it for early Mass on Christmas morning! Ah, my child, enjoy all you can now, for my heart throbs with sadness when I think this is the last Christmas you can ever expect the same degree of happiness you are now enjoying. You will soon learn, when in the world, how little true happiness there is in it; and how much there is of pain and misery even with those apparently the most favoured.[14]

I believe I told you in my last letter that I should spend my Christmas altogether alone. I am right glad such is the case for I shall have full opportunity of enjoying all the church favours on that holy day, after which I can visit you in imagination and revel in the enjoyment fancy shall portray. In all probability this is the last letter I shall write till after Christmas; you must therefore permit me to anticipate the season and wish you and *our* darling little Anna all the pleasure and happiness this holy season can bring and in the most expressive language of all time wish you both a "Merry Christmas and a Happy New Year." . . .

. . . The box of French bon bons, as the writing will inform you, was sent by "Vanity," who called some few evenings ago and asked my permission to do so; of course I freely granted it. When you write, be sure you acknowledge them in a suitable manner.

Did I tell you in my former letter that I had had quite a pleasant talk with Mr Hopkins, and also that he was much gratified with your letter, and that he intended to answer it "about the holiday times." . . .

Papa says, "Give my love to May and Anna and tell them I hope their anticipations of enjoyment may be fully realized." . . .

Goodbye my dear, dear child.<br>
Mama

Baltimore Decr 26th 1866

My dear children

So Christmas has come and gone and henceforth we shall speak of it as the *past*! How many of its hopes and wishes have been realized? How much of the pleasure and happiness anticipated has been enjoyed? Well! if some have been doomed to disappointments, if bright daydreams have been crushed— Christmas! dear Christmas, will banish all pain, by telling of the birth of *such* hopes as can never die—hopes proclaimed by angel lips and wafted over the plains of Bethlehem eighteen hundred years ago—in these words—Glory to

God in the highest and on Earth peace, goodwill towards men. Oh that every heart that is beating throughout Christendom this day might echo the glorious sentiment! and so they would, if all united in the "One Lord, one Faith, one Baptism!" . . .

I rose early and went to Church before five o'clock. Of course I went to St Ignatius Church, and at that early hour the church was crowded. I sat in McNeal's pew and all the family were there but "Van," who attended at a later Mass. I had my dear children, like yourselves, had the happiness of receiving as the greatest of all earthly gifts our Infant Lord. Be assured my dear children I did not forget to beg our dear Lord that his choicest blessings should be poured upon you. . . .

On returning home we took a nice little Christmas breakfast, after which Papa handed me the most acceptable Christmas present I could have rec'd in the form of a delightful, lengthy and affectionate letter from a dear little absent daughter of mine. . . .

At the proper time, Papa left me to make a round of visits to his friends, as most all of them "received" on that day. I also prepared for a call or two, my first visit being to Mrs McNeal's, where I spent a short time most pleasantly. Mrs McNeal and Ella asked after you most kindly and seemed gratified at your mention of them in your letter. I then called at Abells' and it really does me good to think about them and to tell you what a glorious party I met there. . . . Think of ten children and two grandchildren! The boys and girls from Georgetown of course being home. Certainly it was the most elegant establishment, house, children and all, that I have ever seen. They all asked most affectionately for you, and expressed regrets that you were not with them &c &c. Charley and Walter had almost grown out of my knowledge and the girls too. By the way, Mary says she "greatly prefers St Joseph's to Georgetown and she loves the *Sisters* much better than the *Nuns!*"

In the evening Papa and I walked up to Mr Parr's and there we spent a charming evening. . . . Papa was in one of his "eloquent moods," and when that is the case, you know, few persons can be more agreeable than he is. . . . We had a quiet walk home, the weather was charming and the moon shed a flood of light over the city till it was glorious to look upon and thus we reached our little domicile. On entering which, though no cheerful face greeted us, there was still a bright glowing fire in the grate and that, together with a full jet of gas burning, presented so comfortable an aspect that we seated ourselves cozily before the fire and discussed the pleasant events of the day before retiring. . . .

And now my dear children as I am obliged to leave you and dress to attend a dinner party to which Papa and I have been invited at Judge Alexander's, I will close this much of my letter. . . . My cold of which you make especial mention is quite well and I am now, thank God, in the enjoyment of excellent health. Papa also *I think* is very well this winter, but you know his fancy for complaining makes us sometimes feel perhaps he is suffering a little.

Mama

Baltimore Decr 28th 1866

My dear children,

Having a few spare moments this evening . . . I devote them most cheerfully to the finishing of the letter. . . .

You must know I have been taking holiday with the rest of the world this week; consequently, at the proper hour this morning, I dressed myself in my prettiest walking gear and sallied forth to make morning calls! Think of that —Mama making fashionable calls! Well, "When you are in Rome, you must do as Rome does." . . . Among the visits made that morning was one to Mrs Kelly and Agnes. . . . From Mrs Emory's I went to the asylum, and there I had a quiet pleasant visit with my sister and *your* Sister. Sr Leopoldine told me she wrote to you, and expected you would receive her letter on Christmas day. . . . When I reached home, I found Papa had just come in also, and as it was our dinner hour we at once sat down to take our dinner. We dine late, usually about four oclock; of course, when dinner is over it is almost dark. After dinner Papa takes a little nap and I bid him "goodbye for a little while," and go over to the church. They close the doors at six o'clock and then I leave. This has been my habit all winter and I cannot tell you the happiness it affords me. Papa seems to expect it as much as I do, and generally says "Make yourself comfortable before you go that you do not take cold in the church." . . .

I believe I mentioned in the latter part of my yesterday's sheet, that Papa and I were . . . attending a dinner party at Judge Alexander's! . . . I must not forget to tell you about Robby, the dearest little fellow you ever saw. Sometime ago when he and his parents were at our house, I gave him one of your pictures which the Judge has had nicely framed. The little boy remembered *your* name, but could not think of mine, so he calls you "little May" and me, "big Miss May"—very much like Kitty's "Miss Mammy." He is very clever indeed and says the prettiest things at times. His mother took him to church Christmas morning. (The boy you know is just three years old.) The Episcopalians dress their churches beautifully with evergreens on Christmas day. Over the pulpit in St Paul's Church was suspended a large cross made of evergreens; Robby looked at it intently, and then whispered to his mother, "Mama is that the cross our Lord was *killed* on?" Your Father was at the Judge's the other morning and when Robby came in, he ran up and spoke to Papa, calling him by name. Papa said, "How do you know me, Robby!" The little fellow stood still for a minute or two *reflecting*; at length he said, "I know in my *heart*, it is you." Was that not a remarkable expression for so young a child? . . .

So you have been made Godmother to Mrs Ryan's little daughter![15] I am sure I am most happy to know that Mr & Mrs Ryan have paid you the great compliment of giving you this little Godchild and sincerely hope, at some future day, you may be able to fulfill the promises you take upon yourself as Godmother to this dear child. My dear Anna, when you write again to your sister, please make my kind regards acceptable to her and say, I thank her for the great pleasure and happiness she has given May by creating this beautiful tie between my child and her own.

I have not seen "Van" or "Castle" during the holidays. The "Owens" are spending the Christmas week in New York. Theodosia is coming home to-morrow. Crick & Johnny next week. So there will soon be an end of our quiet Darby and Joan[16] mode of living. Now my sweet children I think I have written enough to keep you busy during all your spare hours for the coming week. Good night my dear May & Anna. May our Blessed Mother have you now and always under her protecting wing.

Lovingly Mama.

# 16

## "My Lady Randolph"

MADGE'S FIRST LETTER OF the new year, written just before midnight of January 1, must have pleased May; for it confirms, like all of the mother's letters, the warm affection flowing between the two. The letter suggests a busy day full of holiday pleasure, a returned traveler, afternoon callers. Yet how the letter lies! To read it after reading the diary entry written by the same woman just moments before is to throw into question all the cheerful chronicles within the correspondence of the preceding year.

Whether through historical accident or deliberate suppression, Madge's diary for 1866 has not been found.[1] Thus no countersource exists to belie the cheerfulness of Madge's letters. Madge had always been in the habit of disguising to May her true feelings concerning relationships at home. Now Madge's pleasure in passing the 1866 Christmas season alone with her husband—the warm comfort of the domestic hearth which she had emphasized in end-of-the year letters to May—reverberates against the first page of the 1867 diary. Madge's pained labeling of the newly returned Thede, "those who have made the house pleasant by their absence," and her misery, "where insincerity and deception are the ruling principles in a house," are almost unendurable.

Yet the Thede who appears in that same day's letter to May suggests a warmly received messenger with the latest tidbits of news and the daughter's curl, and the New Year's Day call from the McNeal women is conveyed to May through the mother's letter as affectionate and warm. The letter's content testifies both to the epistolary skill of the writer and to her social restraint. While Madge acted the gracious hostess to her guests, she was clearly enraged over the absence of the other two members of her household. Either they were actually playing cards and thus ignoring these important guests or— worse—pretending to do so as a cover for talk and actions more threatening still to Madge. Yet nothing in Madge's letter, with its warm greetings to the two Sisters most admired by her husband, suggests the least blemish on the person or the behavior of the Sisters' "champion."

---

**Tuesday, January 1, 1867**

*Come here my diary, and thank God with me, that we are once more alone! What a struggle we have had tonight and what a struggle we have had all day to be where the eyes of intrusion should not be upon us. Alas! Alas! it is even worse than I feared it would be, when those who have made the house pleasant by their absence, should return. How long, Oh how long is this fearful life to be endured—something must bring about a change or I cannot live! How quiet, how peaceful, how happy the last three weeks, and how suddenly it has all ended, and what is the cause, can I doubt for one moment the cause? But enough—I had hoped we would have spent a pleasant and happy New Year, but how can happiness exist, where insincerity and deception are the ruling principles in a house? We did not rise as early as usual this morning though we wanted to begin the year right, consequently everything has gone wrong today. Mr Preston has remained home all day, but has not been at all well. "Vanity" called on me this afternoon and immediately after Mrs McNeal and her daughter. While I was entertaining them Mr Preston and Theodosia amused themselves playing cards! It seemed to have put them both into an ill humour for the rest of the evening.*

Baltimore Jan^y 1^st 1867

"Better late than never" is a good old adage: for a modern version of it, let me suggest, "a short letter is better than none at all."

Though the day is almost spent, scarcely an hour left of it, I still must wish you A happy New Year, and to you, my dear child, it will be one, if noble and good resolves and an intention to perform faithfully your duties, go with you on your voyage. May you therefore be happy and may you never know a day less joyful, and may you never feel the cares of life press more heavily than they have done this day.

I had intended writing you and my dear Anna a long letter today; but as it has been universally observed in this city as a holiday, of course Papa remained home: you will see therefore I could not take the time to do it. This evening no one seemed disposed to go to "early bed," but each one sat up to the latest possible hour. After the family retired, I posted up for the year my household book of expenses, wrote the first page of this year's diary, and now I am writing a few lines to my darling child, to assure her I have not forgotten, but through every phase of the day her dear image has been before me.

You do not need to be informed that Theodosia did not reach here on Saturday as I wrote you she would do, but came down yesterday. The most pleasant information she brought me was that she had spent an hour with you on Sunday—that you and Anna were looking very well, and were the happiest girls she had ever seen. Dear Sr Raphael! Thede says she was so sweet and lovely, she does not wonder you and Anna are so happy. How could they be otherwise with such surroundings. I rec'd your little curl this morning as a New Year's gift. So you have had your pretty locks shorn again. I think it was advisable as your hair was falling out so much. I think however my dear child, it would have been *very much better* to have had it cut all over your head leaving it about an inch long; it would then have come out even; now the top part must be longer than around the neck. Even once shaving it would have been better than anything else, but if you are satisfied I am also.

I believe there has been nothing new or interesting taken place that I am interested in since I last wrote to you. Vanity called to see me this afternoon and asked kindly after you and Anna and desired to be respectfully remembered. Mrs McNeal and Ella also made me a New Year's call and sent ever so much love to you. Ella seems to be looking forward to your return with real pleasure as does also someone else. As I do not wish to run too far into the New Year with my letter, I must bring it to a close before the clock strikes twelve.

With love and good wishes to Anna and the girls, in the Happiest of New Years to dear Sr Raphael and Sr Genevieve, I am as you already know, your loving Mama.

With all the love imaginable from each member of the family to "dear May."

---

After Madge had completed this letter, she drew forward again the little brown book—all but one page still blank and unused. In the margin of that page she penned: "Wrote a short letter to May on this New Year." Then she put away the book.

Baltimore January 7th 1867

My dear child,

Instead of devoting this evening to you as I had intended, Papa and I are going by special invitation to spend the evening at Mr Parr's; but I avail myself of a few moments before dressing time to tell you this important fact—to thank you in the name of the whole family for your delightful letter of the 3d inst, and tell you of a little shawl we dispatched by mail to you on Saturday and to send you the four-inch diary you desired.

Your letter was indeed a treat, and so gratifying! as it assured us of the pleasant and happy manner in which you spent your holidays. I can only say, If my letters afford you the tithe of the pleasure and satisfaction yours give me, I am indeed more than compensated for the writing of them. Your description of the fancy ball was most amusing and I can readily imagine, as the grand costumers of the occasion, you and Miss Lotte Hoffman must have had your full share of the fun. I wish from the bottom of my heart that I had been there to have assisted you and to have partaken of the frolic. I have no doubt you manage your plays quite as respectably as these more pretentious boys "over the way." Kings, lord, dukes and cavaliers lose nothing by being represented by the gay and fanciful girls of a clever boarding school. Papa, Thede, and I were at another dramatic exhibition at the college on the 2d of this month. *Hamlet*, as the programme will inform you, was played.[2]

By the way, speaking of plays reminds me of your little allegory, in which your ambition was satisfied, I presume, by personating the Catholic church! I told Papa, it would be strange indeed if he did not now attach himself to the Catholic church, since *you* had become its visible representative. How thoughtful in the dear Sisters . . . to permit you to make a grand toilet, like "young ladies of the world," to show off in the evening entertainment.

I have cut out a slip from this morning's *Sun*, to send you as the head of the church, thinking it will be interesting to you and the Sisters also. It is very evident to me that the Catholic church will, before long, take a position in this country which a few years ago was not dreamed of. The quiet, dignified stand of our clergy during the late troubles impressed even those opposed to Catholicity most favourably and makes them think there must be something in a religion which teaches, "Peace and good will to all men."[3]

. . . Thede told me on her return from visiting you that your little josey looked uncomfortable worn over your dress and yet something seemed to be required more than the dress. Thinking a shawl would be convenient, I send you one. Is it not clever to be able to get such little articles through the mail? It would be well if the Sisters knew this, as occasionally they might have small packages which they would like to send away. You can see what the Act of Congress is, on that subject, by referring to the first page of your "4 inch diary."[4]

Well we made our visit last evening and a delightful time we had. Our invitation was based particularly on meeting with Judge Russell and his wife from Virginia. Judge Russell was a member of the Confederate Congress during the whole of its existence,[5] and a gentleman of high position and great intelligence. Mrs Russell is one of the most brilliant women I have met with for a long time . . . we discovered that we were old schoolmates at St Joseph's. Ask Sister Raphael if she remembers Margaret Moore of Virginia, the "worst girl in school," as she herself now says? She remembers St Joseph's as the most delightful spot on earth. . . . Mrs Russell asked in the most affectionate manner after the Sisters who were at St Joseph's in our time and requested me to give her best love to Dear Sr Raphael and Sr Mary Edward; do not forget to mention her to Sr M. Edward, as Sister was her especial friend . . . Judge & Mrs Russell have suffered severely in many respects during the Rebellion and have settled in Baltimore with the hope of retrieving their fortunes. Mrs Russell is an ardent Catholic, another thing to unite us.

. . . Love to each and all from your loving

Mama

I believe dear Kate will yet be able to go to St Joseph's to receive Baptism and make her first communion, some compromise having been effected between herself and parents. She desired her love to you and wishes you would write.

Baltimore January 13th 1867

My dear child,

I confess to a slight disappointment yesterday when Papa came home in the evening and had no letter for me from you. . . .

We have had during the night and the greater part of the day one of the most beautiful falls of snow—not a blustering, fierce, cold disagreeable snow-storm but a gentle, soft, loving snow, which seems to have quietly and affectionately folded its white mantle round Mother Earth to protect, as it were, her bosom from the keen winter blasts. I rose early this morning to attend six o'clock mass at St Ignatius Church. Just think of my surprise on stepping out of doors to find myself ankle deep in the snow. I went over however and found when I reached there, many others who had evidently come many squares more, to be present at that early Mass. —To me, the very early dawn and the beautiful twilight hour are the most delightful and inviting times of prayer —the mind refreshed from sleep and before the busy cares of the day have troubled it, seems more readily to take in the great and wonderful goodness of God and we feel it easier to offer that loving homage which is so justly due the Great Ruler of this Universe and to beg his blessing upon the labours of the day, and again, when the calm and holy hour of twilight comes over the earth and mind and heart and body are wrung and pained and wearied with the toils, the anxieties and duties of our stations in life—how refreshing to enter the House of God and lay the broken heart, the wearied body and the over-tasked mind at the foot of His Altar and beg Him to accept them for Christ's sake.

I had a pleasant visit from Kate today. Dear child, she was kind enough to trudge through the snow to come and see me, to tell me of a kind and beautiful letter she had rec'd from dear Sr Raphael. Kate, you know, has been disappointed by not being able to go up to St Joseph's at this time . . . but I think

. . . she will meet with no opposition about Easter times, and Kate, by the advice of the Archbishop, yields graceful obedience to her mother's wishes and looks forward to that period with all the ardour of a young and zealous heart. . . .

I believe I told you in a former letter that Johnny had returned from his visit to his parents in Washington.[6] The boy was much pleased but well satisfied to get home again. Thede also seemed to think Loyola Place a more agreeable spot than Mountain View, at this particular season especially. Crick has not yet come down, and I trust he will not—at least till there is a possibility of his getting a situation, as I am convinced the life he leads here is well calculated to unfit him for any situation requiring constant attention. Papa has been very busy and very active in his profession . . . just now he is suffering with a cold contracted whilst superintending the putting up [of] a stove in the cellar of the house in Fayette Street, which stove is intended to heat the offices and do away with the necessity of stoves in them. Papa thinks it is quite a success so far and talks strongly of adopting it in this cellar, so as to do away with fire in the parlour. I forget whether I have ever told you how delightfully comfortable we find our new house. Our dining room is a perfect little gem, the parlour not *quite* as pleasant when the weather is very cold as we would like, but *our* room is charming, and we think your room would be sufficiently warm for all sleeping purposes with the door left open between the rooms. I like our house and the situation more and more and I think you will also. I have not seen Van or Castle since I last wrote, though Castle was here last Monday evening while we were at Parrs'. Goodnight my darling child; and believe me your loving Mama. . . .

### Thursday, January 17, 1867

. . . *Mr Preston went to his office this morning and did not return all day; when evening came and he was not home, Thede and I went down to his office and not finding him there, we went to Barnam's from there to Daugherty's and then to Mr Abell's, from there home, where we found him, having just returned. I think he was mortified at having caused us such anxiety though he did not say so. Mr Preston was evidently excited about something but being fatigued he retired early and I suppose I shall not now hear it till tomorrow. Father Clark called . . . today and was very particular in inviting Thede to come over to see him. Thede seems greatly pleased with the good Father.*

### Friday, January 18, 1867

. . . *Papa has been engaged writing an article for the sun paper this evening.*[7]

**Saturday, January 19, 1867**

*[Earlier Madge had given Johnny some clothes for a Negro woman living near the mill to launder for them.] Johnny came in this morning and brought with him the clothes the old woman had washed & ironed, or attempted to wash. They were so badly done that I shall not give her any more to do. They almost sickened me with the smell of a tobacco pipe. . . .*

Baltimore 20th 1867

My darling child,

I am so nervous and so depressed from the fearful storm we have had the greater part of the day and are still having that I fear I am not able to write you a suitable letter. . . . You know the peculiar effect a storm of any description has always had on me, consequently can understand how greatly I must be affected by the fearful one now raging.[8] I am constantly reminded of that terrible snowstorm you and I witnessed in Phila years ago, and from the effects of which dear Papa was so unfortunate as to break his leg, and suffer, as you may remember he did, for many months afterwards. I am sure there must be fearful suffering throughout the country and also in the cities during the prevalence of such weather. It is said the winter, thus far, all over the country has been intensely cold and the storms unusually severe. A few days ago the city of Boston was visited by one of those dreadful Yankee storms and during its continuance, the papers stated that one hundred and seventy-three women and children were conveyed to their respective houses by the police, who perhaps otherwise would have perished in the snow. . . . Perhaps the very consciousness of my own personal comforts and freedom from exposure makes me more painfully alive to the sufferings of those less tenderly cared for and who are obliged to face the dangers of the weather. I trust I am not unmindful of the many blessings so lavishingly bestowed by a kind Providence. . . .

Dear Kate! She is, as you say a dear, good, girl, and deserves to be happy herself, for she tries so hard to make all those happy who come within her influence. I have not seen her since last Monday, but will give her your message when I do see her. . . .

Did I tell you in my last letter that I took your report . . . and showed it to "your Sister" and also to Sr Louisa? They were much pleased with it, and Sr Leopoldine told me . . . she would not be at all surprised to see you with a medal round your neck! I do not know when I have seen Papa as much pleased as in the perusal of your report and the kind and affectionate note appended to it by dear Sr Raphael. You are a dear, good, child, to give us so much pleasure by your attention to your studies and your amiable and satisfactory deportment in and out of class. Again I embrace you most lovingly.

I was pleased to learn that our dear little Anna had had the gratification of seeing her brother. I hope there are many more such visits in store for her from other brothers and loving friends; give her my love and tell her I think, as her "Aunt and Uncle," we also should have had her report. . . .

I must not forget to tell you I called last Monday on Father Clark at the college; the next day the rev'd gentleman returned my visit, and when I introduced Thede to him, he seemed to be quite interested in her and gave her the kindest invitation to come over to see him, and to let him give her instruction in the Catholic religion; she promised to go and I am in hopes she will make him a visit tomorrow, as she was perfectly charmed with him and calls him, "her Father." Thede sends her love to you and to Anna. . . .

Yours lovingly, Mama

### Thursday, January 24, 1867

. . . *Yesterday morning Mr Preston called over to see Father Clark about Johnny's going to school. Papa was quite pleased with Father Clark. God grant that it may continue and be the means of bringing Mr Preston to the church.* . . .

### Saturday, January 26, 1867

. . . *Today the people of the Holiday Theatre gave an afternoon performance for the benefit of the Southern Fund. As Mr Preston could not go and Thede did not wish to go, I sent a note to Mrs Parr asking her to call for me on her way down. She did not come but sent Florence and another child to accompany me. We went and succeeded in getting good seats. The house was crowded. Mr Jefferson played Rip Van Winkle in the play of that name, and played it grandly.*[9]

### Monday, January 28, 1867

. . . *Mr Preston did not come home till near 7 o'clock this evening and then he & Thede played a game of chess, with the usual result!*

### Tuesday, January 29, 1867

. . . *From the game of chess last night, I knew what would follow this morning and was not disappointed. Both parties were excessively nervous and before breakfast was over, it fulminated in a regular blow out!* . . . *Things are not going on very pleasant about the house as I am not disposed to forget the doings of yesterday.*

**Thursday, January 31, 1867**

. . . *We had an unfortunate circumstance occur this evening. Catherine fell down the steps with a pan of hot water in her hand & scalded herself quite badly. The skin came off of her hand & arm and the poor thing seemed to suffer so patiently. Mr Preston dressed it in his way and we were obliged to look on and submit. . .*

**Friday, February 1, 1867**

. . . *When I got up this morning, I was glad to find Catherine up and as she told me, feeling tolerably well, poor thing! On examining her arm I was shocked to find it terribly blistered and I am sure it must be fearfully painful though she bears it like a good Christian, as I am sure she is. Johnny came in this morning and remained all day, giving us much assistance. I did the ironing today and the work generally. Thede helping some. . . . Mr Preston and Thede played chess this evening, and I sat in my room darning stockings.*

**Saturday, February 2, 1867**

. . . *Johnny came in from the mill this morning, reaching here before 8 o'clock, and after breakfast Mr Preston took him over to the college and entered him at school. The boy on his return seemed quite pleased with the irricative.[10] Poor boy he will have a hard task, riding in and out from the mill daily, attending to his duties there, and going to school and learning his lessons. . . .*

St. Joseph's. Feb. 6th 1867

My dear Mama,

I avail myself of the kindness of dear Sr. Agnes, who will go down to Baltimore to-morrow, to make a request of you that I think will please you though I fear it may give you a little trouble. You may remember having asked me in one of your letters . . . if I had thought any more of the slippers I intended to work for Mr. Hopkins. Now I do not remember having ever said anything to you about my desire to do so, although I had for some time intended to make them and thought I had kept my design a secret from even yourself. Not only have I begun them but they are finished, and Sr. Ameilia my teacher in that branch much pleased with them.

I would now like to make dear Papa a handsome smoking cap, for this being my last year at school I think I could do nothing more pretty or appropriate than to offer him . . . a proof of my success in that truly graceful and feminine accomplishment, needlework. But as I do not want him to know anything about it, I am obliged to write thus quietly to you. I had intended and wished to use my pocket money for that purpose so that not even you should partake of my pleasant little secret . . . but I remembered that if I did that I would have to call upon you so soon for spending money that I abandoned that plan & chose this—of writing to you. . . . The materials that I will require are three quarters of a yard of purple velvet, for the cap is made lengthways of the stuff, a spool of purple machine silk No. B or C, a quarter of a yard of florence silk if wide and a half a yard if narrow for the lining, and some wadding. Now dearest Mama if you will be troubled by the getting of these things, do not think of sending them. I will choose something simpler. . . . If you get them I forgot to say if the velvet is light, the sewing silk must be two or three shades darker, if dark the silk must be two or three shades lighter. The lining either purple or crimson silk, whichever you like best. Love to my dearest Sister and Cousin Thede and to Papa when he is asleep so that he will not know how he got it. Lovingly your little

May. . . .

Monday evening<br>Feby 11th 1867

My dear child,

I have spent the greater part of the day looking through the stores of Baltimore for the articles you desire for Papa's smoking cap or rather reading cap, in as much as Papa does not use the noxious weed in any form. I have purchased the velvet, which I am sure you will pronounce exquisite, and have taken the liberty to select white silk as a lining instead of crimson thinking it prettier. . . . But my dear child, I find it utterly impossible to get any machine silk such as you desire. I could get embroidering silk in skeins that might suit, but not knowing whether you could make use of it, I deem it best to ask you about it. When you write, put this little matter on a slip of paper by itself. Papa will not read it. If you think of any other color that would contrast well with it, perhaps I might be able to get it, but to tell you the truth the assortment of such articles is very inferior in Baltimore—Perhaps the Sisters might be able to send to Phila. . . .

Is the black ribbon such as you wished?—Good night, lovingly your

Mama. . . .

St. Joseph's Feb. 10th 1867<br>Feast of Saint Scholastica

My dear Mrs Preston,

Your letter expressing the great gratification caused by May's report was received a few days ago. Yes, I am happy to say that May is pursuing her studies most pleasantly to herself & to those who have charge of her. Our hours of reading & recitation pass most delightfully. Sister Mary Ann, with whom May & Anna are reading Schlegel & dipping into Logic, seconds my assertion in their favor.

May did not tell you of her composition on "Language," which was read aloud at the concert by Anna, who gave it effect—the subject was a very extensive one, but May treated it very well. . . . [11]

After this composition is finished, she and Anna will commence a very *momentous one*, & I know they both would be pleased for me to ask you to say a prayer *daily* for their success, as they must be written *carefully* & bear *criticism*. Can you guess the *subject?* May will write in *verse* & Anna in *prose*. There will be no conflicting of interests whatever, but I want both to be good, good. The dear children harmonize so well together in their studies & pastimes, that it is a pleasure to direct them. . . .

. . . Mother & all the Sisters unite in love to you & kind regards to Mr. Preston.

Yours affectionately
S M Raphael

St. Joseph's. Feb. 15th 1867

My dear Mama,

You cannot imagine how much pleasure your delightful letter, brought by dear Sr. Agnes, gave me! . . .

Anna was delighted with your mention of us together in such an affectionate manner. She always says when we get to the end [of] your letters, "Oh! why does your Mother ever finish, I never get tired of her letters!" She also sends you and dear Papa much love. . . .

Has Cousin Thede seen *her* "Father" yet? I am anxious to know what she thinks of him. If she coincides with everyone else who is intimately acquainted with him, she will be sure to like him. I enclose her the "Remember" printed by the St. Joseph's press, and hope that she will say the little prayer daily for my intention. How does little Johnny succeed in his school duties? I feel much interested in them and look forward to much pleasure in assisting him in pursuing them. . . .

Most lovingly
Your little May. . . .

[On separate notepaper enclosed in above]
My dearest Mama,

How can I thank you as much as I want for the things you sent me by dear Sr. Agnes. I do indeed think the velvet is beautiful. Such a lovely shade! . . . I regret dear Mama that you should have had such a long walk for the silk, which in the end you were not able to obtain. Do not feel at all worried about it as we have decided to work the cap with shades of green silk. This I think you can get without any difficulty in Baltimore; if you are able to do so, the amount I will require is one skein of yellow green, one skein of olive green, and one skein of blue green twisted embroidery silk. Not the deep blue but that which has just enough of it to seem like a dark green. I forgot to say *shaded* silk, the same as I did Papa's slippers last year; they will do for a guide. But, my dear Mama, if it will be any trouble to you do not feel at all anxious about getting them. . . . Everything was just what I wished; how could it be otherwise when sent by my dear Mother. . . .

Now I must stop and write so that Papa may see my letter too; but before doing so I wish to thank you again and again, dearest Mama, for all you have sent me.

Your grateful little
May.

### Thursday, February 14, 1867

*The weather still continues unpleasant it having rained the greater part of the day. This morning, My Lady Randolph*[12] *considered herself insulted by a remark of mine relative to her performing sundry duties about the house, and in consequence she has preserved an unbroken silence to me the entire day. . . .*

### Friday, February 15, 1867

*. . . Thede is still in the huffs, which I do not regret as I think I get along quite as well without her talk as with it.*

### Saturday, February 16, 1867

*. . . Lady Randolph is still on her high horse. I am somewhat surprised that Mr Preston has not noticed it and stopped it. . . .*

### Sunday, February 17, 1867

*A glorious morning and a delightful day! But to me most unhappy! I went to church at half past 7 to the cathedral and remained till near ten o'clock. On my return I found Mr Preston much fretted in not being able to find a paper he had mislaid, and seeing the table waiting for me, as I have no breakfast before going to church, he became very angry and it ended in one of our most unpleas-*

*ant scenes. I feel certain that poor unfortunate woman was in some way the cause of it.*[13] *I went to bed this afternoon sick with headache. . . .*

---

May was enjoying her French classes more and more. On February 17 she wrote again in that language—this time to her mother. She was also enjoying, with Anna Northrop, the perquisites of senior class status. Her French letter was full of the special privilege the two girls shared on the chilly winter mornings of accompanying Sister Raphael and a half dozen other Sisters on their morning walk. "I'll leave you to judge," May wrote her mother, "with what pleasure we accompanied them in that charming hour."

Her letter bubbled on also about her music. At the last concert May and Anna had performed a piano duet. "I love music so much," May apostrophized, "that I would always like to have a piano near me, but I prefer to play by ear than by reading the notes."

Loyola Place
Feby 18th 1867

My dear child,

I suppose you have rec'd my shadow of a letter, telling you why the substance did not come on Monday evening, as you have good reason generally to expect it. It was a great disappointment . . . not being able to enjoy my Sunday evening conversations with you and my dear little niece—by the way, I am not so certain that the *diminuitive* applies to Anna with the same appropriateness (Mercy! what a big word for a small object.) that it does to you; when I come to reflect properly upon *that object*, the child looms up to a very respectable sized young lady!

It was right selfish in me too, to regret, or be annoyed at the manner in which we spent our evening, for dear Aunt Christie was so sweet and lovely and so entertaining, full of a kind, cheerful pleasant gossip that did no one any harm, but informed us many things quite pleasant to know of our country friends and neighbours. . . . Your young friend Willie Fowler has been, as it were, snatched from the grave; for days it was a terrible struggle between life and death, but thanks to a kind and merciful Providence, life conquered and the dear boy has been restored to his devoted parents and numerous friends. In the other place, death came off the victor—perhaps *there* he felt he had the right, for he had for so many years passed by the door and left them in such undisturbed enjoyment of all the pleasure that this world can give that each and all of that devoted family thought of no other happiness—almost of no other Heaven! You will know I could mean no other family than "Grandpap's"[14] "Uncle Joseph"—after a long illness in which all that medical skill

& the most gentle and tender nursing could do to spare the life of this beloved son and brother was employed, but all in vain. Death had marked him for his own and love and skill were powerless to arrest the blow. . . .

Scarcely any of the Stansbury family were able to be present at the burial. Aunty Stansbury was suffering so much with rheumatism or, still worse, what is feared to be dropsy, and Mary Lizzie not yet considered well enough to go out and poor little Alice confined to bed with cold—so you see just now the "dark day" is upon that family. . . .

As it is quite late, I will not begin another sheet, but wish you a good night and pleasant dreams.

Mama

19th of Feby 1867

I wonder if you remember my darling child that this is one of my pet days—this same 19th of February? I expect if you could look over the letters of each year during your absence, you would find I had written to you always on this day. I think in one of my letters I told you the pleasant little incident connected with it in years gone by and which has thrown a halo round it, to me, for all time? . . .

. . . Our friend Mrs Barnum, now Mrs Barnum no longer but Mrs Gordon, is going to France and her son Frank accompanies her. You will be pleased to learn that Frank has become a Catholic; he was baptised in St Ignatius Church last Saturday week, being one of Father Clark's converts. Mrs Barnum made no opposition to Frank joining the Catholic church, as she says the boy was old enough to decide for himself. You can readily imagine Mrs Gordon's friends are not very well pleased with this hasty remarriage, and the so soon forgetting her good and excellent husband Mr Barnum. The gentleman she has married is much younger than herself, and strange to say she scarcely knew him one month before she married him; another strange thing is that Frank is perfectly satisfied with the whole affair. . . .

On my return home judge of my surprise and delight to find your delightful French letter stuck up in the most conspicuous part of the mantelpiece. I eagerly seized it, and still stranger than all of the above, I was able to *read* nearly every word of it. *That* is really very wonderful, when you reflect that I have not read a line of French excepting in your letters for years. The fact is, I think I read your letters by instinct. I intuitively know what you are or would write about. Why my dear baby, you are a perfect little wonder! . . . Papa don't say much; he hemms! and haws! and looks pleased, and when I say, "Dear child! how she exerts herself to please us all," Papa says, "O you are so foolish about that child, you really think she is a piece of perfection." I answer, "Perfection or not, I am very glad she is mine." . . .

Remember me in all kindness to dear Sister Raphael and tell her I think I shall be a parlour boarder at St Joseph's next year or enter the Senior class as I am so much in love with all your doings. . . .

"Castle" spent the evening with me, I say with *me*, because I was left entirely to the entertainment of the great "Castle," Papa and Crick being engaged in the dining room playing chess and Theodosia not feeling disposed to make her appearance.[15] I am perfectly satisfied that neither of us felt the want of other company. The subject of our conversation being quite interesting enough. . . .

Good night my darling child
lovingly Your Mama.

### Wednesday, February 20, 1867

. . . *I wrote a note this morning intending to send it to Theodosia, but on giving it to Mr Preston to read, he became violently excited, of course saying I was wrong and others right. This I think is the last appeal I will ever make to Mr Preston to act the part of a true, honest man by me. I have made up my mind to quietly submit to my fate let it be what it may, and hope for a change when May comes home. . . .*

### Thursday, February 21, 1867

. . . *We had quite a scene this morning. My Lady Randolph insultingly asked me a question and I said to her, Theodosia when you address your conversation to me do it in a proper manner, call me by name, do you understand me? Her reply was I understand that I will do exactly as I please. Upon which Mr Preston rose up and told my Lady her conduct was improper &c &c—Of course she cooled down and was quite amiable, though she has not condescended to hold communication with me yet. . . . Mr Preston had another squabble with me this evening and went to bed on the strength of it.*

# 17

# Converts and a Hold-out

PRESTON'S STERN REBUKE OF Thede seemed to clear the air, and the original power balance between niece and aunt appeared reestablished. For Madge a short sojourn in the old country neighborhood offered a respite from the tension of her own household.

---

Loyola Place
Feby 26th 1867

My very dear child,

When Aunt Christie was in the city last week, she made me promise to return with her to Eudowood. . . .

The roads were in such a shocking condition that I almost regretted having placed myself in a position to be frightened *out of my life*, as I really was, before I reached there; but the kindly welcome awarded me by dear good Cousin Eudocia and the rest of the family amply repaid me for the terror I had undergone to get to the dear old spot again. Everything looked natural and wintry, and as I stood by the window and saw through the opening in the woods the gable end of the old cottage at P. Plains and the comfortable storehouse of Auntie Stansbury, I could almost imagine we were still living in the country and I had surely come over to pay one of my old-fashioned visits; but as time wore away, and being constantly confined to the house became a little irksome (as walking out of doors was an utter impossibility), I mentally thanked my stars that being in the country *for me* was simply a question of days, and that good fortune had located me in the city for the winter at least. . . .

I was pleased to find everything had gone quietly and pleasantly at home during my short absence, and Papa was very well and *un*complaining. . . . In a letter rec'd from Charley[1] a few days before I went to the country, he tells me he has entered Seton Hall College in Orange County, New Jersey. It must have been a most unexpected event to the poor boy, as he knew nothing of his going till the day before he left. Of course I was most gratified to know his mother had had the courage to send him from her, as I think it ought to have been done long ago. Charley wrote me a . . . most affectionate letter, which I answered, giving him such counsel and advice as I thought might benefit him in his new position. . . .

> Love to Anna and the girls.
> Your loving
> Mama.

> Loyola Place
> March 3d 1867

Well my little pet, I suppose you see in your "mind's eye," if you are in a meditative humour tonight, the vision of an old lady, seated at a convenient and comfortable looking writing desk, with paper and letters and envelopes, books &c &c scattered in an apparent wild confusion over it, and by looking a little closely you are made conscious that old lady is your own dear Mama, and she is engaged in the pleasant task of writing to her darling child. The vision is a reality, my little one, and here I am prepared for a good long talk with my sweet children this stormy sabbath evening. As an evidence of my great satisfaction with both of you, let me open my conversation by thanking each of you for the great pleasure we have all had in reading your *really very clever* Essay on Language. I thank you both. You, for having written it and dear Anna for having read it (as Sr Raphael says) so beautifully at the concert. Papa thinks "the little thing deserves credit," and again, "I am much gratified with May's Essay; the ideas are good and original and indeed beautifully expressed." So you see, my child, while you are faithfully pursuing your studies, we are . . . appreciative . . . about all you do.

In a most delightful letter . . . from dear Sr Raphael, she said you and Anna were . . . beginning a most important task, one which she was desirous you should perform in an admirable manner, and she would leave me to "guess" the subject, at the same time requesting a *daily* prayer for your success. Of course I have "guessed" it, and of course you have my earnest prayers for your success. If it be true, as many writers have said, that an author must have his *heart* in his *subject* to do full justice to it, then surely we may hope that you and Anna will not fail. I suppose it is almost time to begin to look forward to the Distribution? Only think, four months, and your happy school days will come to an end. I sometimes don't know whether to rejoice or feel sad about it. You know the trials and troubles and you also know the pleasures and happiness of school life—but you do *not* know the cares and anxieties, the painful struggles and annoyances that even the most favoured experience in their intercourse with the great world: but fortified as I hope you will be with the pious instructions and beautiful examples of those kind Sisters who have had you in their keeping for the last five years, you will be able to fight the great battle of life and come off victor. . . .

Mrs Owens and Laura came in from Aigburth on Friday, intending to take me out with them that same evening . . . but sundry little things which required my attention at home prevented my accompanying them. The most important one, and which I did not tell them, however, was the losing my Sunday visit to you—nothing that is offered to me can in any wise compensate for that deprivation. I feel the want of it the whole week following and am not satisfied till the next Sunday gives me the chance of making up the disappointment. Independent of the pain to me, I would not unnecessarily deprive you, my little darling, of what evidently gives so much pleasure and which I must say are appreciated from beyond their worth (my letters). . . .

By the way, speaking of letters reminds me of one I rec'd yesterday . . . it came from Charley, and you really must forgive me if I trouble you with its perusal. . . . Poor boy! You know exactly what I think of him and how thoroughly I feel convinced that Charley has been more "sinned against than sinning." I knew there was no one to write him a word of advice or [to] counsel him . . . in fact, no one to say even a kind word of encouragement to him, and I thought if a word of mine would comfort or cheer him and make him happy in the consciousness there was one person really interested in him, willingly and gladly would I give up my little pleasure I might have in going out . . . and stay home and devote the time to him: how the act was appreciated I have you to judge by the dear boy's letter to me. . . . [2]

Good night, with affectionate remembrance to Sr. Florence, Sr Maria, Sr Aimee and Sr Ann Scholastica and all my dear children I am your loving

Mama. . . .

Loyola Place
March 10th 1867

Indeed, my dear child, I am afraid my senses are all washed away by the incessant rains of the past week—rain, rain, rain, splash, splash, splash, mud, mud, mud, and then it begins again . . . till we are almost disheartened—disheartened, though we are not in the country any longer and you would think it was only country people who feel so depressingly the effects of bad weather —not so, even in the city . . . muddy streets, leaden skies and a watery atmosphere are anything but pleasant, yet with these we have had to struggle for so long a time that sunshine, fine weather, and dry pavements are now only counted as of the past, and remembered as among the things that were. Poor Papa's patience has been considerably exercised of late by the unfavourable condition of the weather. Our friends at the "mill," having moved nearer the city . . . the place in consequence became vacant, and John Ensor our good old standby, wishing to occupy part of it, Papa has rented it to him, but alas! the poor man has been waiting and watching so long for just one glimpse of sunshine to enable him to move his family down, and yet it comes not, that Papa said this afternoon on returning from the mill where he had spent a few hours, "that John was the most lugubrious creature that could be imagined." . . .

The only thing of interest that I have to tell you is the faithful continuance of our friend Mrs Nickerson in receiving instructions on the subject of the Catholic religion from Father Clark. She calls over to see me nearly every day after her visit to the Rev'd Father, and it is really edifying to witness her earnest efforts to learn the truth, and practice it. She is making arrangements to go out to St. Louis, to live permanently with her son Edward, and expects to go, I think, next month. I fear she will not be able in so short a time to pass through the ordeal to which Father Clark will subject her, as I am told the Rev'd Father is very particular. In her case, I am in hopes he will put aside a little of his vigour and permit her to join the church before she leaves this part of the world. If she goes among her Protestant friends without being fortified by the seal of the church, it will be so easy for her to forget or become indifferent to her good resolves. . . .

. . . Theodosia has not yet made a visit to Father Clark, and . . . I am nearly certain she will not do so. I cannot tell you how much I regret her apathy and indifference and how assured I feel that the excellent opportunity now so graciously extended to her, if not availed of, will at some future day cause her bitter regrets and many sorrows. I feel a conviction that Theodosia is trifling with graces bestowed upon her and I am unhappy in consequence, yet it will answer no good purpose for me to urge her to do otherwise; the peculiarity of her disposition is to *oppose.* I therefore think it best to say no more on the subject to her, and so I told the Rev'd Father in my last interview with him. Of course you must not mention the above as I do not wish her to know I have written thus to you.

I, or rather we, had a pleasant visit from Mrs Owens yesterday and while with us Papa, she and myself went out *house hunting.* Mr Owens has partly promised to purchase a house for her in the city for a winter residence and they as well as ourselves would like to be in our neighbourhood. We *found* a house in St Paul Street, not quite finished, but will be in about ten days. It is pleasantly situated and a beautiful house, and pleased Mrs Owens. Next week will decide the purchase; till it is a "fixed fact" of course you are to know nothing about it. . . .

Everyone about the house send lots of love to you and Anna, as does also

Mrs McNeal. . . . "Vanity" went into *business for himself* the first of February.
Good night lovingly Mama

Loyola Place<br>March 17th 1867

My dearling child,

I wrote you a few hurried lines and sent them off on Saturday morning,
hoping you might have the pleasure of reading them . . . on the termination
of the happy retreat . . . you have just made. . . .

I was thoughtful and kind of you to write your little explanation why we
would not receive the Friday letter due us this week. I always think I will be
very philosophical, *till I am tried,* and then I find if I do *not* hear from you, all
the unpleasant reasons that can be imagined come thronging to my mind,
and despite of the good resolves that have been made, I end by being very miserable and—but you need not hint it, Papa is also. Poor, dear Papa is very
much of a stoic on most subjects, but on some, he is as weak as a child! . . .

. . . On arising this morning, we feared we were to have the worst snow
storm of the season, and I looked longingly over to the church, wondering
how I was to wade through the heavy banks of snow . . . having a little cold, I
thought Papa would surely veto any attempt of mine to brave the storm . . .
but about eight o'clock the storm . . . began to lull off and in a short time the
sun shone out bright and beautifully and with thick rubbers I went over to
church and returned again without feeling any *bad* effects physically, but
mentally and spiritually delightfully and happily refreshed and strengthened.
My prayers and offerings were made . . . for May and for Anna. I prayed to
God to bless my dear children, to keep them always lovingly united in mind
and heart, and even though their paths in life might be separated and each
would walk through thorny and intricate ways, beset by temptations and trials,
that our Blessed Mother would at last lead them hand in hand to the feet of
her dear Son.

I felt though I was not with you that each knew intuitively I was thinking of
you all the morning and I flattered myself too that my little girls had not
forgotten me in their prayers, and I *thought* I felt the influence of their tender
and innocent supplications in my behalf. . . .

Love to dear Sr Raphael [and] Sr Genevieve . . .

St. Joseph's. Mar. 19th 1867.
St. Joseph's day.

My dear Mama,

We did have . . . a most happy Retreat. Who can say, but those who have
experienced it, what a happiness it is to pass through such a blessed season of

retirement ! I should be particularly thankful to our good God for permitting me to make not only one, but five Retreats. Anna and I are very grateful to you for the prayers you offered for us, and both answer most heartily to that part of your letter in which you express the hope that we prayed for you. "Yes ! Certainly we did." . . .

Could not Papa find time to write now and then to me; if you did not tell me all about him I would never know anything concerning my father. . . .

Our dear Sister Genevieve has been obliged to give up her duty and go to the Sisters' Infirmary. Sister felt leaving us so much, and *we* fear that her place, at least in our affections, can never be filled. She left the kindest of messages for yourself and dear Papa, and took your last letter over with her in her knitting bag. I think if you would write to Sister she would be most happy to hear from you. Your loving little

May.

### Wednesday, March 20, 1867

. . . *Mr Preston has rented another office and is arranging to move in a day or two. Catherine cleaned out the new office today and Crick and Johnny carried to the mill in the market wagon sundry boxes &c &c that were at the house. Mary O'Brian came this morning and washed a very large washing of clothes and very fortunately we succeeded in getting them dry this evening.* . . .

### Thursday, March 21, 1867

. . . *Mary O'Brian came this morning and ironed the clothes she washed yesterday, and did them beautifully. . . . Mr Preston notwithstanding the heavy rain insisted on our going to see Mr Owens play Solon Shingles at the Holliday St Theatre.*[3] . . .

Loyola Place<br>March 24th 1867

My precious child,

Your welcome favour written on St Joseph's day, was duly received, together with one of your poetical compositions, which some dear good child, I think our little Annie, was kind enough to write off for me and dear, thoughtful Sr Raphael enclosed with your letter and sent to us. . . . I cannot tell you my dear little girl how much your literary efforts gratify both Papa and myself, and we flatter ourselves that with industry and perseverance you might do something *very respectable* in that line. Tell dear Sr Raphael, I *have* "guessed" the subject on which you are now engaged, and in which she is so kind as to be deeply interested, and like herself, I want it to be "good, very good" as also dear Annie's *prose* composition on the same subject. Every day since I have known of your being thus engaged, I have made an especial visit to the Blessed Mother's Altar in St Ignatius Church to offer a prayer for my children's success *in that,* and all their other studies. I hope to continue my daily visit till the prize is won! . . .

I have only taken this half sheet of paper on which to finish my letter. I promised Papa this evening that I would go to bed every night this coming week at ten o'clock, and as it is so near that time, I shall not have time to write more than this page. Aunt Louisa left us last Tuesday for Mountain View. Crick is still looking for something to do and Theodosia has not yet made up her mind to visit Father Clark. . . .

Poor Papa! when he read your note, he said, "I should indeed, be sorry not to see Sr Genevieve when we visit St Joseph's this summer. I feel as if Sister Genevieve was especially *my* Sister, having met her before I knew the other Sisters."

Good night my darling child. . . .

### Thursday, March 28, 1867

*. . . This afternoon I went to Dr Winchell's and had two teeth filled and the rest of them cleaned, the whole costing me 3 dollars.*

### Friday, March 29, 1867

*. . . This is the anniversary of Uncle Wickham's death, his death took place 34 years ago. Mr Chandler and Aunt Eliza are the only two links binding that epoch and this together.*[4] *. . .*

> Loyola Place
> April 5th 1867

I can readily imagine, my dear children, with what joy you will greet your young friend, the bearer of this note.

Dear Kate has persevered bravely and at last has overcome the opposition so strongly made by all her family to the dear child's desire to unite herself to our holy church. You children who have been so fortunate as to be born Catholics can scarcely appreciate the efforts required to eradicate early prejudices, and wipe out as it were from your mind the wrong teachings of many years: but the grace of God can work miracles, if we only yield to its divine promptings, and the once stubborn, unbelieving creature may become the docile, humble and regenerated Christian.

I hope you will both find it in your power to be a good deal with Kate during her novitiate; you are both so well grounded in your religion, that you can in many graceful ways and without seeming so to do, give her much instruction, and perhaps she herself may feel easier to ask you many things she would like to know and understand and yet hesitate to ask of others.

I feel so happy in knowing Kate will make her first communion at St. Joseph's. I think it would have been almost impossible for the dear child to have segregated herself from the worldly doings at her home sufficiently to have the same dispositions that I am sure she will have from the pious instruction, the good examples and holy surroundings with which she will now be favoured. God grant her the greatest blessing in this world, a *good* first communion. On the happy day in which she makes it, give her, from me, an affectionate embrace and heartfelt congratulations for the great blessing she has enjoyed. If you can let me know at what hour you hear Mass on Easter Sunday, I will endeavour to hear Mass at the same time and if found worthy to receive a visit from our dear Lord will meet you in Spirit at his altar.

And now my dear children let me ask you if you remember the happy times we enjoyed this time last year? My heart has been hovering round your sweet home all this week, and I have been wishing it *was last year* and I was now with you all. . . .

Good night my dear May and Anna

Yours lovingly
Mama & Auntie

St. Joseph's. April 5th 1867

My dear Papa and Mama,

You see how much I thank you for the pretty little note paper and envelopes you were so kind as to send me, by my using them the first time, in writing to you. They are just the kind I wanted! . . .

Do you ever hear anything about Kitty? If any of you knew for one instant how anxious I feel, *and always will feel*, about her you would be sure to tell me anything that you would hear concerning her. . . .

You wish to know, dear Papa and Mama, what I will want for Distribution. You see, dearest Papa, I include you particularly in these arrangements for I flatter myself that, though they do not exactly belong to your sphere, you will be just as much interested in their success as my dear Mama will be. Now won't you, Papa? Well to begin. You know, Mama, first a very fine, pretty swiss dress; with regard to the making of it I would like one of those pretty full skirts that you like so much with a very deep hem and no tucks, the body puffed, plain or made with little narrow tucks. . . . If the sleeves are made with the swiss double, they need not be lined, the body too requires nothing more than a swiss lining. Around the neck only a little ruse[5] of a piece of lace. Several yards of narrow white velvet for my hair and neck, white-kid gloves, a handkerchief and, if you would like it, a little fan. . . . I believe you have my measure at Perry's for gaiters. . . . I will need too a new pair of corsets. Dear me! I nearly forgot to say anything about my sash; it must be a broad white one, plain or watered.[6] Now dearest parents, you will see I have told you everything I could think of, and I now leave it to you to choose whatever you like best. . . .

With much love and many prayers for my dear, good Father and Mother,

I am your devoted little<br>May.

Loyola Place<br>April 11th 1867

My dear child,

Having returned from Eudowood I avail myself of the first spare moment I have to answer properly your pleasant and interesting letter of the 5th. . . .

. . . We were greatly pleased with the beneficial arrangement Sr Raphael has made relative to your examinations; and the reading of those "standard works," whatever they may be, is the very thing of all others I could have desired. I am so anxious you should possess that kind of general information which can only be obtained by a regular course of judicious reading, and I cannot imagine anyone more capable of directing young persons in that way than dear Sr Raphael. I am sure both you and Anna feel the importance of it, and can therefore appreciate the advantages you are now enjoying. . . .

Be assured Mama does not forget or neglect to pray for you. My "twilight hour," at which time I have you most particularly in my heart and thoughts, is to me the happiest part of the day. What shall I do when you and Anna no longer need my affectionate anxieties about you?—Ah! me, I fear they will have but begun, when I have you with me *in the world*!

You ask me about poor dear Kitty. I, like yourself, shall never cease to feel the deepest interest and affection for that poor child, and, were it left to myself to do, would surely have her with me. —I could so much better than anyone else make great allowances for her shortcomings; but as Papa is not now willing to submit to her failings, we must only hope and pray that she may overcome them, and then when she is an improved girl, perhaps Papa will have her again with us. The last time I saw the child, was a few days . . . before Christmas, at which time she came to see me and of course was in a condition to excite all my sympathies. I looked over my storeroom and hunted up such articles as I thought would be useful and suitable for her and gave them to her; she was apparently most grateful and certainly most delighted with her

"Christmas gift." Since then I have never seen her and perhaps shall not, till she needs some more of "Miss May's old clothes." You must not mention the above in your letters, as I keep such doings to myself. . . .

And now my dear child with regard to that "grand toilet for the interesting occasion." . . . You have written for narrow white velvet ribbon; do you prefer *that*, to white watered ribbon, matching your sash? I should like you and Anna to be dressed as nearly alike as possible, therefore if Anna's dressing is already arranged and you could let me know about it, I would make yours to suit it. . . .Love from Papa, Thede and Crick.

Lovingly Mama

When you write again let me know something about your "curls."

Loyola Place<br>April 15th 1867

My darling children,

If I had been the fortunate possessor of Aladdin's lamp, or one of the equally famous wishing carpets, yesterday, you would have found yourselves transported by their magic aid, from your present loved home to a pretty little rugged spot near the York turnpike called the "mill" property.

On waking quite early yesterday morning, Papa asked me if I would not accompany him to the "mill" and spend the day rusticating with him? As Papa had been hard at work *professionally* all the week and had gone to bed wearied and careworn, I could not but feel that it would literally be a "day of rest" to him to wander through the quiet woods or sit calmly musing by the clear stream as it flowed quietly over its sandy bed or at times rushed impetuously over the rugged rocks. . . . I at once cheerfully consented and proposed that the whole family should go with us. Papa seemed well pleased—so I rose and prepared myself and started *over the street,* to six o'clock Mass: at which time I had the happiness of receiving Holy Communion.

On returning home, I found the family all up, breakfast ready and each one eager to do his and her part for the furthering of the anticipated pleasure of a "day at the mill"! Now you will readily understand, as it was Palm Sunday, I had hoped and intended to have gone to High Mass at the cathedral; but of this, I said nothing—but with the rest of the family *seemed* cheerfully bent on the country visit. Crick went in cavalier style, riding Black Hawk. Thede and Catherine, to add a new feature to the frolic, started off to walk to the York Station, where they were to await the coming of the car and Papa and I, like a good old "Darby and Joan," took seats in the car and rode out expecting to overtake the youthful pedestrians, pick them up, and all should proceed together to the "turning off point" on the road and then walk down to the mill—but judge of our surprise on reaching the station, to find our young adventurers had gone on and were actually out of sight, neither did we ever overtake them, but only once we caught a glimpse of the two, in the far distance, standing on the brow of a long hill, apparently looking their last on the *slow coach* they had left so far behind them. . . . When Papa and I reached the "mill," we found the rest of the party quietly seated and evidently quite elated at the wonderful feat they had performed of *walking all the way out.* Papa and I humoured the thing and pretended to think it an Herculean task.

After relieving ourselves of sundry wrappings which the heat of the day made rather superfluous and resting a little, we started for a ramble through the woods. . . . We spent an hour or two in thus roaming over hills, through woods, and along streams, till at last fatigue and hunger admonished us to turn our steps . . . towards the "mill" . . . and in a short time, with Thede and Catherine's assistance, and now and then a little bothering from Papa and Crick, our simple picnic dinner was placed upon the table. Said dinner consisting of cold ham, spendidly boiled potatoes, good bread and butter, and a delicious cup of tea, for dessert some of Papa's old Pleasant Plains wine, nuts & apples. You will perceive our bill of fare was quite sufficient for people not given to epicurianism; indeed we, in our simplicity, thought it quite luxurious—but with regard to the service on which it was placed, perhaps it would be well to be silent, as neither silver nor gold, glass nor china flourished in any extravagant profusion; if the truth must be told, on several occasions plates fell short of performing their duty—or rather, I beg pardon, they performed double duty, Papa kindly giving me the loan of part of his to put my ham on, and if I did not pay attention to him, forgetting in his eagerness to satisfy his appetite that it was mine, and Thede passing over to me the *one good fork* that the place boasted of possessing. However through all these little pleasantries, we managed to make quite as hearty a meal as we could have desired. . . .

While we were at the "mill," John returned from church, bringing with him some blessed palm, which he shared with me and which I brought home to ornament the altar. We left the mill at three o'clock, took the car at the "turn of the road," and by half past four . . . found ourselves safe and comfortably at home. You can readily imagine it was not long before we were all refreshed by a good wash and clean clothes. I found it necessary to rest my wearied limbs by half an hour's doze on the bed, after which I rose, feeling bright and happy and well pleased that the sacrifice I had made of my own feelings had been the cause of pleasure and satisfaction to the rest of the family. . . .

How are you girls getting on this week? You are enjoying dear Kate's being with you I am sure. Give my love to her and tell her her dear Mama was with me some time this afternoon. . . . Mrs Parr sends love to you, and I suppose will write to Kate this evening as she intends to send Kate's veil through the mail tomorrow. . . . Papa has just come up in my room and, as he says, wants to talk to me, so goodbye and good night with love to Anna, Lizzie and Stella. . . .

Mama

Suppose you send by Kate the length of your dress and tell me if you would like it to trail behind.

St. Joseph's. Apr. 17th 1867

My dear Mama,

What shall I do! I have only a short time to devote to my letter this morning. . . . I was so much obliged to you for writing to me by Kate. . . . As for Kate, I think she is as happy as she can be; nor is this at all odd, for everything that could make her feel once more at home has been done for her. . . . What a blessed lot hers has been! When she first came to St. Joseph's she seemed to have anything but a partiality for Catholics; now she would relinquish everything else for the sake of being one. She sends you much love and begs that you will pray for her at this all important time. . . .

You ask us to tell you, if we may, when our examinations will terminate. We do not exactly know. Meanwhile we thank you very much for your prayers at "twilight," or any other time you may feel like offering them for us. I too love that hour, and thinking as you have mentioned it so often, you would like to know what we are doing at that time, I will tell you. We go to music at half past five, come down at six, generally have a few moments' recreation on the porch (it being just after general studies) and then go to supper, which usually occupies the time until half past six. Coming downstairs we almost always have the full benefit of our beautiful Mountain sunsets, which *we* think like everything else at dear St. Joseph's is the most perfect of its kind in the world. . . .

The bell has rung. With love to dearest Papa and cousins I am Your loving little

May.

Loyola Place<br>April 19th 1867

My darling child,

I have just returned from church and, late as it is, I must write you a few lines before retiring. It being, as you will perceive from the date of my letter Good Friday, the happy privilege has been granted me of spending the greater part of the day in church. The ceremonies at St Ignatius' Church are perfectly grand. . . . The chanting by the Priests, there were about twenty-five in the sanctuary, and as many boys, was glorious. . . . The ceremonies of today as performed at St Ignatius were entirely new to me and . . . I have enjoyed them greatly. Yesterday also the Procession with the Blessed Sacrament and placing it in the repository was very imposing. . . . Mrs McNeal has with great kindness given me constant access to her pew at all hours; consequently I have been enabled to be present at all the ceremonies of the present week. This evening "Vanity" took me to church and came home with me. "Vanity" as well as Mrs McNeal and Ella made the kindest of inquiries about you. . . .

I am pleased to know our dear Kate is so happy and looking forward to a still greater happiness on the coming Sunday! I shall not forget her in my prayers on that morning. . . .

I had almost forgotten to tell you a most pleasant and agreeable surprise I had a few days ago. I was called to the parlour to see a gentleman who had just come in and, opening the door, judge of my surprise and pleasure at seeing Hillen Sanders. *The dear boy* has grown to be a great man but he was still the boy Hillen to me. I don't know when I have seen anyone so wonderfully improved; if I except his sister Mollie, whom I saw the day after, and whom I assure you has grown to be a pretty & elegant looking girl. They each asked a thousand things about you and sent a thousand messages together with ever so much love to you. I gave them *your picture* as an evidence of my great regard for them. The whole family are going out to St Joseph's in Missouri in a month or two, so it is not probable you will see them again for years, if ever. . . . Goodnight

Mama

## Sunday, April 21, 1867

*How little can we calculate upon in this world. I have looked forward all this week to a happy Easter, have prepared myself to the best of my ability for a proper spending of it — but what has been the result. Alas! I have not even had the happiness of hearing Mass today. Another of our Sunday disturbances took place early this morning, and all through that poor unfortunate girl. Will she ever leave the house and will I ever have the satisfaction of being alone again.[7] I cannot understand the strange doings about this house. One would suppose Mr Preston abuses me to gratify the other party. Mr Preston, after all his unkindness to me, went to the mill and returned about 1/2 past four. Rose came in the 1 o'clock train and remained with me till 7 o'clock. She is now stationed at Cockeysville. . . . I have left the family downstairs and have retired to my room miserable & unhappy.*

**Tuesday, April 23, 1867**

*. . . Mr Preston, as is always the case when we are alone, is quite pleasant tonight!*

**Thursday, April 25, 1867**

*. . . Mr Preston rose early and went down stairs, made the fire and set the table for me; of course I had a good hearty laugh about the "Biddy" when I went down and found what was done.*

**Saturday, April 27, 1867**

*Thede and Catherine had been at mill several days to clean it. Thede says there is still another room to clean up. I can't help thinking they have been very slow about their work but it won't do to say so. . . .*

St. Joseph's. Apr.25th 1867

My dear Mama,

I would not have you think, as your little note seemed to suppose, that I had been for such a length of time in possession of the box that you sent on Saturday, and for which my dearest Mama I thank you a thousand times. How good of you, my sweet Mama, to remember that at the termination of Lent some good things would be most acceptable. . . . As you desired . . . I selected the nicest of the oranges and arranged them for our dear Sr. Genevieve. Sr. Raphael was so kind to me about the little decorations for them and, besides the geranium leaves, gave me some beautiful helitrope and several little white flowers; with these I was able to make the plate quite pretty and I hope refreshing to the eyes of dear Sister. Sister also permitted me to write a little note sending much love and respects from you and Papa and begging that she would accept it together with the accompanying preserves and fruit. How I wish you could have heard the many kind messages dear Sister sent in return. . . .

This morning Kate and I got up and went to early mass, this being the last that we would perhaps forever assist at the Holy Sacrifice at St. Joseph's together; as we were coming out of church, we met Sr. Genevieve and had quite a pleasant little chat with her. She was able to walk to church and back without her crutch, and really seems to be improving. She told me how much pleased she was with your delightful long letter to her (the note enclosed to me I received yesterday afternoon); she then renewed all her kind messages, adding many others which from the mutual bond of friendship existing between your heart and dear Sister's will doubtless be suggested to you without my writing them. . . .

I feared after I had written the letter concerning my Distribution things, that I had led you to suppose that my dress must be only of the plainest style. If there is anything in the way of ornament that you wish to have about it, use your own judgment and taste entirely. I have but one request to make . . . my dear Mama. . . . It is that *no matter what any one* says to the contrary you will not make my dress with a great sweeping train. . . . My reason for being so particular on this point is that as Distribution day will be the last on which I can be a real schoolgirl, I would not for all the fashions in the world nor for all the begging of companions relinquish that last right to be a girl. After that you may make my dress from here to Baltimore if you like, for then I will return to my old indifference about what I wear; but for that one I am decided. . . .

Sr. Raphael expects to visit the city some time in May; she will tell you any little thing that you may like to know much better than I could, for instance about the ribbon & so on. . . . This visit my dear Mama you must not mention as Sister would rather make it quietly. . . .

Again we all thank you and with much love to your dear self, my Papa & cousins, Sister & all kind friends, I am your own little girl

May.

Loyola Place April 28th 67

Many thanks my darling child for the long and interesting letter written the day before our dear Kate left St Joseph's and which she was the prompt bearer to me. . . . As soon as I could after dinner, I went round to see Kate and know from her all . . . about St Joseph's and its dear inmates, but unfortunately Kate had started on the same mission and we missed each other. I made however a pleasant visit to Mrs Parr, and just as I was leaving the door Kate came up and in a few hurried sentences she told me how pleased and gratified she had been with her visit &c &c and finished by saying she would come down in a day or two . . . yesterday in compliance with Papa's request, I went with him to the mill and remained till three o'clock, when we took the car and reached the city at half past four. I had just time to refresh myself by a good wash and seat myself to write to you and had about one dozen lines of the first page written when a ring at the front door announced a visitor and in walked Kate, sweet, fresh, and lovely; letter was once laid aside, and *alone* in the parlour we had a good long talk. Poor dear Kate, in the midst of her narrative, stopped suddenly and said, "Oh Auntie it is such a satisfaction to come to you and talk all these things; now Mama is as sweet and kind as she can be and pleased to know I am happy, but then she can't so fully *sympathize* with me as you do and just now, I feel it so necessary to be occasionally with someone *who thinks and feels as I do.*" I said, in reply—"Never fear Kate, it will all be right in God's good time; I see *that* in the distance, which will bring your mother to the knowledge and love of God, just as surely as I saw *you* last spring in 'my mind's eye' in the bosom of our holy church now."

Kate remained with me till it was almost dark, and then she left, promising to see me whenever she could spare the time. She intends calling on the Archbishop this morning, but I very much fear she will not see him, neither will he be able to confirm her before he leaves for Rome. After tea last evening, Papa became interested in conversation about sundry things of importance, and I felt it would not do to leave him even to write to you, consequently my darling child must forgive me for being behind time.

My visit with Papa to the mill yesterday was really one of great self-denial but you know it is *part of my religion* to gratify Papa in all his little whims and wishes; very likely if I had told Papa my *reason* for not going to the mill, he would at once have yielded his wish to have me with him but then you know it would have been a great disappointment to him and the disappointment had better fall on me than on Papa.

At St Ignatius Church yesterday morning at the 1/2 past 10 o'clock Mass a mission was commenced, conducted by Revd Father Smarius and Father Duncan. You can readily imagine it would have been very gratifying to me to have been at the opening, but as that satisfaction was denied me, I shall endeavour to attend the other exercises as often as I can. . . . I shall see or write Kate a note to attend in the morning; as it is expected the instruction will be most excellent. . . .

We laughed heartily over the fear you seem to have had that we intended to deprive you of the pleasure and satisfaction of being "a girl" for the last time at Distribution. Now my dear child you must "have grown a feet" if the measure you sent me for the length of your dress does not give you a train starting at Baltimore and stopping somewhere between this and St Joseph's! 38 inches by 44 ! My wildest ideas of a *train* will be more than gratified by those dimensions, but I shall make your dress by those measures *exactly* and then you will be obliged to sweep in the room leaving the rest of the ranks—feet behind you. I hope you will practice in the meantime the managing of your train, so that the *graceful girl* may not be unintentionally merged in the *awkward woman*.

We are so happy to know that Sister Genevieve is "really improving" and that she will come to see us when we go up to the Distribution—and the *last* Distribution too! till I take my grandchildren up to have the finishing touch put to their educations by Sister Raphael, who will occasionally intersperse her instructions with some kindly remembered trait or anecdote of their Mama's young days, not forgetting to mention with equal pleasure the words and doings of their dear Aunt Anna!! . . .

I rec'd another long letter from Charley, which really has astonished me. The dear child had been in retreat before Easter and his remarks about his views and his feelings were excellent, most excellent. God grant the dear boy may be all I wish him to be. . . .

Mrs McNeal, Ella and Vanity send love and respects to you. Papa and Thede also send love to you and the girls. . . .

> Good bye, love & kisses to Anna
> lovingly Mama. . . .

### Sunday, April 28, 1867

. . . *Mr Preston and I went down to Holliday St and there took the car, we reached the mill about half past ten and as it was cold we made fire, after which we began the inspection of the house and certainly I never saw cleaner cleaning in my life. It was thoroughly and perfectly done. Mr Preston seemed to be greatly pleased with my satisfaction. . . .*

### Thursday, May 2, 1867

. . . *I went over and went to Confession to one of the mission fathers. . . . I found him a delightful, kind & good confessor. After my Confession I spoke to the good Father about Thede and he told me to bring her over and introduce her to him and he would instruct her with pleasure. Of course I came over at once and begged Thede to go, but she declined. I shall from this time give up the hope of her becoming a Catholic. . . .*

# 18

# The Schoolgirls' Farewell

ALTHOUGH INTIMATIONS OF TENSIONS within the household were still surfacing in Madge's letters and diary entries throughout the spring, stray comments also suggest that all parties were trying to reduce the level of friction. Madge joined in the festive jaunts to the mill, putting on a semblance of enjoyment, even though she described these trips to May as a personal sacrifice. Preston tried once to smooth over Madge's anger at himself by setting the breakfast table—an action so extraordinary and unforeseen that Madge had to laugh. And Thede, with Catherine's help, did her best in cleaning out the house at the mill. Even Madge was pleased. Madge is of course silent about whatever annoyance she might have been to both Preston and Thede as a result of her efforts to arrange opportunities for their respective conversions. At last Thede made her objections unambiguous; the apparent finality of her refusal seems to have cleared the air, though later she may have had second thoughts.

With only two months now remaining till May and Anna would put aside their schoolgirl roles, Madge had plenty of special missions to carry out for the two graduates and pleasant conspiracies to share with the girls and with Sister Raphael. All would lead, they hoped, to a triumphant end.

---

**Sunday, May 5, 1867**

*. . . Kate & Mollie called to see me this afternoon to tell me Sr Raphael was in the city. . . . I went to the asylum and saw Sr Raphael & Sr Matilda. Sr R has given me the pleasant intelligence that May has written the "Farewell" and it is beautiful. She also asked me to purchase for Anna such articles for the Distribution as I would get for May. I shall therefore go out tomorrow and get them for Sr Raphael that she may take them up when she returns.*

**Monday, May 6, 1867**

*I rose at our usual hour and . . . prepared myself for my shopping expedition. I
went at once and bought Anna's dress, getting it the same as one I purchased
for May on Saturday. I then went up to see Mrs Parr & Kate; from them I went
half through the city looking for pretty ribbon for a sash for May & Anna. I
bought May's but I am not quite certain about Anna's. . . .*

Loyola Place
May 6th 1867

My darling children,

You can readily imagine what a pleasure I have enjoyed in being with dear
Sr Raphael. . . . Dear Sister, with a kindness that took me altogether by surprise, sat down and without waiting for me to ply her with questions, began at
once to tell me, what she knew would be the most interesting for me to know.
That was everything about my dear children, how they were looking, what
dear good children they had been during the year, how much they were beloved in consequence by Sisters as well as companions—how attentive and
industrious they had been in their studies. What *wonderful* and satisfactory
progress they had made—how *beautiful* the valedictories they had written,
and in consequence of all of the above, what *rewards* she had in store for
them, and how *elegant* she wanted them to look on "Distribution day."

Now comes the amusing part of our discourse, and that which made dear
Sr Matilda laugh quite heartily—Sister Raphael and I *discussing the fashions!*
"Well," said Sr Matilda, "I really did not know my country cousin was so well
informed in these worldly subjects!" It really was interesting to see dear Sister's
evident pleasure at the prospect of her "dear children" having everything of
the best and prettiest. You may be sure I seconded her in all her views—perhaps if the truth must be told—rather set the example of some little extrava-
gancies, which truth again bids me say found a ready and willing coadjutor in
dear Sister. Sister paid me the compliment of placing Anna's purse in my
hands and telling me to buy such articles for Anna as I intended to get for you.
So you may both look forward to having the prettiest toilets for the grand occasion in which you appear for the last time as "schoolgirls" that *my affection*
and *taste* can procure for you. I also purchased for Anna material for a dress; it
is the same as one I got for you but which I shall not have made till you return. Made up prettily for an evening dress, I think it will be lovely. I was out
all the morning making purchases or rather *looking up* such articles as I
needed, the sashes giving me most trouble; but I feel I have been amply repaid
by the beauty of those I got. With regard to ribbon for the hair, I rather

preferred watered ribbon which, if you think is not narrow enough, I will try and get other, by letting me know in your next letter. . . .

You are right my dear child in knowing I have been pleased with my opportunities of attending the mission at St Ignatius Church. The mission is still progressing, and I judge from the crowded house daily and nightly that it is doing much good. . . . I have also persuaded Thede to attend some of the instructions for those preparing for their first communion, and I send Catherine every night—poor Catherine also went to Confession on Saturday. . . . Papa went one night, by invitation from Father Clark, and sat with the Priests in their private gallery.

. . . Thede . . . sends her love to you. And Papa smiles and looks proud whenever anything clever is said about you and says, "Tell May, if I don't write it is not because I do not think constantly of her but you (meaning me) fill your letters so full there is no room for me to add a postscript. Give my love to her and Anna, and tell them I look forward to seeing them with great pleasure." If the weather is good, and there is the hope of being able to get enough to eat at the hotel in Emmitsburg this summer, I think we will have quite a pleasant party with us at Distribution. . . .

You see I have filled my sheet without telling you how . . . much I, and Papa also, have been pleased with your "French letter." To give you some idea of my estimation of it, I intend to take it to Father Clark, and let him see what my little girl is capable of doing. I can never cease to feel the warmest gratitude to the dear Sisters who by their judicious kindness and attentions made that study so pleasant and agreeable to you. . . .

And now goodnight my dear children; it is just striking twelve o'clock. lovingly

Mama and Aunty.

## Tuesday, May 7, 1867

*. . . After breakfast we all went out shopping. . . . I purchased the ribbons, laces &c &c for May & Anna, and took them up to Sr Raphael, who was really as much pleased with the finery as the girls will be themselves. It was quite gratifying to see her evident delight. I also took Sr Matilda a pound of cream crackers, which I think she will like. . . .*

## Monday, May 13, 1867

*. . . Miss Anne Loveday has promised to come tomorrow and cut and fix May's Distribution dress. I went to May prayers this evening. . . .*

St. Joseph's. May 12th 1867

My dear Mama,

How shall I thank you as I wish for all that you have done relative to our Distribution things, and for being so kind as to tell us the evident pleasure you have received from dear Sr. Raphael's kind remarks about us! Imagine how anxiously the whole house awaited Sister's return, and then think of our delight in greeting her and hearing the loving messages she bore from the friends of all the Baltimore girls. Dear Sister, though tired and exhausted with her day's journey, would not retire until she has showed Anna and I the extent of her and your shopping. I can only say that we were *delighted with everything.* It is particularly pleasant for me to say this for Anna as well as for myself. She was perfectly satisfied with all you had done, indeed so much so, that she intends writing to you herself on Friday, our letter day. Our sashes are perfectly beautiful! And we happy as larks at the fulfillment of our great desire to dress alike. Anna thinks her little handkerchief and fan lovely gloves and ruse "ditto." I feared very much when I saw my gaiters that they would be too small for me, so yesterday before I tried them on I said a fervent "Hail Mary" that they might fit for of all things I think these long delays and sending backwards and forwards of things before they suit is about the most disagreeable. But my prayer put an end to all that, for Cinderella like my shoe fit me perfectly. The corsets also. You need therefore feel no anxiety about them. Do you think I had better have my dress on as soon as I get it? We think the narrow watered ribbon the prettiest thing we could have for our hair, so you see dearest Mama, we "Valley girls" are not so wedded to our own opinions after all. . . . I hope everyone at home admires our sashes and other things as much as we do, and all here who have seen them. Our blue dress too have given the greatest satisfaction they particularly please us by being the same pattern for both. . . .

For the present I will only say that dear Sr. Raphael told me many pleasant things about you and my dear Papa. I am most happy to hear that all of you have been so much pleased with the Mission. . . . Tell Catherine how much your good news about her pleased me. . . .

Your children
Anna & May

**Tuesday, May 14, 1867**

. . . *I sent for Anne this morning and she came up and remained all day and we together have nearly finished May's dress. Much to my gratification Mr Preston went to the mill this morning and did not return till evening.* . . .

*before dusk I went to night prayers and on my return found Mr Preston &
Thede engaged in packing [May's] box.*

### Thursday, May 16, 1867

*. . . Mary came this morning and ironed the clothes she washed yesterday. I
made May's book muslin skirt[1] this morning and we think it looks very well.
Mr Preston came in about two o'clock today for the purpose of going to the mill
and being unusually amiable, I asked him to let me accompany him. Papa
seemed quite pleased, and off we went, returning about half past seven o'clock
having had a pleasant afternoon and the satisfaction of bringing in a bottle of
good milk. We were playing a game of cards when the bell rung and Mr Abell
& Mr Swain were announced, George Abell & Willie Swain.[2] Of course we
were most delighted to see them and they seemed pleased with their visit as they
stayed till after eleven o'clock.*

### Friday, May 17, 1867

*. . . I had quite an agreeable surprise today. A bundle was brought here from
Perkins directed to me, but I thought it was for Mrs Owens. It remained the
greater part of the day; at length I concluded to open it. When lo and behold! it
was a pattern for a dress for May of green silk which the Owens had presented
to May as a birthday gift together with a kind note to May. I shall send the
note to May, with mine and her father's long letter of 18 pages written in
rhyme for her birthday. Dear child, how happy she will be on Sunday when she
gets all these evidences of our love for her.*

Baltimore 19 May 1867

To Miss May Preston
on her eighteenth birthday

i

Of all the pleasures known to time
There are but few above
A rambling letter fram'd in rhyme,
Address'd to those we love.

ii

Therefore dear child in genial mood,
I seize my old goose quill,
And dip it in the inky flood
From old Parnassus' hill.

iii

Strange! that a stream, as Lethe dark
The cherish'd means should be
To keep alive the brilliant spark
Of life-long memory. . . .

---

Preston's verse went on for many stanzas in the same jog trot. Once again he recounted the scene at May's birth, followed her through childhood days with doll and hoop and then to her departure "For good St. Joseph's door." After compliments to the piety of May's teachers and to the excellence of his daughter's education, Preston brought the verse to a close with his little joke:

lii

And now farewell—I must have done
'Tis time to go to bed—
Line after line I've rambl'd on
And very little said—

liii

But said enough my daughter dear
To perfect my design,
Which was a *page for ev'ry year*
For *ev'ry month a line*—

liv

Good bye—God bless you—ev'ry friend
Remember your birth day—
And one and all, they kindly send
Their "love to little May"—

WM P. PRESTON

## Sunday, May 19, 1867

*A clear bright morning, for which I was very glad—rose early and went to six o'clock mass, and had the happiness of receiving our dear Lord in Holy Communion—returned, took breakfast and prepared the family to go to the country—Mr Preston, Theodosia, and Catherine all going. After they left, I cleaned and fixed up the house—and then sat down to write May a long letter—about her box—her birthday—Anna's dress and everything I thought interesting to the dear child. The day passed most pleasantly because I was alone. I went to Vespers and remained to make the six Sundays in honor of St Aloysius; from church I walked down to the asylum and spent an hour most pleasantly with the Sisters, who all told me they had remembered it was May's birthday. . . .*

---

Madge had earlier predicted that she, as Preston's substitute, would be called on to make the annual pilgrimage to Philadelphia to consult with Mrs. Simmons on the complicated business concerning her late husband's estate. On the day after May's birthday, Madge wrote from there.

Philadelphia
May 20th 1867

My dear Mr Preston:

After one of Mrs Simmon's generous slices of roast-beef and a cup of good warm tea, thoughtfully made by Sarah, I am glad to tell you I feel very much better than I did this morning when I left home. Our trip to Phila seemed shorter to me than usual and on my mentioning that to a lady sitting with me, she said it really was so—since the completion of the bridge across the Susquehanna and the travel on it, the time between the two cities was shortened at least three quarters of an hour, and *that* you know is considerable in this fast age of ours. Tell Thede, neither she nor I proved good physiognomists this morning, as we were both free in our remarks about the lady with the lunch basket, whom we thought looked cross at the gentleman who seated himself beside her. —The said lady was a Mrs Schriver of Westminster and proved an agreeable and acceptable companion during my trip to Phila—very ladylike and quite intelligent, notwithstanding, in our shortsightedness, we thought otherwise. . . .

After reaching the city I hastened up as quickly as possible to our little friends. . . .

You will perceive thus far I have not been able to settle business matters with Mrs Simmons—we . . . do those things *only when alone,* and the opportunity has not yet offered. Mrs Simmons expressed herself as greatly disappointed at not seeing you this time, but she says, as soon as you are sufficiently well to come on, you must do so, as the *executors want you.*

As it has brightened so nicely, I think I will go down this afternoon and see Aunt Eliza. Goodbye with love to Thede, who I hope reached home without getting wet. Affectionately yours

Madge

Baltimore 1/2 past 9 A.M.
21st May 1867

Dear Madge

I have just recd your letter of yesterday announcing your safe arrival at Mrs Simmons. . . . I am glad that you found Mrs S. and Willie as well as usual. I feel quite an interest in the boy and unless I am much mistaken he will make a good and useful man. I do not think he is *selfish*—which is the best security for his being naturally *innocent*. Selfishness is the parent of more vice than is generally ascribed to it. . . .

Have you read Booth's Diary?—I do not envy the feelings of the blood-thirsty miscreants who kept back that document on the so-called trial of the unfortunate Mrs Suratt. . . .[3]

With my love to you and kind regards to Mrs Simmons & Willie. . . .

Wm. P. Preston

Philadelphia May 22d 1867

My dear Mr Preston,

Having been looking anxiously all the morning for a letter from you, I am at last rewarded by receiving yours of yesterday morning kindly written by you before going into court. . . .

I managed . . . yesterday afternoon to run down between the showers to see dear Aunt Eliza. You would have been amused to have seen her look of surprise, nay, almost of consternation when she opened the door and saw *me* standing there. "Oh you dear child," she exclaimed, "I thought, from not receiving my usual birthday letter that you really must be sick or something very strange had happened to you. Why did you not write to me?" I replied, "I thought I would come myself this time instead of sending a letter!" "Oh yes I am glad to see you, but I was so much distressed about you." Here the dear good creature broke down and ended with a hearty cry. I, laughing in the meantime, and telling her it was the first time I ever heard of letters being more welcome than their writers. . . .

Goodbye dear Papa, do take good care of yourself—love to Thede and a sincere wish that she has not had a headache since I left home.

Affectionately
Madge

St. Joseph's May 20th /67

My dear Mrs Preston

Ever since my return I have been promising myself the pleasure of giving *my* version of my meeting with May & Annie & making you laugh at all their exclamations &c &c. . . . Since I returned May & Anna have passed an excellent examination in Schlegel's philosophy of history, they have accomplished their exams & they are now comparatively as light and as bright as birds.

—Everyone feels interested for them, & they are behaving so beautifully—this part of their schoolgirl life will be one of happy remembrance. —Now May's birth-day—On Saturday after the receipt of your letter I sent into town 3 or 4 times to enquire for the box, but not till *Monday* morning did it enter the village & it was immediately dispatched to us. However the receipt of her Father's beautiful letter dictated from Parnassus & under the auspices of the Sacred Nine,[4] made ample amends for the delay of the *material* part. . . .

May was delighted at the faithful & tender sketch that her father made of her brief span of eighteen years.

Shall I tell you, we had Mr. Preston's letter read aloud in our community room during our recreation.

You have my dear friends lavished much tender care on this dear child but I am happy to say it is not lost, she is deserving of it, & I believe would make any sacrifice to please you or respond to your desires in the smallest point. Of this I am certain. . . .

Mother, Sr Genny, *all*, all unite in love to you.

Yours sincerely
S. M. Raphael

Philadelphia
May 23d 1867

Dear Mr Preston,

Your hasty note of yesterday, enclosing Sister's welcome favour, was rec'd this morning just after breakfast, for which I thank you with all my heart for I know it must be quite a tax on you to send off even these few lines before you go to your ten o'clock duties. . . . Dear Sister's letter is satisfactory in as much as it assures us of the safe arrival, though somewhat tardy it is true, of the birthday box. . . . The *document* however *did* reach her in time, and I doubt not gave all the pleasure that you wished it to give. You see I was not mistaken when I predicted "its being read in the Community room." Now you may not understand exactly as well as I do, how great an honor *that* is—nothing but what is considered of real merit, and containing the purest and best of sentiments and principles, ever finds its way into that hallowed place. The dear Sisters! I can just see what a pleasure the reading of that little domestic poem must have given them. . . .

Dear Papa, you will think me the most vacillating of all creatures when I tell you I shall *not* be home till Saturday afternoon. Mrs Simmons says, "*Dere is no use, Mr Preston don't expect you home before the last of the week, just write to him and say I won't let you go.*" So, hoping that it fills you and Thede with inexpressible grief that I do not come tomorrow, and love to Thede & Catherine, I am yours truly & affectionately

Madge . . .

### Saturday, May 25, 1867

*. . . Mr Preston handed me a letter from May, written in rhyme, in response to his "big letter" on her birthday. I think Papa will have to look to his laurels or May will win them from him. Her letter is* excellent![5] *. . .*

### Monday, May 27, 1867

*Clear beautiful day, and I took advantage of it to have my room cleaned up, Catherine swept and dusted very nicely though she was nearly all day at it. I cut out a linen body for May this morning and also a pair of linen drawers. . . . After tea Mr Preston went down to the Daughertys' and remained there till after 12 o'clock, making me quite uneasy about him.*

### Tuesday, May 28, 1867

*. . . After breakfast I went to the depot to see Sr Matilda off to St Joseph's, and sent a packet containing 2 white bodies and a little apron, also a bottle of lotion for rheumatism to Sr Genevieve. . . . I then . . . went to church and before coming home I called on Father Early and gave him 10$ as my contribution to the new sacharista they design to build. . . .*

### Sunday, June 2, 1867

*I rose early and went to six o'clock Mass and rec'd Holy Communion; on returning home, I found things all gone wrong—Thede angry and Catherine just returned from church, where she had gone without doing any of the morning work. On remonstrating with her, she got into one of her ugly spells and became so nervous and miserable that when she brought up the hot water she let the pan fall and the water going on her foot scalded it fearfully. Of course there was quite an unpleasant scene, Mr Preston plaguey, and in the midst of it poor Catherine had to suffer. . . .*

Loyola Place
June 2d 1867

Dear child

Having written a long letter to Mrs Bateman and just closed it I fear it leaves me but little time to devote to you. . . . In your little slip "to Mama," you ask me to send you a tassel for Papa's cap—now darling do you want a black tassel or a yellow one? as you have not specified the color I suppose *any* thing I send would be acceptable! . . . I have not the slightest idea in what colors you have worked your cap, consequently can form no idea of what would be appropriate, would either a gold or silver tassel suit, or would white silk be better?—In your next if you want any particular color of silk, send me a specimen and I can have one made of any color or of any size, only specify what you want.[6] . . .

The other day, when we were to have our May Procession at St Ignatius Church—the clouds gathered up in the afternoon and the wind rose—and altogether it seemed we were going to have a fearful storm—but a few drops, scarcely more than enough to moisten the ground, fell, just as the children were leaving the college. You can't imagine anything more beautiful than it was—little girls ranging from about five or six to young ladies—boys of the same size and ages. The girls of course were robed in white with blue or white sashes, and the larger ones all with veils, wreaths of flowers on their heads and wreaths, bouquets & baskets of flowers in their hands—which they carried as offerings to our Blessed Mother, and which were rec'd by Father Foley at the altar, who delivered a beautiful and appropriate address to the children on the occasion. This is the only church in the city where they have these processions and as they are somewhat of a novelty, of course they attract considerable attention. Owing to the threatening aspect of the weather, the procession only went as far as Monument Street on the side of the college—then crossed over and came up on our side as far as Madison Street, crossed over again, entered the church and then made the circuit of the church, after which they presented their offerings and when all were laid on the altar, it was literally covered. Father Foley then addressed the children; at the close the priests chanted a hymn to the blessed Virgin, and Father Foley gave the Benediction of the Blessed Sacrament and then they all formed in ranks again and singing the Litany of the Blessed Virgin they walked out of the church to the college and thus it ended. Of course you know this took place on the evening of Ascension Day. . . .

I am so pleased to know dear Sr Genevieve is well enough to go over to her old quarters. I can never think of Sister with half the satisfaction any other place than in her own little corner looking over the church and waiting for Our Lord to call her there. Remember me always lovingly to her. Only think, my child, scarcely more than three weeks and I shall be with you and then a few days and you will be home again. I fear now the time is approaching for you to leave your dear old home, you will just begin to realize how *very* sad a thing it is. I am sorry to tell you that dear Papa is, and has been, suffering dreadfully with the worst cold I have ever known him to have; for several days the pain seems to have concentrated itself over the left eye and causes him great suffering. . . . I send you his love and also Theodosia's. . . .

Dear Kate came up the eve before Ascension Day to tell me she had just come from Confession to Father Foley and hoped to receive Holy Communion on the following morning—dear Kate! You do not know what a self-sacrificing child she is—and so sweet and good.

Good night lovingly
Mama

## Monday, June 3, 1867

*This morning Thede & I made a very important move in our house arrangements; we put the sewing machine in the storeroom and design making that the sewing room in future. We think it a great improvement as it will enable us to leave our work each day without the trouble of fixing it up at night.*[7]

## Thursday, June 6, 1867

*. . . I returned [from church] and found Catherine so poorly that I was obliged to put her to bed and attend to her foot, which has become fearfully swollen and is very painful; poor thing I do pity her so much. . . .*

## Friday, June 7, 1867

*. . . This morning I went up to market & was obliged to ask Martha, the colored girl living next door, to go with me, which she did cheerfully. I purchased 8 qts of strawberries and on my return Thede and I picked them and pressed them, making three jars of preserves, which seem to be very nice. Mary (O'Brian) came over from church this afternoon and has promised to come and wash next week. . . .*

St. Joseph's. June 5th 1867

A happy birthday to my dearest Mama.

And now it is my turn, my beloved Mama, to write a birthday letter, wishing you all the happiness that a daughter can desire for her devoted Mother. But how is the pleasure of performing so sweet a duty enhanced when I think (at least I hope) that this is the last time I will be absent from you on your birthday! Dear Mama, next year I can give you a birthday kiss in place of a letter. Now if my letters were beautiful ones like dear Papa's, I might almost wish that, for a part of that day, we might not be together, so that you could have the pleasure of receiving such a delightful package. . . . How much I have to say to you, my dearest Mother! How many thanks to offer for a thousand acts of kindness from you in this year alone! The older I grow the more forcibly do I feel all that you have ever done for me; meanwhile my debt of gratitude is increasing and I do not know that I find myself more capable of repaying it. Before I began to write I thought of a dozen particular things that you had done, and which as they had made me particularly happy I wished to mention, and now I feel as if I can only say Mama! dear Mama! and then leave you to understand the rest. Have you ever felt so much that you could say nothing? . . .

But do not flatter yourself, my dear Mama . . . that I am not as great a talker as ever; no indeed, in three weeks you will find out (I fear to your sorrow) that "the little member" is as active as formerly and that one more year of school chatter instead of blunting said instrument has on the contrary sharpened it. Yes those three weeks—they are all the subject of our conversations now. It is such a consolation for me to think that my Mother can sympathize with me when I speak of leaving our dear, dear St. Joseph's. Those girls whose parents do not feel as mine do, with regard to their attachment to the dear old place and its inmates, must experience very different emotions from such as myself, who know that every word they say on this subject strikes a corresponsive chord in the hearts of their father and mother.

Dear Sr. Raphael just now came in to the library where I am writing to send you a message, which when you understand the import of it will make you heartily wish the same thing. She said, "Tell your Mama I wish she were here to take supper at the grotto with us this evening." You know the entire month of May was so rainy that we were not able to have our supper as usual in the grounds; today being thought dry enough for us to enjoy that pleasure, the whole house has turned out en masse, and I am now the only one, with the exception of three or four Sisters, and two girls in the infirmary (the latter are to go down in a wagon after while, I believe, so that they will be in the frolic too) in the house. Do not be distressed at that, dear Mama, I am much happier writing to you than doing anything else, and then when I finish I will join the rest. . . .

How is my dear Papa now. I feel so anxious about the bad cold with which he has been suffering. . . . Tell Papa that his letter, or rather *my letter*, for I like to call it all mine, has been and still is going the rounds, every where exciting universal admiration. I was not able to go to confession today dear Mama for your birthday. . . . I went on Sunday and fearing that something would prevent my doing so today, I offered my Communion then, that God would bestow his choicest blessings on the best and loveliest of Mothers, your own sweet self.

Love to my dear Papa, Cousin Thede, my Sister and to all kind friends

Your devoted and grateful little May.

St. Joseph's June 7th /67

My dear Mrs Preston

I write . . . to deliver a message from our good Father Burlando to Mr. Preston & you will please to be the medium—Father desires me to say that he expects Mr Preston to be his guest at the Distribution without any further formality. It was an idea so established in his mind, that he imagined we would all of us understand it—so now while we hold you captive pro tem, he will be in durance with our Father. . . .

Yours—
S.M. Raphael

**Monday, June 10, 1867**

*. . . Catherine is getting much better and is able to be about again; she helped me pack up some winter clothes, and I have trimmed May's body with the lace. . . .*

St. Joseph's. June 8th 1867.

My dear Mama and Papa,

Would you like to hear some of the doings of the birds in the orange grove? Anna and I are so delighted with the pretty poetical name dear Sr. Raphael has given us that we do not intend to lay it aside in a hurry. You remember when I last wrote I told you we were to spend the evening at the grotto; well when I finished my letter to you, dear Mama, I *titivated* a little bit and then went down with the rest of the girls. Just imagine what a pretty sight they must have presented. They were all coming up to the verandas to get their supper (we take it quite early on such evenings as that) and choosing shady places, where they sat in groups to eat it. "Our Lady of the Grotto" is over on the hill above the lake, and lately we have had two new verandas made in place of the old one. One was occupied by the older Sisters, and the other by those who have charge of us, and by the girls. The table in the summer house was filled with baskets of cakes, rolls and biscuits, jars of preserves and plates of ham, while outside several of the Sisters, ladle in hand, were giving out hot tea and coffee from the large buckets in which it had been brought down. As each one got her supper on her tin plate, she joined the crowd that had collected round the Sister who had the preserves like a swarm of young flies (do pardon the comparison), and then taking a large tin cup went for her share of tea or coffee. The large blocks of wood that the carpenters had left after their work were very useful as chairs and tables, and in a little while the recipients of the good cheer were doing it ample justice. As for Anna and me we had the honor of being placed between Father Burlando and Sr. Raphael. . . . After supper we went off again to walk about and enjoy the cool of the evening, until the signal for us to return to the limits of the yard. Anna and I had ever so much fun playing pastorals, for as we have been reading Virgil's Eclogues lately, we constantly take now, in our "make-believes," the characters of rustics. We are both very fond of clover blossom wreaths and that evening we made very pretty ones. . . .

What a pleasure you must derive, my dear Papa and Mama, from dear Sr. Raphael's letters! I think it is so kind of her to take every opportunity to write to you and tell you such kind things about your children. . . .

Lovingly and expectingly your little May

### Sunday, June 16, 1867

. . . *This morning I gave Catherine permission to go to church and to remain till half past two o'clock. Just after she left, Kate Parr came in, and remained till near three o'clock; during the time she was here we had a nice lunch of strawberries &c &c. Kate made me quite sad by telling me that Mollie Bank had been clandestinely married on last Monday. Of course the family & friends are greatly distressed. . . .*

### Monday, June 17, 1867

. . . *I went to church; after that I went down the street to a mattress maker and told the man to come up and take mine away, which he did and promised to return it by Thursday evening. I then went to Mrs Wendhall and got her to retrim May's little hat with green ribbon, which I think is better for the summer than the brown velvet. . . .*

### Thursday, June 20, 1867

. . . *This afternoon I went down the city—and sold my gold duck for $11.25 cts. With some of this I purchased two prayer books, one for May & one for Anna to be given to them the day they graduate. . . .*

## Friday, June 21, 1867

. . . *After breakfast I went to church and returned home and set to work fixing up the altar, packing my trunk, and making sugar cakes for May. Mrs McCoy and Kate Parr called this morning to see about going to St Joseph's. I went out this afternoon & purchased a little present for May to give Sr Raphael. . . . I am going to St Joseph's in the morning and God willing I shall be with May to-morrow night. . . .*

## Saturday, June 22, 1867

*This has been a glorious day & we have enjoyed it greatly. I rose early & went to church heard Mass & rec'd Holy Communion, returned, took breakfast and dear Thede & Papa interested themselves so kindly to get me off in the car all comfortably & pleasantly. We found Kate there and . . . were on our way to St Joseph's rejoicing. We reached Gettysburg all right & Dr Tate brought us over to St Joseph's in an omnibus; we reached here about five o'clock, and [I] soon found myself in the arms of my darling little child. May does not seem to me to be looking well, but then she has done so well that I can think of nothing else. Sister Raphael & Sr Domitius met me with great kindness & soon made me feel at home. I miss Sr Genevieve but Sr Domitius takes her place very cleverly. Kate & I occupy the [illegible] room and May sleeps in the dormitory.*

## Monday, June 24, 1867

*This has been a day of rain but we hope the clouds will exhaust themselves and the two following days may be clear. I have spent a most happy day. Most of the Sisters with whom I am acquainted have called over to see me, and I have had the satisfaction of seeing the drawing room arranged for exhibition. The work of the girls is really beautiful and I have been much gratified to find that May has done some few articles—a smoking cap for her father and a pair of slippers for Mr Hopkins and a pair for me together with a box and watch stand for Papa. Kate & I have had the privilege of going in ranks with the girls to Mass, she & I heading them.*

## Tuesday, June 25, 1867

*Another day of rain. Indeed it has rained incessantly all day. It is to be regret-ted in as much as most of the children's parents & relatives are expected today. Mr Preston & Thede are to leave Baltimore today, and I suppose have done so. . . . I have spent a delightful day—enjoying privileges rarely awarded to strangers in this house. The "girls" were taken to the Distribution room today and drilled in their performances, and I was allowed to witness the whole of it. I have also had a pleasant interview with dear Sr Genevieve and most of my other Sisters during the day.*

### Wednesday, June 26, 1867

*The cloudy weather still continues, but notwithstanding, a good many strangers have been here. Mr Preston came early this morning, and was delighted at seeing May & all the Sisters. We have just heard that the Rev'd Mr Northrop, Anna's brother, will not be here on Thursday. Of course it is a great disappointment to the dear child. Aunt Louisa and Thede were also here and were greatly delighted with the exhibition in the drawing room, as were also Judge Alexander, who very kindly came up to witness May receive her honor. The Judge seems much pleased with all he has seen.*

### Thursday, June 27, 1867

*The clouds still hang around the mountains and spread over the valley but everything is cheerful & pleasant at St Joseph's for this is the great day of Distribution. At an early hour we rose and prepared ourselves to attend Mass, but owing to certain causes we were not able to go. After breakfast the "girls" came to the Infirmary to dress; we had arranged their "finery" the night before and everything was in order for them. Consequently we soon had them dressed and they really looked very sweetly. Kate & I then dressed ourselves and went to the parlour and from there to the Distribution room, where we were soon seated amidst a number of friends. The exercises of the day began and May & Anna rec'd their honors amidst the plaudits of the audience. Papa was much affected, but I felt cool & collected to a very singular degree. The whole of the ceremonies passed off beautifully. After they were over, most everyone came up and congratulated me and Mr Preston upon May's success. We remained a good while in the study room talking &c &c, after which the "girls" were sent over to Sr Genevieve & the dear Sisters over there; they had a delightful visit, but alas! on May's return, she came to the Infirmary and I was obliged to undress her & put her to bed with one of her fearful sick headaches, where she has remained all the rest of the day. Papa & the Judge, together with Aunt Louisa & Thede were over the greater part of the day, walking round the grounds & the green yard, and admiring everything. They then left us, to remain in town all night, and start [for] the city in the morning. May is better this evening, but will sleep in my room.*

## Friday, June 28, 1867

*Well this is to be my last day at St Joseph's and May's also; poor child, how I feel for her. We have spent the afternoon walking round the grounds and taking the last look at dear old familiar scenes, and saying goodbye to the Sisters. . . . Tho' the evening has been spent pleasantly, I as well as May have felt very sad—knowing it was our last night. . . .*

## Saturday, June 29, 1867

*Another lovely day, and though disappointed in not getting off from St Joseph's, I am only too happy in being here over Sunday. May is as much pleased of course as I am and the dear Sisters as well as Mother try to make me feel comfortable in still remaining a guest at St Joseph's. . . .*

## Sunday, June 30, 1867

*The weather still continues fine, and the day has been spent charmingly. We rose at a rather late hour, and did not go to Mass till eight o'clock. . . . We have . . . made arrangements to leave tomorrow and the evening has been devoted to saying goodbye to Sisters and girls. Farewell, dear St Joseph's. Farewell, I hope not forever!*

# Afterword

May and Madge took an extended trip to Europe together in 1868 and 1869, traveling through Germany and Italy. At some time after her return, Madge copied into a bound volume all the letters she had written home from her trip abroad. This volume is in the Rare Books Room of the Milton Eisenhower Library at Johns Hopkins University. It is pleasant to speculate that this may have been Madge's personal gift to their elderly friend, the founder of the university. The inference, however, cannot be proved since no list remains of the books in the private collection of Johns Hopkins. The volume, according to library records, was donated anonymously.

May married "Vanity," Joshua Vansant McNeal, and they had four children—a daughter, Stella, who never married; a son, Mark, who became a Jesuit priest and died in the Philippines, where he was a missionary; a son, J. Preston W., who died in Harford County in 1954; and a daughter, Marie, whose husband, Renato Tittoni, was for some time foreign correspondent in Washington, D.C., for an Italian newspaper. Another daughter died in infancy. The Tittonis' twenty-six-year-old son, Tommaso Preston Tittoni, was buried in the McNeal-Preston plot in 1937 in Baltimore's Greenmount Cemetery. I have been unable to trace further any of these descendants. Stella died in 1965, when the family home was sold and its contents, including the personal papers, were sold at an auction.

Madge and William Preston lived separately throughout most of the decade of the 1870s. In failing health—and apparently considerable mental deterioration—he stayed at the mill property he had bought when the family moved into the city. Madge's niece Theodosia cared for him there till his death in 1880. Madge remained in the city, trying to cope with a financial reversal brought on after Preston co-signed a loan for a casual acquaintance who later defaulted. Preston, forced to sell most of his properties to pay off this debt, asked for and received assistance from Baltimore philanthropist Enoch Pratt, who bought the properties. In 1878, two years before his death, Preston became a Catholic.

Van McNeal was employed for most of his life by the Baltimore & Ohio Railroad, of which he was treasurer at the time of his retirement in 1916. He

was then a widower, May having died in 1913. In the first years of their marriage the McNeals lived in Indianapolis.

Madge lived alone, with a succession of maids, till she sold the Calvert
Street home around 1888. During her final years (she died in 1895), she lived
with the McNeals.

# Location of Documents

The family papers of the William P. Preston family are primarily divided between two repositories—the Historical Manuscripts and Archives Section of McKeldin Library, University of Maryland, College Park, and the Manuscripts Collection of the Maryland Historical Society, 201 W. Monument Street, Baltimore. One bound volume, a fair copy of Madge Preston's letters from a trip to Europe in 1868–69, is held in the Rare Book Room of the Milton Eisenhower Library, Johns Hopkins University, Baltimore. Another volume, a copy of Madge Preston's business correspondence of 1888, is in private hands. The collections include some of William P. Preston's papers from his law practice, his youthful correspondence, exchanges of letters among members of the family and friends, account books, memorabilia, and fourteen volumes of Madge Preston's diaries, written between 1860 and 1893.

The Maryland Historical Society also owns a few photographs from the Preston estate. One tiny picture of a woman (about half an inch square), unlabeled, is probably May. Two photographs depict William Preston in his role as lawyer; but apparently no photographs remain of Madge.

The locations of documents reproduced in this book or referred to are as follows:

## Manuscripts Division, Maryland Historical Society

### DIARIES

| | | |
|---|---|---|
| Ms. 1861 | Madge Preston | 1862, 1863, 1864 |
| Ms. 978 | William P. Preston | 1860 |
| Ms. 978 | May Preston | 1865 |

## CORRESPONDENCE MS. 978

*Madge Preston to May Preston*
  1863—Aug. 23
  1864—Mar. 28; Apr. 8, 10, 22
  1865—ca. Feb. 20; Nov. 14, 21; Dec. 17, 21, 22
  1866—Jan. 2; Feb. 16, 22; Mar. 11, 19; Apr. 6, 24; May 17, 27, ca. 29; June 4;
       Oct. 4, ca. 11
  1867—Feb. 11, 18, 19; Mar. 3, 10; May 6

*May Preston to Madge Preston*
  1863—Apr. /?/ 13
  1865—Feb. 13; ca. Apr. 26; June 14; Oct. 22
  1867—Feb. 6, 15; Mar. 19; Apr. 5, 17, 25; May 1, 12, 30; June 5, 8

*Madge Preston to William P. Preston*
  1863—Apr. 25
  1865—ca. Jan. 26; June 30
  1866—Mar. 26; July 2, 3, 4; Nov. 22

*William P. Preston to Madge Preston*
  1863—Apr. 22; Sept. 25; undated note concerning the making of whiskey
  1865—July 23, 25; Aug. 1; Nov. 2
  1866—July 2
  1867—May 21

*William P. Preston to May Preston*
  1865—May 19
  1867—May 19

*May Preston to William P. Preston*
  1867—Jan. 20

*Sister Raphael to Madge Preston*
  1866—Feb. 16; May 28, 29; Oct. 10
  1867—Feb. 10

*May Preston to Kitty Mason*
  1865—Jan. 19

## University of Maryland

## DIARIES

Madge Preston      1860, 1865, 1867

# CORRESPONDENCE

*Madge Preston to May Preston*
　　1862—Sept. 20, 26; Oct. 5, 10, 30; Nov. 6, 13, 17, 29; Dec. 3, 9
　　1863—Jan. 9, 14, 19, 23, 27, 30; Feb. 3, 4, 9, 13, 19; Mar. 10, 13, 18; Apr. 3,
　　　　13; May 10, 26, 31; June 6; Oct. 11
　　1864—Jan. 1, 8, 10, 24; Feb. 4, 11; ca. Mar. 1; Apr. 29; May 1, 8, 15, 16[?], 19,
　　　　30; June 5; Oct. 17, 24; Nov. 1, 16, 25; Dec. 8, 18
　　1865—Jan. 10, 23, 26; Feb. 9, 16; Mar. 6, 12, 26; Apr. 24, 28; May 7, 29; June
　　　　8, 12, 16, 21; Sept. 11, 17, 25; Oct. 1, 13, 31; Dec. 28
　　1866—Jan. 5, 12; Feb. 1, 3, 5; Apr. 18; May 3; June 11; Aug. 4; Oct. 23, 28;
　　　　Nov. 1, 9, 18, 26; Dec. 2, 10, 17, 20, 26, 28
　　1867—Jan. 1, 7, 13, 20; Feb. 26; Mar. 17, 24; Apr. 5, 11, 15, 19, 28; June 2

*May Preston to Madge Preston*
　　1862—Sept. 30; Oct. 3; Nov. 7; ca. Dec. 3
　　1863—Jan. 13, 30
　　1864—Jan. 30; May 6
　　1865—Mar. 30; May 5; Oct. 15
　　1866—Jan. 30; Feb. 2, 24; June 1

*Madge Preston to William P. Preston*
　　1864—Aug. 10
　　1865—Nov. 3
　　1867—May 20, 22, 23, 24

*William P. Preston to Madge Preston*
　　1862—Dec. 30
　　1863—Feb. 2
　　1865—Feb. 15; July 26, 27; Aug. 2
　　1866—July 4

*William P. Preston to May Preston*
　　1862—Dec. 22
　　1863—Dec. 25 (continued on Jan. 3, 1864; May 19, 1864)
　　1866—Mar. 27; May 19

*William P. Preston—A letter from battlefield of Gettysburg, July 7, 1863*

*Sister Raphael to Madge Preston*
　　1862—Nov. 5, 20
　　1863—Feb. 2
　　1866—Feb. 24
　　1867—May 20; June 7

*Mollie Sanders to Madge Preston*
　　1864—Jan. 30

# List of Characters

Abell, A. S. Publisher and founder of the *Baltimore Sun*. Close friend of William P. Preston.

Abell, Charley. Son of A. S. Abell. Student at Mount St. Mary's.

Abell, Mary. Daughter of A. S. Abell. Student at St. Joseph's.

Abell, Ned. Son of A. S. Abell.

Abell, Rose. Daughter of A. S. Abell.

Abell, Walter. Son of A. S. Abell. Student at Mount St. Mary's.

Adolphus. See Schaeffer.

Alexander, Judge. Baltimore official and friend of Prestons.

Alice. See Stansbury.

Alice, Aunt. Wife of Uncle Jim Henry, black employee.

Ann Scholastica, Sister. Staff member at St. Joseph's.

Ann Simeon. Mother Superior at St. Joseph's.

Anna. See Northrop.

Archbishop. See Spalding.

Aunty. See Carlon.

Bartlett, Mr. Acquaintance and houseguest of Prestons, probably a lawyer.

Bateman, Kate. Internationally acclaimed actress, first starring as a child in a European tour with Barnum. At age seventeen (in 1860) she starred in New York as Evangeline. Friend of Prestons.

Bateman, Mr. and Mrs. Kate Bateman's parents. Residents of Brooklyn, New York.

Beer, Louis. Son of Preston's housekeeper of Baltimore townhouse.

Beer, Mrs. German immigrant housekeeper.

Blenkinsop. See Sister Euphemia.

Bruce, Miss. See Thompson.

Burlando, Father Francis. Chaplain at St. Joseph's.

Caleb. See Taylor.

Camilla, Sister. Business manager at St. Joseph's.

Carlon, Aunty. Madge Preston's closest friend. Resident of Baltimore.

Carman, Mrs. Rachael. Member of the Stansbury establishment at Eudowood, the farm neighboring Pleasant Plains.

"Castle." Nickname for an unidentified young man, apparent suitor for May.

Christie. Hired man at Pleasant Plains.

Christie. See Monks.

Catherine. Servant to Prestons.

Clark, Father. Staff member at Loyola College, Baltimore.

Codori, George. Madge Preston's nephew by marriage, married to Louisa
Smith's daughter Josephine.

Codori, Josephine. Louisa Smith's oldest daughter.

Crick. See Smith.

Delia. See Owens.

Dielman, Dr. Henry. Musician and music teacher at Mount St. Mary's and
St. Joseph's. Recipient of first honorary doctorate from Georgetown University.

Domitius, Sister. Replacement for Sister Genevieve at St. Joseph's Infirmary.

Eliza, Aunt (Mrs. Meigs). Madge's Philadelphia relative.

Ensor, John T. State's attorney, prosecutor in Mount Hope case.

Eudocia. See Stansbury.

Euphemia, Sister (later Mother Superior at St. Joseph's). Also known as Mary
Blenkinsop, defendant in Mount Hope case.

Faber, Mr. and Mrs. Tenants at Preston's mill property.

Foley, Father. Close counselor to Madge Preston.

Gandolfo, Father Hippolitus. Assistant to Father Burlando.

Genevieve, Sister. In charge of Infirmary at St. Joseph's.

George. See Codori.

Georgy (Georgiana). Servant at Fayette Street house under Mrs. Beer.

Gilmor, Col. Harry. Confederate officer; Baltimore native.

Gittings, Mr. Baltimore attorney, colleague of Preston in Mount Hope case.

Giustiniana, Father. Staff member at St. Ignatius Church, Baltimore; originally at St. Joseph's.

Goldsborough, Major. Baltimore friend.

Greppo, Ellen and Mr. Greppo. The former Ellen Bateman, famous child
actress. Brooklyn friends of Prestons.

Grindle, Mary Elizabeth. Daughter or wife of Mr. Grindle, a Catholic
friend.

Hamilton. See Smith.

Harriet, Aunt. Hired cook for Prestons, a black woman.

Hartman, Isaac. Childhood friend of Madge Preston, prospector in California.

Hillen. See Sanders.

Hillen, Col. and Mrs. Wealthy neighbors of Prestons near Pleasant Plains.

Hood, Mr. and Mrs. Business associates of Preston in Philadelphia.

Hopkins, Miss Hannah. Sister of Johns Hopkins.

Hopkins, Johns. Baltimore philanthropist.

Jim, Uncle (surname Henry). Former slave of Patrick Henry, hired by Prestons after Emancipation.

John. Hired man at Pleasant Plains, probably Kaniff.

John or Johnny. Orphan boy. See Mathews.

Johnny. See Stansbury.

Kaniff (or Caniff), John. Hired man at Pleasant Plains.

Kitty (Mason). As a three-year-old, given as a slave to six-year-old May Preston.

Lelia (Duffell). Young student at St. Joseph's.

Lizzie (Johnson). Preston servant, a free black. Listed on 1860 census as thirty years old, a mulatto born in Maryland.

Louis. See Beer.

Louisa. See Smith.

Louisa, Sister. Assigned in Baltimore with Sister Leopoldine. Former classmate of Madge Preston's at St. Joseph's.

Louise. See McN____.

Lyman. Father. Priest at church in Govanstown, Baltimore County, near Towson.

Leopoldine, Sister. May's favorite among staff at St. Joseph's, later transferred to Baltimore.

Mamie. See Stansbury.

Martin, Dr. Homeopathic physician.

Mathews, John. Orphan boy taken in by Prestons, in charge of dairy.

Matilda, Sister. Probably witness in Mount Hope case. Staff member at St. Joseph's.

McGrew, Louisa. Louisa Smith's daughter, niece of Madge Preston.

NcN____, Louise. Somewhat mysterious visitor.

McNeal, Ella. Joshua Vansant McNeal's sister.

McNeal, Mrs. Joshua Vansant's mother, a prominent Catholic in Baltimore.

McNeal, Joshua Vansant ("Vanity"). May's suitor, eventually her husband.

Monks, Christie. Neighbor from Union Hall, Stansbury estate, near Pleasant Plains.

Mother Superior (at St. Joseph's). See Ann Simeon.

Mulgrew. See McGrew.

Nancy, Aunt. Former slave of Prestons.

Newberger, Mrs. Laundress and housecleaner, day laborer hired for heavy work.

Northrop, Anna. May's closest friend at St. Joseph's, from prominent Charleston, South Carolina, family. An orphan.

O'Brian, Mary. Laundress in Baltimore.
Owens, Delia. Daughter of John E. Owens.
Owens, John E. Internationally known actor, famous comedian. Neighbor of Prestons near Pleasant Plains on estate called Aigburth Vale.
Owens, Mrs. John E. Wife of the actor and close friend of Madge Preston.
Parr, Mr. Baltimore leader.
Parr, Mrs. Mother of Kate Parr, student at St. Joseph's.
Parr, Kate. Student at St. Joseph's and Catholic convert.
Patterson, Dr. Physician at St. Joseph's.
Pauline. See Stump.
Pent, Mrs. Clementine (or Pentz). German housekeeper for Prestons.
Pent, William. General handyman at Pleasant Plains.
Potee, Mr. Farm manager for Mrs. Eudocia Stansbury.
Raphael, Sister. Principal of St. Joseph's Academy, Emmitsburg.
Rachael. See Carman.
Roder, Adolph. Farm tenant.
Roder family, tenants at Prestons' Glen May property.
Rogers, Alexander H. Prosecuting attorney in Mount Hope case.
Russell, Captain George W. Captain of passenger ship *Louisiana*.
Russell, Judge (and Mrs.). Former member of Confederate Congress.
Ruthy. See Sheridan.
Sanders, Mr. and Mrs. Beverley. Baltimore friends, parents of Mollie and Jeannette, May's schoolgirl friends.
Sanders, Hillen. Older brother of Mollie and Jeannette.
Sanders, Jeannette. Schoolgirl friend of May Preston.
Sanders, Matilda. Black servant of Prestons, wife of "Skipp" Sanders.
Sanders, Mollie. Schoolgirl friend of May Preston.
Sanders, Nettie. Older sister of Mollie and Jeannette.
Sanders, Skipp. Husband of Prestons' black servant Matilda.
Schaeffer, Adolphus. Son of seamstress.
Schaeffer, Mrs. Hired seamstress.
Scharf, Mr. Tenant at Pleasant Plains after Prestons' move to Baltimore.
Sheridan, Emily. Black cook, former employee who was rehired.
Sheridan, Millie. Emily's child.
Sheridan, Ruth. Emily's youngest child.
Simmons, Charley. Son of Philadelphia friend and former business partner.
Simmons, Mrs. Widow of Azariah Simmons, for whose estate Preston was executor. Resident of Philadelphia and close friend.
Simmons, Willie. Son of Mrs. Simmons in Philadelphia.
Simon. See Codori.
Smith, Anne. Madge's niece.

Smith, Crichton ("Crick"). Son of Dr. Joseph and Louisa Smith, Madge's nephew.

Smith, Hamilton. Son of Madge's brother. Killed in railroad accident.

Smith, Dr. Joseph. Country doctor near Bendersville, Pennsylvania.

Smith, Louisa. Madge Preston's older sister, often called Aunt Louisa.

Smith, Rose. Niece of Madge Preston, daughter of Louisa.

Smith, Theodosia. Niece of Madge Preston, daughter of Louisa.

Smith, Thomasene. Widow of Hamilton Smith.

Sophia. Laundress.

Spalding, Martin John. Archbishop of Catholic church. Based in Baltimore.

Stansbury, Alice. Childhood friend of May Preston, next door neighbor, daughter of William Stansbury.

Stansbury, Eudocia. Widow. Owner of Eudowood, next door neighbor, north of Pleasant Plains.

Stansbury, John. Son of Eudocia Stansbury.

Stansbury, Mary Elizabeth (or Mamie). Daughter of William Stansbury, childhood friend of May Preston.

Stansbury, William. Prosperous farmer, owner of Union Hall. Great grandson of a German count who received extensive land holdings from Lord Baltimore.

Stansbury, Mrs. William. Neighbor at Union Hall. Former Christiana Taylor.

Stansbury, Willie. Son of William Stansbury.

Stephans, Clara. Former housekeeper for Prestons at Pleasant Plains.

Stevens, Mrs. Mother of Mrs. John Owens.

Stewart (or Stuart). Husband of Sanders' daughter Nettie.

Stokes, Dr. William. Physician at Mount Hope Insane Asylum.

Stout, Emmanuel. Young son of Delaware friend.

Stout, Mrs. Friend in Dover, Delaware.

Stuart, J. E. B. Confederate general.

Stuart, Nettie. Married sister of Jeannette and Mollie Sanders.

Stump, Judge. Close friend of Preston.

Stump, Pauline Coffin. Former student at St. Joseph's, daughter of Judge Stump.

Stuntz, Mrs. Probably sister of Mrs. Beer.

Swain, William. Preston's business partner in Philadelphia.

Sweet, Mrs. Stansbury relative, resident of Brooklyn.

Tate, Mary. Louisa Smith's daughter in Gettysburg.

Tate, Dr. Theodore. Gettysburg physician, Louisa Smith's son-in-law.

Taylor, Caleb. Neighbor near Pleasant Plains, later fiancé of Mamie Stansbury.

Theodore. See Tate.

Thompson, Mary Bruce. Schoolgirl friend of May's at St. Joseph's, from Louisiana.

Tommy. See Smith, Thomasene.

Treanor, Hugh. Hired hand at Pleasant Plains.

Whiteford, Mr. Miller south of Towsontown.

Wickham, Marine. Late uncle of Madge Preston, Yale University graduate.

William. See Pent.

# Notes

INTRODUCTION

1. Orlando Brown, *Memoranda of the Preston Family* (1842; reprint, Frankfort: University of Kentucky Reprints I, 1963).

2. Carl Bode, who uses some of the Prestons' correspondence of the 1850s in his *Maryland: A Bicentennial History* (New York: W. W. Norton, 1978), 107–12, infers a happy relationship between Madge and William, as at that time it may have been. No diaries of this period exist to tell us otherwise. But psychologist Gordon W. Allport warns of the possible distortions in letters which may idealize relationships "in periods of absence." "Both the artificialities of letter writing and the effects of distance between writer and recipient must be explored," Allport cautions, "before correspondence can be taken as a true message of the relationship." In *The Use of Personal Documents in Psychological Science*, Bulletin 49 (New York: Social Science Research Council, 1942), 109.

3. Mark Twain satirized the lugubrious style of the nineteenth century in the Emmeline Grangerford section of *The Adventures of Huckleberry Finn*. As we shall see, Preston often affected it in his own letters. Elizabeth Hampsten, in *Read This Only to Yourself* (Bloomington: Indiana University Press, 1982), 121–30, explores the imagery of death in the letters of Midwestern women from 1880 to 1910.

4. Jean H. Baker, *Ambivalent Americans: The Know-Nothing Party in Maryland* (Baltimore: Johns Hopkins University Press, 1977), 39. I am indebted particularly to the initial chapter of this book for the wider context in which the Know-Nothing party emerged. Percentages of those born outside the United States for 1850 are given on p. 17. Figures on the percentages for 1860 are drawn from p. 12 of her other book, *The Politics of Continuity: Maryland Political Parties from 1858 to 1870*, Goucher College Series (Baltimore: Johns Hopkins University Press, 1973).

5. Bode, *Maryland*, 98.

6. J. Thomas Scharf, *History of Baltimore City and County* (Philadelphia: Louis H. Everts, 1881), 787, as quoted in Bode, *Maryland*, 99. Bode chronicles the movement in a section of his bicentennial history which he calls "The Rise and Fall of Homegrown Fascism," 95–102.

7. Ms. 619, William P. Preston Collection, University of Maryland (hereafter referred to as UM). For locations of all documents used in this book, see Appendix A.

8. Preston's behavior after the assault fits the description by Frank A. Elliott of the dyscontrol syndrome that follows from injury to a certain segment of the brain. The injury may result from an accident, such as happened to Preston, from tumors, or epilepsy. Elliott describes the manifestations as "frequent episodes of intense rage . . . triggered by trivial irritations . . . and accompanied by verbal or physical violence." Yet between occurrences the sufferer will be friendly and gracious. Although most patients show remorse after violent episodes, Elliott notes a few who seemed "untroubled," others who denied their violence. See "The Neurology of Explosive Rage: The Dyscontrol Syndrome," in *Battered Women*, ed. Maria Roy (New York: Van Nostrand and Reinhold, 1977), 101–4.

9. Bode, *Maryland*, 112.

10. See Baker, *Ambivalent Americans*, 152, and Baker, *Politics*, 25–31.

11. Asher C. Hinds, *Precedents of the House of Representatives*, House Report No. 89, 36th Cong., 2d sess., 1907, vol. 2, 2.

12. *House of Representatives Miscellaneous Documents*, no. 28, 36th Cong., 1st sess. Maryland

Contested Election—Third Congressional District. Memorial of William P. Preston, Contesting the Election of the Hon. J. Morrison Harris, of the third congressional district of Maryland. May 15, 1860. See also Chester Harvey Rowell, *Digest of Contested Election Cases* (Washington, D.C.: GPO, 1891), 169–70, which quotes committee member McKnight, upon whose report the committee action was based, that "not over a dozen illegal votes were shown, and not more than 20 persons were prevented from voting by violence and intimidation."

13. Obituary article, *Baltimore Daily News.*

14. According to Baker, *Politics,* 222, Preston purposely destroyed some of his papers during the Civil War. She gives no source for this information. Presumably such papers would have referred to his slave holdings, or perhaps to his law clients, for example, the case of Kaniff, which is discussed in chapter 1.

15. These three letters following the assault are in the Maryland Historical Society (MHS). In the UM collection no business correspondence for Preston is extant between October 26, 1859, and May 29, 1860.

16. See my article, "The Towson Commuter," *Maryland Magazine,* Fall 1981, 42–43. Bode, *Maryland,* 108, also uses the word *commuter* to describe Preston.

17. This information is given in a letter from the UM collection written to May, dated December 24, 1855, from Thomasina Gist Thrale, obviously an elderly woman. Kitty at the time was three years old, as inferred from the 1860 census record.

18. Quoted in Eugene D. Genovese, *Roll, Jordan, Roll: The World the Slaves Made* (New York: Pantheon Books, 1974), 51.

19. See, for example, Susan Schechter, *Women and Male Violence* (Boston: South End Press, 1982), 211: ". . . stress does not 'cause' abuse: men choose to deal with stress in specific ways. The belief in one's right to use violence, batter, and dominate women is what causes a man to relieve his stress by beating his wife."

20. Recounted in an article by John Greenya, "Better All the Time," *Washington Post Magazine,* June 5, 1983, 11, col. 3–5.

21. R. Emerson Dobash and Russell Dobash, *Violence against Wives: A Case against Patriarchy* (New York: Free Press, 1979), 4. Their attribution of a similar law of this period to Maryland is in error. The so-called Bread's Law involved a 1681 application by a Charles County woman, Jane Bread, for protection from her husband, John, who had "grievously and manifestly threatened" her life and "mutilation of her members." The court ordered the sheriff to require bond from the husband not to do "any damage or evil" to her "otherwise than what to a husband, by cause of government and chastisement of his own wife, lawfully and reasonably belongeth." Cited by Julia Cherry Spruill, *Women's Life and Work in the Southern Colonies* (Chapel Hill: University of North Carolina Press, 1938), 342.

22. Dobash and Dobash, *Violence,* 63.

23. Elizabeth Pleck, "Feminist Responses to 'Crimes against Women,' 1868–1896," *Signs* 8 (Spring 1983), 461.

24. For a fuller discussion, see Jane Turner Censer, "'Smiling Through Her Tears': Ante-Bellum Southern Women and Divorce," *American Journal of Legal History* 25, no. 1 (1981), 24–47.

25. Preston's letter, dated May 10, 1856, is in the UM collection.

26. For examples of quotations from such works, see Ben Barker-Benfield, "The Spermatic Economy: A Nineteenth-Century View of Sexuality," in *The American Family in Social-Historical Perspective,* ed. Michael Gordon (New York: St. Martin's Press, 1973), 336–72.

27. Ibid., 336.

28. Letter from C. W. Thompson, Philadelphia, July 29, 1841, MHS.

29. Barker-Benfield, "Spermatic Economy," 337.

30. Catherine Beecher, autho: of the best-selling *Treatise on Domestic Economy*, believed that American democracy would be protected by removing women from the labor pool. She conceded men's superiority in the public sphere in exchange for women's supremacy in the private. Her book, which was first published in 1841, was much reprinted. It is available in a modern edition (New York: Schocken Books, 1977). See also Sara Delamont and Lorna Duffin's introduction to *The Nineteenth-Century Woman: Her Cultural and Physical World* (New York: Barnes & Noble Books, 1978).

31. One thinks of Louisa May Alcott, supporting her parents with her pen, or Mollie Sanford, speculating in her diary on what life may hold: "Will I be a happy beloved wife, with good husband, happy home, and small family, or an abused, deserted one . . . ?" See *Mollie: The Journal of Mollie Dorsey Sanford in Nebraska and Colorado Territories, 1857–1866* (Lincoln: University of Nebraska Press, 1979), 62.

32. Barbara Welter, *Dimity Convictions: The American Woman in the Nineteenth Century* (Athens: Ohio University Press, 1976), 102.

33. The classic work on the history of childhood is Philippe Aries, *Centuries of Childhood: A Social History of Family Life*, trans. Robert Baldick (New York: Knopf, 1962).

34. John and Virginia Demos, "Adolescence in Historical Perspective," in *The American Family in Social-Historical Perspective*, ed. Michael Gordon (New York: St. Martin's Press, 1973), 216–217.

35. Ibid. See also Eli Zaretsky, *Capitalism, the Family, & Personal Life* (New York: Harper & Row, 1976).

36. See Deborah Gorham, *The Victorian Girl and the Feminine Ideal* (Bloomington: Indiana University Press, 1982), 76. An example of how this kind of training by her Calvinist father affected a sensitive girl is provided in an excerpt from the autobiography of Mary A. Livermore (1820–1905) in Gerda Lerner, *The Female Experience: An American Documentary* (Indianapolis: Bobbs-Merrill, 1977), 25–32.

37. From "The Family as Government," *British Mothers' Journal*, May 1856, 99, as quoted in Patricia Branca, *Silent Sisterhood: Middle Class Women in the Victorian Home* (Pittsburgh: Carnegie-Mellon University Press, 1975), 109. Many British child-rearing books were sold across the Atlantic, and the views expressed here parallel those in American books of the time.

38. Ibid.

39. From *The Mother's Assistant* 3 (January 1843), as quoted in Anne L. Kuhn, *The Mother's Role in Childhood Education, 1830–1860* (New Haven: Yale University Press, 1976), 25.

40. Charles McIver, as quoted in Thomas Woody, *A History of Women's Education in the United States* (1929; reprint, New York: Octagon Books, 1974), vol. 1, 403. McIver's views were expressed earlier by Napoleon (ibid., 59).

41. Sara Delamont, "The Contradictions in Ladies' Education," in *The Nineteenth-Century Woman: Her Cultural and Physical World* (New York: Barnes & Noble Books, 1978), 135.

42. The standard work on the subject is Woody, *A History of Women's Education*. Curiously, Woody omits St. Joseph's from his list of Maryland female seminaries in the first half of the nineteenth century, though it was still flourishing when he wrote his book.

43. Jessie Bernard, *Self-Portrait of a Family* (Boston: Beacon Press, 1978), 233.

44. Ibid., 319–20.

45. Robert Fothergill, *Private Chronicles: A Study of English Diaries* (London: Oxford University Press, 1974), 9.

46. Joanna Field, *A Life of One's Own* (1934; reprint, London: Penguin Books, 1955), 200–201.

47. Allport, *Personal Documents*, 131–32.

48. Fothergill, *Private Chronicles*, 41.

49. Margaret Jones Bolsterli, "On the Literary Uses of Private Documents," in *Teaching Women's Literature from a Regional Perspective*, ed. Leonore Hoffman and Deborah Rosenfelt (New York: MLA, 1982), 44–54.

50. C. Van Woodward and Elisabeth Muehlenfeld, *The Private Mary Chesnut: The Unpublished Civil War Diaries* (New York: Oxford University Press, 1984), 18.

51. Pleck, "Feminist Responses," 452–53.

52. Elizabeth Hampsten, *Read This Only to Yourself: The Private Writings of Midwestern Women, 1880–1910* (Bloomington: Indiana University Press, 1982), 120.

53. Walter Ong, in *Orality and Literacy: The Technologizing of the Word* (London: Methuen, 1982), 102.

54. Clyde Kluckholm, "The Personal Document in Anthropological Science," in *The Use of Personal Documents in History, Anthropology, and Sociology*, Bulletin 52 (New York: Social Science Research Council, 1945), 104.

55. For a more extensive development of this idea, see my article "The Fantasy of Posthumous Fame, Lady Mary Montagu's Legacy to Mary Chesnut," *CEA Forum* 15, no. 4 (1985), 4–7.

56. Margo Culley, "Diaries of American Women: The Writer, the Reader" (paper delivered at the University of Alabama, Tuscaloosa, July 1979).

57. See especially Susan P. Conrad, *Perish the Thought: Intellectual Women in Romantic America, 1830–1860* (New York: Oxford University Press, 1976).

58. Jessie Bernard, *The Female World* (New York: Free Press, 1981), 90.

59. Culley, "Diaries." An extended analysis of diary literature is given in her Introduction to *A Day at a Time: The Diary Literature of American Women from 1764 to the Present*, ed. Margo Culley (New York: Feminist Press, 1985), 3–26.

60. Harriet Hunt, as quoted in Welter, *Dimity Convictions*, 61; emphasis mine.

61. Field, *A Life*, 59.

62. Ibid., 22.

63. Quoted by Susan H. Armitage, "'Aunt Amelia's Diary': The Record of a Reluctant Pioneer," in *Teaching Women's Literature from a Regional Perspective*, ed. Leonore Hoffmann and Deborah Rosenfelt (New York: MLA, 1982), 70.

64. William McPherson, "To Capture the Fugitive Day," *Washington Post*, December 4, 1984, A19.

65. Schechter, *Women*, 211.

66. Elizabeth Hampsten, "Tell Me All You Know: Reading Letters and Diaries of Rural Women," in *Teaching Women's Literature from a Regional Perspective*, ed. Leonore Hoffmann and Deborah Rosenfelt (New York: MLA, 1982), 61.

67. It would be an oversimplification to suggest there were only two paradigms. Ellen DuBois, "The Radicalism of the Women Suffrage Movement: Notes Toward the Reconstruction of Nineteenth-Century Feminism," *Feminist Studies* 3 (1975), 63–71, emphasizes an activist model taken by one group of women to gain greater control over their own lives; and Richard Sennett, "Middle-Class Families and Urban Violence: The Experience of a Chicago Community in the Nineteenth Century," in *The American Family in Social-Historical Perspective*, ed. Michael Gordon (New York: St. Martin's Press, 1973), 111–34, shows a passive male model of retreat into the sanctuary of the nuclear family and private home. Sennett does not explore whether violence may have erupted inside that retreat.

68. For an account of Lady Mary Wortley Montagu's letters, see Robert Halsband, "Ladies of Letters in the Eighteenth Century," in *The Lady of Letters in the Eighteenth Century*, symposium volume (Los Angeles: William Andrew Clark Memorial Library, University of California, 1969), 29–51. See also my article, "Letters as Literature: The Prestons of Baltimore," in *Women's Personal Narratives: Essays in Criticism and Pedagogy*, ed. Leonore Hoffman and Margo Culley (New York: MLA, 1985), 29–39.

69. Claire Badaracco, "Sophia Peabody Hawthorne's Cuba Journal: Volume Three, 31 October 1834–15 March 1835," *Essex Institute Historical Collections* 118 (October 1982), 280–315.

70. Carroll Smith-Rosenberg, "The Female World of Love and Ritual: Relations between Women in Nineteenth-Century America," *Signs* 1, no. 1 (1975), 1–29.

71. See my article, "Letters and Diaries: The Persona and the Real Woman—A Case Study," in *Women's Personal Accounts: Essays in Criticism and Pedagogy*, ed. Leonore Hoffmann and Margo Calley (New York: MLA, 1985), 40–47. The article compares Madge's diary entry for January 1, 1867, with a letter to May written within the same hour.

## CHAPTER 1

1. Probably a variant of *jersey*, a close fitting knitted tunic or jacket worn by women. The OED cites an 1864 example of *jersey*, also the spelling *jarsey*. I have been unable to find the word *jozey* outside Madge's letters.

2. Students at Mount St. Mary's College.

3. Mary Grady had given May a farewell gift of a dozen handkerchiefs.

4. The first page of the *Baltimore Sun* departed from its usual bland format to devote almost one and a quarter columns to the events in Pennsylvania. Under a series of headlines in large type—The War News/ Confederate Raid in Pennsylvania/ Temporary Occupation of Chambersburg/ Property Seized—Bridges Burned/ Town Evacuated—the *Sun* quoted from Harrisburg, Philadelphia, and Washington papers concerning Stuart's daring raid into enemy territory and the excitement engendered in the areas he passed through. A report that a bridge at Scotland, Pennsylvania, five miles east of Chambersburg, had been destroyed was contradicted later in the story. More serious was the report that 500 horses had been stolen and the Chambersburg Railroad Depot and much track destroyed. The *Washington Star* stressed the impact of the shortage of horses on the Union Army. Most of the Union cavalry were afoot, the article said, and wagon trains could not move.

   The article concluded with a biographical study of Stuart which doubtless appealed to Southern sympathizers such as the Prestons: "Ready for any enterprise, his military motto seems to be that of the French leader—'De l'audace, encore de l'audace, toujours de l'audace'—and his raid yesterday into Pennsylvania seems to have surpassed his previous acts of audacity." Preston's unexpected return from the city was doubtless prompted by his desire to share the exciting news.

5. Evidently an allusion to the exciting stories from the Hillens' visit to the Confederate forces near Frederick.

6. A purplish red color.

7. A loose, high-necked blouse patterned after the shirts of the Italian general Giuseppe Garibaldi and his soldiers.

8. Possibly a reference to menstruation. On the other hand, both Madge and May were subject to disabling headaches.

9. A figured or striped woolen petticoat, worn under a skirt looped up in front.

10. Probably a *talma*, for the French tragic actor François Joseph Talma. This was a woman's long cape or cloak, often hooded. In the 1860s it sometimes had pleats a little below the waistline in back giving a fitted appearance. See Charlotte Calisibetta, *Fairchild's Dictionary of Fashion* (New York: Fairchild Publications, 1975).

11. Another property owned by the Prestons.

12. Doubtless Aunty Carlon, who attended Madge during May's birth, was particularly solicitous about her younger friend's daughter.

13. A number of Baltimore leaders had been arrested in 1861 for being Southern sympathizers and confined at Fort Warren in Boston Harbor. These were Thomas Parkin Scott, Henry

M. Warfield, and William J. Harrison, members of the state legislature; William H. Gatchell, commissioner of police; Frank Key Howard, editor and owner of the *Baltimore Daily Exchange*; Thomas W. Hall, Jr., editor of the *Daily South*; Robert Hull of the firm of Hopkins, Hull and Atkinson; Col. George P. Kane; Hon. George William Brown, mayor at the time of the arrest; S. Teackle Wallis; and Dr. Charles Brown.

Madge paraphrases the *Baltimore Sun*'s account of November 29: "No cheers were given, and not the slightest noisy demonstration made. The greetings were those of friends and relatives, and did not savor in the least of any political feeling."

14.  Compare the school day when first established by Mother Seton in 1811: "The children rose at a quarter to six, and were in chapel for morning prayers at a quarter after. There was a short study period either before or after Classes began at eight and continued until 11:30, when the children said the Rosary in common. The recreation time after dinner lasted until three o'clock. The girls then went to their respective classrooms and started the afternoon session with a brief 'adoration.' There was another recreation period at five, and then study until supper at 7:15. After supper the older girls listened to the reading of a spiritual book, while the younger ones often went right to bed." From Joseph I. Dirvin, *Mrs. Seton: Foundress of the American Sisters of Charity* (New York: Farrar, Straus and Cudahy, 1962), 325. Not much had changed in fifty years, although the curriculum had been expanded from the original reading, writing, spelling, grammar, geography, and arithmetic. Needlework, music, and languages were taught privately in Mother Seton's time; music still was in 1862.

15.  The speaker was to be the Honorable Erastus Brooks of New York City. His subject was "Franklin and the Early Inventions." The *Baltimore Sun* notice called it "a theme full of promise, and one in which the gifted speaker will not fail to enlist the attention and interest of an intelligent audience."

16.  One among Madge's frequent allusions to Shakespeare—*Othello* and *Richard III* being the most often mentioned of the plays.

## CHAPTER 2

1.  Her letter is dated December 23, his December 22.
2.  For information on Phillips, see *Encyclopedia Britannica*, 1977 edition; for Whittingham, see J. Thomas Scharf, *History of Baltimore City and County* (1881), 139, 151, 654. As was common in slave-owning households, adult black women were referred to as "Aunt." Treanor was the farm manager and Old Christie a hired man. "Andy Handy" is either a mistake or a deliberate revision of the name *Handy Andy*, title of a popular book by Samuel Lover. Buck was a pony and Jewell a dog.
3.  Judge LeGrand, who predeceased her, was either a son or a nephew.
4.  Probably Mr. Sanders, father of Mollie and Jeannette.
5.  A sleeping garment of some sort, probably of gray flannel. The name may be Madge's own coinage.
6.  The lambs are named to honor Willie Stansbury, May Preston, Mollie, Jeannette, and Nettie Sanders.
7.  This letter, in a beautiful script, is written on the blank last page of May's preceding letter.
8.  Made of a gauzy material.
9.  No doubt the French Zouaves, of whom General de Trobriand was a member. This unit were members of the Union army. See chapter 4.
10.  The subject was the history of Baltimore. Notes for the lecture are in the MHS collection.
11.  The Ravels were a family of ten performers who did rope dancing, Herculean feats, and

pantomime ballets. They were popular in the United States from the 1830s through the 1850s.

12. May's favorite doll.

## CHAPTER 3

1. A bonnet of a particular shape.
2. A naval expedition of nine ironclads, under Flag Officer Samuel Francis du Pont, attempted to capture Charleston but was repelled by Southern gunners under General Pierre Beauregard.
3. One of a group of paintings by the American landscape artist Frederick Edwin Church done while he visited Quito, Ecuador. The journey was stimulated by his admiration for the explorer Karl Wilhelm von Humboldt, whose former lodgings in Quito Church occupied. Ruskin wrote of this painting: "An interesting picture. He can draw clouds as few men can . . . he has a great gift of his own." (Quoted in *Dictionary of American Biography*.)
4. The letter is apparently not extant.
5. The Battle of Chancellorsville. Hooker's army was defeated by a Confederate force under "Stonewall" Jackson. The Federal troops withdrew across the Rappahannock during the night of May 5. They lost more than 17,000 men to about 10,000 Confederate casualties.
6. A novel by Mary Elizabeth Braddon, later Maxwell (1837–1915). Her output and popularity are nothing short of astonishing. Titles of editions of her works occupy 27 full pages in the National Union Catalogue volume. Four editions of *Aurora Floyd* were published in 1863, 19 editions in all by 1892. It was also made into a play. Her most famous work was *Lady Audeley's Secret* (22 editions by 1889). Some of her works were translated into German and even into Hungarian. She was apparently English, but her influence on American readers must have been enormous.

## CHAPTER 4

1. J. W. Hering, "Recollections of My Life," as reprinted in *Just South of Gettysburg: Carroll County, Maryland in the Civil War*, ed. Frederick Shriver Klein (Westminster, Md.: Newman Press, 1963), 64. See also 41–51 for a fuller description of the cavalry skirmish.
2. For an account by a participant, see Regis de Trobriand, *Four Years with the Army of the Potomac*, trans. George K. Dauchy (Boston: Ticknor, 1889), 479.
3. Details of the occupation of the campus of St. Joseph's are recorded in the annals of St. Joseph's, unpublished volumes held in the archival collection of the Provincial House of the Daughters of Charity. Most of the accounts of this period are holograph manuscripts. For a fuller description of the occupation of the campus of St. Joseph's, see my article "The Sisters and the Soldiers," *Maryland Historical Magazine* (Summer 1986), 117–133.
4. For further exploration of this theme, see Angela Davis, "Reflections on the Black Woman's Role in the Community of Slaves," *The Black Scholar* 3 (December 1971), 3–15.
5. Annals of St. Joseph's, 561.
6. Eugene D. Genovese's *Roll, Jordan, Roll: The World the Slaves Made* (New York: Pantheon Books, 1974) is the definitive work on the subject of relations between masters and slaves. In particular see his chapter on slave defections and the psychology of the masters, who read these as ingratitude ("The Moment of Truth," 97–112).
7. Letter from Emma M. to May Preston, August 23, 1863, MHS.
8. McLellan ran the main hotel in Gettysburg, which had been turned over to the Sisters of Charity as their headquarters during the weeks after the battle when they were in charge of nursing the wounded.

9.  The omitted passage is almost illegible, as it is closely written in faded ink on paper so thin the darker ink of the preceding page shows through. Madge is discussing the terrain and actions of the Battle of Gettysburg. George Codori was Madge's nephew by marriage. His wife was Louisa Smith's oldest daughter Josephine.

10. Louisa Smith's daughters, Rose and Theodosia, May's older cousins. Madge had written to Preston earlier, requesting permission to bring them back with her.

## CHAPTER 5

1.  See Robert Wernick, "Shakespeare's Most Durable Villain, Richard III," *Smithsonian* 15, no. 12 (1985), 91.

2.  Madge means that the Stansburys are critical of the Catholic institution, believing that the Sisters withhold the students' mail.

3.  See Carroll Smith-Rosenberg, "The Female World of Love and Ritual," *Signs* 1, no. 2 (1975), 323–24.

4.  *Solferino* is a purplish red color, and *Agnus Deis* were pictures of Christ as a lamb, often holding a cross or a flag. The girls mounted them on bits of cloth, which they embroidered. These were customarily given as gifts to favorite Sisters and to friends.

5.  The wage agreed upon was four dollars a month, as noted at the top of the page in Madge's diary.

6.  Madge has the actress's name wrong. At that time Mrs. Bowers was playing at the Holliday Theatre in Augustine J. Daly's play *Leah the Forsaken*. The performance elicited a rave review in the *Baltimore Sun* of March 16: "great, commanding and impressive." Curiously, the same play was running simultaneously at the Front Street Theatre, where the role of Leah was performed by Miss Western. The *Sun* advertisement for the latter drew on the fame of another actress altogether: "Produced in New York and London by Miss Kate Bateman with a success unprecedented by any other play." Such competition between the two theaters was a long-standing tradition. See Francis F. Beirne, *The Amiable Baltimoreans* (New York: E. P. Dutton, 1951), 179–80.

7.  Preston himself had invited this old school friend of Madge's to Pleasant Plains.

8.  President Lincoln was in Baltimore for the opening of the Maryland State Fair, described in a *Baltimore Sun* headline of April 19 as "For the Benefit of the Sanitary and Christian Commissions." A parade of all military units in and around Baltimore made a procession to the fair "to testify to their grateful sense of the noble efforts of the ladies of Maryland in behalf of the sick and wounded soldiers of the national army." Lincoln arrived by special train and was driven from the station in the carriage of William J. Albert to the latter's residence. A squadron of cavalry escorted the carriage.

## CHAPTER 6

1.  Madge usually wrote on quarto-size double sheets. This stationery was a 7¾-by-9¾-inch folded sheet.

2.  Edwin Forrest, "greatest of living Tragedians and Exponents of Shakespeare," as described in T. Allston Brown, *History of the American Stage* (1870; reprint, New York: Burt Franklin, 1969). Although Forrest retired in 1855 at the age of forty-nine, he agreed in 1860–61 to perform 100 nights in major U.S. cities. He played in San Francisco as late as 1864.

3.  *Pages* were clips for holding a woman's skirt in walking. The *Oxford English Dictionary* example is from 1864.

4.  This explanation, which appears interlinearly in the original, is Madge's.

5. To see the black servants on the Stansbury estate.

6. Her last words before she was guillotined on November 8, 1793.

7. *Hamlet*, III, i, 84–85.

8. From Edward Young's *Night Thoughts*, I, line 393, reprinted in *Eighteenth Century Poetry and Prose*, ed. Louis I. Bredvold et al. (New York: Thomas Nelson and Sons, 1939), 511–20.

9. Aigburth Vale was named by John E. Owens after a residence in England belonging to some relatives. He was a native of Liverpool and was brought to America in 1825 at the age of five. After his success in the theater—he was a popular comedian—he purchased his farm property of almost 200 acres in 1853. Subsequently he added to his holdings. In 1892 his wife wrote a biography, *Memories of the Professional and Social Life of John E. Owens*, in which she describes his work on Aigburth Vale, "improving the farm agriculturally and building a mansion which was surrounded with ornamental shrubbery and grounds designed with exquisite taste in landscape gardening." The mansion house was not built until 1867, but the landscaping was already under way, as this letter of Madge's records. See *300th Anniversary Book of Baltimore County* (County Directories of Maryland, Inc., 1959 [?]), 148, 150.

10. The boys' school, Mount St. Mary's College.

11. For local eyewitness accounts of these events, see *Just South of Gettysburg: Carroll County, Maryland in the Civil War*, ed. Frederick Shriver Klein (Westminster, Md.: Newman Press, 1963), 206–9, and H. George Hahn and Carl Behm III, *Towson: A Pictorial History of a Maryland Town* (Norfolk, Va.: The Donning Company, 253 West Bute St., n. d.).

12. The incident described was true but curiously unreported in the *Baltimore Sun*, which instead stressed the widespread circulation of rumors. On page 3 of the *Sun* for July 11, under the heading "War News," were the following paragraphs: "It is hardly necessary to announce to our readers that yesterday was one of the most exciting days ever known in Baltimore. Rumors of every description, calculated to arouse the people, were abundant, but none could be traced to any reliable source. . . .

    "Yesterday morning, between five and six o'clock, the city was startled by a general ringing of alarm bells, and in a short time the streets were thronged by an excited multitude, and the most extravagant stories were put in circulation."

13. The news account in the *Baltimore Sun* reads as follows: "*The War News*. The railroad between this city and Washington and the telegraph line was damaged yesterday at different points by the rebels.—It is said the force of the enemy which crossed the road at Beltsville moved in a southerly direction, and occupied one hour and a half in passing that point. Heavy fighting is also reported as being in progress at an early hour yesterday morning on the north side of Washington by parties arriving from Montgomery County.

    "The damage to the railroad and telegraph communications in the North is now found to be not so bad as was at first supposed, and it is expected that all will be repaired in a day or two. . . .

    "*Major Harry Gilmor's* band of rebel Cavalry were at Towsontown during Monday night. His forces had a skirmish with some of our independent citizen cavalry on the York road between Towsontown and Govanstown, about four o'clock yesterday morning and afterwards started in the direction of Frederick."

    The paper also reported that 4,000 rebel infantry "breakfasted" at Randallstown and were believed headed for Washington.

14. The former Negro driver, who had fled from Pleasant Plains the summer before. Probably the soldiers sought Preston as a Southern sympathizer. The two boys, John and William, hid to avoid conscription.

15. That is, Aunt Louisa's home at Mountain View. Captain Shanabrook, who was in charge

of a ship out of Baltimore, was a close friend of Preston. Apparently he had earlier planned to join Preston in the north.

16. Madge's niece, Louisa Smith's married daughter.

## CHAPTER 7

1. Sister Leopoldine had been reassigned from St. Joseph's to one of the enterprises of the Sisters of Charity in the Baltimore area, probably St. Vincent's Infant Asylum.
2. Narrow strips of used fabric to be woven or braided into rag rugs.
3. The fair was already well into its second week. Almost daily the *Baltimore Sun* ran small articles about the wonders there on display: India rubber goods, saddles and leather goods, showy military ornaments, boots and shoes, enameled wallpaper, bead work made by the blind, furs, clothing, artificial teeth, embalmed natural flowers, carpets, ladies' dress trimmings, silver-mounted show cases, earthenware, movable comb beehives, soaps, extracts, pomatums, portable beds. Large crowds attended, including many soldiers home on furlough or stationed in Baltimore. A blues band was especially popular.
4. Ruth and Millie, Emily's children. *"Your friends"* evidently referred to Sister Leopoldine and the other Sisters.
5. This passage makes clear that in the course of the summer Madge had shared with her daughter at least some of her anxieties about Preston's relationship with Rose Smith. The openness of the comment perhaps also suggests that Madge no longer believed May's incoming mail was being screened by Sister Raphael.
6. The quotation is from the Bible, 2 Samuel 1:20.
7. Evidently a transparent lozenge of some kind.

## CHAPTER 8

1. That is, Anna Northrop, who would become May's closest friend.
2. A former slave. Aunt Nancy and her husband, Uncle Isaac Woodlands, a free black, were frequent subjects of Madge's 1860 diary.
3. Madge does not identify the contents of her green chest. This entry suggests Kitty's sense that she deserves remuneration, like the other workers, now that her slave status has ended.
4. Green was May's favorite color.
5. Rose was employed as a telegrapher.
6. This letter from May to the younger black girl shows that the adopted mother-child relationship between young girls played out also across racial lines.
7. That is, with the horseshoes fixed with long-headed nails to make them grip better in slippery weather.
8. Possibly a reference to a product described in an undated note from Preston:
   Dear Madge,
   I send herewith ten Gallons of purified Alcohol or refined whiskey it is 6th proof and therefore bear 3 quarts of water to each Gallon of Alcohol. You had better take out and lay aside for other use 3 gallons & put it in one of the 3 Gallon demijohns which you will find in the wine cellar—the 3 Gallon demijohns are the *straight* ones and I think there is one or two empty. Having taken out 3 Gallons you will have 7 Gallons remaining in the barrel, to which you may add 21 quarts of 4th proof whiskey to which you may add as many cherries as will fill the barrel as you like, or just such quantity of cherries as you may determine. I think you had better use *all black cherries*.

   In haste Yours truly
   Wm P. Preston

## CHAPTER 9

1. The letter breaks off suddenly; the concluding page was apparently lost.
2. St. John's Academy was a school for girls that occupied the original building housing St. John's Church after the church moved to a new site in 1856. The academy was located on Valley Street near Eager Street. In J. Thomas Scharf's 1881 *History of Baltimore City and County* (Baltimore: Regional Publishing, 1971), 538, the academy is described as operated by thirteen Sisters of Charity and having about 300 pupils. Probably the institution was much smaller in 1865.
3. He was Mrs. Stout's alcoholic former husband.
4. Apparently Anna's stepmother.
5. A hotel in Baltimore.
6. Madge's Freudian slip betrays her extreme agitation.

## CHAPTER 10

1. Made of a certain kind of silk fabric.
2. "The Maiden's Prayer Granted." I have not been able to find this title. It may allude to a song by Thecla Badarzewska, "The Maiden's Prayer," which was published in both Philadelphia and Baltimore, probably in the 1850s.
3. A hardened natural resin imported from Malaysia.
4. The first stop on the B & O Railroad out of Baltimore, the place where the connection was made between the cars and the steam engine. Within the city the cars were pulled by horses.
5. May, of course, is not told the true cause of Madge's indisposition. This passage confirms Madge's sense of her own physical danger.

## CHAPTER 11

1. It seems difficult to imagine that sixteen-year-old May would be anxious to receive her doll, Nannie, in the context of the school activities; but perhaps the doll had some of the same cultural meaning as the stuffed animals so cherished today by teenage girls.
2. Jefferson Davis, president of the Confederacy.
3. Q evidently stands for *query*, Preston's substitute for a question mark.
4. Mrs. Beer, the Baltimore housekeeper.
5. Probably Mrs. Beer's sister, Mrs. Stuntz, and her husband.
6. With the lease of Pleasant Plains, Mrs. Pent, the housekeeper, and her son, William, were let go. Mrs. Beer was apparently being discharged because Madge herself would be taking command of the much smaller household in Baltimore.
7. He is imitating her Germanic pronunciation of *my*.
8. Lady Mary Wortley Montagu was famous for a posthumous volume of letters about her life in Turkey, where her husband had been a diplomat. Madame de Staël was a major Swiss-French novelist, author of *Corinne* (1809).
9. Probably Mrs. Beer's sister's family. This may be a jocular nickname for Madge's amusement, as is the Bear.
10. The letter, which has been preserved in Preston's legal papers (UM collection), is an interesting period piece on drug abuse and alcoholism. It is written in his hand as a draft for Mrs. Owens to recopy. The letter, which is very accusatory, condemns Mrs. Stevens for leaving her quiet place in the country to return to Baltimore, where once again she had access to liquor.

CHAPTER 12

1. The word *brutality* has been scratched out, but with a different color of ink, making the original word still legible. The same is true of *Mr Preston* in the last sentence of the previous day's diary passage. Whether the editing was done by Madge herself or by a descendant is of course unknown.
2. She is sarcastic, remembering his coming late when he waited for Rose.
3. Not to be taken literally. Madge "adopted" several of May's classmates as her nieces. This was common practice at the time.
4. An account in the next day's *Baltimore Sun* described a gathering of thousands of members of the "colored Odd-Fellows" from major cities of the mid-Atlantic region. A procession, which started to assemble at 7 A.M., led from Mount Vernon Square to Monument Square. "The best order and decorum prevailed," the *Sun* reported, "and the procession . . . elicited considerable attention from crowds of both white and colored persons." Prayers and speeches began at 12:30 in Monument Square, and a social gathering in the evening concluded the celebration. Paraders wore "bright regalia" and carried "very many fresh looking and shining banners." A major speech urged the importance of "the new position which the colored race has assumed."
5. Louise McN——, had come to visit the day before. Preston took her to the city in the evening and they remained all night, according to Madge's October diary entry. Although the name is similar, she does not seem to be Madge's niece Louisa McGrew.
6. An allusion to the Stephen Foster song, "Uncle Ned." The first stanza is as follows: "There was an old darkey and his name was Uncle Ned / And he died long ago, long ago; / He had no wool on the top of his head, / In the place where the wool ought to grow."
7. May's dolls.
8. Named for a Baltimore philanthropist. Kelso, who was then eighty, endowed the Kelso Episcopal Orphan Asylum.
9. The battle of Solferino, in northern Italy, was fought on June 24, 1859, with great loss of life. A shade of red was subsequently named for it. Dickens focused the world's attention on the event in an eyewitness account in his periodical *All the Year Round* 13 (July 23, 1859). Baltimoreans may have followed events with unusual interest because one of their own, Elizabeth Patterson, had married the nephew of Napoleon III, leader of the French forces. Another eyewitness, the Swiss Jean Henri Dumont, organized emergency aid for the wounded, an experience resulting in his founding of the Red Cross.
10. From this time Madge frequently addresses her husband this way in letters.
11. *Pie safes* were cupboards with open sides covered by screening to protect food from flies.
12. "Uncle Jim" had been asked to engage Matilda to help with the work at Pleasant Plains. She may previously have been a servant or slave for the Sanders family. This would explain why May later inquires about Matilda's husband.
13. The letter breaks off here, the rest apparently having been lost.

CHAPTER 13

1. Probably two of the Sisters named in the indictments who had been dismissed. The names used in the legal papers are those given the women at birth—not those assumed when they joined the order.
2. Since, as previously indicated, the 1866 diary is lost, no similar passages until 1867 can be included to provide counterpoint to the generally optimistic tone of the letters for this period in Madge's life.
3. *Baltimore Sun*, February 7, 1866.

4. *Baltimore Sun*, February 8, 1866.
5. *Report of the Trial of Dr. Wm. H. Stokes and Mary Blenkinsop, Physician and Sister Superior of Mount Hope Institution Before the Circuit Court for Baltimore Co., Md.* Held at Towsontown, Tuesday, February 6, 1866. By Eugene L. Didier, Stenographic Reporter. / Together with an Introductory Account of the Circumstances which gave rise to the Case, the Preliminary Legal Proceedings, and the Origin of the Sisters of Charity (Baltimore: Kelly & Piet, 1866), 84ff. A copy of this volume, which was privately printed by Preston and for which he wrote the introduction, is in the MHS collection.
6. Ibid., 96, 98.
7. Ibid., 99–100.
8. These are reprinted in their entirety at the end of the private volume, *Report of the Trial*.
9. Sister Genevieve is ironic. Rogers was the opposing attorney in the Mount Hope case, hardly Preston's "friend."
10. The name *Asylum* refers to two different institutions. One is Mount Hope Insane Asylum, where the principals in the law suit, Mother Euphemia and Sister Matilda, probably stayed during their residence in the city. The other was the institution to which Sister Leopoldine was assigned—St. Mary's Female Orphan Asylum. Founded in 1817 and located on Cold Spring Lane near Roland Avenue, it was a home for girls from age seven to about fifteen. See *Directory of the Charitable and Beneficent Societies and Institutions of the City of Baltimore* (Baltimore: The Charity Organization Society of Baltimore City, 1885), 51.
11. Recently named Mother Superior after the death of Mother Ann Simeon.
12. The photograph shows Preston gesturing as if caught in the act of arguing before the court. A copy is owned by the Daughters of Charity, St. Joseph's Provincial House, where it has been kept in an album of the period. The book referred to, *The Report of the Trial*, is also in the archives of St. Joseph's Provincial House; another copy is in the MHS collection.

## CHAPTER 14

1. Receipts from the fair totaled $164,569.97. It was disbursed as follows: Virginia, $27,000; North Carolina, $16,250; South Carolina, $19,750; Georgia, $17,875; Alabama, $16,250; Mississippi, $20,625; Louisiana, $7,500; Florida, $5,500; Arkansas, $5,000; Tennessee, $12,500; Maryland refugees, $10,000; miscellaneous states, $6,069.97. The source for these figures is Col. J. Thomas Scharf's *The Chronicles of Baltimore* (Baltimore: Turnbull Brothers, 1940), 664–65.
2. Kitty, who worked out of Baltimore, evidently kept in touch with the Prestons.
3. Because Madge's diary is missing, the only evidence of her possible unhappiness occurs in comments such as this. The statement may also be read, of course, as a way of hedging against future disappointment.
4. St. Joseph's House of Industry, at the southeast corner of Carey and Lexington streets, was founded in 1863. Female orphans between the ages of twelve and eighteen were taught a trade, usually dressmaking and fine sewing. Sale of completed articles helped to support the institution. (*Directory of the Charitable and Beneficent Societies and Institutions of the City of Baltimore* (Baltimore: The Charitable Organization Society of Baltimore City, 1885), 50–51.
5. The reference is to the Baltimore philanthropist Johns Hopkins. He and his sister took a particular interest in young May Preston.
6. She died. (Her soul left her body almost at the moment she was playing her instrument —perhaps piano or organ.)
7. Meaning *named*. Preston's style is heavily literary. Here he uses the archaism that Edmund Spenser revived in the sixteenth-century work, *The Fairie Queene*.

8. Scapulars are badges in the form of images attached to small pieces of cloth, which are worn on cords over the shoulders hanging front and back. In 1840 the Sisters of Charity were authorized to manufacture a green scapular; in 1847, Pope Pius IX authorized them also to make a red scapular. To this day, at the Provincial House in Emmitsburg, the Daughters of Charity continue to manufacture and distribute both the green and red scapulars. The modern versions, about one by one and a half inches, are laminated in plastic. For the wearer to receive full spiritual benefit, a formal investiture, such as Madge was seeking, must occur.

9. Herbal concoctions.

10. An allusion to Shakespeare's *Richard III*. Madge often quotes this line.

CHAPTER 15

1. The *Baltimore Sun*, July 8, 1866, noted that "Wm. P. Preston, Esq., of this city delivered a very appropriate and interesting address."

2. Marine Wickham was Madge and Louisa's mother's brother—probably a great uncle of one of the infant's parents. I have not been able to identify Sade.

3. Archbishop Martin John Spalding. The book referred to later in the letter in his *The History of the Protestant Reformation, in Germany, and Switzerland, and in England, Ireland, and Scotland, the Netherlands, France, and Northern Europe*, 2 vols. (Louisville: Webb & Levering, 1860). By 1875 fourteen editions had been printed.

4. This reference to some real estate transaction is not otherwise explained.

5. The fire destroyed the shops of a carpenter and a box-maker, a loss estimated at $10,000; a four-story building used by both a carpenter and a house painter ($18,000); and a three-story building used for manufacture of boxes and store shelves. The rear of houses on Fayette Street were also endangered (*Baltimore Sun*, August 4, 1866).

6. Joshua Vansant was active in municipal, state, and national politics. He served two terms as mayor of Baltimore, later represented Maryland in the U.S. House of Representatives.

7. The Second Plenary Council of the Catholic Bishops, described by Archbishop Spalding and quoted by Madge as "the most important as well as the most imposing gathering of the hierarchy" in 200 years. The sessions, which lasted for two weeks, were intended to result in recommendations on various ecclesiastical matters, which would be forwarded to Rome and, if approved by Pope Pius IX, would become canons of the church. The Council was to begin on Sunday, October 7 (*Baltimore Sun*, October 1, 1866).

8. Under discussion is May's proposed return to Baltimore to attend those sessions of the Council that were open to the public.

9. *Fabiola, or The Church of the Catacombs* was by Cardinal Nicholas Patrick Stephen Wiseman (1802–65). The 1854 edition of this popular work was reprinted by the Garland Publishing Company in 1976. The quotation is from the first line of Edward Young's "The Complaint, or Night Thoughts on Life, Death, and Immortality" (1742–45). (See chap. 6, n. 8.)

10. A town in Harford County, northeast of Baltimore.

11. This was the Great Maryland Horse Fair, held at Herring Run racetrack. The purpose of the event, sponsored by an association of gentlemen, was to display famous horses from different sections of the country. The proceeds were to go to the poor of Baltimore and Rockingham County, Virginia. To ensure the comfort of the ladies, a special stand was erected for their use and one of the two entrances to the track was set apart for "ladies accompanied by gentlemen." The Philadelphia Road, which gave access to the track from Baltimore, was graded and filled. The *Baltimore Sun's* November 13 account noted that there would be "excellent police arrangements" and that "nothing approaching rowdyism

will be tolerated." On the fourteenth, General Grant himself, "whose love for fine horses is as well known almost as his fame," was scheduled to attend.

12. May's French letter had described the girls' anticipation at seeing a shower of meteors. People in Baltimore were also excited. If it was seen at night, the fire commissioners were to strike all the fire alarms ten strokes (not a fire alarm signal), the signaling to be repeated three times (*Baltimore Sun*, November 13).

13. Madge's complimentary close to her husband is very formal. In earlier letters she usually signed herself "Affectionately."

14. This sentence seems to support the inference that the Prestons' relationship continued troubled. Madge's letters, however, as noted before, were usually cheerful in both content and tone, however unhappy she might have been in her personal life.

15. Anna Northrop's niece. The mother had been one of the Southern refugees at St. Joseph's.

16. Happily married old couple in an eighteenth-century folk song.

CHAPTER 16

1. In the spring of 1985 I became aware of the presence of another Preston document, Madge's 1885 memorandum book containing her copy of business letters concerning the sale of her home and other financial matters which, as a widow, she was handling. This book was purchased in a second-hand bookshop near Easton, Maryland. Conceivably other Preston documents are in private hands.

2. At Loyola College.

3. The article to which Madge referred occupied fully half of the left-hand column of page 2 of the *Baltimore Sun*. Captioned THE CATHOLIC CHURCH IN THE UNITED STATES, the article noted a recent decision by the Pope to increase the number of episcopal seats in the United States fourfold. The writer—quite possibly A. S. Abell himself—recounted the church's history in the previous fifty years, since Archbishop John Carroll of Baltimore was the nation's sole bishop. Including the four new bishops, there would be twenty-two.

    The article went on to commend the church for abstaining from political activities and for its missionary work, especially among the Indians of the Northwest and of Canada. What drew Madge's strong endorsement was undoubtedly the paragraph that followed: "That same religious enthusiasm and missionary spirit has now opened before it an immense field of labor amongst the freedmen of the South. . . . [I]n the changed relations of the white and black races, there will arise urgent necessity for moral and intellectual culture amongst the negroes of which the Catholic missionaries . . . will not be slow to avail themselves." Such a statement would support Madge's own concern for Kitty's religious education, a concern that Preston had consistently ridiculed.

4. This new policy on shipping packages through the mail may have depended on a contract with a local carrier. Parcel post service, as we know it, began in 1913. In the 1840s private express companies conveyed packages. In succeeding decades, Congress tried to make the U.S. Post Office competitive by reducing rates and forbidding private companies from carrying mail matter. See Clyde Melville Kelly, *United States Postal Policy* (New York: D. Appleton, 1932), 182–183. May's 1867 diary appears to be lost.

5. Judge Charles Wells Russell (1824–1867), chief counsel of the Baltimore & Ohio Railroad. His wife was the former Margaret Wilson Moore, daughter of Henry Moore of the firm of Neill, Moore & Co., which had operated a stagecoach line between Washington, D. C., and Columbus, Ohio. The Russells had lived in Wheeling. Russell represented Virginia as a member of the House of Representatives in the Confederate Congress (*The National Cyclopedia of American Biography*).

6. The comment is confusing because when Johnny came to the Prestons originally, he was described as an "orphan." The discrepancy is not explained.

7. Although *Sun* articles were never signed, a half-column article on January 18, THE ABUSE OF THE APPOINTING POWER, bears Preston's unmistakable style: "To secure equal and just laws for a people is the first duty, but to secure their faithful administration is scarcely less important. . . . Constitutions may be remodeled until men grow weary of change; municipal organizations may be varied at every session of the State legislature, but until some plan is fallen upon which will give to the people honest, capable servants, the same evils will be felt, the same abuses be renewed, the same wasteful extravagance in public expenditure indulged, the same load of taxes imposed upon a groaning people. . . ." After a disquisition on corruption and evils in government, the article concludes: "We cannot point to any specific remedy. We can only deplore the misfortunes, which flow so copiously from the abuse of official appointments of every sort, and trust that public sentiment will operate in some way to compel a reformation of the greatest of political corruptions."

8. A great snowstorm blanketed the northeastern states on January 17, impeding train travel into Baltimore. Then on the twentieth a second storm, described in the *Sun* of January 21 as "violent," hit Baltimore.

9. Joseph Jefferson was donating his services. The advertisement appearing in the *Sun* prior to the event announced: "On Saturday, at midday, doors open at 1, to commence at 2 o'clock. THE BENEFIT OF THE LADIES SOUTHERN AID ASSOCIATION. . . . There will be no expenses on this occasion: Every cent received will be paid over to the Association, Tickets $1, admitting one adult or two children."

   Jefferson had been performing Rip Van Winkle since he first opened in the Boucicault play on Christmas Eve 1860, at the Winter Garden Theatre in New York. A *New York Herald* reviewer had proclaimed his achievement: "His native humor and geniality are fully developed in the earlier scenes. His awakening after the sleep of twenty years, the gradual return to consciousness . . . were delineated with the hand of a master. . . ." George C. Odell, *Annals of the New York Stage* (New York: Columbia University Press, 1931).

10. "The irricative" is probably Johnny's blunder for *indicative*.

11. The document is at the Maryland Historical Society.

12. Thede. Why Madge chose this name is not clear. Possibly it alludes to the daughter of Thomas Jefferson, Martha, who married Thomas Mann Randolph. As her father's White House hostess from 1802 to 1803 and again from 1805 to 1806, and after 1807 at Monticello, Mrs. Randolph entertained representatives of European nobility and intellectuals. Before her marriage, of course, she had participated with her father in French social life at the court of Louis XVI.

   Another possible allusion is to minor actress Victoria Randolph, who was noted for her proficiency in elocution and her readings from classic plays. The title in any case suggests imperious behavior and self-dramatization on Thede's part.

13. The reference is unexplained.

14. The Stansbury children's grandfather, whom May also called by that name.

15. As close as Madge ever comes in letters to May to suggesting her real feelings about Thede. Her next two sentences immediately skirt away from the subject.

## CHAPTER 17

1. Charley Simmons.

2. Madge seems especially to empathize with someone she casts in the role of another victim.

3. Madge was evidently not moved by a description of the previous evening's audience in the *Baltimore Sun* of March 21: "HOLLIDAY STREET THEATRE. —Mr. Owens was most

flatteringly received at this theatre last night by one of the largest audiences of the season. The house was packed, and many persons were compelled to retire, unable to find even standing places. As Solon Shingle, Mr. Owens has won the most valuable praise, both in Europe and America. The character is assuredly one of his best—eminently distinctive and full of genuine American drollery. He will repeat it this evening, with Joshua Butterby, in the amusing comedy of The Victims" (2).

This was a revival of "The People's Lawyer," which ran on Broadway between August 29 and November 19, 1864. According to George C. D. Odell (*Annals of the New York Stage* [New York: Columbia University Press, 1927–49], 8:648), who quotes the *New York Herald* of October 13, 1864, Owens in this New York run "became almost the fashion, and his Solon Shingle at once took rank as one of the very few genuine portraits of American character." "The People's Lawyer" ran as a double bill with "The Victims," in which Owens played the Joshua Butterby role. For a full description of Owens and his most famous role, see also Thomas A. Bogar, "John E. Owens: The People's Comedian from Towsontown," *Maryland Historical Magazine* 79 (Winter 1984), 319–24.

4.  Uncle Wickham was Madge's uncle Marine Wickham, a Yale University graduate. All three persons were Philadelphia friends and relatives.
5.  Ruche or ruching, a frill of lace.
6.  Of watered silk, a fabric having a shimmering pattern.
7.  An apparent allusion to Thede.

## CHAPTER 18

1.  A thin white fabric used for women's dresses.
2.  Boys of May's generation, sons of two of Preston's business partners.
3.  The diary of John Wilkes Booth was published in the middle column of the front page in the *Baltimore Sun* of that day, May 21, 1867. Preston assumes it would have appeared in a Philadelphia paper as well. Five days earlier another front-page article in the *Sun* had related Secretary of War Stanton's refusal to release the diary to the press. "The diary shall not be published if I can prevent it," he was quoted as saying. Other government leaders disagreed, however, including both President Andrew Johnson and the judge advocate general. According to the *Sun* of May 16, the leading "journals" in the country "almost unanimously demanded" its publication.

    The president overruled Stanton following the former's receipt of a letter from the secretary of war—duly printed with the diary—certifying to the diary's authenticity and to its being intact as received. (Some missing pages were believed to have been torn out by Booth himself prior to his death.)

    Preston refers to Mary Surratt, who was executed as Booth's co-conspirator on July 7, 1865: the first woman to be put to death by the U.S. government. Booth's diary makes clear that he was acting alone. (The original diary is now on display at Ford's Theatre, Washington, D.C.)

4.  The nine Muses, in Greek mythology, who inhabited the heights of Mount Parnassus, were believed to be the source of poetic inspiration.
5.  Apparently not preserved.
6.  Madge forgot that in the original letter requesting materials for the cap, May had specified a tassel of the same color as the velvet—that is, purple.
7.  Previously the sewing machine had been located in the dining room.

# Index